T. S. ELIOT

AND THE CULTURAL DIVIDE

T. S. ELIOT
AND THE CULTURAL DIVIDE

David E. Chinitz

THE UNIVERSITY OF CHICAGO PRESS • Chicago and London

DAVID E. CHINITZ is associate professor of English at Loyola University, Chicago.

The University of Chicago Press, Chicago 60637
The University of Chicago Press, Ltd., London
© 2003 by The University of Chicago
All rights reserved. Published 2003
Printed in the United States of America

12 11 10 09 08 07 06 05 04 03   1 2 3 4 5
ISBN: 0–226-10447-8

Library of Congress Cataloging-in-Publication Data

Chinitz, David.
    T. S. Eliot and the cultural divide / David E. Chinitz.
        p.   cm.
    Includes bibliographical references and index.
    ISBN 0-226-10447-8 (cloth : alk. paper)
    1. Eliot, T. S. (Thomas Stearns), 1888–1965—Criticism and inter-
pretation. 2. Popular culture in literature. I. Title.
    PS3509.L43 Z64926 2003
    821'.912—dc21   2002155085

♾ The paper used in this publication meets the minimum requirements of the American National Standard for Information Sciences—
Permanence of Paper for Printed Library Materials, ANSI Z39.48–
1992.

To my parents

CONTENTS

ACKNOWLEDGMENTS

"How do you ever write a book!" Eliot exclaimed to Lytton Strachey in 1920. "It seems to me a colossal task" (*Letters* 393). The knowledge that producing a volume of criticism proved something of a challenge even for T. S. Eliot has brought me some consolation as I've wrestled with mine—though not very much, considering that Eliot's plaint preceded his completion of *The Sacred Wood* by under a month. My own "colossal task" could not have been completed at all without the help and support of numerous colleagues, teachers, and friends. Of their importance to me I can give here only the merest hints.

I must first mention Ann Douglas, under whose inspiring direction at Columbia I embarked on the course of research that would lead to this project. At Loyola, Pamela Caughie, Paul Jay, Andrew McKenna, and Joyce Wexler read parts of the manuscript and gave me valuable and highly appreciated counsel. Christopher Castiglia was a truly indispensable adviser and strategist as the project approached the publication stage. I am indebted, too, to Suzanne Gossett, Timothy Austin, and Frank Fennell for the strong support they have given me as successive department chairs. The kindnesses of these and other colleagues have meant a great deal to me.

I would like to thank Jewel Spears Brooker, Ronald Bush, John Xiros Cooper, James Loucks, Timothy Materer, Ronald Schuchard, and Kirstin Hotelling Zona for the expertise and encouragement they have shared with me in various ways. To Kevin Dettmar and Barry Faulk I am beholden for their cordial skepticism, which forced me to sharpen my argument and intensify my research. To Michael Coyle, for the stimulus of his correspondence and conversation, for his unselfish mentorship, and for his unwavering belief in this project, I owe a greater debt than I can hope to repay.

I am grateful to Loyola University Chicago and to the National Endowment for the Humanities for generous research grants that made the writing of this book possible. I am fortunate, also, to have taught a number of superb undergraduate and graduate students whose insight has enriched this book; among these I should mention Cathy Birkenstein-Graff, Phoebe Stein Davis, Joseph Lamperez, Megan Musgrave, Jody Shipka, Louis Simon, Sunny Stalter, and John Vincler. Besides these, Catherine Ramsden, Tim Randell, Kathleen Ricker, Michele Troy, and Abid Vali, my resourceful and dedicated research assistants at various stages in this project's development, made vital contributions of their own.

I wish to thank my friends and relatives for their understanding and indulgence during the several years in which the demands of this study have made me divide my time between it and them. In this regard, my unfailingly kind in-laws, Devra and Marc Gross, deserve special mention. This book is dedicated to my parents, Carol and Wallace Chinitz, whose efforts to instill a passion in me for the sounds of words and music commenced (so I am told) before I was born. For their love and their patience, my deepest gratitude goes to them; to my sister, Judy Gorman; and to my children, Michael Austin and Raina Joelle. I cannot imagine how I could here suitably acknowledge my wife, Lisa; to say that her support and companionship, and the sacrifices she has made on my behalf and on behalf of this project have been "important," or to offer my "thanks" for them, would be absurdly inadequate. I put my faith in her understanding that either a debt or an appreciation sufficiently profound is finally beyond words.

Portions of chapter 1 were published in an earlier form in *Modernism, Gender, and Culture*, edited by Lisa Rado (copyright 1996); and in *T. S. Eliot's Orchestra: Critical Essays on Poetry and Music*, edited by John Xiros Cooper (copyright 2000); these portions are reproduced by permission of Routledge, Inc., part of The Taylor & Francis Group. Part of chapter 2 appeared in *T. S. Eliot and Our Turning World*, edited by Jewel Spears Brooker (copyright 2001), and is reproduced by permission of the Institute of United States Studies, University of London. Scattered portions of the first two chapters were first published in *PMLA* 110 (1995) and are reprinted by permission of the copyright owner, Modern Language Association of America.

INTRODUCTION

Time, alas, does not necessarily bring detachment. It may merely substitute for a set of prejudices favorable to the poet, another set unfavorable to him.

—T. S. Eliot, "Poetry and Propaganda" (1930)

SIC TRANSIT

A young critic named Richard Foster described T. S. Eliot in 1962 as "a cultivated traditionalist whose rebellion consists in the perpetual dramatization of his withdrawal into a world where he and a few other cultivated traditionalists keep the currents of culture and tradition alive in words" (279). Foster's essay, called "Frankly, I Like Criticism," celebrates the victory of those "cultivated traditionalists," also known as the New Critics, over the older, belletristic literary establishment. "Intensely and seriously interested" in literature, and scrupulous in their renunciation of contemporary society ("the common scene," "mass culture") for an unsullied world of high culture, the New Critics had produced an "extraordinary effect" on the "literate young," who "were investing them more and more with oracular significance" (280–83). What had begun as a reactionary "cultus" had thus grown to become an "institution," winning ascendancy in the academy and building a "community of letters," a "house" of criticism that stood "firm on its foundation principle of the artist for the arts rather than the artist for society" (280). And the chief eminence of this new regime was T. S. Eliot, whose work and character embodied the splendors of authentic culture in all its austerity and purity. The leader's renown is his follower's exultation: Foster's triumphalism culminates in the boast that "Eliot's lecturing in 1956 to a Minneapolis multitude equaling that of three hockey games is now almost legendary" (282). In the exhilaration of this moment, the young critic can imagine only that, even if individual reputations, Eliot's included, will ebb and flow, the Age of Eliot will go on forever.[1] "Things," he announces beamishly, "look pretty secure" (282).[2]

Flash forward now to 1989, where we find a prominent novelist and essayist, Cynthia Ozick, puzzling over the collapse of Foster's house of criticism—and especially the demise of its master, whose present diminution, for those who remembered his former stature, was "inconceivable":

> In the early Seventies it was still possible to uncover, here and there, a tenacious English department offering a vestigial graduate seminar given over to the study of Eliot. But by the close of the Eighties, only "The Love Song of J. Alfred Prufrock" appears to have survived the indifference of the schools—two or three pages in the anthologies, a fleeting assignment for high school seniors and college freshmen. . . . And the mammoth prophetic presence of T. S. Eliot himself—that immortal sovereign rock—the latest generations do not know at all. ("T. S. Eliot" 4)

The exaggeration in this passage is not inconsiderable, yet it does communicate Ozick's sense of a momentous change having taken place, "as if a part of the horizon had crumbled away." Once, in "a literary period that resembled eternity," Eliot had seemed "pure zenith, a colossus, nothing less than a permanent luminary fixed in the firmament like the sun and the moon" (4). Somehow, "in the flash of half a lifetime, an immutable majesty was dismantled, an immutable glory dissipated" (6). What Ozick conveys, through this colorful hyperbole, is the experience of living through a paradigm shift.

This shift, as Ozick understands, involves something much larger than the vicissitudes of a poet's reputation—something even larger than a change in literary-critical regimes. It is not, she notes, that Eliot has been replaced by another poetic colossus; on the contrary, it is "almost impossible nowadays to imagine such authority accruing to a poet." And this is because Eliot represented, and continues to represent, an *idea* whose fortunes have turned:

> He was, to say it quickly, absolute art: high art, when art was at its most serious and elitist. The knowledge of that particular splendor—priestly, sacral, a golden cape for the initiate—has by now ebbed out of the world, and many do not regret it. (9)

In the "Eliot era," art was revered; the transcendent value (and, to a great extent, the composition) of the "canon" or "tradition" was taken for granted; the distinction between high culture and popular culture (synonym: "low taste") was unconditional (11). This modernist vision of cultural "grandeur," which Ozick describes as "immensely elevated and noble"—and which Richard Foster would certainly have recognized—has disappeared under the regime of postmodernism, where "[t]he wall that divided serious high culture from the popular arts is breached" (47). Despite her evident disillusionment with Eliot himself, Ozick confesses to being "arrested in the Age of Eliot, a permanent member of it, unregenerate" (13). She concludes that though the elitism of the modernist worldview must be disclaimed, she and her contemporaries "will probably go on missing forever . . . that golden cape of our youth, the power and prestige of high art" (49).

Ozick's essay provoked a stern reply from Hilton Kramer in the New Criterion—a reply that was probably more passionate than its object warranted. Though Ozick had presented Eliot's fall from grace as more or less deserved (her Eliot is an unpleasant and rather pathetic character), her piece was clearly an attempt at historical analysis and explanation, rather than a "ferocious attack," an "unremitting assault," or "an act of intellectual violence, an act intended to annihilate its object" (5). Kramer's anger was fueled by a sense of betrayal: he hadn't expected this sort of "literary assassination" from Cynthia Ozick, a "sainted literary figure" (9) who had been exemplary, until now, of "intelligence and seriousness" (6). By the end of his response, it is Ozick's reputation, rather than Eliot's, that has been put in doubt: her polemic will be seen, in time, "to harbor a vein of intellectual intolerance and misplaced rectitude not heretofore discernible in her carefully crafted writing, and she will be judged accordingly" (9).

Yet what the ostensible antagonists in this skirmish have in common is more telling than their differences. They begin, for example, from identical appraisals of Eliot's sinking fortunes. "For decades," in Kramer's version, "Eliot had bestrode the literary world as a colossus, but now he had disappeared from that world almost without a trace" (5). Eliot, both parties agree, is no longer a figure of significant concern to present-day readers, writers, and critics of poetry.[3] More significantly, they share with equal assurance the identification of Eliot with high art. For Kramer as well as for Ozick, Eliot represents a particular idea of culture distinguished by high seriousness, traditionalism, and purity or exclusivity—an idea of culture that flourished in the period over which Eliot presided and is today either endangered (Kramer) or extinct (Ozick).[4] Whatever else has changed in the interim, this view of Eliot as a cultural icon has survived intact since the day Richard Foster crowed over its potency. In the destruction of that icon, Kramer reads the cultural calamity of our time. Ozick remains nostalgic for its lost efficacy while conceding the historical necessity of its destruction.

Kramer notes Ozick's "litany of regrets"; nevertheless, he proceeds—as Ozick herself would soon protest—to take "a plaint on behalf of serious art for an attack on serious art" ("Exchange" 5). Since she has repudiated Eliot, she can only be understood to have repudiated "the aspirations of high art." The warmth of Kramer's rebuttal is generated by his perception that to assail one is to assail the other. This equation is corroborated by the exchange of letters published two months later, in which Ozick insists that she had not attacked high art (5–6), and Kramer maintains that yes, she had attacked T. S. Eliot (8). For both writers, in short, to reject Eliot is to renounce what he stands for, which is "high art" in all its exquisite seriousness, distinction, and aesthetic purity.

For Kramer, the cultural vision linked in memory with T. S. Eliot is truly fundamental. What, indeed, has he named his journal, whose avowed purpose is "[t]he defense of high art in a democratic society" ("Note" 4), but the New Criterion? Kramer's editorial mission is thus declared ab ovo to be a continuation of Eliot's. The New Criterion, like the old, is determined to "identify and uphold a standard of quality" (1). And the journal explicitly defines this charge in terms of sustaining, or reestablishing, distinctions among levels of culture. In the present intellectual climate, the New Criterion protests on the first page of its first issue, "the very notion of an independent high culture and the distinctions that separate it from popular culture and commercial entertainment have been radically eroded." The editor of the original Criterion, like his self-styled successor, is understood to have done his utmost to secure the boundaries between "high" and "low" art. As this book will show, however, Eliot's actual relations with popular culture were far more nuanced and showed a far greater receptivity than either his supporters or his detractors, today or during his lifetime, have realized or cared to admit.

THE USE OF ELIOT

Through an ongoing process of critical rereading that began in the mid-1980s, the relations between modernism and popular culture have begun to be better understood. The once secure conviction that modernism was uniformly hostile to the popular has undergone a series of challenges. Andreas Huyssen's landmark study, After the Great Divide, for example, extended the theories of Peter Bürger to distinguish two forms of modernism: a mainstream modernism that was in fact inimical to popular culture, and a "historical avant-garde" that, in its struggle against official high culture and the institution of art, remained receptive to the popular. Yet as Bernard Gendron soon demonstrated in a penetrating article on the Parisian avant-garde of the early twenties, this convenient dichotomy "fails to map completely the space of modernist practice" ("Jamming" 4–5).[5] Modernists, that is, adopted a variety of positions with respect to popular culture that cannot be reduced to either of the poles codified and popularized by Huyssen. With scholars giving increasing attention to the diversity of modernist practices and practitioners (often marked nowadays by the pluralizing of *modernisms*), it has become still more difficult to make sweeping claims about modernist enmity for popular culture.[6] The term "high modernism" has therefore come to stand for all the things (but particularly the regressive things) once associated, unsustainably, with "modernism" as a whole. For many critics, the rediscovered variety and vitality of early-twentieth-century writing does not extend to "high modernism," which one still finds characterized as apolitical (or reactionary), institutional, elitist, and aestheticist. With respect to popular culture, this scapegoat has simply replaced "modernism" at the more doctrinaire and patronizing of Huyssen's poles.

T. S. Eliot remains, of course, the public face of this discredited movement, however designated, though he is sometimes made to share this unlucky distinction with some other high-cultural hard-liner. "Modernists such as T. S. Eliot and Ortega y Gasset," writes Huyssen, "emphasized time and again that it was their mission to salvage the purity of high art from the encroachments of . . . modern mass culture" (163).[7] For Corrine Blackmer, Eliot is a useful foil to Carl Van Vechten, who "dissolves the boundaries between high and popular culture" that Eliot is supposed to have fought to maintain (223).[8] Ellen Berry, similarly, cites Eliot and Pound as "the most vocal of American modernists" in their efforts "to preserve the autonomy and integrity of institutional art" and to "[fortify] the boundaries between genuine art and inauthentic mass culture" (168–69). Even Michael Coyle, who has brought to light the importance of certain popular genres to the poetry and thought of Pound, has found Pound's antithesis in an Eliot who was uninterested in "the relations of high modernism to the low and even vulgar discourses of popular culture" that animated his friend. It is because he shares Pound's concern with the "increasing isolation and marginalization of the arts" that Coyle himself finds these relations to be "of compelling interest" (*Ezra Pound* 245–46).[9] Yet Eliot, as we will see, shared this concern no less profoundly.

For the present, an image of Eliot as the hero or antihero of a losing battle to defend a pristine and sacralized high art from the threatening pollution of "lower levels" of culture remains central to twentieth-century literary history. My goal here is first of all to show that Eliot cannot be characterized accurately by this simple metaphor—that he stood, in other words, for something more than "high art, when art was at its most serious and elitist." The Eliot I portray is a richer and more engaging figure than either the poster boy for an aesthetically minded "beleaguered minority" or the straw man for modernist "contamination anxiety." He is a multidimensional thinker and artist, whose approach to the modern popular, both as theorized in his critical essays and as practiced in his art, is supple, frequently insightful, and always deeply ambivalent.

This culturally elastic Eliot has been glimpsed before—seldom for more than a moment, and yet from a variety of perspectives. At least some of Eliot's contemporaries, for instance, seem to have intuited a significant relation between Eliot's poetry and popular music. The drawing of connections between *The Waste Land* and jazz was commonplace in the 1920s, and the association long outlasted the Jazz Age. In a sour "tribute" to Eliot in the 1934 *Harvard Advocate*, William Carlos Williams wrote, "From the first his lilting talent won us all, intrigued the ear and forced a music upon us as seductive as any popular tune" (73). And in 1948, Desmond Hawkins, who esteemed Eliot as much as Williams despised him, explained that his generation came to venerate Eliot "because the poetry got into your head like a song-hit" ("Pope" 45). The same simile appeared before long in *Time* magazine ("much of his poetry . . . is as catchy as a song hit"), yet few readers, it appears, were inclined to pursue the sources or implications of this perception ("Reflections" 26). One who nearly dared was the cultural critic Gilbert Seldes, whose relationship to Eliot I consider in chapter 2. In *The Great Audience* (1950), he suggested that Eliot's early poetry "indicates that he once was influenced by, and perhaps even took pleasure in, one of the popular arts, in his use of the rhythms of jazz to contrast with the stately phrases of the past" (262). Seldes's tentative qualifiers ("once," "perhaps even," "one of") testify to his difficulty in believing what his ears were telling him, as does his final clause, which takes the usual "out" by reducing the function of Eliot's jazz rhythms to ironic contrast. Still, in detecting Eliot's "pleasure" in jazz behind the purported irony, Seldes comes close here to envisioning the ambivalence that, I argue, permeated Eliot's response to popular culture.

All the same, it has been a rare critic who gives Eliot's relations with popular culture any extended consideration, and Hugh Kenner's "invisible poet," who is always acting, whose nearly every pronouncement is, as Gregory S. Jay has put it, "pure vaudeville" (*T. S. Eliot* 3), provides welcome relief from the received view of Eliot, with his stultifying highbrow seriousness.[10] To be sure, Kenner's Eliot does seem rather *too* arch, too much the confident manipulator of his audiences and critics, too much, perhaps, "Assured of certain certainties" and insufficiently "Doubtful, for a while / Not knowing what to feel or if I understand." Still, Kenner, almost alone, has been able to account for *Sweeney Agonistes,* the "Shakespeherian Rag," the "Marie Lloyd" essay, *Practical Cats,* and *The Cocktail Party* without having to resort to such devices as "ironic contrast," "noblesse oblige," "political expediency," "a game," and "a mask" to explain away a fundamental element of Eliot's art and thought that, because it is not easily squared with most Eliots (the traditionalist, the Christian, the cultural diagnostician, the "high modernist," the aristocratic ideologue, etc.), proves an inconvenience to most critics. "Yet, we need not choose," as Jay concludes, "between Old Possum and Saint Thomas" (3). Indeed, herein I present an Eliot in whom these and other figures perpetually contend, and whose work, in all its brilliancy, fascination, dazzling insight, and maddening blindness, issues from the contest.

Until we have dispensed with the two-dimensional, standard-issue Eliot, he will continue to block our own access to this conflicted and compelling figure. There is a remarkable passage in *Marginal Forces / Cultural Centers*, to take one example, in which Michael Bérubé argues that "modernist imperatives notwithstanding, *The Waste Land* never fully resolves the tension of the relation between high and low cultures" (192). Bérubé can only assume that this happy evasion survives in the poem despite what Eliot must have thought of the matter (here encoded in the phrase "modernist imperatives"). When he considers the "confrontation between . . . high and low cultures" that takes place in both *The Waste Land* and Melvin Tolson's *Harlem Gallery*, Bérubé finds it a "curious thing" that the outcome of this confrontation in *The Waste Land* is "more uncertain than it is in *Harlem Gallery*" (190). What makes this acute observation "curious" is merely that we have learned not to expect such dualism and cultural uncertainty from Eliot. Bérubé can scarcely believe what he himself has perceived:

> In other words, *The Waste Land*'s treatment of modernity's cultural literacy tends in two directions. On the one hand, there are clearly moments of the mock epic in the poem, whereby our culture is dwarfed by the magnitude of its own heritage. . . . On the other hand, "A Game of Chess," whatever its intention, suggests that the spiritual dryness of our world, its inability to die and consequent inability to live, to create and procreate . . . is a phenomenon heedless of class distinctions. (191)

In the phrase "whatever its intention," we see again the strain placed upon the sensitive critic faced with the discrepancy between what Eliot has actually written and what he is supposed to have been capable of thinking. This strain becomes most obvious when Bérubé attaches the disclaimer, "We know, of course, that these are not propositions Eliot would be quick to entertain" (192). What "we know, of course" stands, as always, in the way of what we see.

If a fresh approach to Eliot's relations with popular culture will enable a less incredulous reading of Eliot, it will also help clear the way for a better knowledge of modernism, and thus of our own response to modernity, which is still (whether or not we choose to acknowledge it) conditioned by modernist representations. We needn't revert to an older, narrower conception of modernism as the canonical work of a few individuals to recognize that a misconstrued Eliot remains a major obstacle to a well-understood modernism.[11] At the same time, in the resurgence of academic interest in modernism, scholars have succeeded in establishing that between modernist art and popular culture there was in fact substantial interchange. The recent attention to this traffic across the cultural divide has shed new light on any number of figures and institutions, though less perhaps on Eliot than on many of his contemporaries. Still, the "New Modernist Studies" has introduced new approaches and opened up whole areas of interest that have already begun to prove fecund for Eliot studies. Thus Lawrence Rainey and Leonard Diepeveen have both written fascinating chapters on Eliot's strategic marketing of himself and his version of modernism, while Colleen Lamos and Wayne Koestenbaum have viewed Eliot revealingly through the lens of queer theory. *Gender, Desire, and Sexuality in T. S. Eliot*, a forthcoming collection edited by Cassandra Laity and Nancy K. Gish, promises to add significantly to our understanding of Eliot along the axes of gender and the erotic. And, in a development especially important to any reconsideration of Eliot and popular culture, Rachel Blau DuPlessis, Michael North, and Susan Gubar have insightfully brought cultural and "race" theory to bear on Eliot's poetry. All this criticism, except for Koestenbaum's, has been published since 1994.

New work on T. S. Eliot and the popular will suggest that the current understanding of modernist cultural attitudes, which represent a significant advance over the crude caricatures of the not-too-distant past, still tends to oversimplify. As one frequently encountered position would have it, for example, what modernists disliked was not "popular art," but "a commodified, mass-produced, supposedly 'feminine' culture that took the form of slick-paper magazines, Books-of-the-Month, and big-budget productions from Broadway and Hollywood" (Naremore 44). Modernists, that is, distinguished between categories one might term "popular culture" and "mass culture" (begging the question, here, of whether such a distinction can be reasonably sustained). There is much truth in this generalization, and a glance at Eliot's *Selected Essays* would seem to lend it full support: Eliot could, for example, wholeheartedly applaud a popular music-hall artist like Marie Lloyd while bitterly denouncing the film industry, that new purveyor of mass entertainment, which threatened to take her place (SE 407–08). On closer inspection, however, even so apparently reasonable a formulation fails to contain the intricate unpredictability of real-life modernist views, Eliot's included. There were aspects even of "mass-produced" culture that Eliot not only welcomed but actively supported (the medium of radio, for example); he schooled himself for years to write plays that could be mounted as "big-budget productions" on Broadway; and to other genres that tread the always-indistinct line between "mass" and "popular" (e.g., Tin Pan Alley song), Eliot bore an ambivalent attachment rather than a simple hostility—a complexity of attitude mixing appreciation with irony and at times approaching something very much like camp.

Having now invoked its name three times, I had better put in a word for the much-maligned condition of ambivalence.[12] As a construct, ambivalence has romantic roots and is thus connected from the start with the social conditions that produced modernism; as a construct with a name and a psychoanalytic pedigree, it is itself a modernist phenomenon.[13] The technical sense of *ambivalence* in the literature of psychology dates from 1912, the Imagist year; its general usage goes back to the late teens and thus roughly coincides with Eliot's earliest publications.[14] Today, however, ambivalence has been in academic ill repute for some time, particularly in discussions of poetry, where it still evokes strong New Critical associations. Terry Eagleton sums up the case against ambivalence when he describes the "New Critical poem" as a "delicate equipoise of contending attitudes" and thus "a recipe for political inertia":

> Reading poetry in the New Critical way meant committing yourself to nothing: all that poetry taught you was "disinterestedness," a serene, speculative, impeccably even-handed rejection of anything in particular. (*Literary Theory* 50)

Ambivalence, which Eagleton contrasts with William Empson's more dynamic *ambiguity*, suggests a static opposition within a text—an opposition that inevitably manufactures passive and quiescent readers (51).

If we grant, *arguendo*, that Eagleton generalizes accurately about the New Critical conception of ambivalence, such a characterization must nevertheless be firmly rejected as an account of ambivalence outside the realm of literary criticism. There is nothing "delicate" or "serene" about ambivalence in lived experience, where it is often an intense, unsettling, and even painful condition. Nor is it a formula for inaction; on the contrary, it goes hand in glove with critical evaluation and is therefore an indispensable preliminary to effectual action. Richard Hoggart, to take one example, exemplified a thorough ambivalence toward popular art:

> Assimilated lowbrowism is as bad as uninformed highbrowism. It is hard to listen to a programme of pop songs, or watch "Candid Camera" or "This Is Your Life" without feeling a complex mixture of attraction and repulsion, of admiration for skill and scorn for the phoney, of wry observations of similarities and correspondences, of sudden reminders of the

raciness of speech, or of the capacity for courage or humour, or of shock at the way mass art can chew up anything, even our most intimate feelings. . . . It is a form of art (bastard art, often) but engaging, mythic and not easily explained away. (258)

Yet Hoggart's ambivalence, so far from paralyzing him, moved him to nothing less than the founding of the Centre for Contemporary Cultural Studies at Birmingham. The quoted excerpt comes from his inaugural address.

Ambivalence (not irony, which is merely one of its symptoms) is the characteristic modern disposition, because ambivalence is the one mature response to most of the cultural phenomena of the modern world—rapid transit, Hollywood, television, youth culture, globalization, the Internet, identity politics, postmodernism, consumerism—which are themselves full of contradiction, never monolithic, and seldom coherent. To this list one could add T. S. Eliot himself, another complex product of modernity, whose work is full of contradiction and mood—expansive, sympathetic, reactionary, wise, snobbish, visionary, parochial.[15] To respond to Eliot without some measure of internal conflict is without doubt either to over- or to underread him.[16]

Given the centrality of ambivalence in postindustrial structures of feeling, it is not surprising that a writer who memorably registers a deeply and widely felt ambivalence should win a following. And Eliot made poetry, indeed a career, out of an ambivalent sensitivity to the experiences of modern life. Despite his many idiosyncrasies—for as his biographers have shown, Eliot was almost anything but a representative man of his time—his determined exploration of states of ambivalence under modernity, and the strikingly contemporary poetics he devised for giving expression to those states, resonated with an extraordinarily diverse readership that crossed numerous lines of nationality, age, gender, and culture.

Eliot's prose, as one point of departure for the nascent discipline of cultural studies, suggests other reasons why renewed attention to Eliot's treatment of popular culture is instructive. Despite his politics, with which they had much to disagree, Eliot was not, for the founders of the field, merely an obstacle to be overcome. His characteristic strategy of relating literary phenomena to socioeconomic transformation, his engagement with culture per se as an issue to be analyzed and investigated, and his recognition of its intricacy contributed measurably to the field's early impetus. Though never affiliated with the new discipline, Eliot was an enabling force as it took shape.

In *Culture and Society* (1958), Raymond Williams devotes a chapter to Eliot, most of it given to an incisive critique of *Notes towards the Definition of Culture*. Yet

Williams finds several things of value in Eliot, most of all his inclusive understanding of culture as "a whole way of life" (232–33). Readers have since noted that Williams's own conception of culture as "an organic, cooperative and collaborative activity" bears comparison with Eliot's (Swingewood 42).[17] Williams also perceives, as many others have not, that Eliot, rather than subscribing to the defensive doctrine of "minority culture" propounded by F. R. Leavis and his followers, actually offers a compelling argument for its "inadequacy" (235). A large part of Eliot's usefulness, for Williams, subsists in his refutation of this and other contemporary dogmas. While challenging Eliot's conclusions (on class distinction, for instance), Williams thus credits his "discussion of culture" with having "carried the argument to an important new stage" (227).

If Williams focuses exclusively on Eliot's late works of social criticism, another seminal text of cultural studies, Stuart Hall and Paddy Whannel's *Popular Arts* (1964), is haunted and animated by Eliot's earlier essays, beginning with "Tradition and the Individual Talent." Eliot's brief but powerful tribute to the music-hall artist Marie Lloyd is not merely quoted extensively in Hall and Whannel's chapter "Minority Art, Folk Art and Popular Art": it could well be said to drive the entire discussion. Here and in the following chapter, "Popular Art and Mass Culture," Hall and Whannel's choice of examples—British music hall, Charlie Chaplin, Elizabethan drama, Dickens—replicates several focal points of Eliot's prose where it touches on popular culture. Many key elements of Eliot's critical program recur here: the relation between social change and developments in the popular genres is adduced; the transitional position of figures like Lloyd and Chaplin is noted; the isolation of high art is deplored. "Clearly," the authors write, "one of the great—perhaps tragic—characteristics of the modern age has been the progressive alienation of high art from popular art" (84). If this was indeed clear, Eliot, as we shall see, had helped make it so. To open the question of Eliot's relations with popular culture thus works toward a critical goal aptly defined by Jay: "to suggest his precedent place: how he shares the interests of our day, how he is a major precursor of contemporary theory and poetry in ways neither he nor his progeny might comfortably imagine" (*T. S. Eliot* 4).

Jay expresses another objective that I share: to make Eliot not "better or worse, more or less agreeable, but better understood and therefore more interesting" (8). Though a sympathetic reader by inclination, I have no intention of smoothing over any defective or discommoding features of Eliot's thought. Yet no inquiry is entirely disinterested, and if I am to be honest, I must acknowledge that in writing on Eliot as I have, and in trying to make him "better understood," I am no doubt attempting to account for, and possibly to justify, my own responsiveness to Eliot's work. How can one read with enthusiasm, and without discredit to oneself, an author who is so

widely (and not entirely unjustly) perceived as, in Ozick's typically hyperbolic terms, "an autocratic, inhibited, depressed, rather narrow-minded
and considerably bigoted fake Englishman" (7–8)? The pages that follow
will point up an aspect of Eliot's work and thought to which readers whose
sensibilities have been shaped, as mine have, by postmodernism and cultural studies may respond with something other than guilty pleasure. If this
neglected aspect cannot fully account for my own enjoyment of Eliot
(surely, after all, I am also moved by many of the same stylistic, imaginative,
and philosophical elements in Eliot's work that moved earlier generations
of readers), it does represent a source of pleasure that must heretofore have
been mainly unconscious. I hope that my work, by bringing this element to
light, will make Eliot more interesting and accessible to readers of my own
generation.

A PRODUCTIVE ENGAGEMENT

Responding in 1927 to three recent critical portrayals of Shakespeare, Eliot
declared, "About any one so great as Shakespeare, it is probable that we can
never be right; and if we can never be right, it is better that we should from
time to time change our way of being wrong" (SE 107). If Eliot is not "any
one so great as Shakespeare"—though such rankings of "greatness" are really a barren exercise of which Eliot himself, incidentally, was too fond—he
is at least a large subject on whom a great many identities have been con-
ferred. The proposition that "we can never be right" should give any critic
pause, and I, for one, cannot pretend that the Eliot presented in this book is
the final, the genuine T. S. Eliot. Still, it is assuredly high time that we dispensed with some of our old ways of being wrong about Eliot. In an om-
nibus review of eighteen works on Eliot, for example, Stephen Medcalf
complains that critics have constructed "an Eliot without a sense of humour," an error not unrelated, I would offer, to his placement at the center
of a world constituted entirely by "serious" high culture. Most of Eliot's
critics to date, as Medcalf remarks, have been so far from being able to countenance his immersion in the works of P. G. Wodehouse "that they can rarely
be brought to admit that he wrote *Old Possum's Book of Practical Cats*" (12).
　　The rebuke is just, for the Eliot we have inherited is *terribly* serious—a
very paragon of solemn purpose, tormented vision, and lofty contempla-
tion. And his milieu, while quite varied within its bookish limits, is altogether too polite. One objective of my study is to restore Eliot to a fuller
context, in which not only Wodehouse but George M. Cohan and Noël
Coward, Marie Lloyd and Groucho Marx, Raymond Chandler and Agatha
Christie, cartoons, melodrama, and ragtime belong to the mise-en-scène
and have their parts to play in Eliot's cultural life—and in his writing.[18] At

every stage of his working life, Eliot was productively engaged with popular culture in some form, and neither his work nor the overall significance of his career can be properly apprehended without attention to this engagement. To this end, I offer what is essentially a new narrative of Eliot's career—one that, I hope, restores the popular elements that previous narratives have suppressed.[19]

Chapter 1 focuses on Eliot's poetry up through The Waste Land and explores its relations with the historic flourishing and diffusion of American popular culture that surrounded all of Eliot's early activities. Memorializing their college days at Harvard, the poet Conrad Aiken would later recall the "delight" he and Eliot shared in these developments:

> What did we talk about? or what didn't we? It was the first "great" era of the comic strip, of Krazy Kat, and Mutt and Jeff, and Rube Goldberg's elaborate lunacies: it was also perhaps the most creative period of American slang, and in both these departments of invention he [Eliot] took enormous pleasure. ("King Bolo" 21)

But Eliot's enjoyment of this "rich native creativeness" was distinctly impure, as Aiken obliquely acknowledges when he compares its reflection in "Prufrock" with Eliot's sardonic portrayal of their "dear deplorable friend, Miss X," in "Portrait of a Lady" (21–22). Indeed, I read "Portrait" as a poem about cultural homelessness, a poem that articulates Eliot's inability to locate himself in either the passing Victorian world or the "Americanized" world of the modern popular then coming into being. Eliot's ambivalence toward this new culture finds expression in a number of the apprentice poems published only lately in Inventions of the March Hare, as well as in "Cousin Nancy," which I situate in relation to the pre–World War I social dance craze. In the irony deployed within these poems resonate Eliot's conflicted feelings about his American origins, with which, in those years, he still—sometimes ebulliently, sometimes reluctantly—identified. Of particular concern in this chapter will be Eliot's relations to popular music. I will argue that Eliot's poetic style was formed, at a crucial stage, not only by his oft-cited reading of Jules Laforgue but by the convergence of that influence with the nearly unnoticed influence of ragtime and American popular song.

Gail McDonald has predicted that "attention to more of the prose than that collected in The Sacred Wood or Selected Essays will serve to complicate the Eliot of tradition, hierarchy, and canon" (209). Drawing on a number of Eliot's uncollected essays as well as on more familiar pieces, chapter 2, which concentrates on the years 1921–27, shows that Eliot's theoretic position on popular culture went far beyond the contempt and condescension usually ascribed to him. Although Eliot is often identified as a champion of institutional high art, in reality he offered an increasingly forceful critique of aestheticism and its ideal of artistic autonomy, of modernist hermeticism, and of the prevailing constructs that created an unbridgeable chasm between "high" culture and "low." Eliot regarded the sacralization of high art, which maintained this deleterious cultural divide, as a bourgeois perversion of the nature and function of art. Against this he invoked the holistic relations between primitive aesthetic and social life described in the work of contemporary anthropologists.

Perturbed by the disconnect between the poetry and elite fiction of his own time and any audience but small avant-garde coteries, Eliot persistently interrogated the claims of literature to a special status outside the social realm; of the "serious" novel to freedom from any imperative to "entertain"; and of poetry, in its current form, to fulfill any purpose at all. Following out in his own career the logic of this questioning, Eliot ultimately turned away from poetry as such to devote himself to a new form of public art—a poetic drama based on popular genres—that he hoped would reconcile the dissociated realms of modern culture.

The most visible example of Eliot's interest in popular culture to survive in his canonical prose is his 1922 essay on Marie Lloyd. This brief essay and its construction of the popular is the subject of chapter 3. On the surface, the essay is a poignant work of cultural mourning for a beloved performer and for the popular art form she perfected—a form that, as Eliot correctly perceived, was in its death throes. Considered in depth, however, Eliot's argument opens a number of complex problems. The "popular" nature of music hall, for example, has been long a contentious issue in cultural studies, raising difficult questions about who produced and who consumed this simultaneously demotic and fashionable genre. Eliot's essay also participates in a number of preexisting and emerging discourses surrounding music hall. The genre had been adopted by Eliot's early masters, the 1890s British symbolists, as an outlet for the expression of their own "decadence," as a lever against the "legitimate" bourgeois theater, and, inseparably, as an art form that they passionately relished. Even before World War I, the heyday of the halls was already being viewed with nostalgia; the "Cockney" figure both represented on stage and—to an extent quite debatable in fact but scarcely in imagination—peopling the audience was equally sentimentalized. Eliot, I will argue, was not unaware of these complications; nevertheless his perception of the halls remained partly circumscribed by them. I will probe the implicit politics of "Marie Lloyd" while resisting the tendency of some recent commentators to reduce the essay to a political stratagem.

In the world of literary criticism, almost no one seems to find "Marie Lloyd" within the main current of Eliot's thought. Few of the numerous books on Eliot even contain an index entry for Lloyd; neither she nor Eliot's essay on her is mentioned, for instance, in Lyndall Gordon's otherwise thorough biography. As might be expected, given the usual perception of Eliot, most critics who do mention the essay voice some surprise at its existence. Lloyd's biographer Daniel Farson calls Eliot an "unexpected" admirer (55). Eric Lott praises Eliot's "great essay," in which he finds "a largely persuasive formulation of the place of successful popular arts in the life of the popular classes and of the relation of both to 'respectable' society" (91–92). Yet these, Lott remarks, are "atypical reflections" for Eliot (91). T. J. Clark goes so far as to call "Marie Lloyd" the "best discussion" in its time of the word *popular* (*Painting* 216). After quoting at length from the essay, however, he quickly adds, "This is not exactly the kind of argument, particularly in its closing stages, that one associates with T. S. Eliot" (217).[20] I think it important to reposition "Marie Lloyd," so often treated as a peripheral or merely eccentric essay, at the heart of Eliot's critical thinking—or, better, to refocus our view of Eliot in such a way that "Marie Lloyd" will appear not as an anomaly but as one key document in a long series that embody a genuine receptiveness to popular culture.

Another such document is Eliot's uncompleted first attempt at playwriting, the two fragments eventually titled *Sweeney Agonistes*. Rachel Blau DuPlessis has asserted the importance of restoring this often overlooked work to the Eliot canon for both its unique poetics and its fascinating relation to the Jazz-Age discourses of race, culture, and gender (82). I strongly concur. My chapter 4 traces the play's roots in a variety of popular genres (vaudeville, jazz, melodrama, minstrelsy, and others), the techniques—prosodic, structural, and referential—by which Eliot incorporates these forms in his play, and the relations between Eliot's generic choices and his cultural theory. Rejecting the view that Eliot treats this assemblage of popular forms with a superior irony, I argue that he deploys them in *Sweeney Agonistes* with such powerful intricacy of feeling and complexity of attitude as to keep the spirit of the play profoundly enigmatic; indeed, the delight of this work resides in its unresolvable compound of grotesque disaffection and outright enthusiasm. Like *The Hollow Men*, Eliot's major poem of the same mid-twenties period, *Sweeney* attempts to reground high art in popular culture, and popular culture in ritual. I also pay particular attention to Eliot's adaptation of the popular song "Under the Bamboo Tree," an allusion that he uses, together with other racially inflected elements in the play, to cast suspicion on the very idea of civilization. I end by reconsidering the place of *Sweeney Agonistes* in Eliot's dramatic career. Here I reluctantly dissent from the view expressed by a number of critics who regret that Eliot did not develop his later poetic drama from the platform he established in *Sweeney*, and I suggest that Eliot himself was forced to confront the fact that a popular poetic drama could never have been established on this model.

Chapter 5 follows the trajectory of Eliot's career in drama from *The Rock* (1934) to his late comedies of the 1950s. Like *Sweeney Agonistes,* only less flamboyantly, each of Eliot's plays has a basis in one or more popular genres, and three of them, to judge by their reception, have some qualified claim to be considered "popular" works in their own right. In the course of writing his plays, and particularly as he moved from *Murder in the Cathedral* (1935) to *The Family Reunion* (1939) to *The Cocktail Party* (1950), Eliot strove with growing determination to curb his avant-garde tendencies and reach a workable compromise with the expectations of common theater audiences. And he made this choice even as he recognized that these audiences would comprise not the remnants of Marie Lloyd's semi-mythical working class but, for the most part, the very middle class that Eliot and his fellow modernists had despised for so long.

The signs of Eliot's transition are to be found in the stylistics of the plays themselves, but also, and no less importantly, in the way Eliot allowed himself and his plays to be marketed. In giving himself to the theater establishment in this way, I argue, Eliot made an irrevocable break with the cause of "high art" as this was chastely defined in his time. Many writers and reviewers duly greeted this new project, as its aims became clear, with disbelief and a deep sense of betrayal, while most literary critics did their best to pretend that Eliot's plays never happened. The critics succeeded so well, in fact, that Eliot is almost always discussed today as though he had never written his plays, or as though these labors of twenty-five years need have no bearing on our appraisal of Eliot and what he stood for.[21] My fifth chapter contends otherwise.

The primary goal of my final chapter is to explain how Eliot was reduced in critical consciousness to the familiar fogy who would have no truck with popular culture and did everything humanly possible to protect high art from its invasive pollution. Retracing the historical alchemy that created this Eliot, I find that, sure enough, the Eliot we have inherited is the Eliot who has always been needed by his readers. The critics of the 1930s and 1940s required a "serious" Eliot to help them establish a place for modernism (and for the New Criticism) in the academy; their successors required a Rock-of-Gibraltar Eliot to anchor the post–World War II cultural-political consensus; and critics since the 1960s have too often required a bogeyman Eliot to epitomize the hierarchical, elitist tradition against which they have defined themselves. This is a crude summary, and really I have no wish to demonize any of these groups, to whom my own understanding of Eliot certainly owes a great deal. Yet Eliot has proved extraordinarily useful in each role into which he has been thrust, and the last thing anyone has wanted, to put it baldly, has been a messy, intractable Eliot who unsettles, rather than confirms, the received notions of literature, culture, and modernism. As critics struggle now to recover the anarchic shock that modernist literature delivered in its original moment (Dettmar, *Rereading* 14–15), I believe that such an Eliot is desirable at last. If this Eliot proves no more final than his predecessors, he at least raises uncomfortable, and therefore welcome, questions about our understanding of his own moment, our own moment, and the space between.

As I show in chapter 6, part of the reason why a culturally simplified Eliot has performed so serviceably in the past is that he himself prepared the grounds for his own misreading, both in his late criticism and in the character he famously projected at the peak of his fame. During these last stages of his life, Eliot finally reconciled himself to the everyday culture around him and managed to enter the local human community—a transformation traceable in his creative work from the time of his conversion to its aesthetic peak in *Four Quartets*, and beyond that summit, to his last (and weakest) plays. And yet, reexamining the ceremonious, eccentric, elusively ironic demeanor that Eliot adopted as his public persona during the years of his improbable, more-than-literary celebrity, I discover ample grounds for critical misapprehension. Arguably, Eliot's persona represents his single greatest triumph in the realm of popular culture: the conversion of himself into a world-famous literary legend. That legend, unfortunately, was Cynthia Ozick's Eliot and ours: Eliot, the human embodiment of high culture.

It is not my goal in this book to be exhaustive, and I have not attempted to catalogue every popular reference in Eliot or to investigate every possible interest and influence. Much more could be said about Eliot's lifelong immersion in detective fiction, for instance, about his attraction-repulsion relationship with American English, and about his fascination with nonsense, such newspaper features as comics and crosswords, and bawdy verse.[22] The extent of Eliot's involvement with radio has only just been documented.[23] And what to make of Eliot's enjoyment of boxing remains, at this point, anybody's guess. Even in the areas where I have covered more ground, many stones remain unturned; for example, I am conscious of having said little in this book on the subject of gender. Since the publication of my article "T. S. Eliot and the Cultural Divide" in 1995, it has been gratifying to find scholarship on Eliot and popular culture, of which there had been precious little (and most of that dated), beginning at last to accelerate.[24] That there is so much more terrain to explore than I have mapped in either that essay or this volume seems to me a strong confirmation of my thesis.

Although this book keeps its sights trained on Eliot, it also pursues a mild polemic of a more general kind. It is by now amply clear that a vanguardist intellectualism that looks down from the "vaunting heights of high culture" on the "cultural wastelands" of the popular does nothing to improve the climate for the fine arts (T. Bennett 6); its main result is rather to fan the flames of anti-intellectualism. This was true 150 years ago, when the modern construction of "highbrow" and "lowbrow" first took shape in the United States, and as Andrew Ross has shown in *No Respect*, it remains true today.[25] A secondary function of this book is to promote, even if implicitly, an expansive or flexible, yet considered, stance toward culture. Langston Hughes's student of "English B," who likes "records—Bessie, bop, or Bach," seems to me to be on the right track (*Collected* 410). At the same time, a broad engagement need not be, and indeed must not become, either an exercise in self-congratulation or an excuse for reflexive worship of all things lowbrow. I hope my readers will agree that to deal with a T. S. Eliot who liked a good show, a good thriller, a good tune, as well as a "great" poem, is a refreshing experience. But I also suggest that in such an Eliot subsists an early model— complicated, even deeply flawed, yet still valuable—for our own engagement with culture of all kinds.

On the most important question of all, which is, of course, "How would Eliot have felt about *Cats*?" I must admit that I have no settled opinion. Frank Lentricchia is quite certain that Eliot "would have loved *Cats*" (280), and I think that he is right to a point: it safe to say that, in the abstract, Eliot would have been only too happy to collaborate on the most popular Broadway musical of all time. Still, I prefer to think that Eliot would also have wished, as I do, that the show had been rather better than it was.[26] It is not true that Eliot, in order to enjoy popular art, "temporarily doused his critical faculties," as Anthony Burgess has asserted (104).

And yet, by confronting the world with T. S. Eliot, winner of the 1983 Tony Award for Best Book of a Musical—confirming that Eliot's first Tony (*The Cocktail Party* had won for Best Play in 1950) was no fluke—*Cats* has at least helped to irrigate Eliot's dry-as-a-handful-of-dust reputation. True, it has been fashionable among the intelligentsia to recognize the "irony" in, as one reviewer put it, "the fact that one of the most austere poets of the 20th century . . . should have provided the pretext for such a gigantic extravaganza" (Kissel 196). But the only real irony here, I think, is how little we know what we "know."

A JAZZ-BANJORINE

STRONG WEATHER

Speaking in his native St. Louis in 1953, Eliot recounted the adventure of a certain American native who had survived the arduous voyage to Great Britain:

> In October last occurred an event which, while not as spectacular as the descent of Col. Lindbergh at Le Bourget in "The Spirit of St. Louis," is equally remarkable in its kind. For the first time, apparently, an American robin, well named *turdus migratorius*, crossed the Atlantic under its own power, "favoured" according to the report, by "a period of strong westerly weather." ("American Literature" 50)

Eliot went on to identify this expatriate with the "American language," extending its influence eastward through the mass media, global capitalism, and the other phenomena of postindustrial modernity that seemed to emanate from the United States. Yet it is hard not to identify the robin with Eliot himself, especially when he contrives (as if their parallel courses were not already obvious) to associate the bird's point of origin with St. Louis. Moreover, the "strong westerly weather" that had blown Eliot along his own passage to prominence was essentially the same force that was backing American English. During his rise to what Delmore Schwartz would call "literary dictatorship" (312), Eliot had been an American poet in England—it is not clear that he ever really ceased to be—and his ascendancy seemed related in some mysterious way to the other cultural developments blown over from America by the proverbial winds of change. The conviction that Eliot's work was, somehow, fundamentally connected with jazz in particular has been held with assurance, even taken for granted, by critics since the earliest years of Eliot's career. This chapter will show how that notion, though often vaguely apprehended, contains a genuine insight with a basis in both history and prosody.[1]

In his 1953 address Eliot proceeded to "speculate on the future" of the transatlantic robin. Would it soon be joined by a mate of its own species to populate England with American robins? Otherwise—as seems more likely—

> our lone pioneer must make the best of it, and breed with the English thrush, who is not *migratorius* but *musicus*. In the latter event, the English must look out for a new species of thrush, with a faint red spot on the male breast in springtime; a species which, being a blend of *migratorius* and *musicus*, should become known as the troubadour-bird, or organ-grinder. (50)

Again, drawing a parallel with T. S. Eliot is irresistible. For Eliot was himself, as poet, just that combination of *migratorius* and *musicus*, an original blend of Yankee revolutionary and Great Traditionalist, peripatetic haranguing prophet and patron of the "music of poetry," exile and tribal bard. Eliot himself, to complete the analogy, was the "troubadour-bird," or else—and how much homelier it sounds!—the "organ-grinder." Of these two epithets, the early Eliot at least would have embraced the second. We will see presently how he chose to depict himself as a kind of literary organ-grinder: a rude musician, inelegant, impoverished, unrefined, an American migrant worker in the rich but overcultivated aesthetic fields of the Old World.

To play this role in the culturally conservative enclave of early-twentieth-century London was, for Eliot, to present himself as something of a barbarian at the gates. His status as an outsider was enabling. Only by speaking as an American could Eliot write to Maxwell Bodenheim in 1921, "I have . . . a certain persistent curiosity about the English and a desire to see whether they can ever be roused to anything like intellectual activity" (*Letters* 431). This is Eliot at his most secure, certain that England needed him to rouse it. "This is not conceit," he assured Bodenheim, "merely a kind of pugnacity." By positioning himself as an American intruder, Eliot could critique British culture from a seemingly independent point of view.

Although Eliot found it useful in this endeavor to be an American, his pugnacity found no object in America. He showed little interest in attempting to arouse "anything like intellectual activity" in the United States—considered this, in fact, an unlikely prospect.[2] The letter to Bodenheim explains the English difference: "Once there was a civilisation here, I believe, that's a curious and exciting point" (431).[3] And this opposition of a once-civilized England to an ever-heathenish America gnawed at Eliot precisely because he *was* an American: he feared that his roots would forever snarl him in what he regarded as the morass of American nonculture.[4] In 1919 he told his friend Mary Hutchinson of his struggle to fathom the English national character:

> But remember that I am a *metic*—a foreigner, and that I *want* to understand you, and all the background and tradition of you. I shall try to be frank—because the attempt is so very much worth while with you—it is very difficult with me—both by inheritance and because of my very suspicious and cowardly disposition. But I may simply prove to be a savage. (*Letters* 318)

Shortly after this letter, Eliot was writing "Tradition and the Individual Talent" and attempting to reassure himself that tradition "cannot be inherited, and if you want it you must obtain it by great labour" (4). If so, then being born, as Pound was to put it, "[i]n a half savage country" was no disqualification (*Selected Poems* 61): *everyone* had to labor to obtain "civilization," a term Eliot uses interchangeably with "tradition" in his letter to Hutchinson. But this idea could not dispel the anxious concern that Eliot, as an American, had simply missed out on the opportunity to be civilized. Civilization, he wrote to Hutchinson, "forms people unconsciously—I don't think two or half a dozen people can set out by themselves to be civilised" (*Letters* 317–18). Thus Eliot himself, for all his efforts, might "simply prove to be a savage." He would like to have been Henry James in Rome, but dreaded that he might instead be Burbank, or even Bleistein, in Venice.[5]

Six months later Eliot was writing again to Mary Hutchinson in what appears to be the same tone of self-doubt: "I am glad to hear that you enjoyed yourself and didn't get tired, and that Lytton's life is so perfect. But it is a jazz-banjorine that I should bring, not a lute" (*Letters* 357). While it is impossible to reconstruct the full context of this enigmatic remark, it appears that Hutchinson, addressing Eliot as a troubadour (i.e., poet), had invited him and his "lute" to a social occasion.[6] Perhaps Eliot's lute was to balance Strachey's prose instrument. What is clear, at any rate, is the denial in Eliot's reply that he is the sort of poet who sings to the classic lute; it is rather the "jazz-banjorine" that suits him. Correcting his friend's characterization of his poetry, Eliot bases himself in America rather than Europe, in the contemporary rather than the classical, and in the "jazz movement" of modernism rather than the Great Tradition.

Eliot's seizure of the jazz-banjorine is, on its face, self-abnegating. The banjo, popular in stage entertainment and parlor music, certainly lacked the cultural cachet of the lute; in fact, it had a reputation as a crude instrument with little expressive range:

> With its African percussiveness and short sustain on stopped strings, the banjo was ill suited for the slow legato melodies of much European music, and so seemed, by European aesthetic standards, to be emotionally limited and incapable of musical profundity. (Linn 2)

And since the banjo was still best known as a fixture in the minstrel show, Eliot's comment effectively cast him as a blackface comic—or even as the plantation "darky" such a comic would play. By consigning his talent to the banjo, Eliot is forgoing any claim to the bardic mantle in which Mrs. Hutchinson's reference to the lute would wrap him. He is no troubadour, but merely, as he would describe himself to Herbert Read in 1928, a "southern boy with a nigger drawl" (qtd. in Read 15).

Eliot's selection of the "banjorine" in particular only intensifies his self-denigration. Variations on the banjo proliferated during its heyday: there were mandolin-banjos, zither-banjos, banjolins, cello-banjos, tenor-banjos, and so on.[7] Eliot's instrument of choice (often spelled *banjeaurine*) was a diminutive, high-pitched member of this family. In assigning himself a jazz-banjorine, Eliot was making the humblest available selections in both genre and instrument.

Yet when Eliot offers to play his jazz-banjorine, there is a deeper claim to power underlying his modesty. For seventy-five years, the banjo had spearheaded the "Americanization" of Europe—the infiltration of American popular culture into European life. The instrument seemed to have been present at every turn. In 1843, when the minstrel show first stormed England, the banjo (then a novelty) led the charge. By the 1880s it had made its way into more "elevated" performance settings, becoming in the process an acceptable study for respectable ladies and gentlemen. By the 1890s, it had become positively "a fixture in fashionable . . . parlors" (Winans and Kaufman 13). The fashion became a rage around the turn of the century, when even the Prince of Wales began taking lessons. As ragtime reached England, American banjo virtuosos were on the scene again to facilitate its entry, so that in the early twentieth century the instrument was commonly associated with ragtime (20–21). By the time Eliot claimed to wield a jazz-banjorine, the humble banjo had ushered in an enduring taste for the "unofficial" artistic expression of American popular culture. And so the banjo prepared the arrival of Eliot and his modernism—his own challenge to the official culture of England. For Eliot, to play the jazz-banjorine was to be an agent of change.

There is another, related sense in which Eliot's banjorine signifies a kind of modernist bravado. As Michael North has shown, Eliot and Pound's assumption of African-American "trickster" personae ("Old Possum" and "Brer Rabbit") in their correspondence, together with their appropriation of black dialect, functioned as a private code, a "sign of [their] collaboration against the London literary establishment and the literature it produced" (*Dialect* 77). By "blacking up" in their communications with each other, the two poets affirmed their mutual shame and pride in being American "savages" in exile. But in claiming to play the banjorine, in thus professing his abjection to Mary Hutchinson, Eliot is not only blacking up: he is also concealing his strength from his British correspondent while pretending to weakness. This is, of course, precisely the strategy of the trickster in African-American folklore, and in the enormously popular semi-authentic tales of Uncle Remus, which functioned as the sourcebook for Eliot and Pound in what North calls their "racial masquerade."[8] Meanwhile, by wearing blackface, Eliot again associates himself with the popular culture that was America's most important export—for the African American was always at the center of its development.

"It is a jazz-banjorine that I should bring, not a lute": Brer Rabbit himself could not have framed a brag with warier calculation. Yet its anxious humility is genuine too. Eliot's deliberate association with the emerging American popular culture, and with its largely African-American roots, provided a way of laying claim to revolutionary cultural power while simultaneously acknowledging ambivalence about his relationship to it.

KISSING COUSINS

Even in so early a work as "Portrait of a Lady," a poem written several years before Eliot's emigration, the sense of cultural homelessness is already strongly felt. Implicit in the encounter between the young male narrator and the older woman who seeks to befriend him is a conflict between a degenerate high culture and an inadequate modern alternative—a skirmish fought out largely in the realm of music. As the poem begins, the pair have just come from a Chopin recital, to which she responds with cultivated cliché and he with irony (the pianist who "Transmit[s] the Preludes, through his hair and fingertips" is only "the latest Pole" in an implied succession of uncoiffed Slavs). The lady's musty romanticism is likewise embodied in musical terms:

—And so the conversation slips
Among velleities and carefully caught regrets
Through attenuated tones of violins

Mingled with remote cornets
And begins.

(CPP 8)

These "attenuated" sounds are the outmoded culture of the lady's Victorian world. Where one might expect the speaker to be cast as simply antithetical, though, he turns out to be rather more interesting.

Interrogating his own position throughout the poem, the young narrator asks essentially what he, as a modern, has to substitute for the lady's decaying high culture. He finds no single answer to these questions but proposes several partial solutions, as when "Inside my brain a dull tom-tom begins / Absurdly hammering a prelude of its own" (9). The modern comprises, among other things, the primitive—a tom-tom capable of disrupting the meticulously arranged world of the lady. Uncontrollable and destructive, however, this "Capricious monotone" seems to offer no basis for a modern successor to the lady's disintegrating world.

A passage in the second section of the poem—Eliot's earliest canonical work[9]—approaches the speaker's problem along a different axis:

You will see me any morning in the park
Reading the comics and the sporting page.
Particularly I remark
An English countess goes upon the stage.
A Greek was murdered at a Polish dance,
Another bank defaulter has confessed.

(10)

Popular culture, then, including such favorite Eliot pastimes as comic strips, drama, boxing (on "the sporting page"), and sensational murder stories, might offer an alternative to Chopin, were it not associated so immediately with vulgarity and materialism. Later, Eliot would complain that the newspapers were "filled with nonsense and personalities" (*Letters* 230)—in fact, with "an infinity of trivial matters" (220). These remarks date from 1918, when Eliot wrote to thank his mother for a shipment of American newspapers: "They are the first I have seen for a very long time, and they seemed very strange and also wasteful of paper." All was not lost, though: "The part that usually interests me the most is the sporting news" (220).

The speaker in "Portrait," similarly, finds the tabloid diverting enough to read daily but does not feel at home in its world:

I keep my countenance,
I remain self-possessed
Except when a street-piano, mechanical and tired
Reiterates some worn-out common song

With the smell of hyacinths across the garden
Recalling things that other people have desired.

(10)

In these lines Eliot encapsulates a simultaneous yearning for and fear of the
popular and of ordinary feeling. The very possibility of belonging to the
mass is both craved and dismissed. The street piano grinding out its "common song" has moved the speaker where Chopin has failed—but only by
reminding him that however much he enjoys the comics, he is no less excluded from the quotidian life surrounding him in the park than he is from
the lady's "buried life" of tea and lilacs. He remains trapped between these
two worlds to the very end of the poem. The lady has her conventions and
clichés, her preludes and "velleities"; it is somehow the narrator, though he
will survive her, who is "really in the dark" (11). The declining romantic
high culture and the ascendant popular fight to a draw, while Eliot's speaker
can only observe gloomily his own alienation from both.

In "Cousin Nancy," a poem of 1915, Eliot—now ensconced, though
still precariously, in London—gives an updated and more impersonal treatment to a similar network of anxieties. Nancy challenges the stale New England tradition of her aunts through her participation in the nascent culture
of what we have since learned to call the Jazz Age:

Miss Nancy Ellicott
Strode across the hills and broke them,
Rode across the hills and broke them—
The barren New England hills—
Riding to hounds
Over the cow-pasture.

Miss Nancy Ellicott smoked
And danced all the modern dances;
And her aunts were not quite sure how they felt about it,
But they knew that it was modern.

(CPP 17)

The second stanza situates the poem historically by alluding to the craze for
"social dancing" that was sweeping across the United States and blowing on
to Europe at just that time, an extension of the popularity of ragtime. American restaurants were laying dance floors and hiring bands in 1912; by the
next year, theaters and ballrooms were beginning to sponsor dance con-
tests, and department stores were advertising thés dansants (Ewen 181–82).
Nancy Ellicott's "modern dances"—the Grizzly Bear, the Texas Tommy, the
Lame Duck, the Fox-Trot, and so on—followed each other in rapid succession. And the establishment, of course, made known its disapproval.

Eliot was not about to range himself with that reflexive opposition and its expressions of alarm. His endorsement of Nancy's offensive against social authority is signaled by his comic portrayal of her aunts' befuddlement and by the parenthetical description of the matriarchal New England hills as "barren." But Nancy's unconventionality also makes Eliot sufficiently uncomfortable that he must parry it with irony, chiefly by making Nancy a romantic heroine of gargantuan dimensions. As a metaphor for her indulgence in tobacco and the tango, the image of Nancy bestriding and breaking the hills is simply out of proportion, an effect corroborated when "Riding to hounds" is juxtaposed with "Over the cow pasture." Nancy's rebellion is thus rendered nearly as absurd as her aunts' reaction.

Yet in its original setting in *Prufrock and Other Observations*, "Cousin Nancy" appears among such other satires of high-bourgeois society as "The *Boston Evening Transcript*" and "Aunt Helen." In this context, Nancy's subversion remains, on balance, admirable, rather like the disturbances of Mr. Apollinax. The poem's final lines go so far along this ambiguous trajectory as to align Nancy with George Meredith's "Prince Lucifer" against the heavenly order of Victorian culture:

> Upon the glazen shelves kept watch
> Matthew and Waldo, guardians of the faith,
> The army of unalterable law.

(CPP 18)

Although the grandiose association of Nancy with Lucifer continues to ironize her, this ending, as Ronald Bush points out, moves "beyond social satire" (24). By 1915 the cultural "law" of Arnold and Emerson is hardly "unalterable": Eliot shrewdly perceives that Nancy's modern dances and the insurgent modernity they represent are in the process of altering it beyond recognition, leaving Matthew and Waldo scowling from their glazen shelves. But the poem offers no clear point of view on this paradigm shift. It registers a certain enjoyment of Nancy's transgressions, the confusion of her aunts, the discomfiture of the two sages—and it qualifies this appreciation with an evident uneasiness with the new paradigm (and, doubtless, the New Woman) that Nancy represents.[10] Like "Portrait of a Lady," "Cousin Nancy" is an expression of a profound ambivalence in which Eliot deliberately yet reluctantly allies himself with the modern, and with popular culture, against an unpalatable and moribund tradition.

Eliot's mixed reaction to Nancy's audacity is symptomatic of his uneasy alliance with the American, the modern, and the popular. Truth to tell, he and Nancy were virtually kissing cousins. Privately he "confess[ed] to taking great pleasure in seeing women smoke"—so he told his real cousin Eleanor Hinkley around the same time he wrote the poem (*Letters* 96).

Moreover, he liked the "emancipated Londoners" he was meeting in 1915; they were "charmingly sophisticated (even 'disillusioned') without being hardened," and "quite different from anything I have known at home or here" (96). Vivien Haigh-Wood, one of the charmingly sophisticated women mentioned in this letter, became Eliot's wife two months later. Vivien, incidentally, smoked and danced all the modern dances extremely well.

Eliot himself, as a matter of fact, danced all the modern dances—and fretted when he couldn't. In Oxford late in 1914 he had complained ironically of his disconnection from American cultural developments: "I really feel quite as much *au courant* of [Boston] life as anyone can who has not yet learned the fox trot" (*Letters* 70). It was too bad: he'd had such "great fun" on his Atlantic crossing four months earlier, dancing with various girls "to the sound of the captain's phonograph" (*Letters* 39). At least he was "able to make use of the fox trot"—or of his unfamiliarity with it—in a debate at Merton College on the question, "Resolved that this society abhors the threatened Americanisation of Oxford":

> I supported the negative: I pointed out to them frankly how much they owed to Amurrican culcher in the drayma (including the movies) in music, in the cocktail, and in the dance. And see, said I, what we the few Americans here are losing while we are bending our energies toward your uplift . . . ; we the outposts of progress are compelled to remain in ignorance of the fox trot. (*Letters* 70)

Playing up his Americanness, even playing up his Missouri drawl ("Amurrican culcher in the drayma"), Eliot relishes his difference from the society that "abhors" the incursion of American popular culture. He is not altogether bluffing when he portrays Britain as practically an American colony, dependent on the New World for cultural "uplift" by missionaries such as himself ("the outposts of progress"). As for the fox-trot, Eliot has correctly discerned that such innovations in the dance are "one of the spearheads of the American cultural penetration of Europe" (Hawkes 90). Apparently Eliot's audience also saw the point: his side "won the debate by two votes" (*Letters* 70).[11]

Terence Hawkes has observed that for Eliot, gauging English culture from a foreigner's perspective, stodgy British dancing reflected a deficient modernity that similarly vitiated British literary and intellectual life (91). If English dancing was "very stiff and old fashioned" (*Letters* 97), English letters was blighted by an analogous "critical Brahminism, destructive and conservative in temper" (314). "Novelty," Eliot wrote John Quinn in 1919, "is no more acceptable here than anywhere else, and the forces of conservatism and obstruction are more intelligent, better educated, and more formidable" (314–15). Or, as he declared in "Tradition and the Individual Talent," if tradition signifies mere resistance to change, to modernization, then "'tradition' should positively be discouraged," for "novelty is better than repetition" (4).[12] So Eliot was, and allowed himself to be, a fox-trotting American in England, even if he did "terrif[y] one poor girl . . . by starting to dip in my one-step" (Letters 97).[13] As a conscious and self-mocking evangelist of the new, he maintained a paradoxical attitude of ironic affection for the popular—an essentially camp sensibility that leaves many traces in his art. It was here, as much as in his formal innovations or in his urban phantasmagoria, that Eliot's modernism lay.

A "BLACK AND GRINNING MUSE"

For a poet to portray himself as playing a "jazz-banjorine" around 1920— in fact, for a poet to have any truck with jazz at all—was not only to claim a certain currency but to take sides in an ideological battle over the significance of modernism in the arts and of modernity in general. To unpack fully the meaning of Eliot's self-fashioning we must consider the meaning of jazz itself.

Inevitably, Eliot's conception of jazz would have been more expansive than ours. As Howard Rye asserts, minstrel songs and what we have since isolated as jazz and blues formed a generic continuum in the 1920s rather than a set of discrete musics (45). The "symphonic jazz" of the era also belongs to this continuum, as do ragtime and certain strains of "sheer Tin Pan Alley pop" (Douglas 352). Bernard Gendron has argued sensibly that an "essentialist construction of 'authentic' jazz" was imposed on the Jazz Age by later criticism, creating an insupportable dichotomy between the "genuine" and the "counterfeit" (Between 90–91). For present purposes, then, it makes sense to imagine jazz in the comprehensive sense it took on in twenties discourse—a sense that includes the "classic" blues, ragtime, any sufficiently syncopated music of the vaudeville stage, the "sweet" jazz of orchestras such as Paul Whiteman's, and jazz-inflected popular songs and dance music, as well as the "hot" New Orleans style to which the term jazz is now usually limited.

The popularity of ragtime in the United States dated back to the 1890s, with Britain not far behind, but the smash success of Irving Berlin's "Alexander's Ragtime Band" initiated a second wave in 1911 that introduced millions of Europeans to African-American musicianship, the "modern dances" of Nancy Ellicott, and the joys of continual syncopation. At this point a strong sense developed that something permanent had changed in music and in leisure, and that this change heralded or represented in its own right a seismic shift in Western culture. Its way thus prepared by ragtime, jazz was laden with extramusical meanings from the moment the larger public began to hear of it. Despite its subtitle, for example, Edmund Wilson's essay of 1922, "The Aesthetic Upheaval in France: The Influence of Jazz in Paris and Americanization of French Literature and Art," barely mentions music; the article deals instead with French literary modernism and with the invasion of such phenomena as the skyscraper, the machine, and the motion picture. Jazz, that is, was nearly synonymous with the modern, and the modern with American mass culture. Because of its connection with nightlife, and because of its African-American origins, which allowed it to be figured as a "primitive" alternative to Western culture, jazz stood not only for skyscrapers but for social informality, for relaxed sexual strictures, for leisure rather than industry, for skepticism rather than faith, and, generally, for moral and aesthetic relativism (Leonard 70). Jazz signified, in short, a rejection of the entire Victorian system of value (North, *Reading* 143–45). Eliot's "Portrait of a Lady" invokes this symbology when the "dull tom-tom" in the young narrator's brain reflexively hammers out its own rebellion against the lady's romantic worldview.[14]

For a poet to write *jazz* was inevitably to open a window on this discourse, especially since artistic modernism itself was often associated with jazz. As a columnist in the *New York Times* sneered in 1924:

> Jazz is to real music exactly what most of the "new poetry," so-called, is to real poetry. Both are without the structure and form essential to music and poetry alike, and both are the products, not of innovators, but of incompetents. ("Topics")

And the American critic Robert Underwood Johnson complained that modern free verse "disdains the lute, the harp, the oboe, and the 'cello and is content with the tom-tom, the triangle, and the banjo" (265–66)—a comment that further illuminates the context within which Eliot declined the lute for the banjorine. Johnson's first example of "this so-called modern American poetry" was part I of Eliot's "Preludes" (268–69).

Despite such criticism, other poets willingly accepted and even pressed the same associations. In "A High-Toned Old Christian Woman," which dates, like *The Waste Land,* from 1922, Wallace Stevens taunts a member of the ancien régime while specifically linking the "New Poetry" with jazz. Modernity, which the old woman parses as "bawdiness," is "converted" by the poets "into palms, / Squiggling like saxophones" (*Collected* 59). Stevens's habitual figuration of the imagination as tropical coincides conveniently here with popular representations of "jungle jazz." Modern poems (Stevens's "novelties of the sublime") are verbal analogues to the quintessentially modern music identified with the saxophone and the banjo, whose staccato the poem imitates as "tink and tank and tunk-a-tunk-tunk."

Stevens's "Of Modern Poetry" similarly defines the modernist timbre as the "twanging [of] a wiry string" (240). Jazz is the "skeptical music" of modern poetry that offers to supplant all preexisting systems of belief (122).

The most vociferous opposition to jazz came from religious, political, and community leaders as well as self-appointed moralists (Stevens's "hightoned old Christian woman") who read in the enormous popularity of the new music a threat to established values and social structures. Its proponents did not dispute this perception; rather, they treated the disruptive power of jazz as a positive force. Gilbert Seldes's defense is typical in this respect: "Jazz is roaring and stamping and vulgar, you may say; but you can not say that it is pale and polite and dying"—as opposed, that is, to "conventional pedantry . . . and a society corrupted by false ideas of politeness and gentility in the arts" (qtd. in "Effort" 29–30). Wilson likewise contrasted American mass culture with the morbidity of a Europe strewn with "monuments of the dead": American "films and factories and marimbas [i.e., jazz] are at least of the living world" ("Aesthetic" 100). Jazz, like electric signs, was one of those "triumphs and atrocities of the barbarous" that the New World offered a new age. By asserting an alliance with jazz—by offering to play his jazz-banjorine at Mary Hutchinson's soirée—Eliot depicts himself as a similarly barbarous invader, confessing his atrocity ("I may simply prove to be a savage") but expecting, like jazz, to triumph.

To an even greater extent than ragtime, jazz was embraced by avantgardists and progressive intellectuals as a symbol of their onslaught against sterile mores and "traditional" aesthetics. For these groups, jazz became the cornerstone of a new, more broadminded attitude toward popular culture, often leading to a call for commerce between high culture and the popular. Yet an inability to escape the ideological implications of the high-low binary almost always qualified this position. Jean Cocteau, for example, prided himself on being "very good at jazz"; playing it, he wrote, gave him "a score of arms" and made him "a god of din" (193). Together with the poster, the skyscraper, the circus, and the café-concert, jazz represented for him the arrival of a new age. In 1918, Cocteau counseled artists to immerse themselves in popular culture because "The music-hall, the circus, and American negro-bands" were more full of the "life force" than all the deliberate "audacities" of the avant-garde (21).[15] Yet Cocteau values jazz most for what he, as an artist, can make of it. One fills one's imaginary pockets by experiencing the popular—by collecting African sculpture, attending the café-concert, and putting a record on the gramophone—but these things in themselves are "worthless bric-à-brac." Cocteau's advice is to absorb these sources and then to "substitute gradually your own voice for the phonograph and raw metal for the trinkets" (35). In the end, what Cocteau promotes is the aestheticist ideal of an autonomous high art nurtured in an atmosphere of flânerie or slumming (Gendron, *Between* 95–97). For all its bravado, his argument leaves the categories of high and low intact, even unquestioned.

Cocteau's approach is manifest in *Parade*, the ballet he created in collaboration with Apollinaire, Picasso, Satie, and Massine and envisioned as "a kind of renovation of the theater" (Steegmuller 167). Its emblematic characters—acrobat, Chinese magician, lively American girl—dance a "transposition of the music-hall" to the accompaniment of modernistic mechanical sounds (typewriter, dynamo, train, siren), words spoken through a megaphone, and a musical score with ragtime inflections. "For the first time," wrote composer Francis Poulenc, "the music hall was invading Art with a capital A" (Steegmuller 185). Nevertheless, *Parade* was quite evidently *not* music hall: it appropriated popular culture but was never meant to be popular. On the contrary, Cocteau hoped for—and got—a scandal. Eliot, as we will see, was more complicatedly torn between a similar contempt for public opinion and an intense desire to establish a rapport with a large audience.

Of course there were also a good many intellectuals, even in avant-garde circles, who wanted nothing to do with jazz. Clive Bell of Bloomsbury launched one of the ugliest attacks in a 1921 essay called "Plus de Jazz." For Bell, jazz is much less an ethnic music than an artistic movement, a subgenre of modernism, "a ripple" on a larger wave "which began at the end of the nineteenth century in a reaction against realism and a scientific paganism" (93). The "inventors of Jazz," Bell speculates, considered nineteenth-century art to have been excessively dedicated to "beauty and intensity"; they founded jazz, therefore, in rebellion against Nobility and Beauty. Their impudence, motivated by a "childish" hatred of culture and intellect, finds its "technical equivalent" in syncopation (93). By the "inventors of Jazz," Bell means European and American avant-gardists, for African-American musicians, in his view, are merely pawns in an aesthetic contest beyond their scope.

When it comes to the work of artists he ascribes to the "jazz movement," Bell is somewhat more sensitive. Cubism was often identified outright with jazz, and Bell concedes that in their exploration of that generally unprofitable territory Picasso and Braque have "produced works of the greatest beauty and significance" (95). Stravinsky, too, has been "influenced much by nigger rhythms and nigger methods" and thus belongs to the jazz movement as much as any great artist can be said to belong to a movement (94).

Jazz in literature, according to Bell, appears in syncopated rhythms and in distorted "sequences [of] grammar and logic." Its truest exemplars in poetry are Cocteau and Cendrars, who he says are worth, together, perhaps a half-hour's attention. But Eliot, whom Bell calls "about the best of our living poets," is also a product of the jazz movement. In a bizarre conceit Bell figures jazz—Eliot's "black and grinning muse"—as midwife to Eliot's "agonizing labors" of composition:

> Apparently it is only by adopting a demurely irreverent attitude, by being primly insolent, and by playing the devil with the instrument of Shakespeare and Milton, that Mr. Eliot is able occasionally to deliver himself of one of those complicated and remarkable imaginings of his: apparently it is only in language, of an exquisite purity so far as material goes, but twisted and ragged out of easy recognition that these nurslings can be swathed. (94)

I will be arguing presently that there is something to this. Certainly when Eliot published *The Waste Land* a year later, with its "Shakespeherian Rag" and its ragging of Shakespeare, Bell must have looked positively prophetic.[16]

More telling than Bell's specific judgments, though, is his assumption that there was such a thing at all as a "jazz movement" in the arts; that its methods were in some way connected with the musical techniques of jazz; that its aesthetic goals were embodied in the "meaning" of jazz; that it was socially and culturally revolutionary. Despite his respect for certain "jazz" artists, Bell is determined to range himself on the side of Beethoven, Beauty, and Nobility against a faction that (he claims) elevates popular culture over Art. It is a grievous mistake, he suggests, for artists to take seriously either waltzes or ragtime: the divide between popular and high art must not be violated (94). This is the sort of argument that is now often taken to characterize modernism's unalloyed horror of mass culture—usually in contrast with postmodernism's embrace. Yet Eliot's position, for one, is considerably more complex and less hysterical; and as Bell realized, Eliot's genius was thoroughly entangled with his "black and grinning muse." Indeed, Eliot had accepted his place in the jazz movement a long time before.

WHAT, YOU WANT ACTION?

Eliot's forgotten career in ballroom dance is matched by a disposition to crooning. Undeterred by vocal abilities considerably less than, say, Joyce's, he was known to unleash a vaudeville tune or a bawdy ballad among his sometimes unprepared acquaintances.[17] In the fifties he sang to his friend and "guardian" Mary Trevelyan selections ranging from African-American spirituals to pop (Gordon, *Eliot's New Life* 198, 212–14). Robert Giroux recollected Eliot's singing, in a single evening, "the verses of more [George M.] Cohan songs than I knew existed" (343). And Valerie Eliot later found her morning ritual of shaving her husband rendered "hazardous" by his spirited interpretations of comic music-hall numbers (T. Wilson 45). Popular song marked the stages of Eliot's life, as it does for others; his first visit to London, in 1910, for example, remained for him "always associated [with] the music of 'In the Shadows' by Herman Finck" (*Letters* 17). Perhaps Eliot could have erected internal barriers sufficient to keep such influences out of his work. But he did not.

On the contrary, the poems in Eliot's early notebook (published in 1996 as *Inventions of the March Hare*) illustrate the importance of jazz-inflected popular song to the formation of his verse style. "Suite Clownesque" (1910), for example, includes a vaudeville-comic staging of Prufrock's urban wanderings rendered as Tin Pan Alley pastiche:

> If you're walking down the avenue,
> Five o'clock in the afternoon,
> I may meet you
> Very likely greet you
> Show you that I know you.
>
> (35)

If such cadences were not recognizable enough, the persona soon makes their origins explicit, exclaiming "It's Broadway after dark!" and even alluding to "By the Light of the Silvery Moon," the familiar song hit of the previous year (171). A stage direction prescribing an accompaniment "on the sandboard and bones" introduces a minstrel element into the mix. The poem's colloquial is colored with "Americanisms" and other slang of recent vintage ("get away with it," "cocktails," "I guess," "up to date," "very likely," "I'm all right").[18] In an unusually healthy adolescent twist, Eliot gives his comedian-hero an entourage of "girls" (enough to turn heads) and stands "looking them over" later on the beach. Through the mask of the clown, Eliot is able to project a side of his own character normally obscured by self-consciousness and ambivalence; for once he feels "Quite at home in the universe." Immersing himself in the strong popular rhythms that supply his poetic medium, he celebrates his young, American self, genially "Shaking cocktails on a hearse" as if to bury the corpse of the Victorian past in manhattans and martinis. He is "First born child of the absolute / Neat, complete, / In the quintessential flannel suit" (35). The suit fits Prufrock, who also wears flannel on the beach; but in "Suite Clownesque" the lullaby of Broadway has momentarily soothed the Prufrockian breast. The poem's confidence proves short-lived, however, for even here, anxiety finally prevails:

> I guess there's nothing the matter with us!
> —But say, just be serious,
> Do you think that I'm all right?
>
> (35)

With this uncomfortable plea, the poem ends, leaving the reader to wonder whether the youthful optimism of the preceding lines was just bravado after all.

Eliot's harlequinade and his use of song rhythms both owe a great deal to Jules Laforgue, the French symbolist to whom Eliot had apprenticed himself early in 1909. In his "Complaintes," where the Pierrot figure makes his first appearances, Laforgue, too, experiments by incorporating popular song into his poetry; thus "Complainte de Lord Pierrot" begins by parodying "Au clair de la lune," and "Complainte de cette bonne lune" (which Eliot would later quote in "Rhapsody on a Windy Night") opens with an imitation of "Sur le pont d'Avignon." In these poems, as Anne Holmes argues, Laforgue rewrites familiar materials to "complicate and fuse worlds": the nostalgic, bucolic realm evoked within the musical allusions, and his own sophisticated, urban milieu, in which the songs are heard (34). The technique clearly made an impression on Eliot, whose own allusions frequently perform a similar function. It may even suggest a Laforguean and popular prehistory for the "mythical method," whose purpose is likewise, according to Eliot, the fusion of dissevered worlds ("*Ulysses*" 177–78).

The rhythmic model of popular song played a critical role in helping Laforgue break with the "formal Alexandrine" of traditional French prosody (Collie and L'Heureux 5), just as it may have helped Eliot reduce iambic pentameter to the "ghost of [a] meter" (Eliot, "Reflections" 187). At the same time, Laforgue's use of popular music in the *Complaintes* reveals certain limitations not present in the early Eliot. Laforgue's popular songs tend to be isolated within their host poems, their simple verse forms engulfed by the poems' own complex structures of rhyme and mutable line-length (A. Holmes 81). It could be argued that these "intricately patterned stanzas" are themselves songlike, as in Donne's *Songs and Sonnets;*[19] but if so, their musical quality remains quite different from that of the songs they actually quote. It can hardly be said, for instance, that "Complainte de Lord Pierrot" as a whole is suffused with the cadences of "Au clair de la lune."

The more consequential Laforguean model for Eliot's musical prosody is his posthumous *Derniers Vers,* a book that did much to establish *vers libre* in French. Eliot's early poems even show a prosodic development parallel to Laforgue's: "Spleen" and "Conversation Galante" borrow their versification from the *Complaintes,* while the poems that follow work their way toward *Derniers Vers:*

> "Portrait of a Lady," "Prufrock" and "La Figlia che Piange" are all in free
> verse of the kind toward which Laforgue's poetry evolved: irregular lines
> representing emotive ideas compose a stanza-sentence, with irregular
> rhyme and assonance lending firmness to fluid structure. . . . Through

most of his first book Eliot exploits the instrument developed by Laforgue in his last. (Ramsey 202)

Eliot must have been thinking of *Derniers Vers* when he told Donald Hall in 1963: "My early *vers libre*, of course, was started under the endeavor to practice the same form as Laforgue," which required "rhyming lines of irregular length, with the rhymes coming in irregular places" (D. Hall 97).

One of the powers of this loose "form" is its ability to echo the "shifting play of emotions" expressed in the words (A. Holmes 129), a capacity that depends on a ductile, songlike patterning rich in unpredictable aural effects. Just as the words of a popular song adhere to a musical substructure that is hidden when the lyrics are printed alone, Laforgue's lines seem to take shape around a concealed framework:

Je fume, étalé face au ciel,
Sur l'impériale de la diligence,
Ma carcasse est cahotée, mon âme danse
Comme un Ariel;
Sans miel, sans fiel, ma belle âme danse,
O routes, coteaux, ô fumées, ô vallons,
Ma belle âme, ah! récapitulons.

(*Derniers* 213)

The manuscript of "L'Hiver qui vient," the first of Laforgue's late poems, shows Laforgue working backward from "long Whitmanesque lines" (he had recently been translating the American poet) toward a more "musical" effect produced by short, irregular lines saturated with repetition, rhyme, near-rhyme, and internal rhyme (A. Holmes 119–20). It is really in these last poems—rather than in the *Complaintes*, with their song quotations—that Laforgue earns his laurels as the "Watteau of the café-concert." For in the *Derniers Vers*, the songs of the French music hall have fully permeated the poetry: the use of song is no longer separable from the quality of the verse itself. This achievement is Laforgue's most significant gift to Eliot, surpassing even the better-noted attributes of urbanity and self-reflexive irony.

Yet Eliot's poems also have a rhythmic suavity quite distinct from the ejaculatory style of *Derniers Vers*, with its jagged syntax and concentration of exclamation points; the later poet produces the effect of syncopation with considerably less strain. No doubt the difference derives in part from the linguistic gulf between French and English, but it also inheres in the two poets' underlying musical models, for Eliot's world of popular song is not Laforgue's. What the apprentice poems of *Inventions of the March Hare* now enable us to see is that the acknowledged influence of Laforgue was complemented by the nearly suppressed yet indispensable influence of American jazz. It was the *convergence* of these elements—or their chemical interaction in the presence of the poet's mental catalyst—that produced the masterpieces of the *Prufrock* period. Laforgue showed Eliot how to adapt his voice to the popular material around him, and jazz gave Eliot a way to bring Laforgue into contemporary English—that is, a way to incorporate the inflections of his own language in a form of verse derived from another.[20]

The crucial text, an untitled poem written in February 1911, makes the confluence of Laforgue's modernity with the experience of jazz all but explicit—enacts, in fact, the process by which Eliot put them together. The narrator of this poem sits in a Parisian cabaret, where he languishes among

> The smoke that gathers blue and sinks
> The torpid smoke of rich cigars
> The torpid after-dinner drinks . . .

(Inventions 70)

The attitude of sophisticated ennui owes much to Laforgue as well as to Arthur Symons, who introduced Eliot to Laforgue. The languorous smoke, a fin-de-siècle cliché, echoes such poems as Symons's "At the Cavour," which is already derivative of, for instance, Laforgue's "La cigarette." After the mesmeric and abstract opening stanza, the speaker's drifting attention is finally caught by the live music around him, and Eliot's verse, heretofore as fatigued as Symons's, swerves abruptly into an entirely new form:

> What, you want action?
> Some attraction?
> Now begins
> The piano and the flute and two violins
> Someone sings
> A lady of almost any age
> But chiefly breast and rings
> "Throw your arms around me—Aint you glad you found me"
> Still that's hardly strong enough—
> Here's a negro (teeth and smile)
> Has a dance that's quite worth while
> That's the stuff!
> (Here's your gin
> Now begin!)

(70)

Though it is impossible to say to what extent the enthusiasm of the closing lines is sincere and to what extent ironic, the flattery of imitation is unmistakable. Eliot's stanza remarkably depicts proto-jazz performance and dance, quotes an actual lyric, includes appropriate slang ("action," "the stuff"),[21] and strikingly replicates the angular rhythms and sudden, un-predictable rhymes of popular ragtime lyrics of the period. The italicized excerpt from the chorus of Harry von Tilzer's "Cubanola Glide" nestles comfortably among Eliot's original lines. Ragtime, as Philip Furia explains, "licensed the vernacular as a lyrical idiom and forced the lyricist to con-struct a lyric out of short, juxtaposed phrases marked by internal rhymes and jagged syntactical breaks" (49). An ear for these qualities helped make Eliot, like the band leader of "Alexander's Ragtime Band"—another com-position of 1911—a "ragged meter man."

Eric Sigg has posed the question, "Is it too much to suppose that American popular music, whether from ragtime or Tin Pan Alley, helped to cultivate Eliot's ear for rhythm?" (21). The question need not be posed rhetorically: on the evidence of *Inventions of the March Hare* we can be sure that the influence of American popular music was indeed critical. It would be no exaggeration to call a poem like "The smoke that gathers blue and sinks" jazz poetry *avant la lettre*. Eliot's lines anticipate the musical techniques that would be exploited by Langston Hughes at the height of the Jazz Age.

Still, Eliot's precocity would be of no more than passing interest if he had merely experimented with such a verse form and then moved on. In reality, however, the explicit references to popular music in "Suite Clownesque" and "The smoke that gathers blue and sinks" foreground an element that is no less vital, only better assimilated, in the famous lines composed a few months later. Compare, for instance,

> First born child of the absolute
> Neat, complete,
> In the quintessential flannel suit
>
> ("Suite Clownesque," *Inventions* 35)

with

> And indeed there will be time
> To wonder, "Do I dare," and, "Do I dare?"
> Time to turn back and descend the stair,
> With a bald spot in the middle of my hair
>
> ("The Love Song of J. Alfred Prufrock," CPP 4)

or

> And I must borrow every changing shape
> To find expression . . . dance, dance
> Like a dancing bear,
> Cry like a parrot, chatter like an ape.
> Let us take the air, in a tobacco trance.
>
> ("Portrait of a Lady," CPP 11)

Though these lines drape loosely over a skeleton of iambic pentameter, what gives them the particular character that one recognizes as Eliotic has no source in classical metrics. Nor is this inflection lost in *The Waste Land*—

> O City city, I can sometimes hear
> Beside a public bar in Lower Thames Street,
> The pleasant whining of a mandoline
> And a clatter and a chatter from within
> Where fishmen lounge at noon. . . .

(CPP 45)

—nor even years later in *Ash-Wednesday*:

> The new years walk, restoring
> Through a bright cloud of tears, the years, restoring
> With a new verse the ancient rhyme. Redeem
> The time. Redeem
> The unread vision in the higher dream.

(CPP 64)

Eliot's patented cadences—his characteristic rhythms, the ways he uses rhyme, the tonal contours of his lines—were discovered in the sounds of popular music circa 1911. It is "Amurrican culcher . . . in music, in the cocktail, and in the dance" that gives Eliot's poetry its distinctive resonance.

THE SPIRIT OF ST. LOUIS

That Eliot should have absorbed the cadences of popular music, and that jazz should have been an important constituent of his poetry, ought to be less surprising than it now seems. Through much of Eliot's criticism runs the idea that, whatever else the artist may draw upon, the wellsprings of art lie in the ambient culture, in the broadest sense of the term. In "*Ulysses*, Order, and Myth," he defines the "classical tendency" as "doing the best one can with the material at hand" (177). The mind of each poet, Eliot speculates in *The Use of Poetry and the Use of Criticism*, is "magnetised in its own way, to select automatically, in his reading (from picture papers and cheap novels, indeed, as well as serious books, and least likely from works of an abstract nature . . .) the material—an image, a phrase, a word—which may be of use to him later" (69–70). And "of course only a part of an author's imagery comes from his reading" (141). In "The Metaphysical Poets," it is the "great variety and complexity" of modern civilization that the poet must work into an increasingly "comprehensive" art (248); in "Marie Lloyd" it is the details of popular experience (e.g., "what objects a middle-aged woman of the char-woman class would carry in her bag") (406). The stuff of a poet's work "comes from the whole of his sensitive life since early childhood" (UPUC 141).

Some of the material Eliot had on hand since his early childhood explains a great deal. St. Louis became the acknowledged birthplace of ragtime during the first decade of his life, and sheer proximity placed him virtually in the thick of things. Just after remarking that his poetry showed "traces of every environment in which I have lived," Eliot recalled in a late lecture that his family "lived on in a neighborhood which had become shabby to a degree approaching slumminess, after all our friends and acquaintances had moved further west" ("Influence" 421–22). It was the African-American poor who were gradually surrounding the Eliot homestead at 2635 Locust. Its site (for the house itself has not survived) now abuts streets named for Martin Luther King, Redd Foxx, and—just a few blocks to the north—baseball great James "Cool Papa" Bell of the Negro Leagues. W. C. Handy composed his "St. Louis Blues" in a nearby bar (Hughes, "Songs" 160). By 1900, only Baltimore had a higher concentration of African Americans than St. Louis (Lipsitz 17). Sheltered though he must have been as the scion of St. Louis's most respectable family, Eliot, who always had an ear for the vernacular, could not have failed to take something from these increasingly racialized surroundings.[22]

Sigg has pointed out that the Eliot home "lay only a short walk from the Chestnut Valley 'sporting district,'" where ragtime floating out of the saloons and honky-tonks almost literally "filled the St. Louis air" (20–21). Eliot grew up, in fact, exactly two miles from a center of popular entertainment with more than local consequence—though he was not likely to have ventured inside. This was Babe Connors's African-American "resort" on South Sixth Street, not far from Tony Faust's restaurant (Ewen 81–82).[23] A monumental exhibition of glitz and glamorous showgirls, Babe Connors's anticipated by three decades the elegant Harlem clubs of the Jazz Age. Its featured performer during Eliot's childhood was the legendary Mama Lou, a forerunner of the great female blues singers of the twenties, who broke new ground in nightlife by performing for a white clientele (Ewen 82).

It was Mama Lou who popularized "Frankie and Johnny," the quintessential African-American ballad that Eliot was later heard to sing (Lucas 47); she also introduced audiences to "A Hot Time in the Old Town" and "Ta-ra-ra-boom-de-ay," which Lottie Collins turned into a London music-hall sensation in 1892. These songs and others emanating from Babe Connors's place were well known in St. Louis before Tin Pan Alley songwriters picked them up, bowdlerized their lyrics, and made them into national and international standards.[24] In England, where Collins's naughty rendition of

"Ta-ra-ra-boom-de-ay" provoked endless discussion, its source remained a puzzle. One pundit traced it to "'an Algerian *danse du ventre*' (belly-dance) or the 'barbaric orgies of Central Africa'"; another identified it as "a 'mock coon song' written by a London musician" (Koritz 21). But St. Louisans knew its true origin.[25] From a brothel by the Mississippi it had "crossed the Atlantic under its own power," favored by the same "strong westerly weather" that would propel ragtime, the "St. Louis Blues," and T. S. Eliot to Europe.[26] In seeking the rhythmic source of Eliot's fox-trotting feet and eclectic vocal repertoire—not to mention his poetry—we need look no farther than the muttering retreats and sawdust restaurants of old St. Louis.

Yet Eliot, so far as one can tell, was no expert on jazz; and rather than to portray him as a jazz critic *manqué*, I am content to point out that he seemed to have an ear open to the music—open enough for it to have profoundly affected his work. Eliot emigrated in 1914, early enough to have missed the advent of jazz in America but quite late enough to have known ragtime and its derivatives as staples of American popular culture—especially, as I have been arguing, considering the site of his upbringing. There is no question, either, but that through his patronage of English music halls and dance halls in the 1910s and 1920s, Eliot was exposed to jazz as it evolved. In Eliot's day, numerous African-American musicians found steady work in English venues. Drummer Louis Mitchell, for example, who "claimed, not entirely incredibly, to have been the first man to bring jazz to Britain," arrived in England exactly when Eliot did, in the summer of 1914. The next year Mitchell left his band to begin touring the music halls, where he gave early jazz wide exposure (Rye 47). By 1915, the American ballroom dance craze was making inroads in Britain, and the *Chicago Defender* could report on May 22 that black musicians were "being called from America to take the place of Germans in London hotels and cafes" (qtd. in Chilton 47). From 1919 onward, following the success of the Original Dixieland Jazz Band at the brand-new Hammersmith Palais de Danse—an immense (27,000-square-foot) rehabilitated roller-skating rink that employed eighty dance instructors and accommodated as many as 5,000 dancing Londoners at a time—African-American bands practiced in the emerging New Orleans style of jazz found themselves exceedingly popular (Rye 50; Chilton 48). The most important of these groups, the Jazz Kings, featuring Sidney Bechet, played regularly at the Hammersmith Palais from 1920 through 1922. The fact is worth mentioning because the patrons at the Palais appear to have in-cluded—on how frequent a basis we do not know—Tom and Vivien Eliot.[27] While there is no direct evidence that T. S. Eliot danced to the music of Sidney Bechet, the possibility is breathtaking. In any event, it is clear that Eliot, like any middle-class Londoner with a social life, would have had to work hard not to encounter African-American jazz in this period. Certainly the scene was set when *The Waste Land* descended upon the world late in 1922. It was not only American readers who recognized jazz when they heard it—or read it.

DOWN AT TOM'S PLACE

The influence of jazz on *The Waste Land* has been a source of speculation for many years. While later readers have assumed that any relation Eliot might have borne to jazz would have been purely oppositional, Eliot's contemporaries, for whom the existence of a structural correlation between modernism and jazz was a "commonplace," were inclined to think the opposite (North, *Reading* 146). Thus Louis Untermeyer detected "jazz-rhythms" among what he considered *The Waste Land*'s poorly orchestrated "jumble" of ingredients ("Disillusion" 151–52), while John McClure imagined Eliot as "drowning in a sea of jazz" (170). Even much later, Ralph Ellison paid tribute to the poem that, more than any other text, had launched him into a literary career:

> . . . *The Waste Land* seized my mind. I was intrigued by its power to move me while eluding my understanding. Somehow its rhythms were often closer to those of jazz than were those of the Negro poets, and even though I could not understand then, its range of allusion was as mixed and as varied as that of Louis Armstrong. (160)

That Ellison, like Untermeyer, made no mistake in tracing Eliot's rhythms to jazz sources we have seen already; that he was right as well about Eliot's use of allusion we shall see presently.

There is more, too, to the subject of jazz in *The Waste Land* than Ellison could have known, for the poem Eliot originally wrote was quite different from the poem that was published. Although Ezra Pound's own use of popular genres has been demonstrated by Michael Coyle, somehow—whether because Pound did not particularly share Eliot's fondness for contemporary popular music or because he mistook Eliot's intent—Pound's editorial work eliminated the majority of Eliot's subliterary allusions from *The Waste Land* and ultimately collapsed its levels of cultural reference while leaving its internationalism and historicism intact.[28] The poem was thus recast, ironically, as the first major counteroffensive in high culture's last stand. Pound is not to be blamed for this turn of events. To be sure, nearly all of his emendations constitute decided improvements to Eliot's draft, and Eliot acceded to the recommendations of "il miglior fabbro" in almost every instance. Nonetheless, part of Eliot's original impulse in composing *The Waste Land* was lost in this collaborative process. Had he labored to improve the condemned passages instead of agreeing to delete them, he might have given literary modernism a markedly different spin.

Such speculation is inevitably somewhat tenuous.[29] What is certain is that the manuscript of The Waste Land shows Eliot drawing on popular song to a greater extent than he uses the Grail myth in the final version. For the long idiomatic passage that was to have opened the poem he considered several popular lyrics. The seventh and eighth lines of the original typescript quote George M. Cohan's "Harrigan," from the 1907 musical Fifty Miles from Boston. Cohan, of course, is best known for his Yankee Doodle persona, his insistent Americanism; but "Harrigan" has a somewhat different slant, emphasizing rather the defiant self-respect of the Irish-American: "Proud of all the Irish blood that's in me / Divil a man can say a word agin me."[30] The sentiment is appropriate to this opening section, which recounts in demotic language the adventures of a rowdy group of Boston Irish out on the town. The association of Irish immigrants with the American popular stage and its music may have been part of the stimulus that produced this episode; Joyce's Ulysses was, doubtless, another. For the opening scene of The Waste Land was, as Lyndall Gordon has noted, a "Boston version of the visit to Night-town" (Eliot's Early Years 145)—an observation that Peter Barry has extended by pointing out the particularly close parallels of Eliot's scene to the final pages of "Circe," which Eliot had only just finished reading as he began work on The Waste Land (239–40).

By late 1923 and "Ulysses, Order, and Myth," Eliot had decided that the "mythical method" was Joyce's most significant literary contribution in Ulysses. There is reason to believe, though, that despite the tendency of critics to account for the poem in the terms of the later essay, Eliot had not formulated this theory by the time he completed The Waste Land (Kaufmann 76–80).[31] The canceled opening of the poem suggests that in 1921 Eliot was strongly impressed with Joyce's integration of popular song into his text—for Ulysses, which "revels in the language and forms of popular culture" (Thompson 35), is saturated with song. Apparently Eliot planned to follow Joyce by locating his poem in a similar cultural matrix, conjoining high culture, ancient mythology, and popular allusions in the new American style. His failure to conceptualize such an artistic design without resorting to a Joycean band of inebriated Irish ethnics in an urban red-light district may explain the apparent ease with which Eliot was persuaded to drop the passage.[32] It may even have been the derivative quality of this passage that led Eliot to write to Joyce in May of 1921, apparently speaking of "Circe," "I wish, for my own sake, that I had not read it" (Letters 455). But he was serious about using this episode to introduce his poem—serious enough to have typed his working title, "HE DO THE POLICE IN DIFFERENT VOICES: Part I," at the top of the page, and the extant subtitle, "THE BURIAL OF THE DEAD," beneath it (*WLF* 5).

Next to the lines from "Harrigan," Eliot has jotted, either as an alternative quotation or as an additional one to be worked into the poem, "Meet me in the shadow of the / watermelon Vine / Eva Iva Uva Emmaline." Here he has altered and telescoped lines from two songs: "By the Watermelon Vine," a 1904 "coon song," and "My Evaline," first performed in a 1901 vaudeville-minstrel act (North, *Dialect* 85). Eliot probably heard "My Evaline" at Harvard, where it was often sung as a barbershop quartet. Clearly he had as long a memory for lowbrow as for highbrow materials. Bracketed in the margin just below are the lines "Tease, Squeeze lovin & wooin / Say Kid what're y' doin'," taken almost verbatim from "The Cubanola Glide," the very same song Eliot had drawn on a decade earlier in "The smoke that gathers blue and sinks." Popularized in 1909 by Sophie Tucker—the model, perhaps, for the zaftig chanteuse in the earlier poem—"Cubanola" was a ragtime number of some significance as one of the first American tunes to incorporate "tropical" rhythms (Ewen 173). The composer, Harry von Tilzer, is better known for "A Bird in a Gilded Cage," "Wait 'Til the Sun Shines, Nellie," and "I Want a Girl Just Like the Girl That Married Dear Old Dad," but "The Cubanola Glide" contributed directly to the nascent social dance craze and paved the way for such successors as the Grizzly Bear, the Bunny Hug, and the Turkey Trot (Spaeth, *History* 310). Both its "racial" diction and its eponymous dance, a relative of the cakewalk, added African-American overtones to the Cuban reference of the lyrics. With a light tango rhythm that foreshadows the Latin element in the American popular music of the succeeding decades, "The Cubanola Glide" was in its day an influential transitional work.

After a disruptive stop in a theater, the raucous crew of Eliot's discarded page drop in to a bar that Eliot himself frequented as a college student after attending the melodrama at Boston's Grand Opera House (*WLF* 125). The coincidence hints at a partial identification between the poet and his characters—an identification anticipated in the very first lines of the poem, in which the young men drink with a friend named "old Tom." Tom, as it happens, is "boiled to the eyes," a description that, as Virginia Woolf and other friends noticed, all too often fit Tom Eliot himself at Jazz-Age parties. Being boiled to the eyes, old Tom is "blind," and thus an avatar of Tiresias, *The Waste Land*'s central observer and raconteur. Eliot's identification with the crude, boisterous youths of the opening scene is particularly interesting because, as Gregory Jay argues, the passage vividly displays both sides of Eliot's ambivalent relation to mass culture. His "often affectionate imitation of [working-class] voices," which "conveys a respect for . . . ordinary lives and feelings," is offset by an "almost physical disgust for the materiality of existence—for the object world that dominates the lower classes" ("Postmodernism" 236–37). The episode may therefore be said to repeat a pattern that we have found in the earlier Eliot and that will reach its ambiguous zenith later, in *Sweeney Agonistes*. Eliot strains toward a Joycean sympathy in the abandoned opening of *The Waste Land*, but the strain shows.[33]

Eliot and Pound's editorial decision to omit the Boston Irish sequence had important consequences for *The Waste Land* as a whole. With the deletion of this section, the poem's surviving first line places it squarely within the "Great Tradition" of English poetry, beginning with Chaucer, instead of the contemporary and fundamentally American world of popular culture (Jay, "Postmodernism" 237). As A. David Moody points out, the long narrative on the wreck of a New England fishing boat, which Pound cut from the "Death by Water" section, would also have highlighted the poem's American roots. The cancellation of these two major passages, Moody argues,

> meant that the setting of the poem, along with its great range of cultural reference, became exclusively English and European. The only authentically American detail left in the poem is the hermit thrush. ("T. S. Eliot" 81)

Although Moody is forgetting the "Shakespearian Rag," his observation is otherwise accurate. And likewise, the hints of popular song that survive in the published poem are decisively eclipsed by the more erudite classical and European allusions that predominate. A long poem called *The Waste Land* that begins, "April is the cruellest month," largely shaped the course of literature and criticism for years to come. One can only imagine the effect of a long poem called *He Do the Police in Different Voices* beginning, "First we had a couple of feelers down at Tom's place."

THAT SHAKESPEHERIAN RAG

There are other and perhaps deeper senses, too, in which popular culture penetrated *The Waste Land*. Because the song excerpts on the original first page are, as North notes, "the first examples in the draft of [Eliot's] famous techniques of quotation and juxtaposition," the minstrel or coon-song associations of three of those songs lead him to posit a connection between the minstrel show, an "art of mélange," and the distinctive form of *The Waste Land* (*Dialect* 85–86).[34] Minstrel shows were in fact full of allusions—to Shakespeare, to melodrama, to opera. All genres, high and low, took on new meaning through their absorption into the minstrel setting, as they do in Eliot's poem:

But at my back in a cold blast I hear
The rattle of the bones, and chuckle spread from ear to ear.
A rat crept softly through the vegetation
Dragging its slimy belly on the bank
While I was fishing in the dull canal
On a winter evening round behind the gashouse
Musing upon the king my brother's wreck
And on the king my father's death before him.
White bodies naked on the low damp ground
And bones cast in a little low dry garret,
Rattled by the rat's foot only, year to year.
But at my back from time to time I hear
The sound of horns and motors, which shall bring
Sweeney to Mrs. Porter in the spring.
O the moon shone bright on Mrs. Porter
And on her daughter
They wash their feet in soda water
Et O ces voix d'enfants, chantant dans la coupole!

(CPP 42–43)

This passage, a virtual dramatic performance in its own right, eerily invokes the minstrel context in its second line, where the phrase "rattle of the bones" conjoins two vastly different frames of reference: the phantasmagoric cityscape of the succeeding lines, with their drowned bodies, and the minstrel stage, where the ear-to-ear grin and the bones, qua percussion instrument, were essential elements of the act. (Eliot may even have known Stephen Foster's "Ring de Banjo," which proclaims, "De ladies nebber weary / Wid de rattle ob de bones.") This minstrel reference follows the first of two allusions to Marvell's "Coy Mistress" and precedes a transposition of Shakespeare's *Tempest* into the Gothic mode. Similarly, the brilliant closing lines fly from seventeenth-century lyric (Marvell and Day) to a bawdy popular parody of the sentimental song "Red Wing"—into which Eliot imports his own character, Sweeney—and finally, through the common element of the footbath, to the romance of the Grail Quest by way of a Verlaine sonnet on a Wagner opera.[35] The whole generic crazy quilt that is *The Waste Land* is replicated on a small scale in these eighteen lines, tellingly under the sign of the minstrel show. In a sense, then, it does not matter whether "My Evaline" or the "By the Watermelon Vine" ultimately made it into the published *Waste Land*: the minstrel show leaves its trace in the form of Eliot's profoundest innovations.

At the same time, one need not overemphasize the minstrel show as the inspiration behind Eliot's method, for *The Waste Land*, even on its excised opening page, gestures in other directions as well. Neither "Harrigan" nor "The Cubanola Glide" is a minstrel number, and the musical environment in which Eliot sets his Boston scene is fundamentally a ragtime milieu.[36] Nor is the minstrel show the only popular genre that bears analogy to Eliot's practice of "quotation and juxtaposition." American vaudeville and English music hall, both of which even incorporated minstrel acts among their "turns," were similarly miscellaneous, as was, for that matter, the circus. Jazz-Age popular music may offer an even more potent analogy, for jazz musicians engaged so abundantly in quotation, imitation, and parody that such practices were often taken to be the essence of the genre. Its critics frequently denied that jazz had any substance of its own, preferring to characterize it as merely a technique of willful distortion applied to preexisting music.[37] Of course the same charge was leveled by literary critics who considered Eliot's work, and particularly The Waste Land, nothing more than a species of plagiarism.[38]

The point is not that Eliot extracted his montage aesthetic from jazz in a direct way, but rather that there is a fundamental convergence between Eliot's poem and the principal popular music of its era, particularly in the areas of structure, rhythm, and allusion. There are other parallels that might be and sometimes have been drawn between the characteristic musical traits of 1920s jazz and the new literary techniques explored in modernist texts like The Waste Land. Such synesthetic correlations inevitably seem a bit impressionistic, and I do not want to overreach my evidence. Still, both jazz and The Waste Land were read at the time as expressing, through their very form, the conditions of modern life—its instability, its rapid pace, its "variety and complexity"—as well as the rebellion against it. It should not seem too remarkable, then, if between their structures there is a kind of synergy.

It is thus unfortunate that critics have made so little of Eliot's quotation of the song "That Shakespearian Rag" in lines 127–30 of The Waste Land:

> But
> O O O O that Shakespeherian Rag—
> It's so elegant
> So intelligent

Sigg has speculated interestingly that the allusion may be self-referential. Like a ragtime pianist who has "spliced together strands of melody and patches of harmony" to generate a new composition, Eliot advertises (or perhaps ironizes) his own poem as "a kind of rag, a rhythmical weaving of literary and musical scraps from many hands into a single composition" (21). The Waste Land, by this reckoning, not only quotes the "Shakespearian Rag": it is a Shakespearean Rag. Beyond this suggestion, not much else that is cogent has been written about these lines. Taking for granted that The Waste

Land proposed simply to discredit the barren present by comparison with the fertile past, readers have long assumed that the song represented a degraded (i.e., contemporary and popular) version of Shakespearean high culture—in essence "what Shakespeare had come down to" in their own and Eliot's time. As one critic has asserted, popular culture in *The Waste Land*, this allusion included, "exists as an index of the degradation of the modern age" (Thompson 35).[39] Thirty-five years elapsed after the publication of *The Waste Land* before a scholar named B. R. McElderry finally took the trouble to identify the song as a long-forgotten tune from the 1912 Ziegfeld Follies; but even for McElderry, this discovery was material only for a brief scholarly note. Once he had disparaged the lyrics as "utterly tasteless," there was little more for him to say (185). For McElderry, as for so many others, Eliot used the song merely as a "symbol of vulgarity," or a "proper symbol of public taste" in the early twentieth century.

If we overcome the urge to dismiss the song out of hand, we discover that it actually does shed light on *The Waste Land*. For "That Shakespearian Rag" attempts to undermine exactly the position taken by Eliot's explicators on the value of contemporary popular culture in relation to canonized high culture—the position then blithely attributed to Eliot himself. Shakespeare, the song tells us, is pure caviar, all elegance and intelligence. Ragtime, naturally, is a great deal more fun, and had Shakespeare's characters experienced it, they might have averted their various tragedies:

> "*As you like it*" Brutus,
> We'll play a rag today.
> Then old Shylock danced,
> And the Moor, Othello, pranced,
> Feeling gay, he would say, as he started in to sway,
> "Bring the rag right away."

(3)

Shakespeare's poetry, the song predictably avers, is exceedingly "high-browed" and outdated; fortunately, however, ragtime has come along to give "that old classical drag" new life in a syncopated setting.

At the same time, the song's attempt to sustain an attitude of impudence comes across as rather forced, for the lyrics seem altogether too self-conscious about their own culturally inferior relation to Shakespeare. They protest too much that times have changed and that a rag—"yes, a rag," the song insists—can now be "grand." In this uneasy self-assurance lies an intriguing analogy to Eliot's own unsettled position as a cultural interloper within the placidly civilized London literary scene—as a crass American "savage" bursting into the English drawing room declaiming his verse ("War-Paint"). Eliot's personal admixture of cultural anxiety and confidence, his ambivalence toward the modernity he was compelled to choose, is mirrored in "That Shakespearian Rag," as it is in *The Waste Land* as a whole. Even his readjustment of the established canon is comically figured in the song as the ragging of "Bill" Shakespeare.

Despite its pretensions to outrageousness, the original "Shakespearian Rag" was hardly revolutionary; it was rather a latecomer to a fad for similar titles, such as "That Lovin' Rag" (1908), "That Beautiful Rag" (1910), and "That Mysterious Rag" (1911). Its debunking of Shakespeare adopts a formula established on the nineteenth-century American comic stage. And despite the "Rag" in its title, not to mention its extravagant praise of syncopation, the song is itself rhythmically uninventive and only occasionally syncopated. (Eliot compensates in *The Waste Land* by inserting the extra syllable in "Shakespeherian," beating composer David Stamper at his own game.) The lyric banks its bid for humor on the shock generated when a culture's most revered texts are treated with an unceremonious familiarity. Perhaps audiences in 1912 found the mere presence of such famous tags as "Friends, Romans, Countrymen" and "My kingdom for a horse" in a rag sufficiently funny; at least, there is not much else of the comic to be found in the verses.[40] The application of contemporary slang to what is supposed to be highfalutin "stuff" has comic possibilities, and the song exploits this technique with deliberate audacity but without real cleverness, as in the chorus:

> Desdemona was the colored pet,
> Romeo loved his Juliet,
> And they were some lovers, you can bet, and yet,
> I know if they were here today,
> They'd Grizzly Bear in a diff'rent way,
> And you'd hear old Hamlet say,
> "To be or not to be,"
> That Shakespearian Rag.

$$(4-5)$$

The rhymes are pedestrian, the assertions trite, and the concluding lines, which create the expectation of a verbal coup de grace as the music rises to a crescendo, anticlimactically fail to deliver the anticipated double meaning. One has only to compare "That Shakespearian Rag" with Cole Porter's "Brush Up Your Shakespeare" to see how much more can be done with the same concept. Yet whatever the aesthetic shortcomings of "That Shakespearian Rag," Eliot clearly understood that the ragging of Shakespeare—his own as well as the song's—had explosive potential to amuse or to offend; to link history and contemporaneity, or to push them apart; and to register the widening gulf between art and popular culture. In connection with the last idea, Shakespeare, who was popular in his own day but elite fare by the time of the "Shakespearian Rag," would seem to provide the supreme illustration.

Interestingly, the "Shakespearian Rag" allusion in "A Game of Chess" seems to emanate from the silent husband in response to the wife's last hysterical attempt to draw him out: "Are you alive, or not? Is there nothing in your head?" If the "Shakespearian Rag" is meant as an answer to that question, it may represent the same response—with the same unapportionable degree of irony—that a much younger Eliot had given his similarly abulic speaker in "The smoke that gathers blue and sinks." In both cases, a responsiveness to jazz is the one indication of a life within. At the same time, the most obvious, immediate effect of the song quotation in "A Game of Chess" is to provide an instant of (Shakespearean?) comic relief in the midst of one of the most painful sections of The Waste Land. In "The Fire Sermon," the ballad of Mrs. Porter performs a similar function, breathing momentary life into an otherwise bleak passage on cultural decay.

Its various contexts considered, Eliot's "O O O O that Shakespeherian Rag" thus gestures in several directions at once. The "degradation of the modern age" is perhaps one of those directions, though certainly not because popular culture always functioned for Eliot as an "index" of such degradation.[41] On the contrary, given his other "lowbrow" interests, one does not doubt that Eliot, in his quizzical, elusively ironic way, enjoyed "That Shakespearian Rag" for its blend of brash irreverence and outlandish vacuity. Ironically earnest, delectably vulgar, its self-regarding cheek neatly balancing its evident inanity, the "Shakespeherian Rag" in The Waste Land is a sliver of Eliotic camp.

THE VANISHING AMERICAN

Among Eliot's "creative" work, it is in his next project after The Waste Land, his unfinished verse drama Sweeney Agonistes, that popular influences, including jazz, make their presence felt most openly. We will look at that play in some detail in chapter 4. Meanwhile, it is worth observing that Eliot makes a distinct break with jazz in 1927—a date that coincides, and not by chance, with his conversion to Anglicanism and his assumption of British citizenship.[42]

Eliot was by no means the only one to repudiate jazz at about this time. By the mid-twenties, a consensus had formed among the English intelligentsia that jazz was a fad, and its imminent demise was predicted regularly. In this respect Clive Bell, who had proclaimed in 1921 that "Jazz is dead, or dying at any rate," was ahead of his time. In 1927, the British music critic Ernest Newman begged to assure the American public that in his country, the age of jazz had already passed, and he voiced doubt that "a single musician of any standing could now be found . . . to say a good word for it" (3). There was some truth to this, for jazz was losing support even among its boosters. In 1921–23 William Walton had composed Façade, a brilliant, jazzy setting of poems by Edith Sitwell; in 1926 Walton rejected jazz "in a fit of disgust" because the music—and indeed the "whole atmosphere" of the Jazz Age—had become tedious (Craggs 109).[43] Across the Channel a few months later, a still more prominent advocate, Darius Milhaud, similarly renounced jazz (Gendron, Between 116). Rejecting jazz around 1927 was apparently à la mode in European intellectual circles.

So long as Eliot sought, however ambivalently, the role of the outsider, the "Amurrican," the barbarian invader, he had no reason to squelch speculation about black midwives and seas of jazz in his poetry. By 1927, though, he can no longer permit such loose talk about his offspring. In the January Nation & Athenæum—incongruously, the same month that his jazzy "Fragment of an Agon," from Sweeney Agonistes, appears in the Criterion—he takes his stand in a harsh review of Gertrude Stein's "Composition as Explanation." He credits Stein's rhythms with "a peculiar hypnotic power not met with before" and associates her style with the saxophone and the Charleston— i.e., with jazz. But Stein and jazz then go down together in an apocalyptic flourish: "If this is of the future, then the future is, as it very likely is, of the barbarians. But this is the future in which we ought not to be interested" ("Charleston").[44] Eliot has come a long way here from the ambivalence of the 1910s. On the verge of publicly declaring himself "classicist in literature, royalist in politics, and Anglo-Catholic in religion," he is seeking to exorcise the enfant terrible, the jazz poet, and the pagan in himself.

At this same moment, Eliot seems largely to have abandoned the "racial masquerade"—the game of African-American identification played out in dialect—in which he and Pound had engaged for years, and which was intimately related to both writers' anxieties over their Midwestern provinciality, their American and middle-class roots, and even the spoken accents that marked them as "metics" in the cultural center to which they were laying siege (North, Dialect 77–81). Clearly the impulse toward racial masquerade that generated Africanist references and minstrel borrowings in Eliot's work is closely connected with his receptivity to jazz. As Eliot works to enter the British establishment he had formerly been seen as subverting, at least one window open to popular culture has closed.

Eliot could choose no longer to play the "Amurrican," but no public pronouncement, however definitive, could really banish the American in Eliot or clarify his muddy feelings. His confession in a 1928 letter to Herbert Read draws from the same deep well of ambivalence that had saturated his letters to Mary Hutchinson a decade earlier:

> Some day, I want to write an essay about the point of view of an Ameri-
> can who wasn't an American, because he was born in the South and went
> to school in New England as a small boy with a nigger drawl, but who
> wasn't a southerner in the South because his people were northerners in
> a border state and looked down on all southerners and Virginians, and
> who so was never anything anywhere and who therefore felt himself to
> be more a Frenchman than an American and more an Englishman than a
> Frenchman and yet felt that the U.S.A. up to a hundred years ago was a
> family extension. (qtd. in Read 15)

Eliot misses the point that to be "never anything anywhere," if that implies
an identity that is never quite stable or finally settled, is precisely to *be* an
American. He will work hard for the remainder of his life to be an Englishman; he will play the part so well, in fact, that his American background will come to seem for many years a mere curiosity, while he himself
takes on the legend of the quintessential London man of letters—wry, eccentric, fastidious, tradition-bound, with one foot already in the Poets' Corner at Westminster. But this mask is for others. From the moment he puts it
on Eliot knows that he cannot really escape his history.

The essay Eliot projects in his letter to Read, his cri de coeur, is not entirely hypothetical. Just as he is abandoning his American citizenship, Eliot
begins to reminisce, in print, about his American past. His 1928 preface to
Edgar Ansell Mowrer's *This American World* contains many nostalgic hints.
Between boasting that he himself was "a descendant of pioneers" and
informing us that his grandmother "had shot her own wild turkeys for
dinner," Eliot explains:

> My family were New Englanders, who had been settled—my branch of
> it—for two generations in the South West—which was, in my own time,
> rapidly becoming merely the Middle West. The family guarded jealously
> its connexions with New England; but it was not until years of maturity
> that I perceived that I myself had always been a New Englander in the
> South West, and a South Westerner in New England; when I was sent to
> school in New England I lost my southern accent without ever acquiring
> the accent of the native Bostonian. In New England I missed the long
> dark river, the ailanthus trees, the flaming cardinal birds, the high lime-
> stone bluffs where we searched for fossil shell-fish; in Missouri I missed
> the fir trees, the bay and goldenrod, the song-sparrows, the red granite
> and the blue sea of Massachusetts. (xiii–xiv)

The wan sense of homelessness evident in these lines seems to say that Eliot
had not chosen his exile: exile, rather, had been thrust upon him.[45] His

meditations in his *Landscapes,* in "The Dry Salvages," in "American Literature and the American Language" (with its analogy of the transcontinental robin), and elsewhere all indicate that the conscious effort to become English only made Eliot more aware that he could not forget his forsaken birthright. As late as 1963 he told Donald Hall that his poetry (both *migratorius* and *musicus*) was "a combination of things. But in its sources, in its emotional springs, it comes from America" (110). As the First Tempter in *Murder in the Cathedral* reminds Thomas, "A man will often love what he spurns" (*CPP* 184).

Even after his published comments on Stein, Eliot wasn't through with jazz—not, at least, in his private life. Virginia Woolf wrote to Roger Fry more than a year later that she was going to visit Eliot not only to discuss his new poems but (she complained) "to drink cocktails and play jazz into the bargain" (*Letters* 6: 523). "We're gona sit here and drink this booze," as Sweeney predicts; "We're gona sit here and have a tune" (*CPP* 84). But as for "Amurrican culcher in the drayma (including the movies) in music, in the cocktail, and in the dance"—though their influence never left him, Eliot could no longer, after 1927, seek to develop a poetics based on these particular sources. If the "classical tendency" is to do "the best one can with the material at hand," it was now clear that the "material at hand" had changed, for him. While his national and religious conversions did not mark the end of Eliot's engagement with popular culture, they did, inevitably, mark an important shift in his *conception* of the popular. At any rate, it was no longer suitable for Eliot to be seen strumming a jazz-banjorine.

THE DULL AND THE LIVELY

THRILLERS

"Dullness" is the launch point for the *Criterion* and its seventeen years' inquiry into the condition of modern culture. No welcome, no editorial, no declaration of purpose precedes it: one turns past the front cover of the first issue to find "Dullness" staring up in bold type from the top of the first page.

A lively essay under that title purports to inquire why so much literature seems dull, and it answers unequivocally that the culprit is actually "the reader who finds things dull" (7–8). The fault, dear Brutus—for *Brutus*, of course, means dullard—is not in our texts, but in ourselves. The modern mind is notable for its "curious 'passivity,'" for the "expectation that everything shall be done for it; that at every moment there shall be some external machinery, apparatus, conspiracy of other folk to occupy, amuse, caress, cajole it" (6). We demand of our reading that it not demand too much of us: "Anything that does not at once provide the indispensable and sacred 'good time' deserves contemptuous condemnation and gets it" (2). Mass culture is to blame: we live in "an age of tabloids" (5); we are subjected from childhood to "that specially soul-destroying invention the cinema" and have, moreover, picked up a bad "habit of attending professional football matches" (7). The article concedes that dullness in literature does exist—many books, in fact, are "hopelessly dull" (12). But what is dull is not the great literature that most people consider dull: it is rather the "literature of recreation," the literature that sells, that is genuinely dull (13). The novel, especially, is dullness's chosen breeding ground. "When prose-fiction, after its strange and millennial birth struggles, got itself born at last, Dullness saw her chance and took it" (13).

This argument exemplifies a form of intellectual elitism that is often associated—mistakenly—with the name of T. S. Eliot. As it happens, "Dullness" was written by an older and then more famous scholar, George Saintsbury, who had been invited to appear in the first number of the *Criterion* as part of Eliot's strenuous effort to give his journal credibility. The survival of the *Criterion* and the ascent of Eliot's reputation attest to his success. Ironically, though, the credibility of the journal, so purchased, was offputting to many of Eliot's existing supporters, who complained from the outset that the *Criterion* itself was dull. Most dangerously, Lady Rothermere, on whose patronage the *Criterion*'s very existence depended, was not pleased. As Eliot reported to Pound: "her only comment on the contents is that it is Dull and that Saintsbury is bad" (*Letters* 592).

Pound had already anticipated this reaction. "Of course if she says it looks like a corpse, she's right, mon POSSUM," he had written three days earlier (Eliot, *Letters* 589). Pound meant this as a compliment to Eliot's editorial savvy. He believed that Eliot was making the journal dull by design, its polite gravity a Trojan horse within which the subversive works of modernism ("our own stuff") would steal their way through the seemingly impregnable fortifications of Britain's literary establishment. The *Criterion* was dull because the journal itself was "PLAYIN' POSSUM"; so much the better, then, if Lady Rothermere could not penetrate the camouflage (589).[1] Pound realized only gradually that the joke was on him—that if the *Criterion* was dull, it was earnestly and not strategically so (Levenson 219–20). But until the journal was securely established, Eliot had to watch his step. His immediate response to Pound's letter was to write to F. S. Flint, asking him to translate a manuscript by Ramón Gómez de la Serna that would "provide relief" for readers "who find the review too dull and indigestible" (*Letters* 591).

Eliot's letters do not show how Saintsbury's article was solicited or who suggested its topic. But the subject of dullness was of exceptional concern to Eliot, and the placement of "Dullness," whatever its genesis, at the head of the *Criterion* was not merely a flagrant attempt to capitalize on Saintsbury's standing. Nevertheless, in most respects Eliot's take on dullness was precisely opposite to Saintsbury's. Saintsbury insists on the reader's assiduous effort to make the text interesting: if readers would just get over their "indolence," they would find that all literature (saving the popular) was stimulating to the active mind (7). Eliot's criticism, on the contrary, returns again and again to the responsibility of the writer to entertain, to excite the reader's interest. A play, for example, must "hold the audience all the time," and "it will not do that, if the audience is expected to do too much of the work." "This," he adds, "is a very good exercise for poets, who seem to forget often that poetry, even to be readable, should be interesting" ("Audiences" 4).

As for fiction, the success of what Saintsbury dismisses as "the lowest class of mere dime novels" (7) only demonstrates, for Eliot, the need to take seriously the emotional resources that give an art such popular appeal as it has. In an important 1927 essay called "Wilkie Collins and Dickens," Eliot groups these resources under the banner of "melodrama"—a term that refers both to a popular genre and to its characteristically strong, direct appeal to the emotions. Eliot suggests that when literature, in obeisance to "higher" aesthetic aspirations, excludes the element of melodrama, the result is dullness.

The demand for aesthetic purity, moreover, is historically contingent. Noting the passing of the "golden age" of the melodramatic stage within his lifetime, Eliot describes the disjunction between the "high" and the "popular" as a sort of iron curtain that has only recently descended across the arts. "Those who have lived before such terms as 'high-brow fiction,' 'thrillers' and 'detective fiction' were invented," he writes, "realize that melodrama is perennial and that the craving for it is perennial and must be satisfied" ("Wilkie Collins" 409). Modern highbrow fiction, increasingly independent of any popular impulse, has evolved into a literature without thrills:

> In the golden age of melodramatic fiction there was no such distinction.
> The best novels *were* thrilling: the distinction of genre between such-and-
> such a profound "psychological" novel of today and such-and-such a
> masterly "detective novel" of today is greater than the distinction of
> genre between *Wuthering Heights*, or even *The Mill on the Floss*, and *East Lynne*.[2]
> (409–10)

Dickens may be the obvious evidence that an opposition between melodrama and profundity, between popularity and "art," has not always been inevitable. But Wilkie Collins, a writer of less genius, is also to be respected as a "master of plot and situation," of melodrama and suspense (411), and therefore as an artist (417–18). Contemporary "serious" fiction risks a collapse in its audience as it abandons melodrama in its insistence upon aesthetic autonomy. "If we cannot get this satisfaction out of what the publishers present as 'literature,'" Eliot predicts, "then we will read—with less and less pretense of concealment—what we call 'thrillers'" (409).

As a declaration of Eliot's own intentions, at least, this was no empty threat: he was himself turning from "literature" to "thrillers" and abandoning any pretense of concealment. Eliot personally reviewed twenty-four works of crime fiction and two nonfiction works on the subject of murder in the 1927 *Criterion*, as if to prove he was in earnest.[3] And thirty-five years later he told Igor Stravinsky that he had read no " 'serious' prose fiction" since 1927 (Stravinsky 92).[4] This confession surprised the composer, but it was old news. Eliot had already publicized his indifference to the novel in 1950, declaring in the London *Sunday Times*, "I never read contemporary fiction—with one exception: the works of Simenon concerned with Inspector Maigret" ("Books").[5] There were, in fact, further "subliterary" exceptions, such as P. G. Wodehouse, Raymond Chandler, Agatha Christie, and Peter Cheyney.[6] If entertainment was to be divorced from "literary" profundity, Eliot, it seems, would opt for the former.

In the long run Eliot did not expect others to choose differently. Literature, he complains in "Wilkie Collins and Dickens," "nowadays more and more [is] dull" (416). And since what is dull is not read, "serious" fiction will be condemned to social irrelevance, and perhaps to extinction, unless its practitioners manage to "reassemble the elements which have been dissociated in the modern novel" (410). The divide between high culture and popular culture, in other words, must be breached; our *Mill on the Flosses* must come back together with our *East Lynnes*. Thus Eliot ends "Wilkie Collins and Dickens" with an admonition to his "literary" contemporaries, who are "too conscious of [their] 'art' " and too little of their audience: "We cannot afford to forget that the first—and not one of the least difficult—requirements of either prose or verse is that it should be interesting" (418).

Eliot was not a systematic thinker, and his ideas on any particular subject are, more often than not, scattered across a large number of prose essays on a variety of tangentially related topics. The problem raised in "Wilkie Collins and Dickens," as I have already suggested, is one recurrent motif developed over a number of critical texts. Eliot defines outright his series of "London Letters" in the *Dial*, for example, as an effort to analyze the "dullness" he perceives as endemic in the arts on both sides of the Atlantic.[7] In his first "London Letter," dated March 1921, Eliot begins with the Georgian poets, of whom he takes John Drinkwater to be representative:

> The most obvious thing to say, the thing which makes it difficult for the critic to say more, is that the work of Mr. Drinkwater is dull, supremely dull. But when one turns to view the work of a numerous host of Drinkwaters, incipient Drinkwaters, decayed Drinkwaters, cross-bred Drinkwaters, this adjective ceases to satisfy the intelligence. Any social phenomenon of such dimensions must present more interest than that. (450)

That dullness in the arts should immediately become a "social phenomenon" is typical of Eliot's evolving pattern of thought, which is less and less purely concerned, or more and more impurely concerned, with strictly "literary" matters. Only on the surface is dullness a literary problem: "The dullness of the Georgian Anthology is original, unique; we shall find its cause in something much more profound than the influence of a few predecessors" (450). Much of Eliot's criticism of the 1920s and beyond is occupied with this "something much more profound"—that is, with the cultural conditions under which dullness not only thrives but becomes inescapable.

THE LIVELY ARTS

Despite the obvious Popian resonance of a campaign against dullness, Eliot's discussion of the problem continually complicates, even while it invokes, the elitist cast of such Augustan associations. At least two meanings can be extracted from Eliot's application of the term "dullness" to literary works. When he calls Georgian poetry "dull," Eliot invokes the notions of conventionality and banality one would expect a modernist to wield against a relatively conservative school of art. At the same time, Eliot's usage of the word never strays too far from its everyday function as an antonym of "entertaining," "interesting," or "dramatic." Dull writing in this sense is likely to be self-indulgent and neglectful of its audience's attention—an accusation summed up in Eliot's references to the perennial craving for melodrama that serious fiction fails to satisfy. This dullness is intimately connected with the disintegration of the arts into such categories as "highbrow" and "popular." As writing becomes an increasingly autonomous "high art," it becomes possible for practitioners to ignore, or even to repudiate, the elements of their art that might attract (and once perhaps did attract) a sizable audience. Eliot defends these slighted elements as "perennial" human demands and thus as essentials ("first requirements") of art. With the rejection of external checks summed up in the phrase "Art for art's sake," what Eliot calls "dullness" becomes a perpetual threat.

Despite his assurance that "what is uninteresting is unreadable, and what is unreadable is not read" ("LL [Apr. 1922]" 513), Eliot knows that there is in fact an audience for dull books, and even for dull poetry. When the "serious" becomes identified with the "pedantic," even a Drinkwater will sell (*Letters* 255). "Culture is traditional, and loves novelty," he declares; "the General Reading Public knows no tradition, and loves staleness" ("LL [Mar. 1921]" 451). The apparent paradox is unlocked by Eliot's concept of tradition as a living organism rather than a static order (Menand 97–99). When art is reverenced and not relished, when it is expected to be "improving" and not entertaining, dullness is simply accepted as a sine qua non of high culture.

Like other modernists and avant-gardists since Flaubert, Eliot views the sacralization of art as a reflection of middle-class ascendancy, a product of the bourgeois craving for "culture" as a token of respectability. In the "London Letters" he maintains that the will of "the respectable mob, the decent middle-class mob" has co-opted the valuation and therefore the production of art. Averse to "adventure and experiment," it has cast its "particular torpor or deadness" over the entire cultural scene ("[Apr. 1922]" 510–11). The purveyors of culture, such as Harold Monro and J. C. Squire, are addressed to "the insurgent middle class" whose influence is "[t]he subtle spirit" that moves and regulates the arts ("[Mar. 1921]" 451). Under the circumstances, it is fruitless to "dwell upon the dulness of this book [the *Georgian Anthology*]; that the writers cannot help" (451). Having thus matter-of-factly countenanced the "death of the author," Eliot focuses instead on a failure of cultural leadership:

> The Georgian public is a smallish but important public, it is that offensive part of the middle-class which believes itself superior to the rest of the middle class; and superior for precisely this reason that it believes itself to possess culture. (452)

The remainder of the middle class, seeking cultural capital, follows the tastemakers by reading Georgian poetry—a relationship to the arts that Eliot identifies with consumerism (451–52).

This first "London Letter" is conspicuously bleak—as, indeed, its immediate proximity to the composition of *The Waste Land* would lead one to expect—and it maintains an unwavering tone of disheartened pessimism. So relief comes unexpectedly near the end of the essay when Eliot suddenly remarks, apropos of nothing, "the Palladium has at this moment an excellent bill, including Marie Lloyd, Little Tich, George Mozart, and Ernie Lotinga" (452–53). When he agreed to write the "London Letters" for the *Dial*, Eliot had pledged to Scofield Thayer, "I will endeavor to spot any germs of vitality that appear, lest our American public should find the London spectacle too depressing" (*Letters* 413–14). Apparently these germs of vitality are to be found at the Palladium—that is, in England's *popular* culture, and not, for the most part, in its fine arts. Eliot finds little comfort here, because, as he laments in several later "London Letters," music hall is itself in decline. Yet he invokes popular culture, here and elsewhere, as a corrective to a stultifying bourgeois misappropriation of the whole concept of "art."

Eliot's 1923 appreciation of Marianne Moore's poetry goes a step further, arguing that popular culture and the fine arts are really two phases of the same enterprise and that it is the way in which we *speak* of the arts that creates and sustains the divisions between them. Eliot faults Glenway Wescott's introduction to Moore's *Marriage* for making an "artificial and unimportant distinction" between popular culture and high culture. Such distinctions, Eliot warns, have "dangerous consequences"—meaning the current impoverishment of the arts and its perpetuation or further progression ("Marianne Moore" 594). The popular is not a degradation of high culture: "Fine art," Eliot insists, "is the *refinement*, not the antithesis, of popular art" (595).[8]

This passage in "Marianne Moore" has been read as a call for the elite artist to intervene in the popular realm—as an assertion that the function of the artist is to improve ("refine") the base material of "low" culture to produce a society's *real* art (Faulk, "Letter"). Eliot does occasionally use the verb "refine" to mean "improve"; in "The Metaphysical Poets," for instance, the statement "The language went on and in some respects improved" is equated with "the language became more refined" (247). Even here, the qualifier "in some respects" implies that a more refined language is not altogether a better one. But elsewhere in Eliot, "refinement" takes on quite different senses entirely. In a 1914 letter to Conrad Aiken, "refinement" refers to the decorum and inhibition that preserve a male virgin from sexual temptation: "One walks about the street with one's desires, and one's refinement rises up like a wall whenever opportunity approaches" (*Letters* 75). And in "Tradition and the Individual Talent," the major passage on the poet's relation to tradition explicitly rejects any assimilation of "refinement" to "improvement":

> He [the poet] must be quite aware of the obvious fact that art never improves, but that the material of art is never quite the same. . . . That this development, refinement perhaps, complication certainly, is not, from the point of view of the artist, any improvement. (6)

To call fine art a "refinement of popular art," similarly, proposes a high culture that is relatively decorous, cultivated, and delicate. But none of this implies any innate superiority, except in satisfying aesthetic demands that "The Metaphysical Poets" nearly dismisses as "fastidious" (247). The terms "fine art" and "popular art" merely designate more and less "refined" expressions of what a given culture, at a given moment, has to express. Eliot's definition is an assertion not of hierarchy but of contiguity where most intellectuals, including Glenway Wescott, saw opposition.

Far from upholding the need for an uncontaminated elite art, Eliot seems determined, rather, to render the boundaries between the high and the low more fluid, to affirm the value of popular culture, and to theorize the possibility of crossover works. The available terms make such a discourse difficult, for even to speak of "popular culture" and "high culture" reinscribes the very categories one is seeking to contest.[9] ("I gotta use words when I talk to you," as Sweeney twice complains [CPP 83–84].) Still, Eliot's tendency is clear. "The notion that popular culture is a degraded art form," as Jon Thompson writes, "is a ubiquitous one in literary studies" (34). This consensus is precisely what Eliot seeks to challenge.[10]

Yet if the high and the popular represent a cultural continuum, Eliot also identifies another species of art that is inimical to these. This, not surprisingly, is the middlebrow. While the popular and the fine arts are native elements in a thriving culture, the middlebrow—which Eliot calls "much more artificial than anything else"—leads an unnatural existence perpetuated by the sacralization of the aesthetic ("Marianne Moore" 594–95). If the popular-high continuum expresses existing structures of feeling, "middle-class art" voices thoughts and feelings that are affected for art's sake: it "plays with sham ideas, sham emotions, and even sham sensations."

Here Eliot's thinking bears an instructive resemblance to the theory of culture being formulated at exactly the same time by the American critic Gilbert Seldes. Eliot had in fact known Seldes since 1912, when they met at Harvard (Howarth 246), and though they were never close friends, the two men kept up amicable relations for many years. When Seldes published an analysis of Eliot's work in December 1922, Eliot considered his remarks on *The Waste Land* superior to Edmund Wilson's influential essay (Kammen 60). Eliot also admired Seldes's review of *Ulysses*, which anticipated his own reading of that novel in important respects, beginning with the judgment that Joyce was "possibly the most interesting and the most formidable writer of our time" (Seldes, "Rev. of *Ulysses*" 211).[11] As managing editor of the *Dial*, Seldes even helped arrange the publication of *The Waste Land* after Eliot and Scofield Thayer had quarreled over it—an intervention for which Eliot was sincerely grateful (Eliot, *Letters* 586; Kammen 59).

Meanwhile, Seldes was also beginning to write seriously about popular culture, a critical project whose first and most important result was *The Seven Lively Arts* (1924), still regarded as a "pathbreaking" text in cultural studies (Douglas 38). Beyond its criticism of various popular artists, the book makes a theoretical argument that has a good deal in common with the ideas we have been tracing in Eliot's essays of the same period. Seldes divides the arts into the "serious," the "lively," and the "bogus," the last category being associated with bourgeois aestheticism:

> For at bottom there is a vast snobbery of the intellect which repays the deadly hours of boredom we spend in the pursuit of art. We are the inheritors of a tradition that what is worth while must be dull; and as often as not we invert the maxim and pretend that what is dull is higher in quality, more serious, "greater art" in short than whatever is light and easy and gay. (*Seven* 265–66)

For Seldes, as for Eliot, the real threat to the fine arts is not the popularity of the "lively arts" but rather the pretentious intellectualism that privileges a solemn and reverential approach to culture. Like Eliot in "Marianne Moore," Seldes argues that there is no conflict between the "serious" or "great" arts and the "lively" or "popular," though both are "opposed in the spirit to the middle or bogus arts" (294). What is more, Seldes claims, for the most part the popular arts in the 1920s are "more interesting to the adult cultivated intelligence than most of the things which pass for art in cultured society" (295)—just as Eliot, in "Wilkie Collins and Dickens," justifies a preference for thrillers in the face of "what the publishers present as 'literature' " (409). Both men have trained their sights on dullness.

To be sure, Seldes is more dedicated than Eliot to supporting his theory as an active critic of popular culture. On the other hand, Eliot goes significantly further in critiquing the highbrow/lowbrow binary. Seldes's categories of "serious" (sometimes "major") arts and "lively" (or "minor") arts are fixed entities that he projects through history.[12] Eliot is well aware of the historicity of these constructs and their relation to social change. Seldes embraces the high/low dichotomy and urges his readers to accept the value of the low; Eliot recognizes the entire distinction as contingent and wishes to transcend it.

What Eliot thought of *The Seven Lively Arts* is now something of an enigma. After its appearance he wrote to Seldes offering his compliments and expressing approval. Yet it seems that, at this point at least, Eliot had read only a portion of Seldes's wide-ranging book, for he "wrote as though *The Seven Lively Arts* was primarily about comedians" (Kammen 103). This mistake is intriguing, because for Eliot the music-hall comedian was the central exemplar of authentic popular culture; apparently he identified with Seldes's views sufficiently to graft his own preoccupation onto his colleague's thesis.

There were indications that Eliot planned to review the book himself in the *Criterion*, but that task eventually went to Conrad Aiken (Kammen 103–04). In his review Aiken considers Seldes to be at his best when he writes "with gusto" about particular artists (e.g., Charlie Chaplin, Ring Lardner, Al Jolson, George Herriman); when he "indulges in theory" Seldes is inconsistent and superficial. Aiken's central complaint focuses on Seldes's bugbear, the "bogus arts": "The bogus, or *faux bon*, appears to Mr. Seldes to be a dreadful menace—a kind of monster which must be slain; he seems to know exactly and shudderingly what it is; but what it is he never makes quite clear" (149). Seldes attempts to construe the "bogus" as an independent category—he claims, for example, that it originates in negative emotions ("longing and weakness and depression") while "[t]he great arts and the lively arts have their sources in strength or in gaiety" (*Seven* 272). Aiken considers this argument "remarkably naive" and arbitrary in application.[13] In the end he disposes of Seldes with the brutal judgment that his book demonstrates "a critical bankruptcy almost complete" (150).

Aiken is right to notice a kind of ingenuous ardor in Seldes, a quality that results at times in a rather breathless prose style—one recognizable enough that Langston Hughes could parody it a decade later ("Rejuvenation" 75). The more sophisticated Eliot is never so heady; of the many epithets that have been applied to him, "remarkably naive" would probably rank among the rarest. Yet Eliot, too, never worked out his conception of "middle-class art" with much precision. It is also true, as Aiken suggests, that the *faux bon* was already beginning to function as a sort of Questing Beast, a shadowy but seductive target for American modernist critics; it thrived well into the twentieth century under such rubrics as "midcult" and "kitsch." For Eliot, as for Seldes, the "dull" functioned as a ritual scapegoat whose expulsion permitted the divided brethren of high and low culture to make their peace.

It would appear, in any case, that Eliot did not concur with Aiken's harsh assessment of Seldes's powers, for it was after the publication of *The Seven Lively Arts* that Eliot began to solicit Seldes's contributions to the *Criterion*, including a "New York Chronicle" similar to the "London Letters" Eliot had written for the *Dial*.[14] Since Seldes had left the *Dial* by the time Eliot requested his contributions, Eliot had nothing to gain from him except his point of view.[15]

"NOT VERY MUCH INTERESTED"

I am aware that my portrait of a Seldesian Eliot will give rise to several quite reasonable objections. How, after all, could the author of a poem so abstruse that it required endnotes have been genuinely committed to narrowing the distance between popular culture and high culture? Wasn't modernism itself, by the same token, complicit in widening the cultural divide? And wasn't there even something purposeful in this process—didn't modernists exhibit a relentless insistence on artistic autonomy and a quite deliberate rejection of popular readership? Indeed, modernist complicity, including Eliot's, cannot be denied.[16] But the notion that high modernist writers abandoned the ideal of popularity readily or without misgivings is a false one: Yeats, Conrad, Woolf, Lawrence, Joyce, and Pound, to take six major instances, all evinced complicated attitudes toward popularity and at various points in their careers actively sought, and occasionally found, a wide audience.[17]

Eliot's focus on dullness skirts this issue; it allows him to express his concern over the high/low fissure without acknowledging modernism's own contributions to the problem. It is one thing to find John Drinkwater dull; it is another thing to militate against the cultural divide while you are proudly publishing extracts from the *Cantos* and *Finnegans Wake*, works that, whatever their virtues, are clearly not doing much to narrow the gap. Eliot's well-known defense of modernist opacity in "The Metaphysical Poets" is an attempt to evade this incongruity; he argues that in a complex civilization "[t]he poet must become more and more comprehensive, more allusive, more indirect, in order to force, to dislocate if necessary, language into his meaning" (248). Eliot is careful to premise this imperative on historical conditions: "We can only say that it appears likely that poets in our civilization, as it exists at present, must be difficult." Evidently this would not be the case under more favorable conditions. Obscurity is an unfortunate if unavoidable by-product of rapid and unassimilated social change. Even such esteemed writers as Joyce and Henry James, as Eliot admitted ever so gingerly in "Wilkie Collins and Dickens," were symptomatic of the troubling dissociation of culture in their tremendous distance from popular fiction (410).[18] With what he himself had wrought he was harsher, finally—and startlingly—ascribing the difficulty of his early poetry to artistic immaturity (D. Hall 105). As for obscurity being a device adopted purposely to put off the common reader, Eliot said categorically in 1933, "I doubt whether this ever happens" (UPUC 22). It is demonstrably untrue that such a design had never entered Eliot's mind,[19] but the disavowal indicates that in the long run he could not reconcile himself to such vanguardist thinking.

In the short run, Eliot was inconsistent. As much as he resisted it he was steeped, like other modernists, in the romantic ideology of the artist, and he could muster effortlessly feelings of contempt toward most of humanity. The elitist view that "true art is always unpopular" was sanctioned by the conservative French philosophers Eliot admired, such as Julien Benda (Howarth 230). Still, Eliot ultimately refused the comfortable aestheticism that such a position offered.

The process by which Eliot reached this refusal leaves clear traces in his career. The first step is taken around 1920: to read Eliot's 1917–19 essays in the *Egoist* together with his 1921–22 pieces in the *Dial* gives a strong impression that something important has changed. The *Egoist* presents us with an incisive, aesthetic Eliot, intensely focused on "literary" issues. The *Dial* Eliot is the urbane man-about-town, interested in a variety of cultural happenings and vitally concerned with the relations of art and society. No doubt Eliot realized that the critical austerity of his writing for the avant-garde readers of the *Egoist* would not do for the broader audience of the *Dial*; but the fact remains that Eliot desired a venue like the *Dial* and did not merely adapt to or settle for it.[20]

"What we want is to disturb and alarm the public," writes the *Egoist* Eliot, "to point out that . . . the forces of deterioration are a large crawling mass, and the forces of development half a dozen men" ("Observations" 69).[21] This Eliot insists that criticism confine itself to the objective appraisal of the artwork ("The Perfect Critic" 12–15); he assumes an essential difference between "human emotions" and the "emotions of art" ("Noh" 103); he imagines the artist as aloof, and as possessing a unique consciousness not shared by outsiders ("Tarr" 106). He sometimes equates history and literary history, a reduction he would later abjure.[22] However, when Robert McAlmon warned Eliot in a 1921 review that his criticism was impoverished because "he continually relates literature to literature" rather than to "reality" (10), Eliot called his remarks "quite shrewd" (*Letters* 454).[23] He was already beginning to move in the direction McAlmon prescribed.

By the time Eliot wrote his preface to the 1928 edition of *The Sacred Wood*, he felt that he had moved far beyond the range of concerns addressed in that 1920 collection of early essays. He did not, he said, "repudiate" what he had written, but he now considered it only "an introduction to a larger and more difficult subject." He had since "passed on to another problem not touched upon in this book: that of the relation of poetry to the spiritual and social life of its time and of other times" (viii). As Timothy Materer points out, it is not strictly true that *The Sacred Wood* does not so much as "touch upon" this problem (54); nevertheless, it can be said with some justice that Eliot had not, by 1920, found his subject. Beginning with the 1921–22 "London Letters," Eliot's criticism explores most persistently the relations between social conditions and the production of art.

To take one piece as an illustration of this new direction, Eliot's "Experiment in Criticism" (1929) argues that criticism cannot now be strictly "literary." At one time—as recently as the early eighteenth century—literature was "literature, and not another thing"; that is, critics could assume that its end was pleasure for those with the ability and leisure to read it (200). Since then we have come to expect much more from it:

> If you read carefully the famous epilogue to Pater's *Studies in the Renaissance* you will see that "art for art's sake" means nothing less than art as a substitute for everything else. . . . For the earlier period, art and literature were not substitutes for religion or philosophy or morals or politics, any more than for duelling or love-making: they were special and limited adornments of life. (201)

"On each side," Eliot judges, "there is a profit and a loss." In any case, the easy assumptions available to Dryden and his contemporaries are irretrievable: "The awareness of the process of time has obscured the frontiers between literature and everything else" (207). From his reading of Ramon Fernandez, Eliot concludes that "if we should exclude from literary criticism all but purely literary considerations, there would not only be very little to talk about, but actually we should be left without even literary appreciation" (212). Fernandez is in the line initiated by Sainte-Beuve, who was, Eliot explains, "a typical modern critic in that he found himself obliged to brood over the larger and darker problems which, in the modern world, lie behind the specific problems of literature" (208). Eliot himself is in this Sainte-Beuve line, in which literature is conceived "not only as a body of writings to be enjoyed, but as a process of change in history" (204); his constant concern is "the relation of the poetry of each period to the civilization of the period" (206), a study he will undertake most thoroughly in 1934, in *The Use of Poetry and the Use of Criticism.*

Eliot's point in "Experiment in Criticism" complements the earlier, more famous statement about difficulty in "The Metaphysical Poets": in one case the poet is forced by cultural circumstances to be comprehensive and allusive; in the other case the critic is forced to be comprehensive and activist. One might prefer to be confronted with the simpler task of a Dryden in approaching literature as a critic; and Eliot frankly expresses his regret more than once, over the years, at having to give up the idea of an autonomous aesthetic realm.[24] While such a concept retains its appeal for Eliot, at least as an ideal, he constantly puts by his inclinations in order to affirm that it is not now possible to cordon off one's reading from "religion or philosophy or morals or politics," and that it would be irresponsible even to try.

What has been lost, for Eliot, is the sense of literature as *merely* literature, "a means of refined and intellectual pleasure" ("Experiment" 202). In making this point, Eliot is not urging a return to the pure aesthetic; he is warning that literature has less scope than aesthetes since Pater have tended to credit—that it cannot really be "a substitute for everything else." Literature, Eliot stresses, is primarily a source of pleasure of one sort or another. Inevitably this way of defining literature limits and isolates it as a cultural practice, and the harder Eliot insists on it, the more he boxes himself in. The natural culmination of this train of thought is the bombshell that Eliot drops in the opening sentences of "The Problem of Education," a 1934 essay. "At the present time I am not very much interested in the only subject which I am supposed to be qualified to write about: that is, one kind of literary criticism. I am not"—writes T. S. Eliot—"very much interested in literature" (69).[25]

What goes for literature in general goes for poetry in particular. "The poet's first purpose is to amuse," Eliot asserts, "and unless he can amuse, all else is vain" (*Varieties* 287–88).[26] This was in 1933; in 1921 he had opened his essay on John Dryden thus: "If the prospect of delight be wanting (which alone justifies the perusal of poetry) we may let the reputation of Dryden sleep in the manuals of literature" (264). Eliot does not believe that Dryden's reputation should languish, and so he strives to show that Dryden *can* be delightful.[27] What is striking is that Eliot frames the problem in such terms and thereby accepts the necessity of defending Dryden on these seemingly unpromising grounds. With its relatively small audience and declining prestige in Eliot's own time, poetry could ill afford to be dull.

When Eliot defines poetry as a "superior amusement" in the 1928 preface to The Sacred Wood, the first word in the phrase usually attracts our scrutiny; we detect, or suspect, a note of condescension toward other activities that must be inferior by comparison, and we wonder in just what sense Eliot means to call poetry "superior." This is a legitimate misgiving. But Eliot himself puts all the emphasis on the noun rather than the adjective—an emphasis warranted by the historical context of his definition. To say that poetry is any kind of "amusement" is to repudiate the loftier claims made for the genre from Shelley to Arnold and beyond (viii). And Eliot, uncomfortable with his definition, immediately adds, "I call it an amusement . . . not because that is a true definition, but because if you call it anything else you are likely to call it something still more false" (viii–ix). Truth to tell—for he has not finished back-pedaling—"[i]f we think of the nature of amusement, then poetry is not amusing" (ix). But if poetry is an amusement that is not amusing, what is its value? Poetry has significance because it "has something to do with morals, and with religion, and even with politics perhaps"; yet as we attempt to explore these connections we cease to talk about poetry (x).

Against all assertions that poets were unacknowledged legislators, Eliot exhibited a deep skepticism toward the consequence of poetry in contemporary society. When the 1922 Chapbook sent out a questionnaire on that subject to a number of practicing poets, Eliot's responses were laconic to the point of flippancy ("Answers"). "Do you think that poetry is a necessity to modern man?"—a question designed to provoke eloquent effusions from contemporary poets—drew from Eliot only an unelaborated "No." And to "What in modern life is the particular function of poetry as distinguished from other kinds of literature?" Eliot replied, "Takes up less space."

It seems natural to inquire why, if Eliot refused all the available arguments for the spiritual necessity and social importance of poetry, he dedicated his life to the form. This is a question that Eliot himself posed early and often. In January 1920 he projected a future book on "1) the modern public 2) the technique of poetry 3) the possible social employment of poetry," motivated by his perception that "if people ever stopped to ask themselves what they wanted of poetry, the major part of contemporary verse would appear so obviously superfluous that there would be nothing to say about it" (Letters 355). Formalistic concerns ("the technique of poetry") are already bracketed here by cultural ones, but as Eliot pursued his investigations, aesthetics became a matter of decidedly secondary interest to him.

By the early 1930s, Eliot was doubting the efficacy of poetry and the value of poetic achievement with an urgency and regularity that seem remarkable even in those days of modernism's "political turn." In "Christianity and Communism" (1932), for example, he asks directly, "Of what use is my work? . . . Of what use is this experimenting with rhythms and words, this effort to find the precise metric and the exact image to set down feelings which, if communicable at all, can be communicated to so few that the result seems insignificant compared to the labour?" (382). Rather than offer a reassuring answer, Eliot admits the insularity of his existence ("my own narrow experience of living") and doubts his competence to speak on the social questions that now interest him: "why should a person like myself, whose only reasonable notoriety is due to the composition of verses and jingles, in which I have some skill, be talking on this subject?" (382). Having thus thoroughly trivialized his creative activity, having dismissed the bardic or shamanic authority a professional poet might have been expected to defend, Eliot then offers his comments as a layman. He was still apologizing in 1951, explaining that he kept up his publishing vocation because his writing often seemed to him something "not worth doing." At least, then, he could spend the rest of his time in professional activities that he and other people considered useful ("Value" 25–26).

As the phrase "communicated to so few" in "Christianity and Communism" indicates, Eliot's discomfort with poetry was due in large part to its relative lack of popularity. He was not satisfied with the world of coteries, patrons, and little magazines, whatever the debt he owed to each. Eliot's Harvard lectures of 1932–33, published as The Use of Poetry and the Use of Criticism, make quite clear what he wished for instead. "[T]here is no doubt," he avers there, "that a poet wishes to give pleasure, to entertain or divert people; and he should normally be glad to be able to feel that the entertainment or diversion is enjoyed by as large and various a number of people as possible" (22). What in earlier writings had been a prescription and a warning—poetry must give pleasure—has become for Eliot so self-evident that he now presents it as a norm: "I believe that the poet naturally prefers to write for as large and miscellaneous an audience as possible" (146). Yet as Wallace Stevens summed up the situation in 1942, "There is not a poet whom we prize living today that does not address himself to an élite. The poet will continue to do this" (Necessary 29). What Stevens takes as a datum to be accepted, Eliot takes as a reason to question the whole enterprise: "As things are, and as fundamentally they must always be, poetry is not a career, but a mug's game" (147–48).[28]

APPLIED POETRY

Eliot's position in the lectures is consistent with the logic of his essays. If, as he argues in "Marianne Moore," a living art is continuous with a living popular culture, then bourgeois veneration can only perpetuate a sterile form. It is not clear that anything one might do with poetry under these conditions will make it a truly public art—nothing, at any rate, that one might do with poetry as we have come to know it, an independent genre distributed in books and other print media.[29] Eliot's experience in the business of publishing reinforced this point for him; he saw firsthand, as he told a professional society in 1952, that the challenge for any publisher of poetry was "to lose as little [money] as possible" and that "the saturation point of the market for poetry, for poetry even by a very well known poet, is low" ("Publishing" 1568–70). Poetry as such, then, appears moribund, and if the poetic craft is to survive at all, it will have to take on some new shape. Eliot sees this need as presenting an opportunity. The challenge for the modern poet is to reembody the poet's skills with language and rhythm within a popular form.

Thus the one escape from the predicament of poetry lies in the development of a new genre in which the poet could "convey the pleasures of poetry, not only to a larger audience, but to larger groups of people collectively" (UPUC 147). The theater, Eliot hypothesizes, is "the best place in which to do it. There might, one fancies, be some fulfilment in exciting this communal pleasure." And it is not only a question of rescuing a declining literary mode from irrelevance. By working in a popular form the poet also wins the opportunity to engage with a substantial public, to speak to as well as to entertain an audience. The poet, Eliot writes, "would like to be something of a popular entertainer, and be able to think his own thoughts behind a tragic or a comic mask." In this way the poet could claim "some direct social utility," as Eliot puts it, without violating the principle that literature is primarily a source of pleasure (147). Eliot would later call such uses of the poetic craft "applied poetry" (qtd. in Lehmann 5).

Eliot began to speculate about the prospects of a modern verse drama around 1920, at just the point that I have placed the beginnings of his development away from aestheticism.[30] "The Possibility of a Poetic Drama," first published in 1920 in the *Dial*, already presages *The Use of Poetry and the Use of Criticism* in suggesting that the theater is the natural venue for the socially inclined poet and that most poets, indeed, desire the broader engagement the theater promises: "[T]he majority, perhaps, certainly a large number, of poets hanker for the stage" (60). Eliot's criticism would recur to the subject continually in essays and lectures with such titles as "A Dialogue on Dramatic Poetry," "The Need for Poetic Drama," "Poetry and Drama," and "The Future of Poetic Drama."[31]

Why, then—to put the challenge again—did Eliot go on writing poems? The answer, I think, is first that for the most part he *didn't*, producing only about thirty "serious" poems in the last forty-five years of his life;[32]

and second that even when he did, he didn't *mean* to. Eliot's perfectionism is not the only reason for the thinness of his *Collected Poems*. There are clear indications that Eliot intended *The Waste Land* to be his final effort in nondramatic poetry, a peculiar success never to be repeated. Within two weeks of the poem's publication, Eliot was writing to Richard Aldington, "As for *The Waste Land*, that is a thing of the past so far as I am concerned and I am now feeling toward a new form and style" (*Letters* 596). The "new form" was apparently the jazz-inflected, rhythmic drama of *Sweeney Agonistes*, a project he was planning as early as 1920, before the breakdown that precipitated *The Waste Land* (Woolf, *Diary* 2: 68). In September 1924, when Eliot told Arnold Bennett of his work on the play and sought his advice, he mentioned that he had "definitely given up" on poetry and was now "centred on dramatic writing" (Bennett, *Journal* 786).[33] As far as one can tell, Eliot would have been glad at this point to write only plays—which is essentially the point he reached ten years later. All his poems thereafter were either occasional pieces, outgrowths of his playwriting, or compensatory substitutes for playwriting during the Second World War.[34] His agonizing failure to complete *Sweeney Agonistes*, his first play, set back the transition by several years, but even this disaster was eventually overcome. Taken as a whole, Eliot's career from *The Waste Land* forward is a long process of feeling his way back toward a public—of searching for a popular "applied poetry."

In the meantime Eliot composed each of his major poems under severe emotional stress, as a "relief" of personal crisis (*WLF* 1).[35] At almost every point in his career he was predicting that his poetic genius might have spent itself—he suffered from chronic writer's block—and at each such point, after 1922, he anticipated turning his attention fully to drama.[36] There is even, perhaps, an element of wishful thinking in some of his predictions of his poetic demise, as if his inability to write poems released him to the task he would prefer to undertake. When that moment of release was postponed, he could at least theorize about the necessity and probable nature of a contemporary verse drama. As Virginia Woolf sensed in 1935, Eliot finally felt comfortable with his literary career only when he had determined— and when the success of *Murder in the Cathedral* had made it seem possible— that his future was to lie entirely in the theater: "He's determined to write plays about modern life in verse, and rather crusty when reviewers say he's an old fogy. In fact I think he feels that he's only just beginning to write what he wants" (*Letters* 5: 432).

Ultimately, then, Eliot did deal with modernist complicity in the cultural divide, not by betraying his allegiances but by walking away from them: by asserting that he was no longer interested in "literature" as an autonomous practice carried on for "art's sake," and by turning instead to drama as a popular vehicle with "direct social utility." As Frank Lentricchia puts it, "His career in theater is a would-be farewell to the social disdain of high-modernist coterie" (280). When *The Cocktail Party* ran successfully in London and New York in 1949–50, Eliot regarded it as the triumph of a lifetime.

A musty odor clings to the notion of "poetic drama"—enough, perhaps, that Eliot's desire for verse plays that would be popular may seem preposterous. Indeed, the quest proved more or less futile in the end. But Eliot was aware of the obstacles; he merely considered them surmountable. At any rate, he took pains to dissociate his conception of a modern poetic drama from any sense of staleness one might attach to the idea. In the first place, Eliot rejected outright the sort of argument that might be deduced from, say, Saintsbury's "Dullness": that audiences *ought* to like poetic drama and that they should adapt themselves to what is staged for their improvement. The emphasis on "pleasure" that increasingly attends Eliot's criticism of literature in general is especially prominent in his discussions of poetic drama: the audience, he writes, must be "interested and excited," for "[t]he indispensable merit of a verse play is that it shall be interesting" ("Audiences" 4). Eliot was likewise quick to grant that most current renditions of ancient and Renaissance verse plays were tiresome. In his May 1921 "London Letter" he praises a recent performance of *Volpone* for "proceeding," unlike most contemporary performances of Shakespeare, "without a moment of tedium from end to end" (686–87). In an extended critique of a 1919 staging of Webster's *Duchess of Malfi*, he objected that the production "was not only dull: it was ridiculous" ("'Duchess'" 36). The "Duchess," Eliot complains, was presented as a mental exercise for the "intelligentsia," and he denies "that any service has been done to *Art* by such a performance" (37–38). Gilbert Murray's translation of Euripides's *Medea*, similarly, recasts the play in the sterile "poetic" language that people imagine as appropriate to a "classic" play; the result, in live performance, is "the high-brow effect which is so depressing" ("Euripides" 47–48). Eliot will not have a play treated as a museum piece, rather than as living—which for him means popular—theater. For the same reason, he abhors "closet drama" (i.e., plays intended for reading rather than performance) because it fails the basic requirement that drama perform a social function ("Seneca" 60–61). Closet drama, for Eliot, is a private medium masquerading as public art.

Eliot was attracted to Tudor and Stuart drama and treated it often in his criticism largely because this work appeared to solve, in its time, the problem of the cultural divide: it was popular culture *and* it was poetry. This recognition is one that Eliot could hardly have overlooked in the work of his Victorian predecessors.[37] His notes for his 1918–19 extension lectures demonstrate his own attention to the popular background of Elizabethan drama. The course begins with a unit on the "earliest forms of drama" that immediately focuses on the origins of theater in "popular festival and religious rite" before moving on to the miracle and morality plays as successors to this popular tradition (qtd. in Schuchard 45). The third lecture, which introduces the Elizabethan stage, begins with discussion of the "Popularity of the Theatre" and ends by explaining "Why Elizabethan life and thought found its most adequate expression in the theatre" (45–46).[38]

Eliot's "Seneca in Elizabethan Translation"—published in 1927, the year of Eliot's crime-fiction reviews—deals even more straightforwardly with the popular aspect of such dramatists as Kyd, Marlowe, and Shakespeare. Eliot maintains, for example, that "*The Spanish Tragedy,* like the series of Hamlet plays, including Shakespeare's, has an affinity to our contemporary detective drama"; in fact, "besides *Hamlet, Macbeth* and to some extent *Othello* among Shakespeare's major tragedies have this 'thriller' interest," as does *Oedipus Tyrannus* ("Seneca" 65–66). *Arden of Feversham* and *The Yorkshire Tragedy* are "remarkable plays . . . based on contemporary or recent crimes committed in England." To which Eliot adds, with evident regret:

> It is only surprising that there are not more examples of this type of play, since there is evidence of as lively a public interest in police court horrors as there is today. One of the pieces of evidence is associated with Kyd; it is a curious little account of a poisoning case, *The Murder of John Brewen.* (66)

The essay goes on to contrast the popular Elizabethan playwrights with the cultivated "Senecals," those "fastidious spirits" who deliberately sought to create a "classical" drama. The comparative poverty of the Senecals interests Eliot. "Great poetry should be both an art and a diversion," he writes. Because they did not seek to create a public art but rather struggled *against* "the popular melodrama of the time," "the shy recluses of Lady Pembroke's circle were bound to fail" (77).[39] On the other hand, Eliot demonstrates at length that the boundaries between such highbrow drama and "popular melodrama" were not impermeable: "we must not draw too sharp a line of separation between the careful workman who laboured to create a classical drama in England and the hurried purveyors of playhouse successes: the two worlds were not without communication" (77). The interchange was richer, however, earlier in the Tudor period (83), and the growing distance between the "two worlds" of the theater was an entirely harmful development. Eliot's argument here is clearly parallel to the contemporaneous argument of "Wilkie Collins and Dickens," with its similar warning against the isolation of "literature" from "popular melodrama."

Eliot's position is the more interesting when considered in its literary-historical context. In his insistence on the popular nature of drama, Eliot is squarely rejecting the alternative of an "aristocratic" drama proposed by Yeats, who had turned after 1902 from the effort to create a "People's Theatre" to produce what he called "an unpopular theatre" (254). Yeats's theatrical ideal embraced "an audience of fifty, a room worthy of it (some great dining-room or drawing-room), half a dozen young men and women who can dance and speak verse or play drum and flute and zither" (255). At least once, in 1918, Eliot gained entry to Yeats's "audience like a secret society" at a performance of At the Hawk's Well—an experience that sparked in him a new appreciation for Yeats (Eliot, "Ezra Pound" 326). Eliot shared Yeats's symbolist attraction to the idea of a hieratic, conventional, antinaturalistic performance style; he even wrote an early essay in praise of the Japanese Nö plays, a pursuit he shared with both Yeats and Pound ("Noh"). Yet his dramatic works move in precisely the opposite direction from Yeats's. In the same way, Eliot implicitly resists the "Plea for Two Theatres"—one ritualistic, aristocratic, and "durable," the other popular and "perishable"—of Edward Gordon Craig (3–41). For Eliot, whose dramatic theory otherwise corresponds in many ways to Craig's, a split theater could only portend further cultural disintegration. Drama for Eliot was popular by its very nature, and in the end he would even compromise with the devil, the despised middle class, rather than create a coterie theater. This decision, taken gradually over the quarter century spanning Sweeney Agonistes and The Cocktail Party, is the logical consequence of Eliot's aversion to the cultural divide.

THAT BRIGHT CHIMERIC BEAST

Reaching back beyond the Elizabethans toward the origins of the stage in "[p]opular festival and religious rite," Eliot found much to consider in the ancient Greek drama and the related research of the Cambridge anthropologists, such as Jane Harrison, Francis Cornford, and Gilbert Murray (Skaff 80–85). Though Eliot criticized his baroque translations of Euripides, he admired Murray as a scholar, for Murray, "the most popular Hellenist of his time," contributed significantly to the recognition that the Greek plays had begun not as anybody's classics but as public rituals with "20,000 auditors" ("Euripides" 47–48). Echoing the account of the "historical sense" given in "Tradition and the Individual Talent," Eliot's "Euripides and Professor Murray" (1920) calls for "an eye which can see the past in its place with its definite differences from the present, and yet so lively that it shall be as present to us as the present" (50). Along the same lines, "Ulysses, Order, and Myth" repudiates any conception of classical art as "mummified stuff from a museum" (176–77). Once the Greek drama is assimilated to the bourgeois notion of the "classic," with its connotations of grandeur, remoteness, and tedium, it ceases to be recognized for what it was: the sort of popular ritual performance that scarcely survives in modern culture. The ability to restore the "classics" to their radically different cultural contexts, and thus, paradoxically, to resurrect them as living texts, is, for Eliot, the gift of anthropology.

Since modernist primitivism has come under a good deal of scrutiny during the past fifteen years or so, it should be said that Eliot's attention to primitive culture at least went beyond the fashionable interest and casual theorizing of many of his contemporaries. Through course work at Harvard and Oxford, and through assiduous reading, Eliot followed seriously the development of anthropology for more than twenty years. This activity surfaced in Eliot's many early reviews of anthropological works, published in professional journals, and later in the frequent plugs for such books he worked into his essays and editorials (Crawford 177). Eliot had only contempt, however, for primitivism as a vogue. In a short article of 1919, he waxed sarcastic about the reduction of the primitive to a "drawing-room phenomenon." A "smattering of anthropology" was becoming, like a little knowledge of Freud, a part of the miscellany to which every educated person must have some superficial exposure ("War-Paint").[40] So treated, the primitive suffers the same degradation as the "classics": shallow acclaim, in both cases, eviscerates a cultural product that might otherwise point up a viable alternative to middle-class culture.

Eliot's readings in anthropology, from Durkheim and Lévy-Bruhl to Cornford and Murray, impressed on him the thesis that art had developed not for purposes of pure aesthetic pleasure, and certainly not for its own sake, but as a component of ritual (Henighan 606). What we now call the (plural) *arts* were originally neither autonomous nor mutually independent: there was no poetry conceived as a distinct practice independent of music and rhythm, no narrative unconnected with performance in voice and gesture, no drama that was not at the same time poetic and musical. All these artistic practices were folded into tribal ritual and were thus fundamentally religious—though religion, by the same token, could not be conceived as something apart from them (Skaff 88). Art was not a solitary exercise but a public activity, one in which the entire tribe participated.[41] Primitive art, it could be said, is intrinsically a popular form—except that the concept of the "popular" has no real meaning where it has no opposite. In Eliot's understanding of primitive culture there is no possibility of a high/low divide; the issue does not even arise.

Primitive cultural totality reflected the social integration of the tribe; and the sense of belonging to a community cemented by shared values, conventions, and modes of perception is exactly what Eliot missed in his own century—a loss expressed poignantly in *The Waste Land*. Eliot's attraction to the primitive homogenous community reveals an obvious dark side in its exclusion of outsiders, issuing in, for example, the notorious proscription of "any large number of free-thinking Jews" in *After Strange Gods*

(20). Yet its more appealing concomitants, such as an abiding interest in the concepts of community and citizenship, are worth remarking as well. As Jewel Spears Brooker has argued, Eliot's eager search for "common ground," for collaboration and community, underlay virtually all of his work (*Mastery* 65). Eliot's attractions to music hall, to drama, and even to the Anglican Church, as Brooker shows, are all connected with this same need. The ideal of an organic community therefore had immense appeal for Eliot, and it drew sustenance from his study of primitive culture. He absorbed the concept of "group consciousness" from his earliest readings in anthropology and invoked it in various forms throughout his career, most obviously, though not exclusively, in his social criticism (Spurr 273).

Eliot's review of Emile Durkheim's *Elementary Forms of the Religious Life*, one of his very first publications, posits the urge toward "group consciousness" as a universal: "For the savage or the civilised man, a solely individual existence would be intolerable; he feels the need of recreating and sustaining his strength by periodic refuge in another consciousness which is supra-individual." The wellspring of group consciousness is collective participation in ritual: members of a tribe "partake in a common nature which it is the function of the religious festival to arouse" ("Durkheim" 14). Eliot also takes from Durkheim the priority of ritual to myth; that is, he denies the commonsense explanation that rituals are constructed to represent religious tenets. Myths, rather, are invented to make sense of inherited rituals, "in regard to the true origin of which [the primitive] is as much in the dark as the scientific investigator."[42] The form of a ritual takes precedence over any particular doctrine that may be associated with it: ritual is primarily a collective (and unifying) religio-aesthetic experience. The arts, in their primal unity, are intimately related to the sense of community that Eliot considers so valuable in the primitive social model.

Such anthropological thinking lies behind Eliot's formulation of a strong connection between the coherence of a society and the condition of its arts. On one level, this means merely that art is best produced under undissociated conditions, a recurrent and explicit point in Eliot's literary criticism. Dante, for example, benefited from "a mythology and a theology which had undergone a more complete absorption into life" ("Dante [1920]" 163); Blake's work, in contrast, suffered from the absence of such cultural integrity ("William Blake" 280).The "dissociation of sensibility" is another, differently historicized version of this fall (Materer 54–55). An "easy and natural association between religion and art" indicates that "the whole mind of society is moderately healthy and in order" ("Arnold and Pater" 390). Artists who work within the "social-religious-artistic complex" characteristic of primitive societies—yet found in advanced civilizations only at rare and fortunate moments—have an immediate advantage over those who are forced to construct their own edifice (CC 49). These ideas are familiar to every reader of Eliot's prose. That the model of the ritual-bound primitive community also offers a certain political convenience for a thinker committed to the patterned regularity of social class structure is also obvious.

But Eliot's attraction to a primitive cultural unity dependent on ritual also drives another, less widely recognized inquiry in his criticism: the question of whether any art now performs, and especially whether poetry could conceivably recover, something like its original social function. This problem returns us to Eliot's concern with the "use of poetry" and his anxious inquiry, "Of what use is my work?" with a new, anthropological perspective. Eliot himself frames the issue succinctly in a series of provocative questions that appear in his 1924 review of W. J. Perry's *The Growth of Civilization* and *The Origin of Magic and Religion*. Perry's work has again impressed upon Eliot that "The arts developed incidentally to the search for objects of talismanic properties" and that early craftsmen were "not aiming primarily at decoration" (490). Now Eliot finds himself wondering,

> At what point . . . does the attempt to design and create an object for the sake of beauty become conscious? at what point in civilisation does any conscious distinction between practical or magical utility and aesthetic beauty arise? . . . [S]urely the distinction must mark a change in the human mind which is of fundamental importance. (490)

This crucial shift marks the beginning of the aesthetic as something separate and distinct from the rest of life. But Eliot is never quite convinced that the human mind has altered through and through—that even an apparently "fundamental" change is irreversible. So he pursues his line of inquiry to the present:

> And a further question we should be impelled to ask is this: Is it possible and justifiable for art, the creation of beautiful objects and of literature, to persist indefinitely without its primitive purposes: is it possible for the aesthetic object to be a *direct* object of attention? (490–91)

With scholarly understatement, Eliot remarks only that this point has "interesting consequences for art" (490). But these are potentially explosive, even seditious questions from an up-and-coming humanist icon. The doubt expressed here, as in "Wilkie Collins and Dickens," is whether high culture in its present form, with the functions it now performs, is likely to endure. Can fine art continue as an autonomous cultural practice, or is the art object raised to aesthetic icon too precariously situated? Is art, in brief, too useless to survive? In contrast, Eliot argues that certain forms of popular culture retain key features of the ritual ideal. He believes that the English music hall, especially, carries on ritual patterns of audience participation and fosters something like Durkheim's "group consciousness" ("Romantic Englishman"). It is high culture, rather, that is the really new development—one that conceivably may prove to be ephemeral.

Eliot took the issues he raised in the Perry review seriously, to the point of asking whether the whole concept of literature in post-romantic culture was factitious. In the long "Note to Section II" of his major 1929 essay on Dante, he addresses the question of whether, in order fully to appreciate a literary text, a reader must share the beliefs of its author. He agrees with I. A. Richards that "if you hold any contradictory theory you deny . . . the existence of 'literature' as well as of 'literary criticism' " (229); but rather than to take the existence of literature for granted, as Richards does, Eliot admits that "we may raise the question whether 'literature' exists." For the purposes of his essay on Dante, he adds, he has assumed that it does, but the matter is no less contingent for that. "If there is 'literature,' if there is 'poetry,' then it must be possible to have full literary or poetic appreciation without sharing the beliefs of the poet" (230; emphasis in the original). The validity of the aesthetic depends on our willingness to disregard content in the act of appreciating form: without this readerly concession, "Art," as constructed since at least the middle of the nineteenth century, ceases to be. What is especially fascinating is that by the end of his note, Eliot has all but forced himself to admit that he cannot really believe in such a construction: "It would appear that 'literary appreciation' is an abstraction, and pure poetry a phantom; and that both in creation and enjoyment much always enters which is, from the point of view of 'Art,' irrelevant" (231). If extra-aesthetic considerations *always* enter, then by Eliot's own reasoning there is never "Art"; the concept is truly phantasmal. In "Experiment in Criticism," written in the same year, Eliot again steps carefully around this problem—for example, by putting "creative writing" in scare quotes, as he had "literature" and "Art" in "Dante." "So long as literature is literature, so long will there be a place for criticism of it," Eliot writes, pontificating and hedging all at once (213). The primitive "social-religious-artistic complex" bypasses this difficulty, for here there is no concept of an autonomous literature, no attempt to assert what Eliot increasingly perceives as a modern chimera.

THE USE OF THE PRIMITIVE

With his assertive prose style, Eliot is often seen as absolute in his pronouncements, yet philosophically, as Jeffrey Perl has demonstrated, he was always a thoroughgoing relativist. A stress on contingency and on point of view—the product of his graduate studies in Mádhyamika Buddhism and the philosophy of F. H. Bradley—undergirds all his criticism.[43] Attacking evolutionist approaches to the history of religion in a seminar paper he wrote at Harvard, Eliot points out that so long as we ourselves stand within the processes of historical change, we can have no objective basis for describing the development of modern religion as a "progress" (Gray 115). All interpretations of past cultures are "passed through the sieve" of our own consciousness; and because we change over time, "the past is in perpetual flux" ("Introduction to *Savonarola*" vii).[44] Such thinking leads Eliot to an anthropological approach that anticipates, inconsistently but sometimes strikingly, the cultural relativism of Franz Boas:

> Any person, therefore, who is aware of "culture" at all, will be aware that there are and have been various cultures, and that the difference between our own culture and an alien culture is different from the difference between culture and anarchy, or culture and pseudo-culture. ("Commentary [Jan. 1925]" 163)

Though contorted in its phrasing, this sentence cannot be said to express the sentiments of a confirmed Eurocentrist. It is in this spirit that *The Waste Land* "conjoins and relativizes" the various traditions it incorporates, denying, in the grip of what Michael Levenson calls the "anthropological temper," any cultural system a place at the summit of human evolution (202–03). Western civilization, the poem insinuates, is one of any number of "falling towers" in the wreckage of history (209). Eliot's attention to popular culture can also be seen in relation to this anthropological relativism, which suggests that all elements of a culture, high and low—like all cultures—merit serious consideration (Denney 170–71). It has been suggested that Seldes's work was authorized by contemporary anthropology, and Eliot was far more deeply immersed in the subject than Seldes was. Eliot's awareness of cultural difference allows him to perceive the contingency of apparently permanent truths and natural categories. Anthropology shows that the arts, among other things, could alter so completely in social function as to become a different object altogether. The knowledge that there has been radical change in the past makes the prospect of change in the future seem thinkable, even likely, and perhaps even desirable. Anthropological thinking makes it possible to reimagine the possibilities of one's own culture.

Primitive culture interested Eliot, however, not only because of its otherness but because of its ostensibly lineal relation to modern culture—a relation that implies sameness as well as difference. Eliot's work often highlights the continuity of "civilization" and "savagery," an idea that was gaining currency in the early decades of the century, thanks to Freudian psychology as well as anthropology and ethnology.[45] Eliot's *Poems* (1920), *The Waste Land*, and *Sweeney Agonistes* all seem to imply that the distance between the primitive and the contemporary mind is mostly illusory.[46] Indeed, in the years following its publication *The Waste Land* was considered a central document in a broader effort to establish just that point.

One consequence of this view is that the study of the primitive becomes essential to modern self-knowledge, and specifically that acquaintance with primitive conceptions of art is indispensable to an informed understanding of modern art. This much is implicit in the Perry review, where Eliot uses anthropological findings to interrogate contemporary constructions of art. In "The Ballet," Eliot states directly, "Anyone who would penetrate to the spirit of dancing . . . should begin by a close study of dancing amongst primitive peoples" (441). The same applies to literature, for "as it is certain that some study of primitive man furthers our understanding of civilized man, so it is certain that primitive art and poetry help our understanding of civilized art and poetry" ("War-Paint"). Literature as a whole, in fact, "cannot be understood without going to the sources: sources which are often remote, difficult, and unintelligible—unless one transcends the prejudices of ordinary literary taste" ("Beating" 11). Such an attitude is consistent with Eliot's argument in "Tradition and the Individual Talent," where he considers the "rock drawing of the Magdalenian draughtsmen" to be a constituent element of European culture that, like Shakespeare and Homer, is never abandoned or superannuated (6).

A second consequence of Eliot's stress on continuity is a demystification of the primitive. Despite his admiration for the work of Lucien Lévy-Bruhl, Eliot criticizes him for overemphasizing the gap between civilized thought and a "prelogical" primitive mentality. Eliot himself generally rejects the idea that there are primitive modalities of feeling and perception to which the modern lacks access.[47] In "War-Paint and Feathers," a 1919 review of a collection of Native American songs and chants, he dismisses as modish and sentimental the tendency to ascribe to the primitive "gifts of mystical insight or artistic feeling" that are unavailable to the sensitive contemporary. "War-Paint and Feathers" is largely an attack on the chic primitivism of the American intelligentsia, among whose "murmurs of approval" the *sauvage du jour*, the "romantic Chippaway," is credited with "the last word in subtlety, simplicity and poeticality." One understands Eliot's irritation with this fashionable anti-intellectualism; yet his impulse to compensate ends in an unattractive inconsistency. Somehow the Eliot who could affirm daringly that the poet "must be quite aware of the obvious fact that art," including the Magdelanian rock-drawings, "never improves" is also willing to assert defensively that the artist is "the first person to see how the savage, the barbarian and the rustic can be improved upon."[48]

What most irked Eliot about the primitivist dilettantes, however, was that their celebration of "Polynesian, African, Hebridean, Chinese, etc. etc.

say savage and Oriental art in general" was coupled with an ignorance of "what these have in common with our traditional art" (*Letters* 317). The connection is important to Eliot because just as he is "vitally interested in the use of poetry" (*UPUC* 23), he is vitally interested in the use of primitive culture; in fact, the two interests are really one. The capacity of tribal masks or drums to excite the modern spectator is not Eliot's primary concern, and the emergence of the primitive as a fad presents not only a nuisance but a positive obstacle to any consideration of primitive cultural constructs as a serious alternative to modern ones. The primitive "social-religious-artistic complex" represents to Eliot, as late as 1939, something "we should emulate" as a remedy to the dissociation of modern culture (*CC* 49).[49]

Eliot did embrace Lévy-Bruhl's concept of a primitive-mystical consciousness, a holistic mode of thought that intimately connected the human subject to its environment (Crawford 94; Spurr 268). Lévy-Bruhl's "prelogism" seemed to provide a scientific basis for a contrast between the empty rationalism of the modern epoch and the existential security of an earlier age. At the same time, though, Eliot denied that the *mentalité primitive*, with its undissociated relation to immediate experience, was extinct: it survived as a "substratum" of the modern unconscious (Skaff 77; Spurr 270–71). He was also aware of the theories then in circulation that primitive modalities of mind were preserved mainly in the arts. Under their influence Pound called modern artists "the heirs of the witch-doctor and the voodoo" ("New Sculpture" 68), and Eliot himself could write in 1918: "The artist, I believe, is more *primitive*, as well as more civilized, than his contemporaries, his experience is deeper than civilization" ("Tarr" 106). The idea had not lost its appeal by 1933, when Eliot cited the work of two French anthropologists who extended the ideas of Lévy-Bruhl to argue that "the pre-logical mentality persists in civilised man, but becomes available only to or through the poet" (*UPUC* 141). Eliot suggests that, in particular, the primitive symbolic and rhythmic elements of poetry have the ability to arouse "unnamed feelings which form the substratum of our being, to which we rarely penetrate"; our heightened awareness of these feelings submerges us in the "visible and sensible world," the world unmediated by abstraction and analytic reasoning (149). The *mentalité primitive* thus becomes a way of preserving the authority of the poet when the station of poetry within modern culture seems considerably diminished.

Given the importance that this argument accords the poetic, the problem of the audience presents Eliot with a true dilemma. The poet, according to Eliot, "naturally desires a state of society in which [poetry] may become popular" (*UPUC* 22). And poetry itself, as repository of the primitive holistic mentality, offers access to a mode of being that could make such a state of society possible. Yet as an unpopular art, poetry is in a weak position to effect social change. The inevitable result is an aestheticized art that bears little connection with lived experience, coupled with a way of life that suffers from a lack of vital aesthetic experience. The "savage," Eliot concluded from Durkheim, "lives in two worlds, the one commonplace, practical, a world of drudgery, the other sacred, intense, a world into which he escapes at regular intervals, a world in which he is released from the fetters of individuality" ("Durkheim"). The modern has no such outlet, and in a society nearly divested of ritual, art—which might supply the lack—is left marginalized and ineffectual.

Thus it is a mistake, though a common one, to boil Eliot's primitivism down to an aesthetic prescription, a set of principles for creating a modernist art. His allusions to vegetation rites, his preference for a ritualistic theater over a naturalistic one, and the "mythical method" he extracted from Joyce hardly begin to sum up Eliot's ambitions, for none of these things is an end in itself. Even in "Ulysses, Order and Myth," Eliot writes not that the mythical method makes art possible in the modern world, but the converse: that the mythical method is "a step toward making the modern world possible for art" (178). What this familiar sentence really anticipates, then, is an artistic program that will initiate a piecemeal transformation of modern culture. And this will require not just better art of the same general kind (obscure modernist rather than soporific Georgian poetry) but a change in the nature of art.

What Eliot envisions, in other words, is a revolution in the relation between art and society along the lines of primitive communities in which art is a central and not a fringe activity—a regular part of the experience of life, closely connected with what people believe, with their community-building, and in short with their relationship to their world and to one another. Such a transformation will also require, and may even have to begin with, a change in the role of the artist, whose defensive isolation must yield to an altogether different model of conduct. Eliot's poet is a public figure who "aspires to the condition of the music-hall comedian" and whose proper medium is drama, envisioned as a public and ritualistic art (UPUC 22). And the goal in view is not merely the rescue of art from irrelevance or dullness but the simultaneous redemption of modern culture from the twin plagues of skepticism and alienation.

AN "AVANT-GARDE" PROGRAM

It will be apparent to readers of Peter Bürger's Theory of the Avant-Garde that Eliot's anti-aesthetic cultural program as I have outlined it here bears comparison to the programs of early-twentieth-century European avant-garde movements in Bürger's account. Indeed, if this resemblance seems surprising it is only because Bürger's theory has been used, most influentially by Andreas Huyssen, to argue the existence of a strict separation between "modernism" and the "historical avant-garde." The example of T. S. Eliot, which ought to provide unproblematic evidence for such a generalization (indeed, Huyssen cites it as if it did), actually provides important reasons to question it.

Bürger traces the origins of the avant-garde to a process of self-criticism within the "social subsystem that is art" (22). "In bourgeois society," Bürger writes, art is assigned "a special sphere of experience," the aesthetic, and becomes detached from the ordinary, daily components of living, which Bürger calls the "praxis of life" (22–24). For avant-gardists, the dissociation of art from the praxis of life—summed up in the word "autonomy" and in the slogan "art for art's sake"—is nothing less than the "dominant characteristic of art in bourgeois society" (49). The avant-garde arises out of antipathy to this dissociation and to the "social ineffectuality" that comes as the price of autonomy (27):

> The European avant-garde movements can be defined as an attack on the status of art in bourgeois society. What is negated is not an earlier form of art (a style) but art as an institution that is unassociated with the life praxis of men. When the avant-gardistes demand that art become practical once again, they do not mean that the contents of works of art should be socially significant. The demand is not raised at the level of the contents of individual works. Rather, it directs itself to the way art functions in society, a process that does as much to determine the effect that works have as does the particular content. (49)

And herein, for Huyssen, lies the difference with modernism: "In modernism art and literature retained their traditional 19th-century autonomy from everyday life" (163). Modernists engaged in technical experimentation that sometimes resembled avant-garde practices, but they did not, according to Huyssen, try to subvert the "institution of art": "the traditional way in which art and literature were produced, disseminated, and received, is never challenged by modernism but maintained intact" (163). Avant-garde groups, by contrast, sought "to undermine, attack and transform the bourgeois institution art and its ideology of autonomy rather than only changing artistic and literary modes of representation" (192).[50]

Yet what Bürger and Huyssen identify as the avant-garde project corresponds in many ways to Eliot's. To be sure, the conservative Eliot hardly shared the activist agendas (whether left wing or right) associated with most avant-garde movements. And though other, relatively apolitical avant-gardes did exist, such as the Parisian group surrounding Jean Cocteau at Le Boeuf sur le Toit, it is quite true that Eliot, unlike Cocteau, studiously avoided avant-garde shock tactics and spectacle in promoting his aesthetic and social programs.[51] "You let me throw the bricks through the front window," Pound observed to him; "You go in at the back door and take out the swag" (qtd. in Carpenter 264). Yet the consequences of Eliot's thinking, even when developed in an unobtrusive and fragmentary way in his prose, are often radical—a fact that may help to explain Eliot's acknowledged usefulness to leftist writers of the 1930s as well as his later (and less frequently acknowledged) usefulness to cultural studies. Like the earlier avant-gardes, Eliot is keenly aware that the autonomy of art is a recent and local development, and not an immutable and transcendent reality. No less than they, Eliot opposes the middle-class fetishization of art. And we have seen—not only in Eliot's anthropological reviews but in even so well-known an essay as "Ulysses, Order, and Myth"—that Eliot's aim is not simply to alter "artistic and literary modes of representation" but to effect a larger cultural transformation (authorized by Durkheim and Lévy-Bruhl) that would "reinte grate art into the praxis of life" (Bürger 87). That art, suitably modified, might induce such a change is a notion, perhaps an illusory one, that Eliot and the avant-gardists share. They both seek a "reorganization of the praxis of life through art" (59).

Huyssen again follows Bürger when he associates modernist aestheticism with its purported rejection of mass culture. Bürger argues that the "dichotomy between high and low literature" is established by and for the purposes of the "institution of art" (lii). Because Theodor Adorno, for example, spoke from "within the institution that is art," he "almost always viewed serious and pulp literature as radically distinct spheres, thus making the separation that is established in the institution of art/literature his own." In Adorno's work, Bürger explains, "the relation between serious and pulp fiction is barely thematized, precisely because both are assigned to distinct spheres from the very beginning" (liii). Huyssen extends this characterization to the whole of modernism. And Eliot, he asserts,

> felt drawn to the constructive sensibility of modernism, which insisted on the dignity and autonomy of literature, rather than to the iconoclastic and anti-aesthetic ethos of the European avantgarde which attempted to break the political bondage of high culture through a fusion with popular culture and to integrate art into life. (167)

Eliot's criticism before 1920 confirms that he was indeed drawn to the position Huyssen defines as modernist—a position that, as Huyssen neatly explains, attracted American artists because high art in the United States (as opposed to Europe) "was still struggling hard to gain wider legitimacy and to be taken seriously by the public" (167).[52] But Eliot, having escaped this particular difficulty by emigrating, did not need the reassurances of aestheticism for long, and by the early twenties he was engaged, as we have seen, in interrogating the high/low binary. And this questioning is indeed, as Bürger's theory predicts, linked with a reexamination of the institution of art and a desire to realign the relationship of art with "the praxis of life." Eliot's goal is not merely a new and better poetry, but a complete rethinking of the prevailing construction of art.

My objective here is not to abolish all distinctions between modernism and the avant-garde; indeed, a revaluation of Eliot alone would hardly give adequate grounds for doing so. A counterexample of Eliot's magnitude, however, may provide sufficient reason to banish the conviction, from which many invidious conclusions follow, that modernism and the avant-garde are impermeable or mutually exclusive categories. Astradur Eysteinsson identifies some of the "ensuing value judgments and fruitless distinctions," as, for example, "seeing the avant-garde as simply a preparatory stage for the masterpieces of modernism or judging the avant-garde as the only significant revolt, while modernism is merely a classicism in disguise" (178). Eysteinsson's rejection of a "rigid separation" in favor of a more flexible model that recognizes the interpenetration of modernism and the avant-garde is to be commended as both a more "stimulating" and a more accurate representation of early-twentieth-century cultural history.

The efforts of the European avant-garde movements to transform both art and society cannot, evidently, be counted a success. As Bürger bluntly puts it, "the attack of the historical avant-garde movements on art as an institution has failed, and art has not been integrated into the praxis of life, art as an institution continues to survive as something separate from the praxis of life" (57). In this endeavor Eliot prevailed no more than the avant-garde. His methods, on the other hand, could not have been more different. Pound's bricks-through-the-front-window approach was basically avant-gardist: he wrote polemics, assembled conspirators, orchestrated scandals, published manifestos, and sought notoriety. Eliot was more level, more calculating, and more ingratiating; his modus operandi was to infiltrate the system and work from the inside—thus the cultivated "dullness" of the *Criterion* with which we began this chapter. In this way he succeeded, as Pound could not, in dictating artistic principles and canons in a country that was not his own, and ultimately even in capturing the admiration of a significant public.

Aside from the obvious question of whether any modern artist or artists, whatever their aims and whatever their tactics, stood a chance of completely transforming bourgeois culture, two special problems must be acknowledged in Eliot's case. First, Eliot was deeply conservative as well as radical, so that as he insinuated himself into the established "art institution" he was also to some extent co-opted by it, recoiling from and courting the system all at once (Levenson 217–20). As a result, Eliot the icon and champion of English letters has almost totally obscured Eliot the revolutionist in critical and popular perception since the 1930s. Second, Eliot's desire to alter the "praxis of life" was quickly and seamlessly absorbed, after his conversion, into advocacy of Christianity and the Church. Though this shift represents a change of focus rather than a reversal of principle, its significance is so obvious that after 1927 Eliot's project quite naturally appears altogether different from, or even antithetical to, the historical avant-garde's. Both of these problems will be considered in greater detail in chapter 6.

For now it will suffice to observe that although the "mythical method" is usually discussed in connection with The Waste Land—largely because of the light Eliot's analysis of Joyce sheds on his own major work—it is his unfinished play, Sweeney Agonistes, that best exemplifies Eliot's attempt to launch his broader program. It was this new project that Eliot had in mind when he wrote "Ulysses, Order, and Myth," and not the work he had written almost two years before in a genre on which he had "definitely given up." Whereas The Waste Land was torn out of Eliot under great psychological pressure, Sweeney was a calculated first step toward "making the modern world possible for art"—for Eliot did not expect to alter modern culture by writing poems. And not coincidentally, it is in Sweeney Agonistes, his one pre-Christian play, that Eliot today appears stylistically most avant-garde.

BACKSTAGE WITH MARIE LLOYD

VIRTUE, VEGETARIANISM, AND A HEADACHE

For Cecil Sharp, the folk song collector and founder of the English Folk Dance Society, dance, circa 1920, was in a bad way. Social dancing was dominated by "the Jazz," an abominable import associated with second-rate music. Sharp's one consolation here was his conviction that only the Great War could have "unsettled" the English mind enough to allow such an "inferior" type of dance to gain a foothold (31–32). Sanity, and superior dancing, would return in time. More disturbing to Sharp was the deplorable condition of performance dancing. The culprit here was another import, the ballet, which for Sharp was hopelessly artificial and virtuosic. The ballet had taken dance much too far from its popular roots, and the time had come for a revival of, for instance, the traditional sword and morris dances. In a posthumous work of 1924, Sharp proposed that to reform dance,

> the better way . . . and perhaps the line of least resistance is not to attempt an amendment of the existing ballet but to revert to first principles, to start afresh and endeavour to create a ballet founded upon one or other of our national folk-dance techniques. . . . Here, surely, is sufficient material from which to develop a spectacular dance for the theatre which shall consist wholly of movements at once natural and expressive, and possessing the advantage for England that they are cast in the dance-idiom of our own country. (49)

Happily, Sharp could report, a serious effort to revive the native English folk dances was underway, one that might well initiate "a genuine development of the art of the dance which previous efforts"—and particularly those of Diaghilev's Ballets Russes—"have failed to achieve" (32).

The sword dance, it should be noted, was more than a dance: it was a folk ritual encompassing music, costume, dancing, props, and play-acting. Centuries ago, it had sired that ubiquitous national treasure, the mummers' play, and so was often said to stand at the origins of the British dramatic tradition.[1] In such materials, clearly, there is much that would interest T. S. Eliot—the more so when one considers their obvious relationship to the fertility rituals that figure so prominently in his work. The plots of the various local ceremonial dances almost always involve a slaying and resurrection, indicating their descent from seasonal rites (Chambers, English 153– 54).[2] And in 1923 Eliot had speculated about the characters of the Fool and the Doctor in the mummers' play, through which he connected Shakespeare to shamanism and the ritual origins of drama ("Beating" 11).[3]

Yet Eliot did not welcome Cecil Sharp's intervention on behalf of the sword dance. For one thing, it ran afoul of Eliot's cosmopolitanism. The desire for a "native ballet" struck Eliot as an instance of English provincialism, "another 'protectionist fallacy'" ("Ballet" 442). The ballet, for Eliot, exemplified the ultimate development of European high culture; it demonstrated what international collaboration could achieve. In defending the ballet Eliot condemned Sharp's position using the worst term of reproach he knew: he called it middle class. Sharp's nationalism, Eliot thought, gave his writing "a somewhat smug . . . Chelsea-cum-Golders Green flavour."[4] That Sharp professed "some diffidence" in suggesting that the ballet be bypassed in favor of the sword dance did not at all appease Eliot, who considered it "not irreverent" to call the recently deceased Sharp "a confirmed—and I must say dangerous—radical" (442).

More devastatingly, though, Eliot critiqued Sharp's dream of a native ballet "founded on folk-dance technique" from an anthropological point of view. The modern ballet could certainly borrow from English folk dance, Eliot affirmed, but "founding a new ballet on a dead ritual" was "a different matter":

> For you cannot revive a ritual without reviving a faith. You can continue a ritual after the faith is dead—that is not a conscious, "pretty" piece of archaeology—but you cannot revive it. ("Ballet" 443)

To resume a ritual outside the cultural paradigm that had produced it would be merely to supply an exotic confection for the delighted palates of leisured faddists. "Of what value is it to 'revive' the Sword Dance," Eliot asked, "except as a Saturday afternoon alternative to tennis and badminton for active young men in garden suburbs?"[5]

The impossibility of resurrecting a defunct ritual is a recurring theme in Eliot's writing from his early prose to *The Hollow Men*, which, with its meaningless chanting voices, ineffectual prayers, and shattered altars, can even be read as a poetic realization of this idea.[6] Eliot's 1921 critique of *Le Sacre du Printemps* has a similar basis. While Stravinsky's music succeeds in constructing something new out of "the rhythm of the steppes," the accompanying ballet presents only a "pageant of primitive culture" ("LL [Sept. 1921]" 452–53). The self-conscious staging of a no-longer-popular custom has at best only an antiquarian interest. But a modernist high art, if there is to be one, must begin from popular materials that it simultaneously respects and (to borrow Eliot's term from "Marianne Moore") "refines." In his music Stravinsky realized the necessary "interpenetration and metamorphosis" as the balletic reproduction of a fertility rite did not.

For Eliot, in any case, drama was in a much worse way than dance. The London stage, he observed in 1921, was materially threatened by the indifference of its patrons: "Eleven theatres are on the point of closing, as the public will no longer pay the prices required by the cost" ("LL [July 1921]" 213). Two months earlier Eliot had voiced his dismay over the impending demolition of nineteen City churches. The disappearance of eleven theaters inspired only the judgment that "Considering the present state of the stage, there is little direct cause for regret" (213). His one concern was that the resulting vacuum would be filled not by a better theater but by the cinema.

Eliot's antipathy to contemporary drama is often expressed in anthropological terms and often ends in a sortie against the cultural divide. "Dramatic form," he argues, "may occur at various points along a line the termini of which are liturgy and realism; at one extreme the arrow-dance of the Todas and at the other Sir Arthur Pinero. . . . In genuine drama the form is determined by the point on the line at which a tension between liturgy and realism takes place" ("Introduction to *Savonarola*" x). When the modern playwright, beginning with Ibsen, sacrificed this tension for a misguided naturalism, drama "lost its therapeutic value" (xi–xii). Although drama was "originally ritual," modern drama forfeited ritual's "liturgical" formality or conventionalism. And most of all it lacked rhythm: "It is the rhythm, so utterly absent from modern drama . . . which makes Massine and Charlie Chaplin the great actors that they are, and which makes the juggling of Rastelli more cathartic than a performance of 'A Doll's House' " ("Beating" 12). Like Gilbert Seldes, for whom drama in the Ibsen tradition was a "bogus art," Eliot considered modern theater a bourgeois institution, attended dutifully—at least until, as in 1921, ticket prices rose—but without any deep emotional response. To experience the genuine effect of ritual form and rhythm one must go to the ballet, to the music hall, or even to a Chaplin film.[7] Such perceptions underlay Eliot's call for a change in direction: "I believe that the theatre has reached a point at which a revolution in principles should take place" ("Four" 91). To Eliot's mind, that revolution would take the form of a new drama in *verse* that would recover the satisfactions of ritual and thus restore a public to the theater.

No doubt the idea of a popular poetic drama seems quixotic; but Eliot was fully convinced that an unsatiated craving for verse drama existed—a demand "not restricted to a few persons" ("Possibility" 60). The "continued popularity of Shakespeare" suggested to him "that the appetite for poetic drama . . . has never disappeared" and "that a native popular drama, if it existed, would be nearer to Shakespeare than to Ibsen or Chekhov" ("LL [May 1921]" 687). Eliot's desire for a renaissance of poetic drama was not inconsistent, then, at least in his own mind, with his stress on the popular nature of drama. A "not negligible public," he insisted, "appears to want verse plays" ("Possibility" 60).[8]

As his references to Shakespeare indicate, Eliot associated verse drama less with the "serious" theater of his own day than with earlier species of theater that had managed to be simultaneously popular and sophisticated. He found it "curious that the popular desire for Shakespeare, and for the operas of Gilbert and Sullivan, should be insatiable, although no attempt is ever made to create anything similar" ("LL [May 1921]" 687). England was full of "comic talent," he remarked, yet there was "no intelligent attempt [being] made to use it to advantage in good comic opera or revue." In such passages Eliot is not merely calling for a change: he is also preparing himself to fill an opening.

If prose drama was moribund, however, Eliot also recognized that poetic drama in English was a "lost art"—could even be said, by his time, to have "wholly disappeared" ("Poetic Drama" 635). A modern would-be practitioner of verse drama had no living tradition on which to build, a difficulty whose near insuperability a daunted Eliot regularly emphasized. A study of the Elizabethan playwrights, he argued, would show by contrast "how little each poet had to do," since not only each writer but the audience habitually participated in a productive and well-developed theatrical discourse ("Possibility" 64). In a more ideal age "a framework is provided," a set of dramatic conventions, a shared understanding resulting in "a kind of unconscious co-operation" between artist and audience ("Poetic Drama" 635). The lack of such a framework results in plays like The Cenci, whose "relation . . . to the great English drama is almost that of a reconstruction to an original" ("Possibility" 62). "There is all the difference," Eliot adds, "between preservation and restoration"—a point well glossed by his later critique of Cecil Sharp's attempt to resurrect the sword dance. *You cannot revive a ritual*: once it is dead, any attempt to bring it back will succeed only in parading across the stage a "pageant of primitive culture." Modern poetic drama along the old lines is therefore merely "imitation Greek, imitation Elizabethan"—a futile attempt to graft new growth on long-barren stock ("Possibility" 67).

The revolutionary poetic drama Eliot envisioned, then, even if Shakespearean in its relation to its public, would not be Shakespearean in any stylistic sense. Its sources would have to lie in other, more animate genres—Gilbert and Sullivan, for instance. Eliot was at pains to separate his hypothetical new drama from any dreary notion of sacralized "Art." Modern performances of the Elizabethans, he complains, almost invariably solemnize the plays and render them dull (" 'Duchess' " 36). "We want the enjoyment of spoken poetry across the stage," Eliot proclaimed, "the design of a scene of costume, of movement, and the excitement of something very fine taking place before a number of people" (38). What he found instead was a dead ritual periodically resuscitated for the delectation of a few literati:

> Why does the revival of Seventeenth Century Drama suggest virtue, vegetarianism, and a headache, while a performance of "Don Giovanni" . . . may be entirely a pleasure? Because Opera has gone on without interruption. . . . [P]oetry on the stage is Dead, has been dead two hundred years. (39)

Such revivals are "bad archaeology" and nothing more (37).

The challenge facing the modern verse dramatist, then, is to create a work that genuinely engages the audience—not in the patient way that a tolerant elite attends *The Duchess of Malfi*, but in an "intense," "immediate and direct" way that has as its end "the interest of pleasure rather than culture" (" 'Duchess' " 39). This way of experiencing art, so foreign, in Eliot's judgment, to London's bankrupt theaters, yet prevailed in its music halls.

THE ROMANTIC ENGLISHMAN

Eliot's essay "The Romantic Englishman, the Comic Spirit, and the Function of Criticism," published in Wyndham Lewis's ill-fated *Tyro*, presents music hall as the essential living English ritual. Although the modern world is "barren of myths," Eliot notes, the theater, in which communal mythology ought to find its "platform," "affords in our time singularly little relief." The music-hall comedian steps into this gap: "Little Tich, Robey, Nellie Wallace, Marie Lloyd, [George] Mozart, Lupino Lane, George Graves, Robert Hale, and others, provide fragments of a possible English myth"; their comedy embodies, and simultaneously constructs, the English popular character. In this way the music hall succeeds where the "serious stage" fails: it mythologizes—and thus both elevates and criticizes—its audience in a "transformation of the actual by imaginative genius" ("Romantic Englishman").

Music hall, then, as Eliot had already suggested in the *Dial*, provides a viable starting point for a new verse drama independent of the older English tradition that had borne its last fruit two centuries earlier. Distinguishing his own conception from those of other writers from Shelley to Yeats to Middleton Murry, Eliot suggests that "the majority of attempts to confect a poetic drama have begun at the wrong end; they have aimed at the small public which wants 'poetry'" ("Possibility" 70).[9] If indeed fine art is "the *refinement*, not the antithesis, of popular art," then to begin at the right end is first of all to begin with popular and not unpopular materials; only so can the necessary framework, the crucial "unconscious co-operation" between artist and audience, be established ("Poetic Drama" 635). The "problem" facing Eliot's hypothetical right-minded poetic dramatist is therefore to produce a refined music hall that, without abandoning its public, will be poetry.

It is well to acknowledge at once the problematics of Eliot's argument. His attempt to distinguish between music-hall comedians, who are "unconscious" of the seriousness of their "fun," and artists, who rework popular materials with deliberation, condescends to the former and circumscribes the latter ("Romantic Englishman"). And one sometimes suspects, when reading these early essays, that the poet's "refinement" of the popular form really *does* amount to an improvement in Eliot's eyes. When he writes, for example, that the poet should "take a form of entertainment, and subject it to the process which would leave it a form of art," it is difficult to read the art/ entertainment dichotomy as value-neutral ("Possibility" 70).[10] Although we have noted Eliot's attempts to deconstruct this hierarchy, it is not surprising to find him at times slipping back into it.

Most importantly, perhaps, Eliot never makes clear how the modernist playwright is to adapt the popular form without doing it violence. The success of music-hall comedy, as Eliot well understands, depends on a spontaneous rapport between performer and audience. And this, as Amy Koritz points out, is lost when a writer takes the place of the performing comedian:

> Eliot's proposal . . . is not that poetic drama take over the performance style of individual music hall stars, but that it extract the form of their performance and transmute it into art. Music hall performers and their acts become the raw material with which to build a new poetic drama— a drama that, presumably, would not depend on the personality of the performer, the way music hall admittedly does. (146)

Koritz rightly questions whether the vitality of the genre can be preserved when the form of the performance is thus abstracted, and I will argue that Eliot ultimately gets around this problem only by moving away from the music-hall model.

Eliot did foresee other perils, however, and especially the possibility that a refined music hall could become, like primitive art, merely another vogue among self-congratulatory cognoscenti. His first proposal to structure a poetic drama around music-hall comedy is immediately followed by this caveat: "I am aware that this is a dangerous suggestion to make. For every person who is likely to consider it seriously there are a dozen toy-makers who would leap to tickle aesthetic society into one more quiver and giggle of art debauch" ("Possibility" 70). Eliot did not want to encourage, or to be seen as encouraging, a high-low cultural alliance as a matter of fashion.

Whatever needs, emotional or theoretical, music hall fulfilled for Eliot, his own interest should not be dismissed as an affectation. Consider, for example, that Eliot's second appearance in the Criterion—his encore to The Waste Land and, in lieu of any editorial statement, his first contribution in prose— was his elegiac tribute to the music-hall star Marie Lloyd, which had first appeared a month earlier in the Dial as the last of Eliot's "London Letters." The earlier, slightly longer version is worth considering in its own right because it articulates Eliot's feelings before his cautious pen had the opportunity to tone them down. In the Dial, Eliot calls Lloyd's death not merely "an important event" ("Marie Lloyd" 405) but "the most important event which I have had to chronicle in these pages" ("LL [Nov. 1922]" 599). And he concludes with a melancholy and unwontedly personal admission that must have seemed unsuitable outside the relatively intimate context of the "London Letters." Originally the essay ended not with its prediction of the death of civilization but with the sentence, "You will see that the death of Marie Lloyd has had a depressing effect, and that I am quite incapable of taking any interest in any literary events in England in the last two months, if any have taken place" (603). The events that paled, for Eliot, beside the death of Marie Lloyd thus comprehended both the founding of the Criterion and the publication of The Waste Land.[11] Eliot here offers a tacit admission that Lloyd is a more important cultural figure than himself. With that acknowledgment his series of "London Letters" comes to an end.

In his tribute to Lloyd, Eliot claims that her "genius" and her popularity both derive from "her capacity for expressing the soul of the people" ("Marie Lloyd" 406). Other comedians make their audiences hilarious, but Lloyd made them happy, for "no other comedian succeeded so well in giving expression to the life of that audience, in raising it to a kind of art." This point echoes Eliot's argument in the Tyro that music-hall comedy encapsulated the English popular character and supplied a national mythology.

Here, however, Eliot further particularizes this notion: it is specifically "what is called the lower class" that found its life expressed in Lloyd's acts (405). As an example, Eliot mentions the images of working-class (and gendered) behavior Lloyd dramatized in her last "turn" on the music-hall stage, in which she played "a middle-aged woman of the char-woman class" (405). He portrays Lloyd as an organic genius of proletarian London who always drew her greatest strength from urban, working-class audiences (Lentricchia 271). This point gets additional emphasis in the *Dial* version of the essay, where Eliot specifically notes Lloyd's Hoxton origins, and where he suggests that although she toured in America, "she was only seen at her best under the stimulus of those audiences in England, and especially in Cockney London, who had crowded to hear her for thirty years" ("LL [Nov. 1922]" 600−01).[12] Lloyd triumphed through "her understanding of the people and sympathy with them," and her audiences responded by being "invariably sympathetic" ("Marie Lloyd" 405−07).[13]

From Eliot's account of Lloyd emerges a collaborative model for the proper relation of artist and audience. Music hall was a participatory form: the comedians responded to feedback from the crowd, and the audience united with the comedian in song. As Eliot puts it, "The working man who went to the music-hall and saw Marie Lloyd and joined in the chorus was himself performing part of the act; he was engaged in that collaboration of the audience with the artist which is necessary in all art and most obviously in dramatic art" (407). Lloyd's art—and Eliot, to his credit, does not hesitate to use the word *art*—"was not what she did alone on stage, but what she and her audience did together" (Brooker, *Mastery* 72). This collaboration obviously contrasts with the reverential indifference toward art that Eliot considers a consequence of the modern cultural divide. He makes this point forcefully in "Marie Lloyd," predicting that with the eventual death of the music hall and its replacement by the (passively received) cinema, the "working man" will attend with "that same listless apathy with which the middle and upper classes regard any entertainment of the nature of art" (407).

As we saw in the previous chapter, Eliot understood the generation and preservation of a sense of community to be a primary function of ritual. In "Marie Lloyd" this idea undergirds Eliot's implicit suggestion of a causal relation between the decline of the music hall and the disappearance of an authentic English working class:

> The lower class still exists; but perhaps it will not exist for long. In the music-hall comedians they find the expression and dignity of their own lives. . . . With the decay of the music-hall, with the encroachment of the cheap and rapid-breeding cinema, the lower classes will tend to drop into the same state of protoplasm as the bourgeoisie. (407)

No group identity, apparently, can outlive its specific culture, and a culture, in order to survive, requires ritual and the communal sense that ritual maintains. While they lasted, local music halls did indeed fulfill "a craving for solidarity" (Jones 490), and surely they functioned so for Eliot himself, supplying a rare venue in which his modernist alienation was momentarily assuaged by a sense of belonging—phantasmal as any such identification must have been.

MYTHOLOGIES OF THE MUSIC HALL

I say "phantasmal" because it seems scarcely credible, given his family history, social life, and contacts, that Eliot can have known the "working man who went to the music-hall," of whose life and culture he was so solicitous, as well as he thought he did. Still, he was not quite as distant an observer as one might suppose. From 1916 to 1919, for example, he gave several courses in literature for working people in London. His letters are full of excitement about this undertaking: "I enjoy it immensely"; "I am enthusiastic"; it is "[m]y greatest pleasure" (Letters 161, 166, 168). He was impressed with his pupils: they were "very anxious to learn and to think," and some were so "remarkably clever" that, Eliot found, "I have to do my best to keep up with them in discussion" (Letters 168). He reported to his superiors that the students "showed a highly intelligent interest . . . and followed the lectures with closer attention than they merited" (qtd. in Schuchard 31).[14] In "Marie Lloyd" he refers to the working class as "that part of the English nation which has perhaps the greatest vitality and interest" (405), a conclusion drawn largely from his teaching experience. This formulation is in fact drawn straight from his letters, wherein he had already expressed the view that "This class of person is really the most attractive in England, in many ways" (Letters 168–69), that "working people" are "the most agreeable in England" (171), and even that "These people are the most hopeful sign in England" (161).[15] Eliot's sudden discovery of the humanity of the masses even prompted a temporary political conversion: "you see I am by way of being a Labourite in England," he wrote to J. H. Woods, "though a conservative at home" (171). This claim needn't be taken too literally.[16] And yet, although his later published views on higher education are avowedly undemocratic, in the teens Eliot eagerly anticipated the expansion of the Workers Educational Movement and called it a "beneficial change" (Letters 161). None of this makes Eliot the twentieth-century Lost Leader, but it does suggest that the interest he professed in "Marie Lloyd" in the culture and welfare of the populace was of some standing and had at least some basis in lived experience.

The makeup of the audience with whom Eliot shared "communal pleasure" in the music halls would have depended in large measure on which halls he attended. In this regard we have little documentation but some basis for conjecture. In his first "London Letter" Eliot mentions the "excellent bill" at the Palladium, one of the deluxe halls in Leicester Square, where Eliot would scarcely have found himself among the hoi polloi ("[Mar. 1921]" 452–53). On the other hand, the May 1921 "London Letter" briefly discusses, as if from an insider's viewpoint, the type of audience interaction common in "the smaller and more turbulent halls" (688). "Marie Lloyd" also refers casually to similar experiences: "I have seen Nellie Wallace interrupted by jeering or hostile comment from a boxful of Eastenders; I have seen her, hardly pausing in her act, make some quick retort that silenced her tormentors for the rest of the evening" (405). The assertion in the *Dial* version that Lloyd was at her best when performing in "Cockney London" again seems to claim firsthand knowledge ("LL [Nov. 1922]" 660). We also have the testimony of a friend who accompanied Eliot to a music hall in the tough, working-class borough of Islington (Isaacs 147).[17] Although such evidence is not conclusive, these references appear to indicate that Eliot did venture outside the more respectable venues.

Whatever his actual interactions with the working class, Eliot's perception was undeniably inflected by that romanticized figure, the stage Cockney. This character was an invention of the Victorian music hall, one of the means by which it negotiated the demands of the various constituents who formed its mixed audience. The Cockney type assuaged middle-class anxieties about the "uncivilized" and potentially threatening lower orders; it "worked to assimilate otherness into something more compatible [with] middle-class desires" (Faulk, "Aesthetics" 209). And working men, presumably, found the portrayal sufficiently flattering that they continued to patronize the halls. Within a short time, the combined efforts of many musical talents enshrined the Cockney as a permanent fixture in British entertainment (Pearsall 59). Even now the type remains familiar: a working man "strong enough to be gentle," sentimental, self-effacing, rough-spoken but never *too* vulgar, marked by "a sort of chivalry, a gallantry and the saving grace of laughter" (Farson 32). Thus Eliot's Cat Morgan:

> I ain't got much polish, me manners is gruff,
> But I've got a good coat, and I keep myself smart;
> And everyone says, and I guess that's enough;
> "You can't but like Morgan, 'e's got a good 'art."

(Old Possum's 56)

The working-class audience portrayed by Eliot in "Marie Lloyd" is colored—although not, by the standards of the time, cloyingly—by the Cockney type performed on stage. Eliot's working-class audience would jeer at sharp-tongued Nellie Wallace but never at lovable Marie Lloyd; they are cul-turally independent of their social superiors; they remain uncorrupted by mechanical forms of mass culture. In discussing the music-hall portrayal of the "romantic Englishman," Eliot shows himself aware that the comedians mythologize the working class; yet in his own nostalgic affection for that class he seems to reproduce a version of the myth. Like other intellectual observers of the music hall, he could not or would not see around it.

Convenient as such a statement would be to our purposes, we must, then, be on our guard when Eliot later asserts:

> I believe that the poet naturally prefers to write for as large and miscella-neous an audience as possible, and that it is the half-educated and ill-educated, rather than the uneducated, who stand in his way: I myself should like an audience which could neither read nor write. (UPUC 146)

The desire for a large audience in preference to a clique is honest enough, no doubt; we have seen how Eliot expressed such inclinations consistently and with growing intensity in the years following the publication of *The Waste Land*. But Eliot's heavy-handed construction of class types makes the remainder of this often-quoted statement almost tautological. *Anyone*, of course, would prefer an audience of Eliot's stereotyped Cockneys to one of his stereotyped bourgeois. Whether Eliot realistically could have written successfully for working-class audiences is another question. But what he *desired*, as Frank Lentricchia puts it, was "to be the Marie Lloyd of high-modernist literature": to star, somehow, before an uncorrupted, unjaded multitude to whom he would bear an impossible organic relationship (80). Lloyd stands, in Eliot's construction, "as an idealized version of the poet and critic vis-à-vis the community" (Faulk, "Modernism" 606).

If Eliot was somewhat taken in by the ersatz Cockney, his views on mu-sic hall are also subject to the larger question raised by recent cultural histo-rians of whether music-hall entertainment was "popular" culture at all. In Eliot's day the position of the halls appeared uncomplicated: they were a working-class cultural product that accurately reflected proletarian sensibil-ities. As Max Beerbohm wrote in 1901, "The audience is the maker of the form, the form is the symbol of the audience" ("In a Music-Hall" 397). Music hall was made by, and for, the English proletariat, a view accepted and disseminated by critics as well as poets and novelists from the Victorian pe-riod up to Eliot's time and beyond. As late as 1965, John Betjeman could state categorically, "The truth about variety is that it is unselfconsciously the poetry and song of the people" ("Foreword" 8). Dave Russell explains:

> At face value, music-hall songs deal far more directly with the conditions
> of daily existence than any form of English popular music apart from the

industrial folk-song. They abound with allusions to current events and fashions and to real places. . . .The vernacular was often used, enhancing the note of realism. It is hardly surprising, therefore, that both contemporaries and subsequent students of the halls have seen the songs as offering an entree into, especially, working-class lifestyles and attitudes. (89)

In an influential 1974 article on the emergent working-class culture of London in the last quarter of the nineteenth century, Gareth Stedman Jones highlights the resistance of this culture to even the most strenuous middle-class efforts to "dictate its character or direction" (479). The music hall was one site where this resistance was voiced, so that, for instance, working-class antipathy toward the temperance movement was expressed in "the popularity of music hall songs extolling the pleasures of drink and lampooning teetotalism" (472). For Jones, music hall (excluding, of course, the West End palaces catering to the well-to-do) was "predominantly working-class, both in the character of its audience, the origins of its performers and the content of its songs and sketches" (478). The turnout of 100,000 people for the funeral of Marie Lloyd, thirty years after music hall had peaked, confirms the popular character of the genre—as indeed Eliot had argued a half century before Jones in the *Dial* version of his tribute to Lloyd, with its interpolated newspaper account of her funeral and its deliberate stress on her working-class origins ("LL [Nov. 1922]" 660–61).

The conception of music hall as working-class culture, however, is vexed now in ways that Eliot, living in the glow of the genre's sunset, could not have foreseen. Music hall as Eliot knew it was not, to begin with, a "spontaneous popular creation" but the product of an entertainment industry (Russell 94). As such it reflected the views and values not only of its patrons but of its management, which, as many commentators have noted, was increasingly and often actively Tory. That the majority of the performers, including the most famous, came from working-class backgrounds does not mean that the songs themselves accurately represented proletarian attitudes (Jones 494–97). Moreover, the music-hall public was not, after all, strictly working class. Research suggests that from almost the very beginning, large portions of the music-hall audience were lower middle class—ironically, the same clerks and typists whose supposed automatism and pretension so disgusted Eliot (Russell 80).[18] By Eliot's time, the halls had gained full social acceptance among the middle class (though Eliot saw their presence in the halls as culturally parasitic ["Marie Lloyd" 407]); upper-class slummers had penetrated the halls long before. The composition of the audience varied widely from one venue to the next, the clientele depending in each case on location, seating prices, furnishings, and reputation; and to further complicate the picture, each hall attracted a range, often a broad range, of patrons. The performing artists, composers, lyricists, and proprietors were all subject to the different and sometimes conflicting demands of these mixed and shifting audiences. Thus, as Laurence Senelick argues, "It would be a mistake to accept casually the sentiments embodied in stage performances as unalloyed reproductions of popular feeling" (150). Senelick goes so far as to assert that the music hall was "the instigator and not the receptor of popular opinion," a claim echoed by T. J. Clark's argument that the French café-concert "*produced* the popular"—that, in other words, the popular culture (so-called) of the music halls was "a fiction of working-class ways of being" staged for the amusement and reassurance of middle-class consumers and as a means of exerting control over its working-class subjects (*Painting* 220–38).[19]

If "popular culture" is understood to be a working-class mode of resistance, or if, on the contrary, it is defined as the appropriation and standardization of a working-class cultural form, then Eliot's traditional view of music hall can have little validity. But Stuart Hall's insight into the inevitable "double-stake in popular culture, the double movement of containment and resistance" comes partway to Eliot's rescue. "The study of popular culture," Hall observes, "has tended to oscillate wildly between the two alternative poles of that dialectic—containment/resistance" (228). The articles by Senelick and Jones, published only a year apart, provide a textbook illustration of this oscillation, with Senelick critiquing music hall as a form of hegemonic social control from above and Jones commending it as a form of resistance from below. But as Hall sanely concludes of exactly the period in question, the 1880s to the 1920s, "[t]here is no whole, authentic, autonomous 'popular culture' which lies outside the field of force of the relations of cultural power and domination" (232). We cannot, in other words, identify an "authentic" popular culture against which music hall, for example, might be seen as counterfeit (228). The mongrel form that was music hall is not to be contrasted with genuine popular culture; rather, that mélange is what popular culture is, a thing "[n]either wholly corrupt [n]or wholly authentic" (233).

Thus Eliot's conviction that what he found in the music halls was "the expression and dignity" of working-class lives is, on the one hand, an obvious oversimplification. As Russell states, it is "impossible to claim the songs as the property of an individual class" (90). On the other hand, to dismiss music hall as a faux working-class phenomenon would be an equal and opposite oversimplification, as Russell's *mais enfin* indicates: "Despite all these hesitations, music-hall songs do have value as a source of testimony, provided that they are seen as purveying generalized attitudes which *may* have been held by the working class, but were by no means their sole preserve" (95).[20] While Eliot's position needs to be qualified, it is not groundless, for with all the proper caveats in place, "it is probable that cockney attitudes and mentality pervaded the song literature to a considerable extent" (Russell 91). A tune like Fred Leigh's "Don't Dilly Dally," in the hands of a Marie Lloyd, does give voice to popular perspectives and concerns—including the all-important question, "Who pays the rent?" which also happens to occupy Eliot's Dusty and Doris in *Sweeney Agonistes*:

> We had to move away,
> 'Cos the rent we couldn't pay,
> The moving van came round just after dark;
> There was me and my old man
> Shoving things inside the van,
> Which we'd often done before, let me remark.

Such songs may even embody, as Eliot said of Lloyd herself, some of "the virtues which [the people] genuinely most respected in private life" ("Marie Lloyd" 407).

That the working-class "virtues" to which Eliot refers add up to a "profoundly conservative" world view must not be overlooked (Russell 96). This conservatism could be quite directly political. Victorian music-hall hits often brimmed with imperial pride, and several performers, of whom G. H. ("The Great") MacDermott was foremost, spun chauvinism into gold.[21] Topical songs could wax satirical about anyone and anything, but Liberal politicians were targeted with special regularity. This proclivity had the backing of the halls' proprietors, who beginning in the 1880s increasingly allied themselves with the Tories against the temperance lobby and its Liberal advocates (Jones 495).

Still more pervasive than the expression of actual Tory sentiments, however, was the quiescent fatalism of music-hall songs. Over and over they communicated the sense that life was full of hard knocks and that since there was no changing it, the best course was to smile stoically and persevere. The class system in particular was "simply a fact of life" that had to be accepted. The rich might be laughable, but they were entitled; social climbers who tried to improve their status were the single most common target of derision; political activists were full of "hot air" (Jones 493). Though such attitudes probably helped music hall transcend its initial working-class appeal—they were, so to speak, marketable values—they did originate in working-class culture (Russell 97, 110; Jones 462). Eliot's character portraits are saturated in these attitudes. His "small house agent's clerk" in "The Fire Sermon" ("One of the low on whom assurance sits / As a silk hat on a Bradford millionaire") exemplifies the social climber beautifully and is treated with the appropriate contempt, his carbuncles duly noted (CPP 44). The Cockney narrator in "A Game of Chess" lectures Lil on perseverance ("If you don't like it you can get on with it") and chides her friend for her failure to keep a stiff upper lip in the face of serial pregnancy, ill health, and tooth decay:

> You are a proper fool, I said.
> Well, if Albert won't leave you alone, there it is, I said,
> What you get married for if you don't want children?
>
> (CPP 42)

The upper classes may be peopled with fools, from "dowager Mrs. Phlaccus" in "Mr. Apollinax" to Gerald and Violet in The Family Reunion, but they are finally harmless, and their position is never challenged. When Bert, the unruffled Cockney foreman in The Rock, talks down a socialist agitator and exposes his ideas as so much bluster, the scene is again in the best music-hall tradition. Eliot detected in music-hall comedy a manifest expression of popular morality.[22] It was a morality he found both congenial and artistically usable.

A latecomer to the halls, Eliot missed the height of music-hall Toryism by well over a decade. The Great MacDermott was already passé when he died in 1901; and in general, the political and social aspects of music-hall entertainment were considerably toned down after the Boer War and well before Eliot's arrival in England (Senelick 174–80). Marie Lloyd, for one, almost never ventured into politics. Yet the conservative Cockney worldview remained imbedded in music-hall culture, and Eliot recognized it well enough to reproduce it repeatedly in his later plays, whose proletarian characters—the women of Canterbury, Downing, Eggerson—invariably stand fast for order, humility, and quietism. As early as 1917, Eliot found English working people "impressive because of their fundamental conservatism." American workers, by contrast, were "aggressive and insolent," which is perhaps to say merely that they did not accept the social order and their place in it as inevitable or immutable (Letters 169). Music-hall conservatism appealed to Eliot's own desire for cultural stability and for a hierarchical political order that would preserve such stability.

Eliot also accepted the commonplace of an "affinity of outlook" between the upper and lower strata of British society (Jones 496). Another product of music-hall history, this concept dated from the growth of a new leisure-class audience in the last quarter of the nineteenth century and the opening in the 1880s of grand halls such as the Palace and the Empire. The efforts of "purity" advocates such as Laura Ormiston Chant to curb the vices of drinking and prostitution that took root in these convivial settings mobilized both upper- and working-class outrage against middle-class "prudery" and "the fanatics of the suburbs" (Symons, "Case" 501). Disdain for bourgeois aspirations and pretensions united aristocracy and populace, though the alliance was less a political reality than a fiction of the literate imagination.

Eliot often translates the notion of a high-low alliance against the middle into cultural terms. In "Marianne Moore," as we have seen, fine art (which Glenway Wescott had awkwardly labeled "aristocratic art") belongs to the same continuum as popular art, while "middle-class art" is cordoned off (594–95). Eliot uses the high-low alliance, as Koritz notes, as a weapon against mass culture (151), or—for some qualification is necessary here— against certain forms of it that Eliot, like many of his contemporaries, takes to be deadening, depersonalizing, and threatening to human relationship and community. Such forms (the apocalyptic ending of "Marie Lloyd" lists cinema, motor-cars, gramophones, and loudspeakers) Eliot associates post hoc with the bourgeoisie, already in his construction a dehumanized, conformist, insensate mass or "protoplasm"—for the mob, the human multitude Eliot loathes, is always specifically middle class. The middle class threatens to engulf the working class just as mass culture threatens to displace the popular forms Eliot takes to be organic; for Eliot, these changes are integral, cataclysmic, and very likely inescapable.[23]

For Eliot, the slow death of music hall became a symbol of this antici- pated cultural catastrophe. It is a recurrent theme in the "London Letters" from the very first letter, which promises an "important chapter" to come on "the Extinction of the Music Hall [and] the corruption of the Theatre Public" ("[Mar. 1921]" 453). The May 1921 "London Letter" takes up the subject again, as does that of April 1922, with a deeper note of frustration and despondency:

> I thought of Marie Lloyd again; and wondered again why that directness, frankness, and ferocious humour which survive in her, and in Nellie Wallace and George Robey and a few others, should be extinct, should be odious to the British public, in precisely those forms of art in which they are most needed, and in which, in fact, they used to flourish. (513)

But Eliot has already explained that outcome in this essay: art of all kinds is diminished by the growing hegemony of middle-class culture. And this is the answer he will formulate more memorably a few months later in "Marie Lloyd," which begins life as the last "London Letter" and supplies the "important chapter" promised in the first. Eliot knew that the end of music hall, symbolized in the death of Marie Lloyd, was irrevocable. After all, "you cannot revive a ritual."

Popular forms like music hall, associated by Eliot with an organic con- ception of "the people," counteract the alienation and skepticism that de- press the conditions of modern life. Massification, on the contrary, takes art yet further from ritual, with its vital community-making and belief-inducing functions. The mythologizing element of music-hall comedy that Eliot describes in "The Romantic Englishman" is precisely what he finds lacking in the "middle-class" arts; there is no Marie Lloyd, no "expressive figure," in the cinema ("Marie Lloyd" 407). Charlie Chaplin, as Eliot grudgingly admits in 1923, comes closest to bringing the ritual element onto the screen: "The egregious merit of Chaplin is that he has escaped in his own way from the realism of the cinema and invented a rhythm"—this while arguing that the cathartic effect of ritual is precisely a function of rhythm ("Dramatis" 306). But Chaplin was trained in the music halls—he had even appeared, as a boy, on the same bill as Marie Lloyd and had studied her performances from the wings (Farson 53–54)—and carried forward into film many elements of music-hall plot, characterization, and timing. Eliot did not believe that film in the long run would continue the trajectory of stage entertainment, and in this he was right; from early on he understood the fundamental differences in the media. The rapport between a live performer and an audience, in any case, could not be reproduced in a mass medium.[24]

THE DISCRIMINATING AMATEUR

Eliot's devotion to the music hall is in many ways a legacy of the fin-de-siècle writers who valorized the halls against the partisans of the formal theater. Paralleling the advocacy of the Parisian *cafés-concerts* by French intellectuals, and inspired by George Moore's *Confessions of a Young Man* (1888), John Davidson, Max Beerbohm, Arthur Symons, and others scandalously propagated a "cult" of the English music hall in the 1890s (Faulk, "Aesthetics" 73). Symons, whose influence on Eliot is well known, was an extreme devotee who attended music-hall programs obsessively, wrote fervently about his experiences there, and carried on numerous affairs with the young working women of the ballet corps. All these activities, including the affairs, had an aura of slumming: they were a celebration of sin and sensation, a descent into an underworld, an antinomianism cultivated while, as Symons supposed, a hypertrophic civilization collapsed around him. This weltanschauung led him to champion music hall as a cultural expression both more valid and more alluring than the "legitimate" theater. Symons and his allies clashed often with theater critics such as William Archer, who attacked the pro-hall cohort as irresponsible, fanatical, and fashionable. Archer, meanwhile, promoted the naturalistic drama of Ibsen and Shaw. Eliot's later valuation of the halls over the contemporary theater, together with his attack on naturalism, neatly reproduces the conflict played out in this previous generation.

Interestingly, as the music halls—increasingly dominated by large business syndicates eager to expand middle-class patronage—began a determined march toward "respectability" and "family entertainment," the pro-hall intellectuals clung to the older conception of the audience as fundamentally working class and the milieu as raw and disreputable. It may be that supporters preferred not to see that the genre they admired was changing; a more cynical view is that the symbolic capital accrued by championing the halls depended on their maintaining their vulgarity (Elliott 60–61). Of course, as we have noted, what one experienced in the halls still depended on which halls one attended. Symons, however, was professedly "as fond of the seedy Metropolitan in the Edgeware Road as he was of the Alhambra and the Empire," two of the posh halls of Leicester Square; and while he appreciated the different ambience of each hall—"To the discriminating amateur, each music-hall has its *cachet*," he self-congratulatingly remarked—he continued to represent the whole genre as essentially proletarian (Stokes 89).[25] This insistence on the popular character of music hall also lent critical support to the treasured notion that the halls sustained a sense of shared culture and community that transcended class boundaries (Elliott 62). Though it seems convenient to middle- and upper-class interests, there was doubtless something to this idea of a "cross-class consensus" or "community of feeling" to which the halls contributed (Bailey xvii). Its relevance to Eliot's view of music hall, and especially to his conviction that the death of the genre was closely connected with social disintegration, hardly needs to be pointed out. In stressing the socially integrative function of the halls, and in emphasizing their working-class roots to give force to that point, Eliot was again extending and updating the arguments of the late-Victorian avant-garde.

In several respects, then, "Marie Lloyd" is less the expression of an Eliotic idiosyncrasy than, in Frank Kermode's words, the "classic statement" of an existing ideology ("Poet and Dancer" 6). Yet Eliot's approach to music hall also differs in crucial ways from that of Symons and his confederates. Perhaps most importantly, Eliot places himself in a very different relation to the halls. Symons, as Bridget Elliot writes, "Self-consciously creat[ed] a decadent persona complete with matching poetry":

> His obsession with the halls, which he attended night after night, contributed to his image as a restless, cosmopolitan seeker of thrills and experiences. . . . This was the urban *flâneur* at his finest, watching the spectacles that others provided but remaining aloof on the social fringes. (49–50)

Indeed, Symons constantly stresses his distance from as well as his attraction to the activity of the music halls; he is seen ever drifting around the edges of the crowd, lurking in the shadows or just behind the stage door where he contemplates life at a remove, watching the show from a distant doorway or following it in his mind's eye while smoking in the promenade. It is essential to Symons's decadent self-fashioning that he be present yet half absent—a distinctively fin-de-siècle stance that finds its way into Eliot's earliest poems (Prufrock, for one, is a genuine flaneur) but does not seem to enter his writings on music hall. Because he does not emphasize or cultivate a sense of detachment, Eliot's presence in the halls appears—and not, I think, deceptively—less voyeuristic than Symons's "morbid fascination" with a lower order of culture, alluring in its coarseness (Elliott 54). Although the music hall clearly *represents* something for Eliot no less than it does for Symons, his attendance seems motivated by a more ordinary pleasure in the programs themselves.[26] One does not imagine Symons acting out the sketches or rehearsing the songs later to entertain his friends.

What the halls represent to Eliot has its own modernistic spin, in which his trademark concerns—anthropology, audience-artist collaboration, the local or national popular versus the global, and so on—are welded to what Peter Bailey calls the "folk or idealist interpretation of music hall history," a view that "nurses the legend of an industrial or at least urban Volksgeist" and represents the music hall as "part of the World We Have Lost" (xiii–xiv). Still, the genre of the "music-hall lament" in which Eliot's essay participates was already hoary when Eliot dusted it off in "Marie Lloyd."[27] Indeed, by the time Eliot discovered the halls, they had already outlived their heyday not only as a cultural form but as an intellectual fashion. Eliot, well-nigh alone among major critical voices, remained committed to music hall as an art into the late 1930s, when his attention could do nothing, even in theory, to extend its life, and far beyond the point where his advocacy could bring him any avant-garde prestige. He had, seemingly, little to gain by carrying on the fight.

What, then, lay behind Eliot's stubborn devotion to this cultural form? According to Amy Koritz, the answer is "ideology." Eliot, Koritz argues, is determined to forge an alliance with the working class in order to forestall bourgeois hegemony. Ultimately it is his commitment to his own ("traditional intellectual") class that motivates "his attempts to appropriate music hall for high art" (151–52). Without denying the partial truth of this reading, I want to offer an alternative explanation.[28] The preceding chapter showed the extent to which Eliot felt professionally disinherited by the cultural divide—compelled by his modernity to be a modernist poet but never really at ease with his coterie audience and lack of "direct social utility." To have been a Marie Lloyd, or "something of a popular entertainer," was a lost birthright—so Eliot argued along anthropological lines. The music hall, for Eliot, represents a vanishing possibility of reconciliation between diverging levels of culture that ought to have been simultaneously available to him. Marie Lloyd could be both an artist *and* popular; her relationship with her principal audience was organic. Eliot, the loner, the austere patrician, the sovereign of obscurity, was starving for the sort of human connection with an audience that came to Lloyd without contrivance. His loss finds probably its most moving expression in "The Fire Sermon" section of The Waste Land, in a passage I quoted in chapter 1 for its sound:

> "This music crept by me upon the waters"
> And along the Strand, up Queen Victoria Street.
> O City city, I can sometimes hear
> Beside a public bar in Lower Thames Street,
> The pleasant whining of a mandoline
> And a clatter and a chatter from within
> Where fishmen lounge at noon. . . .
>
> (CPP 45)

Here the fishmen's bar, an analogue of the music hall, represents a vestigial enclave of living (popular) culture amid London's commercial center (the "City"). From this oasis, however, the speaker, the poet-flaneur wandering the streets outside, is painfully excluded. The hints of vibrancy, beautifully intimated by the rhythms of the passage, are "within"; the speaker, who may be soothed and tantalized at once, cannot enter or partake.

Eliot would struggle for thirty years, in many ways against himself, to fill the role on stage left vacant after Marie Lloyd's death. His mechanism for doing so was to be, not surprisingly, a marriage of her talents and his in a generically mixed poetic drama whose appeal would, if successful, "transcend the present stratifications of public taste—stratifications which are perhaps a sign of social disintegration" (UPUC 147). A poetic drama rooted in the music hall, in other words, might bridge, or perhaps bypass, the cultural divide and restore to Eliot the popular adulation that was Marie Lloyd's and ought to have been the poet's as well. The sociopolitical apparatus Eliot adopted to account for this loss, tentacular as it was, did not, in my reading, precede the sense of privation.

This explanation, I think, helps to account for the perception common to so many critics that the "Marie Lloyd" essay is an anomaly within Eliot's oeuvre. The stress on mutual sympathy and on an immediate connection between artist and audience does not sound much like Eliot's relation to his own readers. But Eliot was himself cognizant of that gap, to him the deplorable consequence of a fragmented culture. What seems anomalous in Eliot is in reality an expression of yearning for an end to exile. Nothing less can explain the future direction of his career, which would take him out of a waste land and into a cocktail party. There would be, though, a number of "stops and steps" along the way (CPP 63).

SWEENEY BOUND AND UNBOUND

MINSTREL MAN

A young American artist, determined to see what headway he and his banjo could make in the Old World, set sail for London. He opened there with the Sands Great American Circus Company on January 23, 1843. His act delighted the British, and within two years he had given a command performance for Queen Victoria and returned to the United States with "enough money to retire" (Woodward 8). His banjo had, if anything, an even greater success: it inspired numerous imitators, helped establish the minstrel show as a major genre of popular entertainment in Britain, and launched a banjo craze that lasted into the early twentieth century. This episode, in fact, constitutes the first occasion when U.S. popular culture had an appreciable effect on the culture of Europe.[1] The name of the American trailblazer was Sweeney.

Joel Walker Sweeney (1813–60) has not endured in the annals of American culture as have Dan Emmett and Thomas "Daddy" Rice; he did not compose "Dixie" or invent Jim Crow. Still, Sweeney was an influential figure.[2] The legend persisted for many years that Sweeney had added the banjo's fifth string—the "thumb string" that gave the instrument its distinctive rhythmic character. Although historians now discount this claim, the notion that Sweeney added the fourth or bass string to the original African-American form of the instrument is still considered viable, and his importance as the first popular virtuoso of the banjo is beyond question, not least because many of the key early minstrel performers learned their banjo technique directly from him.[3] Yet Sweeney made his greatest *direct* impact in Britain.

Dan Emmett's Virginia Minstrels (whose principal banjoist, Billy Whitlock, had studied with Sweeney) landed in England shortly after Sweeney in the spring of 1843. The group's performances in Liverpool that May represented the first organized minstrel show in Europe.[4] The company soon dissolved, only to regroup gradually around Sweeney, who was still in the midst of his own tour. This troupe carried the minstrel show throughout England as well as to Scotland and Ireland. By the time Sweeney returned home in 1845, he had left an indelible mark. The first native English banjoist, Joseph Arnold Cave, who got his start by emulating Sweeney's technique and covering his songs, even performed on a copy of his master's instrument. George Swayne Buckley, a Sweeney pupil who played with the Congo Melodists, a notable troupe of English émigrés, was billed for several years as "Young Sweeney"; and so it went.

Is "Joe" Sweeney the missing link in the evolution of Eliot's Sweeney? The character's other ancestors have been identified: a Boston pugilist; a London pub-keeper; a St. Louis physician; King Suibhne, the mad hero of a Middle-Irish romance; Sweeney Todd, the "demon barber" of English melodrama. But only Joel Walker Sweeney links Eliot's creation with the minstrel show elements so prominent in *Sweeney Agonistes*, and his audacious assault on fortress England makes this figure a natural object of Eliot's empathy. By 1919, as we have seen, Eliot was representing himself to his British friends as a similar sort, picking his way along on a jazz-banjorine.

It is clear that within a few years, Eliot had developed a certain affection for his Sweeney character and even a tendency to identify with him. One would not have anticipated this from, say, "Sweeney Erect," where Sweeney appears to exemplify the human beast. But in *Sweeney Agonistes*, Sweeney has come to speak for Eliot; he is the one character in the play with spiritual insight—an insight gained through sin and suffering.[5] That Sweeney's alleged sin is the murder of a woman, a crime that obsesses Eliot throughout his oeuvre, strengthens their apparent kinship. By April 5, 1933, Eliot could sign a letter to Pound "F. X. Sweeney" (Carpenter 508). And in 1957 Victor Purcell's *Sweeniad* lampooned Eliot as "Loyola Sweeney," indicating that Sweeney, displacing Prufrock, could now be taken for his creator—a conflation that would have been unthinkable in 1920. Joel Walker Sweeney, whose history Eliot, as an American with a lingering enthusiasm for minstrelsy, may well have encountered in England, completes the chain that links the callous ape of the "Sweeney poems" of the teens to the musical martyr of the twenties.[6]

As discussed in chapter 2, Eliot was preparing in the early 1920s to rechannel his creative energies from the writing of poems to the writing of poetic drama, or what he would later call "applied poetry." He spoke to Virginia Woolf in 1920 about his plans for "a verse drama in which the characters from the 'Sweeney' poems would appear" (Woolf, Diary 2: 68). He also mentioned to Woolf an interest in "people and the creation of caricature," a clear indication that the comic types who would eventually populate Sweeney Agonistes were already forming in his mind. The importance of this project to Eliot at the time can hardly be overstated. The new play was to mark a transition from his brief career as poet—with only about twenty-five poems in print, plus The Waste Land—to dramatist, with all the differences in objective and audience that change entailed. The culmination of Eliot's thanks to John Quinn for his patronage and support is the assurance (in a letter of April 1923) that Quinn's generosity "is the greatest stimulus to me to commence the work I have in mind, which is more ambitious than anything I have ever done yet" (WLF xxiv).[7] Years later, Eliot would continue to maintain that the unfinished Sweeney Agonistes had been his most daring and original work.[8]

MÉLANGE ADULTÈRE DE TOUT

In Sweeney Agonistes, written 1924–25, Eliot turns away for the first time from poetry as a private medium and consciously attempts to reach a popular audience by drawing on vernacular sources. To this end he creates a unique blend of forms, incorporating vaudeville, music hall, melodrama, burlesque, jazz, and minstrelsy—to which performance genres Rachel Blau DuPlessis, in a fascinating chapter on modern poetry and race, adds "tabloid shock, working-class sentimental poetry, true-crime confession, [and] bartender's parable" (99).[9] For a writer who was himself a self-described "mélange adultère de tout," a mixed form of this kind was surely the proper vehicle. But Eliot was not merely trying to suit himself: his objective—and this explains his own sense of his project's ambitiousness—was to forge a new crossover genre that would alter the relationship between the fine artist and the community. If successful, this new form would make the poet, in Eliot's phrase of a decade later, "something of a popular entertainer" (UPUC 147).

The links between style and genre in Sweeney Agonistes, on the one hand, and the thematics of Eliot's early cultural criticism, on the other, are many. Eliot's subtitle for the never-completed play, "Fragments of an Aristophanic Melodrama," points in two directions that Eliot believed to be parallel. "Aristophanic" refers to his plan to borrow the structure of classical comedy expounded by the Cambridge anthropologist Francis Cornford, who mapped Attic comedy to the fertility rites in which it had originated. "Melo-drama" has more immediate antecedents. If *Sweeney Agonistes* contains something of the "thriller" element Eliot calls for in "Wilkie Collins and Dickens," it also resembles theatrical melodrama in its use of stock charac-ters and its sensational plot, which, had the play been completed, would have included a murder. And in the most literal sense of all, the play was to be a melo-drama in its integration of music and action (C. Smith, *T. S. Eliot's* 58). Both halves of its subtitle, then, advertise the play's return to the communal (popular and ritual) origins of drama.

Given the many prompts in Eliot's prose, the variety-show elements of *Sweeney Agonistes* are usually attributed to the inspiration of the London music halls, although one could point as easily to American vaudeville, which Eliot attended assiduously with Conrad Aiken before expatriating, and whose in-fluence, by Eliot's time, had thoroughly infiltrated its British cousin (Gor-don, *Early* 32). The satire, innuendo, parody, and rapid-fire dialogue of *Sweeney* have another important source in burlesque, and this genre, too, had exerted a notable influence on the development of music-hall comedy (Pearsall 68–69).[10] While the play's sexual suggestiveness (Sweeney's per-versely erotic chat with Doris, for example) may be traced to virtually any of these sources, Eliot specifically comments on music-hall bawdry in "A Dialogue on Dramatic Poetry" (1928). And he can hardly have been un-aware of Marie Lloyd's celebrated talent for innuendo.

The "tabloid shock" and "true-crime confession" DuPlessis mentions enter the play in Sweeney's macabre tale of a man, very likely himself, who has "done a girl in." Eliot's own attraction to newspaper accounts of sensa-tional human violence is clearly connected with his appreciation of detec-tive fiction; and it is worth noting the historical relation observed by Jon Thompson, who shows how a series of widely publicized murder cases in the mid-Victorian period "provided prototypes for a new literature focus-ing on the dark mystery within the sacrosanct realm of the middle-class home":

> [O]ne has only to think of the work of Dickens, Collins, Hardy, and of course Conan Doyle (especially in *A Study in Scarlet* and *The Sign of Four*) to see how deeply these sensational elements had penetrated into the Victo-rian literary consciousness. The Gothic novel contained many of these elements, but its locus was usually a fantastic and forbidding setting re-mote from the safety and comforts of the middle-class Victorian hearth. The "Northumberland Street affair" and the Vidil case helped to shift the locus of the sensational from the fantastic to the familiar. (64)

This shift in the location of the horrific is reenacted in *Sweeney Agonistes,* which argues an identity between life under civilization and life on a "crocodile isle," and between the violent impulses of the cannibal and those of "Any man" (CPP 83). Indeed, the penetration of the "dark mystery" of evil into quotidian life, as represented by the respectable home, remains a central theme in almost all of Eliot's subsequent drama.

At the level of style, a key popular element in *Sweeney* is its rhythmic "backchat," a common technique of team comedy in which short phrases rebound rapidly between two speakers. The scene at the end of the "Prologue" that introduces Klipstein and Krumpacker particularly resembles a comic routine, with its absurd nicknames ("Klip" and "Krum"), confusions of identity (each man answers the questions addressed to the other), and anticlimax: "Do we like London? do we like London! / Do we like London!! Eh what Klip?" (CPP 79). But the use of backchat extends beyond such overtly comic episodes to color the whole play:

> DORIS: I like Sam
> DUSTY: I like Sam
>   Yes and Sam's a nice boy too.
>   He's a funny fellow
> DORIS: He *is* a funny fellow
>   He's like a fellow once I knew.
>
> (CPP 75)

Increasingly the comic timbre of such dialogue (reinforced by the lack of internal punctuation) clashes with the dark overtones of the conversation it is used to represent, particularly in the second fragment, or "Agon":

> DORIS: You'll carry me off? To a cannibal isle?
> SWEENEY: I'll be the cannibal.
> DORIS: I'll be the missionary.
>   I'll convert you!
> SWEENEY: I'll convert *you*!
>   Into a stew.
>   A nice little, white little, missionary stew.
> DORIS: You wouldn't eat me!
> SWEENEY: Yes I'd eat you!
>   In a nice little, white little, soft little, tender little,
>   Juicy little, right little, missionary stew.
>
> (CPP 80)

This might be mere flirtation if Sweeney were not in earnest. But we learn to take him quite seriously here when a similar verbal patterning—not to mention the same recipe for stew—governs the tormented speeches to come:

SWEENEY: I knew a man once did a girl in
  Any man might do a girl in
  Any man has to, needs to, wants to
  Once in a lifetime, do a girl in.
  Well he kept her there in a bath
  With a gallon of lysol in a bath

(CPP 83)

The disturbing effect of Sweeney's monologue depends on its bizarre mutation of what is still recognizably a vaudevillian comic device. With this perversion of backchat Eliot creates a new technique of dialogue that can reasonably be said to illustrate his account of fine art as a "refinement" of popular art ("Marianne Moore" 595). The refinement, in this instance, lies in expanding the expressive range of a device normally limited to comic banter.

Like most of *Sweeney*'s constituent elements, the play's adaptation of backchat has multiple antecedents. Beyond the obvious source in the standup routines of the music-hall and vaudeville stages, Eliot himself suggests another, quite different lineage in a 1927 essay:

> Several scholars, Butler in particular, have called attention to a trick of Seneca of repeating one word of a phrase in the next phrase, especially in stichomythia, where the sentence of one speaker is caught up and twisted by the next. This was an effective stage trick, but it is something more; it is the crossing of one rhythm pattern with another. ("Seneca" 72)

"A man like Marlowe," Eliot avers, "or even men with less scholarship and less genius for the use of words than he, could hardly have failed to learn something from this" (73). Eliot himself evidently learned something. Selecting an illustration from Seneca that clearly resembles the first fragment, or "Prologue," of *Sweeney Agonistes*, Eliot goes on to illustrate Seneca's technique of creating "a kind of double pattern by breaking up lines into minimum antiphonal units." Just as *Sweeney Agonistes* is an "Aristophanic melodrama" in genre, it is simultaneously vaudevillian and Senecan in its rhythms. The cross-cultural confluences of style that Eliot perceived, like the cross-cultural mythologies of *The Golden Bough*, doubtless formed part of the inspiration for his play. Eliot's layering of formal devices drawn from various ancient and modern sources may be considered an extension, even a sophistication, of the "manipulation" of historical parallels he defines as Joyce's "mythical method."[11]

Eliot's rhythmic "double pattern" is actually triple, for it also imitates the syncopation of jazz. Crucial as the jazz element is to the play as we know it, it may have entered *Sweeney Agonistes* thanks to a casual exchange with Pound.

"Trying to read Aristophane," Eliot had written to Pound in 1922, while in the early stages of his work on *Sweeney Agonistes*. To which Pound had responded crudely, "Aristophanes probably depressing, and the native negro phoque melodies of Dixee more calculated to lift the ball-encumbered phallus of man to the proper 8.30, 9.30 or even ten thirty level now counted as the crowning and alarse too often katachrestical summit of human achievement" (*Letters* 504–05). Pound's hint apparently inflected Eliot's reading, with the result that *Sweeney Agonistes* became a jazz Aristophanes.

To Arnold Bennett, who read *Sweeney* in draft and suggested revisions, what Eliot was writing was nothing less than a "Jazz play" (*Letters* 286). The convergence of several elements in the play—the slang, the parody, the primitivism, the strong rhythms, the demimondaine female leads, the party atmosphere—made such associations inevitable. This is, without doubt, the effect that Eliot intended, for jazz, as we have already observed, was a "double pattern" in its own right. On the one hand it was a musical analogue to the sounds and rhythms of contemporary life, like "the scream of the motor horn, the rattle of machinery, the grind of wheels" that Eliot found transmuted in the musical modernism of Stravinsky ("LL [Sept. 1921]" 453). The new drama, as Eliot argued just before the publication of the *Sweeney* fragments, would have to be built on a modern rhythmic foundation of exactly this kind ("Introduction to *Savonarola*" xi). On the other hand, jazz was supposed to be an importation of savage ritual, a transplantation of "jungle music." The very allure of this "primitive" music was not infrequently taken to demonstrate the superficiality of civilization and the innate atavism of all human subjects. With its twinned modern and primitive aspects, jazz supplied the perfect medium for Eliot's project. The music was, moreover, immensely popular and would appeal to the wide public that Eliot now sought to reach.

Prosodically, *Sweeney Agonistes* imitates jazz by re-creating the frenetic tempo and rhythmic syncopation that to most listeners of the 1920s were the salient qualities of the music. The play's strong meter generates four implicit stresses in each line—implicit in the sense that though all are felt, any one may be replaced by a "rest" or interval of silence. A variable number of weak syllables separate these musical downbeats. A powerful rhythmic expectancy, reinforced by repetition and rhyme, confines each half line to precisely the same interval of time (Lightfoot 122):

DUSTY: How about Pereira?
DORIS: What about Pereira?
    I don't care.
DUSTY: You don't care!

> Who pays the rent?
> DORIS: Yes he pays the rent
> DUSTY: Well some men don't and some men do
> Some men don't and you know who.

(CPP 74)

The pattern established by the initial questions about Pereira—which are the first lines of the play—indicates that a short pause follows each hemistich of the next exchange ("I don't care. / You don't care!") and that Doris's "Yes" precedes the beat. In this way Eliot's continually shifting pattern of strongly accented beats and weak intermediary syllables creates the effect of syncopation. To strengthen this impression, Eliot suggested more than once that the actors' voices be counterpointed by a drum.[12] *Sweeney* has often, in fact, been performed with a jazz accompaniment.[13]

The play's slang, like the slang in *Inventions of the March Hare*, is à la mode and mainly American in derivation: phrases like "you said it," "do in," and "all right"; words like *swell, slick, gotta, gona, pinched*; and solecisms like "what you going to do," "I seen that," and "that don't apply."[14] Indeed, Eliot's first published title for what he eventually renamed *Sweeney Agonistes* was *Wanna Go Home, Baby?*—a phrase that evokes the primitivist conception of a return to origins but is primarily a Jazz-Age sexual proposition.[15] The action is ostensibly set in London, but Eliot's diction—quite unlike Marie Lloyd's—is not designed to reflect the language of a particular place, nationality, or class. It is rather the international vernacular of a mutually influential assortment of popular arts; it points to the vaudeville and music-hall stages, to the world of sketch comedy, slapstick, burlesque, musical comedy, journalism, jazz, and Tin Pan Alley song. In this sense *Sweeney Agonistes* deals much more squarely with the "popular" as the global, classless, massified—or in a word, Americanized—phenomenon it was becoming than does "Marie Lloyd," which constructs a local and somewhat romanticized ideal of the popular.

UNDER THE BAMBOO TREE

The minstrel show—the Joel Walker Sweeney element—is a complicating ingredient so important in *Sweeney Agonistes* that Eliot considered subtitling his play "Fragments of a Comic Minstrelsy" (Sidnell 263). A public ritual in its own right (one that, arguably, purged the tensions associated with slavery and racial inequality), the minstrel show seems well suited to Eliot's purposes (Lyon 153). Intriguingly, minstrelsy also absorbed and recast from white and black folk traditions a variety of archetypes and plot elements that originated in ancient fertility rites, including, in at least one instance, the myth of the Fisher King.[16] The minstrel element of *Sweeney Agonistes* thus supplements the play's Aristophanic and melodramatic reaching for origins.

In its very structure the play seems to borrow from the "First Part" of the traditional blackface minstrel format, in which a mock-intellectual master of ceremonies called the "Interlocutor," seated at center stage, engages in a futile dialogue with the impertinent "endmen" or "corner-men," the clowns Tambo and Bones (named for their instruments). Misconstrued by and unable to communicate with the characters around him, Eliot's Sweeney takes on something of the Interlocutor's role. The "Olio," or "Second Part," of the minstrel act often culminated in a comic monologue or "Stump Speech" (Zanger 35); Eliot's "Agon," his second part, likewise culminates in Sweeney's grimly absurd monologue on life and death. During the musical numbers, Swarts and Snow, according to Eliot's otherwise sparse stage directions, step forward in the roles of Tambo and Bones. Sweeney himself implicitly blacks up when he casts himself in the role of the cannibal, though in the context of the popular stage, he is already connected by his ethnic name with nineteenth-century stereotypes of the Irishman as "white Negro."[17]

Other relations, serendipitous ones, occurred to Eliot. In "Seneca in Elizabethan Translation," he specifically assimilates minstrelsy to Senecan drama in a passage that obviously gestures toward *Sweeney Agonistes*: "[T]he characters in a play of Seneca behave more like members of a minstrel troupe sitting in a semicircle, rising in turn each to do his 'number,' or varying their recitations by a song or a little back-chat" ("Seneca" 54). Eliot depicts Seneca's dramaturgy as a way of writing about "horrors" (68), and in *Sweeney Agonistes* he adapts Seneca's technique, by way of its minstrel cousin, to deal with his own more metaphysical horrors. The apparent distance between Senecan high tragedy and the low comedy of minstrelsy did not faze him. Even as he worked on *Sweeney*, Eliot was arguing—again citing the authority of Cornford—that "comedy and tragedy are late, and perhaps impermanent intellectual abstractions." Such governing concepts ossify in time and must eventually be discarded through a recursion to the "original dramatic impulse" ("Beating" 11–12). With its marriage of Senecan stichomythia and jazz, of poetry and the rhythms of the comic stage, *Sweeney Agonistes* seems a daring step in the direction theorized in Eliot's essays.[18]

The weird creolization of genres and comic devices in *Sweeney Agonistes* is clearly disorienting by design. At the same time, the underlying connections among its sources animate the play and make its heterogeneity credible. If jazz was *echt*-primitive and *echt*-modern; if preclassical fertility rituals survived in Aristophanes and even, vestigially, in the minstrel show; if burlesque infused vaudeville and both met in musical comedy; if Seneca wrote backchat; then surely, Eliot must have felt, something of the "original dramatic impulse" lay at the intersection. The convergence of minstrelsy and music hall—the American popular ritual and the British—at this juncture is particularly significant. The "comic Irishman" of the British popular stage had influenced the minstrel depiction of black Americans as it developed (Lott 95); in time, Jim Crow, often played by Irish Americans in blackface, then made his way back into British comedy. Thanks to the groundwork laid by Joel Walker Sweeney and the Virginia Minstrels, the minstrel show had an enormous popularity in Victorian England: as a result, minstrel "turns" were a standard feature in music halls from their beginnings into the twentieth century (Pickering 70–73). Backchat as practiced in the later stages of music-hall comedy had minstrel roots, descending in part from the repartee between the interlocutor and corner men (Bratton 138).[19] In the United States, similarly, although the minstrel show per se began to lose its grip on the public in the 1890s, much of its material, as well as its style, was absorbed into vaudeville, and in this way blackface survived as a convention well into the new century (Ewen 85–86).

The racial associations of the minstrel show, as of jazz, are crucial to the meaning of *Sweeney Agonistes*. Because African-American culture in white modernist writing so often functions as an antithesis to the Western culture from which the artist is alienated, "racial ventriloquism"—speaking from behind the mask of the black other—becomes, as Michael North has famously argued, a powerful if never untainted means of subversion (*Dialect* 9). Indeed, the minstrel show was itself a "theater of misrule," a platform for "irreverence and antagonism toward the most prominent aspects of American Victorian high culture," which it punctured relentlessly (Zanger 36). The minstrel element in *Sweeney Agonistes* thus functions something like Nancy Ellicott's fox-trot; it is another pluck—almost the last—at the strings of Eliot's jazz-banjorine.[20]

But Eliot's quarry in *Sweeney Agonistes* is somewhat larger than the Victorian pretensions and bourgeois vacuity targeted in his early social satires: the play interrogates the notion of civilization itself. As DuPlessis argues,

> Eliot has resourcefully bricolaged a packet of racialized materials to jolt, amuse, and sober up a white audience. He is, at bottom, scaring whites with "blacks," with their own dark impulses, cross-coded as African, and with all that "Africa" implies. (105)

The modernist appropriation of Africa as repository and symbol of humanity's base instincts and "dark impulses," whatever its intentions, never quite escapes the specter of racism. What helps redeem a work like *Sweeney Agonistes* is its determination to confront the question "Who, or what, is civilized?" with an unblinking skepticism. Swarts and Snow—whose interchangeable personalities already belie the implicit black-white opposition of their names—morph instantly into Tambo and Bones and back again; Sweeney plays the cannibal only too convincingly; and life in Dusty and Doris's flat is revealed to be indistinguishable from the life of "Birth, and copulation, and death" on a "crocodile isle." "Whiteness" and "civilization" are myths; in this world according to Eliot, *everyone* is fundamentally a savage.

Possibly the most extravagant and sardonic rendering of this point in *Sweeney Agonistes* is the first of the three songs that appear in "Fragment of an Agon," sung by Sam Wauchope and Captain Horsfall to the tambourine-and-bones accompaniment of Swarts and Snow:

> *Under the bamboo*
> *Bamboo bamboo*
> *Under the bamboo tree*
> *Two live as one*
> *One live as two*
> *Two live as three*
> *Under the bam*
> *Under the boo*
> *Under the bamboo tree.*
>
> .   .   .   .
>
> *Where the Gauguin maids*
> *In the banyan shades*
> *Wear palmleaf drapery*
> *Under the bam*
> *Under the boo*
> *Under the bamboo tree.* . . . .

(CPP 81)

The object of this parody is a popular song of greater consequence than either "That Shakespearian Rag" or "The Cubanola Glide." Inserted into the revue *Sally in Our Alley* by singer Marie Cahill late in 1902, "Under the Bamboo Tree" sold 400,000 copies in sheet music within six months (E. Levy 86). The song was among the most sensational hits of early ragtime, outdone only by the ubiquitous "Bill Bailey" (Ewen 173). Eliot could rely on an audience over twenty years later and in another country to remember the tune. His own recollection of it, apparently, reached back to the St. Louis World's Fair in 1904 (Kenner 191).

The historical significance of "Under the Bamboo Tree" exceeds even its considerable popularity, in that its success helped propel its lyricist, James Weldon Johnson, toward his notable career as a writer and race leader. "Under the Bamboo Tree" was the first triumph of the songwriting partnership that teamed Johnson with his brother Rosamond and vaudevillian Bob Cole.

In writing lyrics like "Under the Bamboo Tree" at the turn of the century, Johnson was striving to transform the "coon song" by ameliorating its stereotyped portrayal of African Americans. To this end Johnson strove to portray the black characters in his songs as essentially no different from his white listeners—a daring implication for 1902, though advanced with disarming subtlety. In place of the accepted clownish and rowdy types, Johnson created black figures whose "experiences and emotions [were] common to the human race," and who would therefore arouse sympathy (E. Levy 89).

"Under the Bamboo Tree," for example, describes the wooing of an African princess (the presence of royalty, a mildly Afrocentric touch, is already novel in a coon song) by a "Zulu from Matabooloo." Disdaining any expectations of savage crudeness, the courtship is as modest and decorous as American standards of the time could demand; and the Zulu's famous proposal, which comprises the chorus of the song, is both eager and charmingly shy:

> If you lak-a-me, lak I lak-a-you
> And we lak-a-both the same,
> I lak-a say, this very day,
> I lak-a-change your name;
> Cause I love-a-you and love-a-you true
> And if you-a love-a-me,
> One live as two, two live as one
> Under the bamboo tree.

(5)

The image of Zulus who croon in Pidgin English, court discreetly beneath a tree, and follow European marital customs invites audience identification. Even the dialect, which is mild by the standards of the period, is calculated to elicit a smile without derision. This is in effect a Western courtship transplanted to Africa, with a bit of humor but hardly a trace of exoticism: the African couple "express their love in phrases universal enough to be sung everywhere by young people around parlor pianos" (E. Levy 89). Thus Johnson's mainly white audience is gently maneuvered into recognizing the African "natives" as kin.

Johnson's "Congo Love Song," a subsequent hit, goes so far in its last verse as to call direct attention to this kinship. It explains that the "young maid" of the song

> May have been perhaps a trifle cruder,
> Than girls on the Hudson or the Seine;
> Yet though she was a little Zulu,
> She did what other artful maids do.

(2–3)

The final stanza of "Under the Bamboo Tree" is nearly as explicit:

This little story strange but true,
Is often told in Mataboo,
Of how this Zulu tried to woo
His jungle lady in tropics shady;
Although the scene was miles away,
Right here at home I dare to say,
You'll hear some Zulu every day,
Gush out this soft refrain.

(3–4)

Young American men, Johnson implies teasingly, are Zulus too, pouring out their I-lak-a-you's to their own ladies and queens. When it comes to the human heart, Johnson thus asserts, America is Africa.

One listener who clearly took Johnson's point was T. S. Eliot. *Sweeney Agonistes*, too, seeks to persuade us that America—or England, or Europe—is Africa; only, for Eliot, the common denominator is not love and affection but sin and horror. The identification that Johnson uses to lighten the image of the African is reworked by Eliot to darken the European. Eliot had only to shift the terms of Johnson's equation. He even retained the rudiments of the courtship while converting the original sentimentality to amorous cynicism:

Tell me in what part of the wood
Do you want to flirt with me?
Under the breadfruit, banyan, palmleaf
Or under the bamboo tree?
Any old tree will do for me
Any old wood is just as good

(CPP 81)

—where "flirt," in the midst of a conversation on the facts of life, is patently euphemistic. The overtones of Eliot's refrain are more ominous, draping Sweeney's titillating threat to cannibalize Doris in a cloak of nonsense, so that the promise of romantic love in the original lyrics, "one live as two, two live as one," becomes an incoherent and vaguely menacing "Two live as one / One live as two / Two live as three." There is wooing going on in each song, but Eliot's, with its implied sex and violence, is as lurid as Johnson's is innocent. In such ways Eliot adapts Johnson's denial of racial difference to debunk Western exceptionalism.

SCRAMBLED EGGS

Understandably, the popular elements of *Sweeney Agonistes* are often taken to be implicated in the play's nihilistic vision of modern life. The argument goes that Eliot employs jazz and other forms of popular culture only to expose them as vacuous—as symptoms, in other words, of modernity's spiritual emptiness.[21] But this is to misread the play, which argues not that modern life is particularly deathly, but that *even* modern life, with all its contrivances, is deathly. Marianne Moore's review opens by suggesting an analogy between the Eliot of *Sweeney* and "the men of the neighboring tribes [who] came to Joshua under a camouflage of frayed garments, with mouldy bread in the wallet" (106). In other words, the popular elements in which Eliot had dressed his poetry were very poor stuff indeed, cunningly disguising the play's riches of language and nuance. In Moore's reading, "there is a moment for Orestes, for Ophelia, for Everyman, when the ego and the figure it cuts, the favors you get from it, the good cheer and customary encomium, are as the insulting wigwaggery of the music-halls" (107). That Eliot could have embodied such sentiments in a musical play undertaken in the wake of his essay on Marie Lloyd seems unimaginable. The popular elements in *Sweeney Agonistes* are treated much too affectionately, in any case, to support the thesis that Eliot is only setting them up for a fall. Here Eliot's recollection that "*Sweeney Agonistes* was written in two nights between ten o'clock and five in the morning 'with the aid of youthful enthusiasm and a bottle of gin'" speaks volumes (qtd. in Litz 10).[22] Read without preconceptions as to the poet's dismissal of popular culture, *Sweeney Agonistes* is really rather cagey; as DuPlessis puts it, "the overloaded amalgam of generic allusions drawing on a maximum of theatrical traditions . . . keeps the work mobile—campy, knowing, stylized, sincere, *and* mocking—difficult to fix or pin down" (103). This inscrutable, "campy" effect is perfectly consonant with what we have seen of Eliot's ambivalence toward Americanized mass culture and its ambiguous manifestation in his earlier work.

Sweeney Agonistes is structured as a popular entertainment with Eliotic content; that is, the play's popular elements serve as the vehicle through which Eliot's *Waste Land* vision might be conveyed to a "large and miscellaneous" audience. Despite their considerable differences in genre and style, Eliot employs much the same strategy in his later plays, where theological ideas materialize in drawing-room comedy—or where drawing-room comedy is enlarged to give expression to metaphysical ideas. Such a strategy again seems in accord with Eliot's own theory, expressed in his essay on Moore, that a "fine" art such as poetry is an extension of popular culture. It was in 1923, just when *Sweeney Agonistes* was brewing in his imagination, that Eliot praised Moore not for eluding the jumble of American dialect but for adhering to it and for contributing to its expressive possibilities. Moore's vernacular is a "refinement of that pleasantry . . . of speech which characterizes the American language, that pleasantry, uneasy, solemn, or self-conscious, which inspires both the jargon of the laboratory and the slang of the comic strip" ("Marianne Moore" 596). Whatever the poet's feelings about them—and Eliot's appreciation for the "American language" is always mixed—these are the materials he or she is given. Judged by the standard Eliot here applies to Moore, Sweeney Agonistes must be counted a singular success, for, as Henry Louis Gates Jr. points out, the play achieves a great deal with the "American vulgar tongue" and its rhythms (289).[23]

Why Sweeney Agonistes remained unfinished is an important question that perhaps will never be answered definitively. We know that Eliot was crippled by writer's block as he attempted to work on the play, and that in his frustration he concluded, not for the first or last time, that his artistic career was at an end. Peter Ackroyd speculates that the project was so unprecedented, so revolutionary, that it daunted Eliot, who was used to working within the framework of a literary tradition: "no one had done anything quite like [Sweeney] before, and he did not seem able to trust himself sufficiently with only the non-literary material derived from the ballet or the music hall" (147). My own suggestion, not necessarily incompatible with this, is that the play was based from the start on an unworkable conception. The project fell victim to Eliot's cultural ambivalence, which resulted in irreconcilable conflicts among his goals and premises.

Eliot's first contribution to the Criterion was The Waste Land; his second, as we have noted, was "Marie Lloyd"; his third was "Dramatis Personae," a short essay on the condition of the theater which argues that drama is at a crossroads between a naturalistic recent past and a quite different future. Eliot approaches this thesis by drawing a contrast between the two male leads in a recent production of 'Tis Pity She's a Whore—two actors whose incompatible styles illustrated, for Eliot, the inchoate quality of an institution approaching a turning point. There is, on the one hand, Michael Sherbrooke, whose performance was so realistic that "[he] was not an actor, he was an illusionist." On the other hand, there is Ion Swinley, whose acting is undisguised and conventionalized: "he makes himself into a figure, a marionette; his acting is abstract and simplified." Eliot's preference, unsurprisingly, lies with Swinley and his "mask-like beauty," which, Eliot suggests, "belongs to [the] unrealized stage" (305). The closest approach to this ideal, however, is to be found at present not on the dramatic stage but in the ballet, with its emphasis on formalized "movement and gesture":

> Massine, the most completely unhuman, impersonal, abstract, belongs to the future stage. . . . The realism of the ordinary stage is something to which we can no longer respond, because to us it is no longer realistic. We know now that the gesture of daily existence is inadequate for the stage; instead of pretending that the stage gesture is a copy of reality, let us adopt a literal untruth, a thorough-going convention, a ritual. (305)

Such passages indicate what Eliot has in mind when he speaks of returning drama to its primitive origins.

The influences backing Eliot's endorsement of a ritualized, conventionalized future drama are easily identified. The point was already a favorite with the English symbolists of the 1890s, and it was carried forward to Eliot's time by, most importantly, Gordon Craig, who advocated a marionette theater as a means of eliminating the human actor, and Yeats, whose turn to the Japanese Nö plays was taken up in turn by Pound and by Eliot himself.[24] The effects of these influences culminate in the expressionism of *Sweeney Agonistes*. But how well do they accord with Eliot's insistence on the *popularity* of drama?

Eliot's approbation of Swinley and Massine echoes the terms in which he had praised comedienne Ethel Levey in his May 1921 "London Letter":

> She is the most aloof and impersonal of personalities; indifferent, rather than contemptuous, toward the audience; her appearance and movement are of an extremely modern type of beauty. Hers is not broad farce, but a fascinating inhuman grotesquerie; she plays for herself rather than for the audience. (688)

Apparently these qualities of detachment, inhumanity, and grotesquerie make Levey the "best" in the revue genre (which as a whole Eliot considers inferior to music hall). Yet these qualities contradict, term for term, what Eliot will go on to praise in Marie Lloyd: her sympathetic relationship with her audience, her artistic realization of the minutiae of human lives and character, and even her singular avoidance of the grotesque ("Marie Lloyd" 406−07). The inconsistency is very striking. Eliot emphasizes, on the one hand, a vision of drama as ritual, as when he praises the conventionalized, "inhuman," hieratic qualities of performers like Swinley and Levey—or of the Russian Ballet, which provides the model for a potential new form of poetic drama that is simultaneously primitive and thoroughly avant-garde. On the other hand, Eliot is inspired by the personal, sympathetic, naturalistic Lloyd; she represents the possibility of a new form of poetic drama based on music-hall comedy and thus securely rooted in the "lively" attractions of contemporary popular culture.[25] Eliot's ambivalence toward the popular is nowhere more evident than in his ability to hold these two opposing ideals in tension. And the project that yielded the two fragments of *Sweeney Agonistes* was the apotheosis of that tension.

Eliot's elaborate efforts to structure the play around the ritual model of Attic comedy may be taken as emblematic. The two extant *Sweeney* fragments correspond precisely to the opening movements identified by Cornford: the *Prologue*, ending with the "Parados," or entrance of the chorus; and the *Agon* (Sidnell 91−92). A penciled outline of the remainder of the play indicates that Eliot planned to follow out this structure meticulously (Crawford 163–64). The scenes sketched as *fight, cooking, feast, sacrifice*, and so on were all drawn from fertility-ritual formulas.[26] Eliot later explained that the characters were intended to wear masks, and that Sweeney was to stand center stage "with a chafing dish scrambling eggs" (qtd. in Flanagan 83). It is inconceivable that for any sizable modern public, such a presentation could have appeared anything but esoteric, not to say willfully bizarre. Had Eliot attempted to stage it for a large audience, its debts to music-hall comedy, minstrelsy, and jazz would certainly not have saved the play from an early closing.

Yet we have seen that Eliot (quite unlike a Yeats or a Craig) would have no truck with unpopular drama, and his "jazz play" was intended to mark his first step *away* from coterie art. Anthony Burgess has remarked on Eliot's success in this regard: "To present not only a theology but a vision of hell and a rejection of redemption in the rhythms of jazz is a large literary achievement, and yet nowhere, except in the title, subtitles and epigraphs, is there an evocation of literature" (103). Burgess's point is strengthened by the fact that the epigraphs from Aeschylus and St. John of the Cross were not printed until the play's 1932 appearance in book form. Even the Miltonic title was a later accretion, replacing the demotic *Wanna Go Home, Baby?* In its original 1926–27 publication under that title in the *Criterion*, the play's "literary" apparatus was nowhere in sight, and although its later form gives it a superficial resemblance to *The Waste Land*, the play was meant to be accessible. Intentions, however, are not results.

With Aristophanes and perhaps the sword dance to hand, Eliot may have seen no conflict between a ritualized drama and a popular one. In "Marianne Moore," Eliot noted that ritual itself is a popular phenomenon: "nothing belongs more properly to the people than ritual" (597). But it does not follow that a drama that stages ritual patterns will be popular. Sweeney's scrambling of eggs, for instance, signifies resurrection—but *to whom?* The scrambling of eggs in twentieth-century England, so far as one knows, signifies breakfast. To an audience suckled on realism and increasingly unused to ritual, a heavily stylized, hieratic drama is bound to seem avant-garde, and nothing other.[27] The effect of authentic ritual cannot be aroused in the absence of a live tradition.

"Dramatis Personae," published just as Eliot was beginning work on his Sweeney play, announces his intentions quite clearly in the plea, "let us adopt a literal untruth, a thorough-going convention, a ritual" (305). *Sweeney Agonistes* attempts to resuscitate not just *a* ritual, but Ritual itself, by main force. But conventions, as Eliot was in general keenly aware, cannot be imposed from above; unless they comprise an existing popular tradition, they are futile as a basis for a popular theater. Eliot's reproach to Cecil Sharp is once again apposite: "you cannot *revive* a ritual without reviving a faith" ("Ballet" 443). Eliot penned those words in 1925, shortly after the collapse of his Sweeney project, and in their distance from his earlier remarks we may gauge what he had learned in the interim. He could not complete *Sweeney Agonistes* because he could not revive a ritual; the play was doomed from its inception. Eliot would spend the remainder of his career as a dramatist working out a solution to this problem, essentially a product of his conflicting impulses toward the popular.

DISINTEGRATION: THE HOLLOW MEN

In a letter dated November 4, 1922, Ezra Pound calls Eliot's attention to one English ritual that *has* survived: "This shd. reach you," he begins, "on the anniversary of the Guy Fawks [*sic*] plot" (Eliot, *Letters* 589). In response to Eliot's troubles with Lady Rothermere and the *Criterion*, Pound suggests that Eliot announce his resignation and the founding of a new, more avantgarde journal that might be called the "New Effigy" (590). One wonders what role, if any, this letter played in the genesis of *The Hollow Men*. Written piecemeal during and immediately after Eliot's failure with *Sweeney Agonistes*, that poem is the second child of his designs to derive art from popular ritual. After the *Sweeney* fiasco, Eliot's theatrical aspirations would wait another eight years before inching again toward the footlights. By sacrificing for the present his ambitious attempt to confect a new poetic drama based on popular forms, and by returning to the more familiar sacred grounds of "pure" poetry in *The Hollow Men*, Eliot was able to elude the psychological and theoretical obstacles that had prevented him from completing his play.[28]

The stylistic and thematic relations between *The Hollow Men* and *Sweeney Agonistes*, as one would expect, are many. The connections are particularly strong in the poem's opening and closing movements, the last sections to be written. As Ronald Bush shows, Eliot eventually moved to open outward the interior drama of the earlier versions of his poem, leading to the introduction of the collective voice (the first-person plural) that frames the final sequence (95–98).[29] With this public voice entered the strong rhythms and slant-rhymes of popular song lyrics, in which the outer sections of *The Hollow Men*—"We are the hollow men" and "*Here we go round the prickly pear*"— most strongly recall *Sweeney Agonistes*. Not coincidentally, these outer sections have proven to be among Eliot's most popular verses, to the point where he complained in almost the last year of his life that the poem was overanthologized.[30] The disfigured nursery-rhyme ending—

This is the way the world ends
This is the way the world ends

This is the way the world ends
Not with a bang but a whimper

(CPP 59)

—surpasses even "April is the cruellest month" as Eliot's most-often-quoted lines in the mass media.[31]

But the deepest affinity between *Sweeney Agonistes* and *The Hollow Men* lies in their similar attempts to reground popular forms—whether music hall, jazz, minstrelsy, or children's rhymes—in ritual. In this respect *The Hollow Men* even outdoes *Sweeney* by drawing on a familiar rite, while *Sweeney*, as we have seen, draws rather artificially on ceremonies that had lapsed centuries before. As Bush points out, Eliot's epigraphic reference to Guy Fawkes, which colors the entire poem by attaching an identity to its otherwise faceless speakers, sets *The Hollow Men* within the context of an *extant* popular ritual: "The English people do not simply remember the fate of Guy Fawkes, they re-enact it every year" (97). The Guy is arguably a kind of reverse fertility god: rather than being sacrificed so that he may return to life, Fawkes is re-created annually so that he can be executed. This reversal neatly reflects the poem's themes.

The ritualism of the Guy Fawkes holiday links it in Eliot's poem with other instances of Western fertility rites that continue to be practiced in some form. The broken quotations of the Lord's Prayer seem to imply the inefficacy of another god who suffered death and resurrection; the prickly pear dance in the concluding section puts a grotesque face on the springtime maypole ritual; and the hollow men themselves are good old English mummers. They are effigies, too, to be sure; but their "Rat's coat, crowskin, crossed staves" and stuffed headpieces suggest ceremonial costuming that goes beyond the habits of the Guy. Like ritual dress in many cultures, traditional mummers' costumes are just what Eliot calls them: "deliberate disguises" worn to conceal the human actors and to purge them of individual identity—to render them, in Eliot's terms, "unhuman" and "impersonal."[32] Typically, the players cover their street clothes with an "overlay of floating ribbons or bits of cloth, or of closely laid strips of paper" (Chambers, English 84), and they wear elaborate headdresses that mask the face (Brody 23).[33] The hollow men, like mummers, attempt to carry on a rite long after the passing of the culture (the "faith") that gave it meaning. And in the end, the sacred rites of the hollow men are reduced to children's games just as the mummers' plays have survived at last only as a "favorite schoolboy's exercise" at Christmastime (Brody 127).[34] Even aside from the obvious symbolism of its broken altars and faltering prayers, *The Hollow Men* is in this sense a poem about the death and disappearance of ritual.

By staging a vegetation ceremony, *Sweeney Agonistes*, for all its despair, very nearly implied the vitality of ritual in contemporary culture. Had Eliot carried out his plans, the murder and resurrection of Mrs. Porter would inevitably—despite the lessons of Sweeney's "Agon"—have signified the permanence, the timeless power of the rite. The Hollow Men inverts this optimistic topos, beginning with a subsistent rite, then breaking it down, exposing and mocking its impotence. In writing Sweeney Agonistes, Eliot could carry the play only to the extremity of disillusionment manifested in The Hollow Men, which then stands as a corrective to the uncompleted portions of the Sweeney scenario. The poem could almost be said to dramatize the disintegration of the play. And as Eliot's last work before his conversion to Anglicanism, it marked his abandonment of the notion that ritual could be revived unparticularized, detached from a particular creed. The Hollow Men voiced Eliot's nascent recognition that neither poetry, nor the world, nor himself, if these needed ritual to endure, could survive on a mythic construct of an artist's fashioning. Ritual, rather, had to be discovered somewhere alive, and accepted on whatever the given terms; two of the Christianized Eliot's favorite terms were dogma and orthodoxy. For you cannot revive a ritual without reviving a faith.

THE SUPERIOR LANDLORD

In Eliot's 1935 Collected Poems, the hapless jazz play once known as Wanna Go Home, Baby?—already encumbered for three years with the ponderous title Sweeney Agonistes and with two heavily "literary" epigraphs—found itself reclassified as an "Unfinished Poem."[35] Apparently Eliot was now ready to concede publicly that this work did not point the way toward a new mode of popular drama. Only the previous year, though, he had contemplated giving the Sweeney play one last try. While nearing the end of his 1932–33 stay in Cambridge, Massachusetts, Eliot had received a request from director Hallie Flanagan for permission to put on Sweeney Agonistes at Vassar College. On March 18, 1933, Eliot wrote to give his approval, along with extensive instructions for the play's performance. "The action should be stylised," he wrote, "as in the Noh drama—see Ezra Pound's book and Yeats' preface and notes to The Hawk's Well"; "Characters ought to wear masks. . . . Diction should not have too much expression"; "See also F. M. Cornford: Origins of Attic Comedy, which is important to read before you do the play" (qtd. in Flanagan 83). Eliot professed himself unable to "imagine what anybody can do" with the sketchy drama in his absence. But Flanagan had the good sense to ignore much of his advice, which only tended to make the play more hermetic.

Eliot quite evidently had Sweeney Agonistes on his mind as he composed the often-quoted last of his Charles Eliot Norton lectures, delivered at Harvard on March 31. A few days after telling Flanagan that when he wrote Sweeney he "had intended the whole play to be accompanied by light drum taps to accentuate the beats," Eliot declares in his lecture that poetry "begins . . . with a savage beating a drum in a jungle, and it retains that essential of percussion and rhythm" (*UPUC* 148). He uses *Sweeney* to illustrate the notion that a play can address members of the audience on a variety of levels, commenting memorably at the same time (as we have seen) on the poet's wish to be "something of a popular entertainer" speaking to a "large and miscellaneous audience" in order to achieve the "direct social utility" most fruitfully sought in the theater (146–47). Implicit in this lecture is Eliot's need to gather himself at this moment for his own next attempt at a popular verse drama. The forthcoming production at Vassar, which would mark the first performance of an Eliot play, may have breathed new life into an old desire.

Pleased with Flanagan's staging of the *Sweeney* fragments at Vassar in May 1933, and stimulated both by her wish for a fuller version and by the plan of the experimental Group Theatre to produce *Sweeney Agonistes* in London, Eliot went back to work in the summer of 1934, producing a typescript scenario of a complete Sweeney play called "The Superior Landlord."[36] But the attempt went no further, crowded out by a new theatrical project—one more clearly in line with Eliot's current interests, and one that definitely promised a performance and (importantly for Eliot) imposed a deadline. Offered a commission to write a new play for the following year's Canterbury Festival, Eliot put Sweeney aside, never, as it happened, to return.

The abandonment of "The Superior Landlord" for *Murder in the Cathedral* finalizes a significant change of direction in Eliot's career—a "fundamental" shift, as Ackroyd puts it, in "the nature of his creative life" as religious commitment comes more explicitly to direct his labors (219). Eliot did not suddenly desist, at this point, in his attempt to overcome the cultural divide, but the avant-garde element of his earlier vision had by 1935 become secondary to his desire for a medium that could convey to a large public his own brand of Christian content. Just as Eliot would no longer talk about returning art to some generalized notion of "myth" and "ritual"—since he had by now dedicated himself to a particular creed and a particular array of ceremonies—the goal of reintegrating art into some rather indefinitely modified praxis of life was now circumscribed by a specifically Anglican notion of praxis.

The twenty-five-line scene Eliot gave Hallie Flanagan in order to round off the ending of *Sweeney Agonistes* already reveals, in its contrast with the earlier fragments, how far Eliot had come. The "Agon" had ended with nine ominous knocks on the door, which in the 1933 addendum herald the arrival of an old gentleman who "resembles closely Father Christmas" (qtd. in Flanagan 83). He explains that his name is Time and that he has come "from the vacant lot in front of the Grand Union Depot" where he waits "for the lost trains that bring in the last souls after midnight." He and Sweeney then engage in a catechism—a procedure that recalls, for instance, the ritual questions of Parsifal at the Chapel Perilous. The old gentleman's responses, as David Galef argues, contain "echoes of an Old Testament searching as in Exodus. Here, the trail ends not in the Promised Land but in the wedding-breakfast of life and death, the coming of Christ and a corporeal-spiritual union and dissolve" (507). The themes of death and resurrection have survived from Eliot's original design for the play, but they have now taken on a lightly shrouded Christian significance. The idea of reuniting art and ritual persists, but "ritual" no longer evokes pagan associations: the generic fertility god has given way to the One.

Just as importantly, Eliot's new scene differs sharply from the earlier fragments in rhythm, diction, and tone. Sweeney's anagogical questions, as Galef points out, are uncharacteristic of a man whose typical utterances include "That dont apply" and "We all gotta do what we gotta do" (506):

When will the barnfowl fly before morning?
When will the owl be operated on for cataracts?
When will the eagle get out of his barrel-roll?

(qtd. in Flanagan 83)

The proletarian language of the original play is not the only casualty here. The new scene, largely in prose, is considerably less energetic than the fast-paced earlier fragments; the jittery, manic, modernist quality is greatly diminished; the striking jazz rhythms are gone entirely. In his letter to Flanagan containing the addition, Eliot even writes off the play's "Prologue," where the main interest lies in the syncopated speech rhythms, as "not much good" (83). There can be little doubt, then, that even if Eliot had gone on with "The Superior Landlord," the resulting play would have been quite different from Sweeney Agonistes in tenor and technique. A new Sweeney play at this point would necessarily have resonated with Eliot's Christian sensibility, and with the poetic style this inculcated, as much as the play of a decade earlier had reflected its Jazz-Age context.

In a sense, then, the turn from "The Superior Landlord" to Murder in the Cathedral—uncannily symbolic as it appears—remains only an aftershock of Eliot's earlier, more epochal failure with the Sweeney play. The real pivot point was 1926, when, shortly after he despaired of finishing his play, Eliot began the regimen of religious instruction and observance that would lead to his baptism and official confirmation in the Church of England. So far as jazz is concerned, certainly, the loss of Wanna Go Home, Baby? rather than that of "The Superior Landlord" marks the critical missed moment. The effort to reconcile "literature" with popular culture would proceed, but by other means and on other grounds. No subsequent attempt would generate quite the chilling, demonic, incongruous excitement of Eliot's attempt to mount a "jazz play" in the teeth of *The Waste Land*.

After the performance of *Sweeney Agonistes* at Vassar, Eliot took the stage to lead a discussion of his work. As Hallie Flanagan recalled:

> Philosophic discussion engendered by the play continued most of the night in a flow of Eliot prose and verse which I fervently wish had been recorded. Roaming about the setting of his own play he talked about poetry with impersonal lucidity.
>
> "My poetry is simple and straightforward," he declared; and when the audience laughed he looked pained. (84)

Having brought on himself this depressing reminder that despite the comic songs and jazz patter of *Sweeney* he had never in fact approached anything like the condition of the music-hall comedian, Eliot added dismissively, "It is dubious whether the purpose of poetry is to communicate anyway." Nonetheless, he was about to embark on what was to become a quarter-century's effort to quell the laughter that pained him at Vassar—to make himself over as "something of a popular entertainer" and to communicate, dubiously or not, with a "large and miscellaneous" audience (*UPUC* 146–47). In May 1933, that long, slow process had hardly begun, except, apparently, in Eliot's wishful view. But an opportunity was soon to present itself, and Eliot was prepared to seize it.

"IMMORTAL FOR A WHILE":

THE VERSE PLAYS

BETRAYING LITERATURE: *THE ROCK*

Eliot's dramatic writing after *Sweeney Agonistes* is governed by two competing forces already discernible in his first play: the vanguardist impulse toward austerity, "poetry," and frank ritualism; and the populist or theatrical impulse that urges avoidance of anything that smacks of "literature." At the outset, as we have seen, Eliot had proceeded in the belief that there was no real opposition between these apparent poles since, after all, in its primitive origins drama was quite literally both hieratic and popular. But his experience in the theater from *Sweeney Agonistes* to *Murder in the Cathedral* (1935) to *The Family Reunion* (1939) showed him otherwise, and he was forced into a decision. Faced earlier in the century with the same dilemma, Yeats had dedicated himself to "an unpopular theatre" and a coterie audience—to what he called "not a theatre but the theatre's anti-self." Eliot, as Frank Kermode noted long ago, ultimately made the opposite choice. "After *Sweeney* and the unrepeatable compromise of *Murder in the Cathedral*," wrote Kermode, "Mr. Eliot chose the theatre" ("What Became").

It was a choice that Eliot made with a certain zest, animated by the knowledge that no one expected it from him. In 1949, while Eliot was writing *The Cocktail Party*, Princeton professor Alan Downer asked him "rather impolite[ly] . . . how long he intended to devote himself to playwriting?" Eliot responded tellingly, "Until I can convince people that I know how to write a popular play" (qtd. in Smidt 61). And when the play proved a success, the Episcopalian priest "who suggested to Eliot that The Cocktail Party was covertly all about the Mass" was discomfited by the poet's reply: "I really wanted to write a damn good play, and I hope I did" (Matthews 155).

Throughout the gradual process by which he came to "choose the theater," Eliot found himself pressured by friend and foe alike to reverse his course. A puzzled Leonard Woolf asked him in 1934 to explain why he was writing The Rock, and Eliot "merely chuckled" (Woolf, Letters 5: 256). Virginia Woolf read the play and hated it, not only because of its religious "dogmatism" but because of "the horror of that cheap farce and Cockney dialogue." She avoided the performance, pleading a flu, while Roger Fry "went and came out in a rage" (Letters 5: 315). These dismayed reactions were not limited to Bloomsbury. Conrad Aiken, Eliot's oldest literary friend, admitted to feeling "more than ever uncomfortable about Eliot's present predicament, his present position and direction" ("After" 161). For Aiken and others, Eliot had debased himself by stooping from literature to "propaganda." Ezra Pound was completely unimpressed with Eliot's attempts at popular drama, remarking in 1938, "His fragments of an Agon are worth all his stage successes" ("Musicians" 9). The greater stage successes to come did nothing to change Pound's mind. His private comments were even less encouraging: "Waal, I heerd the MURDER in the Cafedrawl on th radio/ lass' night. Oh them cowkney voices, My Krissz, them cawkney woices! Mzzr Shakzpeer STILL retains his po/ sishun. I stuck it fer a while, wot wiff the weepin and wailin. . . . My Krrize them cawkney voyces!" (qtd. in Carpenter 502).

Others were still more severe, treating Eliot's new mission as nothing less than a betrayal of Art. "The evil he is," seethed Edward Dahlberg, "is in the rabble titles of his volumes, Murder in the Cathedral and The Cocktail Party, which are a claim for cash" (Epitaphs 94).[1] Eliot had run afoul of the postromantic ideology that pits literary professionalism and popular acclaim against aesthetic seriousness and critical esteem: he had pandered to the "rabble" by seeking a large public for his plays.[2] Even Allen Tate, who had championed Eliot for thirty years, was sufficiently disgusted by the success of The Cocktail Party to throw over his idol.[3] And Sagittarius, a satirist for the New Statesman, clucked his tongue in his brilliantly titled "Nightingale among the Sweenies":

> This is the vulgarest success, blasting
> A hitherto immaculate reputation,
> The voice
> Par excellence of the waste land and the wilderness.
> Can the exalted oracle rejoice
> Who, casting

Pearls before swine, wins swinish approbation?
Tereu, twit twit, this metaphysical mime
That should have been
The most distinguished failure of all time
Proves quite the opposite.
Between the conception and the reception, between
The curtain calls the Shadow falls—
The deep damnation of a Broadway hit

. . . .

Has the hautboy of attenuated tone
Become the uncultured herd's unconscious saxophone?

The literary world was not amused by what it took to be Eliot's defection—the apostasy of its revered (and despised) avatar of "austere" high art. Eliot foresaw this response, however, and was prepared to stand to his guns (Ackroyd 215). He even refashioned Yeats as an ally, finding in his predecessor's work "certain principles to which we must hold fast," including the belief that the theater is "an organ for the expression of the consciousness of a people." "I am convinced," he wrote, "that it is only if you serve it in this spirit that you can hope to accomplish anything worth doing with it" ("Yeats" 261−62). And he could take comfort at least from the theater critics, who naturally insisted on evaluating his work *as* theater, and who generally shared his conviction that a playwright's success in captivating an audience, far from being a sin, is a matter of primary importance. But the hostility of the literary world to Eliot's theatrical ambitions gives us some insight into Eliot's difficulties in making his choice as well as the limitations circumscribing it. A quarter-century of hesitation and experimentation separates *The Cocktail Party* from *Sweeney Agonistes*.

It was with his second play, undertaken shortly after Eliot told his Harvard listeners in 1933 that he would enjoy writing for an illiterate audience, that he came nearest playing to the masses. Mounted in the cavernous Sadler's Wells theater by the Anglican diocese of London to raise funds for the construction of new churches, *The Rock* was conceived after the pattern of the open-air pageant, a popular form comprising a sequence of historical scenes exhibited "to celebrate the history either of a place or of an institution," and structurally as near to a parade as to a play (Browne, *Making* 4). To produce the script, Eliot was enlisted by director E. Martin Browne, who first had to overcome the skepticism of the churchmen toward a poet whom they thought "[t]oo modern" and "too difficult" (6). But Eliot at this point no longer strove to strive towards such things: he wished to be "something of a popular entertainer." One of the very few altogether non-canonical works in his oeuvre (saving its choruses), The Rock nevertheless occupies an important place in Eliot's movement from coterie poet to (would-be) popular playwright.

Eliot's decision to work on The Rock marks the end of a phase of his career that had opened with his public announcement (in 1928) of his religious conversion—a period in which he was generally preoccupied with defining a Christian view of culture and was more concerned with the gulf between "orthodoxy" and "heterodoxy" than with the divide between high culture and the popular. This phase culminates in the grim disputations of After Strange Gods, a series of lectures given at the University of Virginia in early 1933. Eliot had then just delivered his longer series of Harvard lectures, which, in returning to such issues as the social "use" of poetry and the possibilities for poetic drama, seem to look ahead to the next phase of his career. It is as though Eliot could foresee the course on which he would embark once After Strange Gods, a work long in the planning, was off his chest. The Rock, as at least some of his friends and acquaintances recognized at the time, was Eliot's Rubicon. That is, in taking on this assignment Eliot was deliberately and consciously crossing a sacrosanct cultural line out of "literature" and into some unexplored terrain lying between high culture, popular culture, and religious expression.[4]

The Rock, which played in the spring of 1934 to audiences of roughly 1,500 a night for two weeks—and which thus may have been seen by 20,000 people, mostly ordinary London parishioners—gave Eliot something like the opportunity he had wished for at Harvard. And the fact that music hall as a popular form was by now clearly moribund (as Eliot had predicted in 1922) did not stop him from emulating Marie Lloyd as far as he could. Subtitled "A Pageant Play," The Rock superimposes upon the formulaic historical tableaux of the pageant the familiar variety-show structure of late music-hall programs, interleaving its serious scenes with comic ones, and both of these with reprises of a theme song. The show's "turns" included a pantomime; a ballet based on the folk legend of Dick Whittington and his cat;[5] a burlesque troupe of fascists who chant in traipsing anapests ("We come as a boon and a blessing to all, / Though we'd rather appear in the Albert Hall"); devotional and satirical poetic choruses; and a rewrite of the familiar music-hall song "In Trinity Church I Met My Doom."[6] The use of music in The Rock extended beyond such occasional flourishes; with the collaboration of composer Martin Shaw, in Browne's words, "the whole piece was conceived in terms of music as well as of words" (Making 12). And the whole was topped off, as one reviewer exclaimed, with the appearance of "a live Anglican Bishop, who, in full canonicals, as part of the final tableau, blessed the audience" (Carter 499). Indeed, the most remarkable feature of The Rock as a popular drama was its sheer spectacle. The play used

330 actors, almost all amateur volunteers—and many of them, it seems, desperately inept—to represent a huge variety of biblical, historical, legendary, and invented characters. Ambitious costumes, scenery, and choreography all bespoke a massive effort of production. The performance was thus a community effort as well as an attempt to confect a popular entertainment—an extravaganza of almost DeMillean proportions in which the cast in effect was drawn from the audience.

The lead characters in The Rock are three Cockney bricklayers engaged in building a church. The foreman, Bert, is intelligent and self-educated; the others, Alfred and Edwin, are good-natured listeners, willing if somewhat complacent learners. Eliot's early experience as an extension lecturer may have influenced these portrayals. Still, the characters are basically flat—modest variations on a comic type. As Randy Malamud notes, "The general tenor of the Cockneys' patter . . . identifies the genre as vintage music-hall: their stage presence is marked by broadly comic dialect, humor, exaggerated earnestness, heavy-handed setups for each other" (Where 35–36). At least one of these "heavy-handed setups" even points directly to the music hall, when Alfred explains that a court jester is "a man what comes on and does the comic turn," and Edwin replies, "Oh, like George Robey" (Rock 25).[7]

The Rock at least went beyond such comic stereotyping in expressing a concern for contemporary social problems. Eliot was disturbed by the effects of Depression-era chronic unemployment on English workers, who were suffering, in addition to financial privation, hopelessness and a loss of self-esteem. "[T]here are at least two million among us," he wrote in 1932, "who have every excuse for thinking that they are not wanted at all" ("Christianity and Communism" 382). The Rock portrays this plight affectingly through the off-stage "Voices of the UNEMPLOYED," who speak in tones very different from the stalwart Cockneys at center stage:

> No man has hired us
> With pocketed hands
> And lowered faces
> We stand about in open places
> And shiver in unlit rooms.
> Only the wind moves
> Over empty fields, untilled
> Where the plough rests, at an angle
> To the furrow. . . .
> Our life is unwelcome, our death
> Unmentioned in "The Times."

(CPP 99)

The language of this chorus, it is true, sounds less like proletarian speech than like Eliot's poetic voice in, say, the final movement of *The Waste Land*. And the play's positing of church construction as the solution to pervasive un-employment is, to say the least, economically questionable. Nonetheless, Eliot's assembling of such voices and issues in a form derived from several popular genres says a great deal about his conception of drama. As one reviewer noted, "Mr. Eliot has always claimed that the poet should be in or-ganic relation with the community: in [*The Rock*] he has achieved that rela-tion, and without any loss to his poetry" (A. M. 643). And an anonymous critic in the *Listener* wrote approvingly:

> Those to whom Mr. Eliot's name is synonymous with "modernist" and "difficult" poetry may be surprised that audiences of bishops, aldermen, church workers, school children and "general public," most of whom are probably unfamiliar with his other works, should be able to join in anything written by him as they do in the last chorus of all. Those, how-ever, who remember the smart rhythms of "Sweeney Agonistes," or the clear lines of the "Journey of the Magi," will not be in the least surprised; but simply pleased that a great contemporary poet should have been given the opportunity of writing directly for a popular audience. (945)

Such comments had to give Eliot some relief at a time when his erstwhile supporters were going sputtering from the theater. But many reviewers were a good deal less generous, and literary critics have generally treated the play as an embarrassment. To Grover Smith, for example, *The Rock* is mere "hackwork," and the Cockney scenes "insult a mature audience" (*T. S. Eliot's* 171). Most often, later commentators have followed the early reviewers who chose to focus on the play's choruses, its most traditionally "poetic" el-ement, while neglecting or denigrating the rest.[8]

Despite its mixed reviews, *The Rock* apparently had some success with its audiences, who, if Browne's observations can be trusted, responded to Eliot's humor and especially enjoyed the political sequence that ended the first act—the one scene that Eliot was able to design and script entirely on his own (*Making* 10, 29–30). Eliot must have felt gratified when the audi-ence, music-hall style, began joining in the choruses, a sign that despite many obstacles, and whatever the critics said, he had succeeded in turning a popular form to his own ends (Davies 361).[9] He would employ the same strategy in his later plays as well, though as music hall receded further into the past he would have to relocate the popular.

Yet the success of *The Rock* in speaking to a larger public did not mean, in fact, that Eliot had made himself over as a popular writer. The churchgoing folk who attended *The Rock* were in large measure, as Eliot quickly realized, an atypical group who came out of a sense of religious duty and felt compelled for the same reason to attend with respect to whatever was put before them. Even before the play opened, Eliot expressed his fear of "a dull and lethargic audience for that sort of affair" (Dobrée 83). One self-described "highbrow" who was present thought he perceived the "simple and devout audience . . . laughing uneasily at the human lines as if they were afraid of being caught laughing in church" (Isaacs 152–53). In this sense, The Rock may be said to have reached an audience sufficiently large but insufficiently miscellaneous to satisfy Eliot's ambitions as "popular entertainer."

THE ARCHBISHOP MURDER CASE

In writing his next play, Murder in the Cathedral, Eliot again faced the prospect of a rather homogeneous audience prepared to give his play the wrong kind of attention. Yet he did not balk when offered the Canterbury Festival commission, seeing an opportunity to develop his stagecraft and to dramatize his meditations on the spiritual quest. As a step in the creation of a popular verse drama, though, Eliot ultimately considered Murder in the Cathedral a "dead end," since the play was written

> for a rather special kind of audience—an audience of those serious people who go to "festivals" and expect to have to put up with poetry. . . . And finally it was a religious play, and people who go deliberately to a religious play at a religious festival expect to be patiently bored and to satisfy themselves with the feeling that they have done something meritorious. ("Poetry and Drama" 79)

To write for such an audience, Eliot came to feel, had been only too easy. The challenge of producing a poetic drama that could achieve the same kind of public success as prose drama, no special allowances made for its being in verse, was still to be met.

Still, in his work on Murder in the Cathedral, Eliot did not abandon the ideal of popularity. Superficially, this is most obvious in the play's oft-noted elements of detective fiction, beginning with its title—"a selling one," Browne approvingly called it—which won out over such contenders as "The Archbishop Murder Case" and "Fear in the Way."[10] Late in the action, the Fourth Knight attempts to recast the assassination of Thomas Becket as a murder mystery ("What I have to say may be put in the form of a question: Who killed the Archbishop?" [CPP 218]). Eliot even interpolated several lines from Conan Doyle's "Musgrave Ritual" into the dialogue, where they passed unnoticed for years by audiences and critics alike. These elements, admittedly, provide only a thin veneer of the popular genre, and the play's overall effect is far more liturgical than melodramatic.[11] Liturgy, however, is not necessarily highbrow, and Eliot recognized religious ritual as community property and thus as a form of popular culture. In his "Dialogue on Dramatic Poetry" (1928), the character E suggests not only that "the consummation of the drama . . . is to be found in the ceremony of the Mass," but that drama itself "springs from religious liturgy, and that it cannot afford to depart far from religious liturgy" (35). While no one character in this dialogue should be simply identified with Eliot—and indeed, B immediately offers important caveats to E's argument—Murder in the Cathedral, with its incantatory choruses and interpolated prose sermon, seems designed with E's point in mind.[12] In its diction and cadences, and arguably in its form (Ayers 580–88), the play approaches the poetry of the church service, a cultural form no less familiar to contemporary audiences than, say, music hall or "thrillers."

Herbert Howarth insightfully grounds Eliot's use of choral speaking in Murder in the Cathedral in England's strong amateur theater movement, "a popular art which looks back to the annual festival plays of the medieval communities and the performances of the craftsmen" (318). Finding the English folk custom of amateur performance still living—after all, it furnished the majority of the original casts for both Murder and The Rock—Eliot "grafted" his play onto this stock. In its beginnings this tradition of popular drama had produced the miracle plays and moralities such as Everyman, on which Eliot openly modeled Murder's versification; and even into the twentieth century, appropriately enough for Eliot's purposes, local theatrical groups were often connected with parish churches (Howarth 318).[13] The more appropriate, too, that Eliot's subject, Thomas Becket, should have been the most popular of English saints, and that his shrine at Canterbury, renowned for its miracles, should have been the destination of Chaucer's pilgrims and was thus associated with the beginnings of the English poetic tradition as well. The critic who cited Murder as "the nearest modern approach to serious art in the popular [theatrical] tradition" was not unjustified (Bethell 26).

As I have argued with respect to Sweeney Agonistes, however, the presence of recognizably popular elements and a deliberate grounding in some popular tradition of drama do not necessarily produce a popular play. And whether Murder in the Cathedral can be considered a "popular play" is a somewhat complicated question. After the original Canterbury production, the play (mounted now with a full professional cast) ran for almost 400 performances in London between the fall of 1935 and the spring of 1937 before embarking on two provincial tours and traveling to New York and Boston. In 1936 it was broadcast on television and BBC radio.[14] Perhaps even more tellingly, an "emergency version" of Murder performed for three years during the Second World War before quite diverse audiences in air-raid shelters, schools, and houses of worship was found to move even working-class audiences from the East End. Of one such performance given in a shelter to a "deeply stirred audience mostly hailing from Hackney," actress Henzie Raeburn recalled, "[f]or the first ten or fifteen minutes the form and language of [the play] seemed strange to them; then they got caught up by it, and it was one of the most 'shared' performances I have ever known" (qtd. in Browne, *Making* 155). The play managed, it seems, to tap into a cross-class reservoir of British communal feeling at a time of crisis.

Still, the play's warm reception should not be overread. It seems characteristic of *Murder*'s success that most of its long run in London took place at Ashley Dukes's tiny Mercury Theatre, the smallest house in the city, with only 136 seats. The 20,000 people who (as Browne later boasted) saw the play in its first seven months at the Mercury would not have filled the house a half-century later for even a two-week run of *Cats* (Browne, *Making* 67).[15] Many an attempt to recover Shakespeare for the masses has "proven" that something of the original popular appeal of his plays survives without restoring Shakespeare, in the long run, to the realm of the popular. *Murder in the Cathedral*, I suggest, achieved something similar. Clearly the right performance under the right circumstances could reach an unexpected variety of audiences. But the play did not therefore point the way to the popular verse drama of the future, and Eliot himself was not fooled by the play's success into believing that it did. He did not want the provenance of poetic drama restricted to "subject[s] generally admitted to be suitable for verse"—those drawn, that is, from mythology or "some remote historical period." Eliot asked no quarter, maintaining that "If the poetic drama is to reconquer its place, it must . . . enter into overt competition with prose drama" ("Poetry and Drama" 81). Henceforth Eliot's poetry would be spoken by characters "dressed like ourselves, living in houses and apartments like ours, and using telephones and motor cars and radio sets," in a form of verse he would struggle to align with modern, colloquial English.

> What we have to do is to bring poetry into the world in which the audience lives and to which it returns when it leaves the theatre; not to transport the audience into some imaginary world totally unlike its own, an unreal world in which poetry is tolerated. (81–82)

What Eliot sought in the wake of *Murder in the Cathedral* was a verse drama no less viable as a form of entertainment than the prevailing forms of theater—a genre that would be genuinely attractive to audiences and not merely "tolerated." In "Audiences, Producers, Plays, Poets," an essay of the same year as *Murder in the Cathedral*, he insisted, "The audience does not care to see what [the playwright] does, in order to rally round a theory, but to be interested and excited. The indispensable merit of a verse play is that it shall be interesting" (4).

Ironically, this article in its original publication was immediately followed by Humphrey Jennings's "Eliot and Auden and Shakespeare," which found *Murder in the Cathedral* to produce an effect precisely opposite to Eliot's intentions. "Mr. Eliot's play," Jennings objected, "has no 'entertainment value'"; it would find itself welcome only in highbrow theaters (6). Michael Sayers similarly found *Murder* "a bit of a bore," adding: "I think the audiences agree with me, for I notice that they rouse themselves for the first time during the performance of this piece upon the entrance of the Shavian knights" (654). Richard Watts's review in the New York *Herald Tribune* would turn the same complaint into a compliment: "For all its occasional obscurity and frequent dullness, [*Murder*] possesses dignity, thoughtfulness, and beauty" (1). The play, in other words, fails as entertainment but triumphs as poetry. What reviewers like Watts and later critics like Howarth found to praise in *Murder in the Cathedral* is just what Eliot would reject and attempt to curb in its successors: its refusal of "any surrender of elevation," its "demanding" verse, its "auster[ity]" (Howarth 320).[16] *Murder* could not, in short, set the pattern for the kind of theater Eliot was hoping to establish.

It is primarily through its versification and its language that *Murder in the Cathedral* maintains its distance from the popular. Eliot had not yet laid one of the cornerstones of his later dramatic theory: the necessity of a completely unobtrusive form of verse. In 1936 he could still recommend as an antidote to the "illusion" of naturalism that the playwright "not let the audience forget that what they are hearing is verse" ("Need" 995). There are many passages in *Murder* where Eliot deliberately introduces "rhyme, even doggerel," that serves as "a constant reminder that [the play] is verse and not a compromise with prose":

> THE FOUR KNIGHTS: You are the Archbishop in revolt against the
>   King; in rebellion to the King and the law of the land;
> You are the Archbishop who was made by the King; whom he
>   set in your place to carry out his command.
> You are his servant, his tool, and his jack,
> You wore his favours on your back,
> You had your honours all from his hand.

> (CPP 203)

The language of the Chorus is patently "poetic" in another way—the way of what Howarth calls "elevation," or what Kenner more incriminatingly calls its "ululating logorrhea, doubling and tripling the image, assailing and bewildering the mind" (242):

> I have lain on the floor of the sea and breathed with the breathing of the
>   sea-anemone, swallowed with ingurgitation of the sponge. I have lain
>   in the soil and criticised the worm. In the air

Flirted with the passage of the kite, I have plunged with the kite and cow-
   ered with the wren. I have felt
The horn of the beetle, the scale of the viper, the mobile hard insensitive
   skin of the elephant, the evasive flank of the fish.

(CPP 207)

This is powerful poetry, but as the speech of the working women of Canterbury it seems even less likely than the *Waste Land*–inflected speech of the
unemployed laborers in *The Rock*. "I had to make some effort," Eliot explained, "to identify myself with these women, instead of merely identifying them with myself" ("Three Voices" 91). He was still trying to pick up
literally where Marie Lloyd had left off in the midst of her final turn as a
middle-aged charwoman. But the speeches Eliot has put in the mouths of
his chorus capture little of the human "tone of voice" Eliot heard in Lloyd;
indeed, they practically shout that they are poetry. Nor is this phenomenon
confined to the choral passages; the dialogue, as well, sometimes calls attention to its own poeticality more than it advances the action:

THOMAS: Whose was it?
TEMPTER: His who is gone.
THOMAS: Who shall have it?
TEMPTER: He who will come.
THOMAS: What shall be the month?
TEMPTER: The last from the first.
THOMAS: What shall we give for it?
TEMPTER: Pretence of priestly power.
THOMAS: Why should we give it?
TEMPTER: For the power and the glory.

(CPP 186)

No matter that the first four of these are the very lines Eliot culled from
"The Musgrave Ritual": if the stichomythic rhythms of this exchange carry
an echo of *Sweeney Agonistes*, their riddling quality gives them a remoteness
and opacity quite unlike anything in the earlier play—at least until one gets
to the twenty-five-line excrescence Eliot produced for Hallie Flanagan in
1933. Other speeches in the play are as thick with paradox as the opening
passage of "Burnt Norton" (a poem that, in fact, coalesced around lines cut
from this play):

Neither does the actor suffer
Nor the patient act. But both are fixed
In an eternal action, an eternal patience
To which all must consent that it may be willed

And which all must suffer that they may will it,
That the pattern may subsist, for the pattern is the action
And the suffering, that the wheel may turn and still
Be forever still.

(CPP 182)

What theater audience, one wonders, could take this in at a sitting? The poetry of *Murder in the Cathedral* is splendidly crafted and often profound, but in attending the play one never does forget that one is listening to poetry. This is not the recipe for a verse drama that will compete on an equal footing with prose drama.

CHOOSING THE THEATER

Eliot quickly reached the same conclusion himself, as he professed in a 1938 letter to Pound:

Opinion about the writing of a play is simply this:

1. You got to keep the audience's attention all the time.
2. If you lose it you got to get it back QUICK.
3. Everything about plot and character and all else what Aristotle and others say is secondary to the forgoin [*sic*].
4. But IF you can keep the bloody audience's attention engaged, then you can perform any monkey tricks you like when they ain't looking, and it's what you do behind the audience's back so to speak that makes your play immortal for a while.
   If the audience gets its strip tease it will swallow the poetry.
5. If you write a play in verse, then the verse ought to be a medium to look THROUGH, and not a pretty decoration to look AT! ("Five")

Notwithstanding the odd epistolary style—here, as often in letters to Pound, pure Poundese—Eliot's five points are perfectly serious. The last, for instance, reflects an imperative he voiced repeatedly in later years: that the audience must be allowed, and even encouraged, to forget that it is listening to poetry. This idea represents a complete reversal of the principle Eliot had adopted in writing *Murder in the Cathedral*. By the time he writes *The Cocktail Party* in 1949, Eliot wishes to see the audience "affected, unconsciously, by the rhythm of the verse, without being consciously aware that it [is] verse they are hearing" ("Aims" 13). The audience, that is, should receive the play as though it were in prose. The verse, Eliot argues, is no less efficacious for its going unrecognized, since "[t]he chief effect of style and rhythm in dramatic speech . . . should be unconscious" ("Poetry and Drama" 73).

The operation of dramatic verse upon the unconscious is a matter of what Eliot's later essays call the "music of poetry"—meaning not a mellifluousness of sound, but the aggregate structure of a work, its changes of pace and tone, the ebb and flow of its emotional intensity, and its marshaling of recurrent imagery to produce a "total effect" ("Music of Poetry" 36). Of the opening scene of Hamlet, Eliot writes, "There emerges, when we analyse it, a kind of musical design . . . which reinforces and is one with the dramatic movement. It has checked and accelerated the pulse of our emotion without our knowing it" ("Poetry and Drama" 76).[17] The artful variation of rhythm and diction in the scene "intensifies the drama" not only for "those members of an audience who 'like poetry' but also [for] those who go for the play alone" (77). These "musical" effects are the "monkey tricks" mentioned in the fourth of Eliot's "Five Points": the operations of the poetry on the unconscious ("behind the audience's back") while the audience is focused on the action.[18] Prose drama, Eliot argues, lacks this power of unconscious stimulation: "I believe . . . that poetry is the natural and complete medium for drama; that the prose play is a kind of abstraction capable of giving you only a part of what the theatre can give; and that the verse play is capable of something much more intense and exciting" ("Need" 994).

The requirement that the verse play at least match the "interest and excitement" of the ordinary play in prose is a constant in Eliot's criticism after Murder in the Cathedral: he is well aware that "People think of [verse plays] as something of a strain on the mind even when not actually boring" ("Need" 994). Unless the play steadily holds the audience's attention—the burden of the first three of the "Five Points"—the excellence of its poetry is for naught. Eventually Eliot boils down his five points to one, telling the Glasgow Herald in 1949: "The first and perhaps the only law of the drama is to get the attention of the audience and to keep it" and that the audience's enjoyment is "the main thing" (qtd. in Browne, Making 236). Still, a successful balance between "poetry" and "theater" would prove an elusive thing throughout his experiments in verse drama.

In The Family Reunion (1939), Eliot more nearly approaches the theater than he had in Murder in the Cathedral by featuring modern characters and by developing a new, subtler poetic line that often succeeds in directing attention away from itself:

> IVY: Yet I remember, when they were boys,
>   Arthur was always the more adventurous
>   But John was the one that had the accidents,
>   Somehow, just because he was the slow one.
>   He was always the one to fall off the pony,
>   Or out of a tree—and always on his head.

(CPP 267)

Nevertheless, Eliot remains caught in this play between "pure" and "applied" poetry, between the popular theater and its Yeatsian anti-self. Although he took great pains "to find a rhythm close to contemporary speech" ("Poetry and Drama" 82), in much of The Family Reunion the suppleness of Eliot's rhythm hardly begins to camouflage his poetry:

> AMY: Not yet! I will ring for you. It is still quite light.
> I have nothing to do but watch the days draw out,
> Now that I sit in the house from October to June,
> And the swallow comes too soon and the spring will be over
> And the cuckoo will be gone before I am out again.
> O Sun, that was once so warm, O Light that was taken for granted
> When I was young and strong, and sun and light unsought for
> And the night unfeared and the day expected
> And clocks could be trusted, tomorrow assured
> And time would not stop in the dark!
>
>   (CPP 225)

The apostrophes to the sun and the light, the ornithological references, the time symbolism, and the heavy parataxis mark the play as unabashedly "poetic" from this, its first moment. Most of Amy's relatives speak more prosaically, but lest they come across as altogether natural, Eliot collects them periodically into a chorus to intone their collective fears and misgivings in a manner not unreminiscent, in tenor or in language, of the Women of Canterbury:

> CHORUS: I am afraid of all that has happened, and of all that is to come;
> Of the things to come that sit at the door, as if they had been there
>   always.
> And the past is about to happen, and the future was long since settled.
> And the wings of the future darken the past, the beak and claws have
>   desecrated
> History.
>
>   (CPP 256)

There are in addition several key scenes in which a figure actually steps out of character to declaim as if in a trance—an awkward effect, as Eliot himself ultimately felt, because it requires "a suspension of the action" for the sake of a "poetic fantasia" ("Poetry and Drama" 83).

The Family Reunion is thus at once a self-concealing and self-advertising piece of high art—a somber, paradoxical, challenging work of poetry. The play's use of a classical myth as its basis (including onstage appearances by the Furies) further heightens the literary effect.[19] Although he had taken several steps in the direction of the theater by 1939, Eliot was not quite

ready to subjugate the "pure" poet in himself fully to the professional playwright. And he paid the price. After four years' writing, The Family Reunion
opened in London to "lukewarm reviews" and closed within five weeks
(Bush 209). No wonder, then, that the next time around, Eliot would follow
out his theorizing to its logical conclusion. At length he returned to drama
determined to write a verse play that would succeed *as a play*, by the ordinary
measure of theatrical success: audiences would line up to see it.

And so the classicizing contrivances of Murder in the Cathedral and The Family
Reunion were scrupulously avoided in The Cocktail Party: Eliot now agreed to
be bound by the conventions of drama as it then existed on stage. In his
important 1940 essay on Yeats, Eliot—while still obviously intrigued by
the possibilities of the chorus—was beginning to see his way toward the
deliberately unliterary style of The Cocktail Party:

> One device used with great success in some of [Yeats's] later plays is the
> lyrical choral interlude. But another, and important, cause of improve-
> ment is the gradual purging out of poetical ornament. This, perhaps, is
> the most painful part of the labour, so far as the versification goes, of the
> modern poet who tries to write a play in verse. The course of improve-
> ment is towards a greater and greater starkness. (259−60).

At this point Eliot retained a measure of avant-garde contempt for the commercial theater; he saw Yeats's plays, for example, as a potential "defence
against the successful urban Shaftesbury Avenue vulgarity" (261). Yet, a
decade later, the TLS could assure potential patrons of The Cocktail Party that
"the author has in this instance shown as much respect for what Shaftesbury
Avenue is supposed to want as for his own sense of reality." The appeal of
this play, as the reviewer perceived, was "not to a small circle of initiates, but
to the main body of theatrical pleasure-seekers who hold very reasonably
that the primary business of dramatic entertainments is to entertain" ("Entertainment").[20] But the virtues of The Cocktail Party are not only negative ones.
The play engagingly converts Eliot's vision of life, human relationship, redemption, and community into a witty and provocative comedy; it also contains, in Henry Harcourt-Reilly and Julia Shuttlethwaite, two of Eliot's most
intriguing stage characters. Though many have found its vision unpalatable,
The Cocktail Party is a successful work of theater. And yet it is in verse.

In The Cocktail Party, Eliot strictly "disciplin[es]" his poetry, "putting it, so
to speak, on a very thin diet in order to adapt it to the needs of the stage"
("Poetry and Drama" 85−86). "Poetry" in this play appears to mean, simply, well-chosen words, a deft but unobtrusive control of cadence and tone,
and a four-stress meter so irregular as to be virtually inaudible. To these features Eliot adds, at moments—but only at moments—a slight elevation of
diction that pushes the limits of conversational speech:

REILLY: To send them back: what have they to go back to?
>   To the stale food mouldering in the larder,
>   The stale thoughts mouldering in their minds.
>   Each unable to disguise his own meanness
>   From himself, because it is known to the other.
>   It's not the knowledge of the mutual treachery
>   But the knowledge that the other understands the motive—
>   Mirror to mirror, reflecting vanity. I have taken a great risk.

(CPP 367)

For the most part, though, the language of The Cocktail Party cleaves to the prosaic:

EDWARD: I know that I invited this conversation:
>   But I don't know who you are. This is not what I expected.
>   I only wanted to relieve my mind
>   By telling someone what I'd been concealing.
>   I don't think I want to know who you are;
>   But, at the same time, unless you know my wife
>   A good deal better than I thought, or unless you know
>   A good deal more about us than appears—
>   I think your speculations rather offensive.

(305–06)

Eliot's stated "ambition" was to ensure that the poetics of his play would impinge on his audience entirely unconsciously, and after its first performance he described himself as "pleased to find . . . that several critics left the theatre without having decided whether the play was meant to be in verse or in prose" ("Aims" 13).

Sharp reviewers saw at once what Eliot had set out to do. E. M. Forster, for one, found that "The difficulties of The Cocktail Party do not extend to its diction. It is most beautifully and lucidly written," using "a demure chatty verse-form which seems to be like prose," but is "full of turns and subtle echoes, and always open for the emotional intensity [the play] occasionally needs" (533). And William Carlos Williams took a break from his Thirty Years' War on Eliot to enthuse:

The Cocktail Party is a very thrilling play which in the reading moved me deeply. The lines begin with capitals so that you see at once that it is all intended as verse. Those who hear the play and have not read it will not know that. I think definitely though that they will feel it to be verse— without knowing and without offense. To me this would be a very considerable achievement on the part of Mr. Eliot. ("It's About" 18)

Eliot had "kept a close rein on the texture of the verse quite as ordinary speech would have it"—a goal of which Williams could easily approve.

Eliot later remarked that in writing *The Cocktail Party* he had imposed on himself "the ascetic rule to avoid poetry which could not stand the test of strict dramatic utility: with such success, indeed, that it is perhaps an open question whether there is any poetry in the play at all" ("Poetry and Drama" 85). In his next play, *The Confidential Clerk* (1953), the verse seldom rises above the pitch of everyday conversation, and some reviewers and many literary critics have questioned whether Eliot went too far in suppressing poetry in this play—whether, in other words, he compromised away his art for the sake of getting and keeping the audience's attention. Brooks Atkinson called *The Confidential Clerk* "at least the second step Mr. Eliot has taken down to the level of the theatre, and . . . the logical result of his long attempt to shake off the shackles of his own genius." "A gifted man," he complained, "has written a commonplace play" ("Comedy").[21] With such criticisms in mind, Eliot could hope that *The Elder Statesman* (1958) "goes further in getting more poetry in, at any rate, than *The Confidential Clerk* did" (qtd. in D. Hall 102). "Getting more poetry in," unfortunately, frequently amounts in this play to the crafting of speeches that no one could mistake for human dialogue. Although most of Eliot's verse in *The Elder Statesman* resembles the inconspicuous near-prose of *The Confidential Clerk*, his attempt to raise the emotional pitch in his love scenes results in the impossible exchanges of Monica and Charles:

> MONICA
> How did this come, Charles? It crept so softly
> On silent feet, and stood behind my back
> Quietly, a long time, a long long time
> Before I felt its presence.
>
> CHARLES
>   Your words seem to come
> From very far away. Yet very near. You are changing me
> And I am changing you.
>
>   (15–16)

The stilted air of such passages is just what Eliot had striven for so long to avoid in trying to bring poetic drama to the modern stage. Though there may be wisdom in this very late play of penitence, forgiveness, and love, Eliot stands awkwardly with one foot in and one foot out of the theater, to the satisfaction of neither his critics nor his audiences.

Whatever the aesthetic value of his three last plays, the principles Eliot adopted in writing them were consistent with a line of his thought we have followed up from around 1919. Drama, for Eliot, was a popular art, and an elite theater was symptomatic of a destructive cleavage between high art and popular culture—one that a popular poetic drama might go some way toward healing. As the TLS observed of The Cocktail Party, "The purpose of the verse is not to paint scenery in the Elizabethan way, nor to make verbal patterns, nor to create emotions in excess of the matter under discussion, but to give the dialogue the finest possible precision and intensity" ("Entertainment"). That is to say, Eliot's dialogue in this play was a selection and distillation of common speech woven into an artistic whole—the very achievement for which Eliot had praised Marianne Moore in 1923.

IN THE WORLD OF ENTERTAINMENT

In The Use of Poetry and the Use of Criticism, Eliot had described the poet as being "incapable of altering his wares to suit a prevailing taste" and thus eager for "a state of society in which they may become popular" (22). In time, however, he concluded that poets, like it or not, would have to adapt to their conditions. As we have seen, Eliot did indeed alter his wares in several important ways. First, he gradually made his peace with the dramatic realism he had once excoriated. Second, while he continued to write in verse, the verse was increasingly well disguised—almost, in the end, to the vanishing point. And third, though Eliot continued to draw on classical Greek drama for his plots (Alcestis for The Cocktail Party, Ion for The Confidential Clerk, and Oedipus at Colonus for The Elder Statesman), none of the plays after The Family Reunion required the audience's recognition of the relevant myth. Eliot now spoke of the Greek originals as "points of departure," or "a sort of springboard," rather than as "models" (qtd. in D. Hall 103).

Given Eliot's oft-advertised allegiance to detective fiction, it is not surprising that the detective element persists and even expands after Murder in the Cathedral. Wishwood, the isolated old country house in The Family Reunion, furnishes just the proper scene for a murder mystery, and it is peopled, as Gordon points out, by "aunts and uncles . . . out of English detective fiction from Conan Doyle to Agatha Christie: the old buffer of the club, the retired Indian army officer, the spinster of the vicar's teas" (Imperfect 326). Although, when the play opens, Harry's murder of his wife has already occurred—if (for that is part of the mystery) it occurred at all—hundreds of miles away, Eliot is still clearly playing with the conventions of crime drama. The detective element is alive and well in The Cocktail Party, which begins with the mysteries of Lavinia's disappearance and of the "Unidentified Guest," who turns out to be something of a private investigator (complete with a staff of undercover snoops). It is present, too, in The Confidential Clerk, with its multiple puzzles of parental identity and its twisting series of Poirotian revelations in the final scene, and again in *The Elder Statesman*'s exposure of the dark secrets of a prominent man's checkered past. This was how Eliot knew best to maintain the necessary quotient of "melodrama" or "thriller" interest in his plays, as his essay on Wilkie Collins had demanded years before.[22]

As significant as any alteration in Eliot's "wares" was his revisioning of his own position as a professional artist. Having chosen the theater, Eliot worked diligently with directors and actors, listened (selectively) to reviewers, and struggled to master the "well-made play" in the style of the English comedy of manners. He also permitted himself to be mass marketed, allying himself from 1949 with the British impresario Henry Sherek, who took the poet "at one bound into the world of entertainment" (Browne, *Making* 181). Sherek's backing ensured that Eliot's plays would be given a real chance as show business. When the London theaters, leery of Eliot's highbrow reputation, balked at *The Cocktail Party*, Sherek—overriding the anxious playwright—bypassed them to bring the play at once to Broadway, an ingenious business gamble that succeeded not only because the 1948 Nobel Prize had recently raised Eliot's celebrity to a new peak but simply because Eliot had in fact achieved a rapprochement with theater audiences and their expectations. *The Cocktail Party*, starring Alec Guinness as Harcourt-Reilly, ran for 409 performances on Broadway, grossing an impressive $7,000 per day.[23] A second cast led by Rex Harrison finally brought the play to London in May 1950, where it chalked up another 325 performances. Eliot's royalties netted him a comfortable living; and though there were sneers that he was grasping for money, he turned down a £30,000 offer for film rights (Malamud, *Drama* 136). Meanwhile, the printed edition of the play made the *New York Times* best-seller list.[24]

Perhaps most striking of all is the fact that in making the move to Broadway and Shaftesbury Avenue, Eliot finally allowed himself to compromise with the bête noir of his early criticism, the middle class. Eliot's late plays make no pretense of being designed for an ostensibly illiterate music-hall audience: their settings and characters, their wit, and even the problems they pose are designed to attract the mainly middle-class audiences who attended plays. If a new verse drama was ever to take root, Eliot realized, the practical course was to begin with the existing theater audience and the available generic materials. His course from *Sweeney Agonistes* to *The Cocktail Party* thus took him progressively, inexorably, into the provenance of what he had once disparaged as "middle-class art." By choosing thus to treat with the middle class, Eliot gained the opportunity to perform his "monkey tricks" behind their backs—to rattle, if he could, their triumphalist secularism and moral complacency, not by offending them, but by presenting an alternative vision. In this way Eliot won a sizable public that he could attempt to nudge toward his own worldview. What he lost is harder to define.

It has often been remarked that Eliot, to his detriment, received little adverse criticism of his last plays from a literary world that stood too much in awe of him. "Towards the end of Eliot's life," as Peter Levi has put it, "a strong body of rather silent opinion had grown up that his verse plays were a disaster" (132); yet only with Eliot's death in 1965 could the "disaster" be openly admitted and the playwright whisked off the critical stage in favor of the poet and man of letters.

Suggestions of an underlying discontent began to surface in the very late 1950s, not long after—and probably, in part, as a result of—the premiere of *The Elder Statesman*. In Hugh Kenner's 1959 "Supplementary Dialogue on Dramatic Poetry," the interlocutor Y sounds the note that would eventually swell to a full chorus:

> I agree . . . that [Eliot's] concern with the audience's attention is misplaced. It leads to plays written for an audience who will swallow the poetry if they get their Noel Coward; it leads to the West End stage and Mr. Martin Browne; it leads to plays more dignified, literate, and intelligent than the West End stage has supported in its time, or than Broadway has commonly occasion to mount; but not to that "new drama (if a new drama ever comes)" which was to owe something to the music hall and the ballet and the invention of a new form, elevating contemporary life into something rich and strange. (188)

In other words, Eliot had gone off track by failing to develop the possibilities imminent in his prose writings on verse drama and in *Sweeney Agonistes*, and by yielding, instead, to the demands of the existing theater. Kenner's Q refers to this argument as "The party line of our literary bureaucracy's more benevolent wing" (189), and indeed, few judgments on Eliot's career have been as consistently rehearsed since his death. Robert Speaight, the actor who originated Eliot's Becket, confessed himself haunted by the wish that Eliot's drama "had developed on the lines of *The Waste Land*," as *Sweeney Agonistes* had seemed to promise. "T. S. Eliot has arrived on Shaftesbury Avenue," wrote Speaight, "and the English actor owes him much. But if he had chosen to go elsewhere, I think that gratitude might have been even greater" ("Interpreting" 78). Alan Downer, the Princeton don to whom Eliot had voiced his resolve to "convince people that I know how to write a popular play," thought that "this determination led to the increasing ineffectiveness of his later work." Eliot had "abandoned" the discoveries of *Sweeney* "too readily for the conventions of domestic comedy" (qtd. in Smidt 61). And Clive Barnes, demolishing a revival of *The Cocktail Party* in the *New York Times*, found it "difficult to believe that Eliot wrote [that play] at all. Here is a man who in the dramatic fragment *Sweeney Agonistes* seemed to hold the clue of modern theater in his hands offering this tawdry and shallow nonsense."[25]

Although most of this Sweeniolatry was posthumous, one should not, I think, dismiss it as mere second-guessing. No one who at all relishes the disturbing excitement of modernist experiment can fail to appreciate the diabolic energy, the teasing ambiguity of tone, and the expansive, anarchic fun of Sweeney, beside which all the later plays seem, except at moments, comparatively studied and conventionally "literary."[26] There is, in short, something (or several things) to the sort of view expressed by John Gross:

> Sweeney Agonistes is incomplete and obscure, but as far as it goes distinctly promising. It suggests that Eliot could have developed his own brand of expressionist drama: he uses music-hall patter much as the German expressionists used vaudeville, along with jazz-rhythms, parody, fantastic imagery. . . . But as it is, Sweeney Agonistes remains the only hint of what might have been. (49)

Gross concludes that Murder in the Cathedral represents the "unique success," the "one indubitable theatrical triumph" in Eliot's oeuvre (50).[27] As for the remainder of Eliot's dramatic output, he asks, "Was it a mistake?" and immediately answers, "In all probability, yes" (48). But this is a complicated question and not necessarily a decidable one, for there is no one yardstick that can take the measure of the various contending answers.

I argued in the previous chapter that Sweeney Agonistes was doomed from the start by Eliot's conflicting impulses toward the popular. In Sweeney Eliot brews popular elements to form a compound that can appeal only to intellectuals, and only at that to the subset of intellectuals who go in for avant-garde art and its provocations. In his later plays, it is true, Eliot adopts a very different cultural matrix as his starting point rather than attempting to domesticate Sweeney; he does not find, and does not seek, a way to preserve the experimental qualities that had animated his first play. And that is a loss—but to whom is it a loss, other than to the very coteries from which Eliot was attempting to escape? As Gross sees, Eliot might have developed a fascinating and original expressionist drama out of Sweeney Agonistes, but who, if he had done so, would have gone to see it? Surely, if Eliot had chosen this path, critics would now be citing his expressionist plays alongside The Waste Land as evidence of his incurable elitism, a further display of disdain for the comprehension and attention of the ordinary reader or theater patron. I myself could wish, with Speaight and the rest, for another five plays along the lines of Sweeney. Yet how can one not respect Eliot's stand against "unpopular" theater, and the risks he took with his hard-earned literary reputation in order to mount his quixotic foray across the cultural divide? Even assuming that one could apply a simple label like "failure" to Eliot's efforts in poetic drama, it does not follow that the attempt was a "mistake."

For some, Eliot's armistice with the middle-class audience is explanation enough for the "failure" of his last three plays. As this argument would have it, Eliot dedicated himself to an essentially unworthy project. This is the position Kermode adopts in his insightful review of *The Elder Statesman.* "Having renounced anti-theatre," he explains, Eliot had "committed to an audience largely made up of middle-class groundlings, incapable of full participation in his whole design. . . . In a sense it is the audience he has considered so carefully that has sabotaged Mr. Eliot's theatre" ("What Became"). To create a public art for a middle-class public was profitless; Yeats had made the truer and more productive decision in "considering only an elite, ignoring the 'shopkeeping logicians' of Shaftesbury Avenue and refusing to supply 'what the blind and ignorant town / Imagines best to make it thrive.'" Such deprecation of the bourgeois is of course a time-honored modernist practice, but it is ungenerous. To whatever extent Eliot's late verse drama is counted a failure, we must look to Eliot, and not to his public, for an explanation.

Eliot might, for example, have chosen any number of models for his popular poetic drama; he decided on drawing-room comedy, a genre that can hardly be said to have been forced on him by his audience, since it was already passé when he took it up.[28] Eliot seems to have felt comfortable in this medium, which provided many opportunities for well-spoken, well-mannered (even if banal) characters to articulate states of mind and their relations to the world and to each other. At the same time, the genre narrowed the range of Eliot's drama in several ways; for example, by restricting his characters socially to the upper-middle and aristocratic classes and their courteous servants, and by severely constraining the plays' diction. Gone is the demotic vividness so effective in the language of *Sweeney Agonistes* (Hayman 6). The late plays are bounded in other ways by the conventions of stage realism; there is nothing in them like the frisson of that moment in *Murder in the Cathedral* when the Four Knights suddenly step out of their century to address the modern theater audience directly.[29] The genre similarly circumscribes the plays' sources of conflict and action, which, by the final two comedies, come to seem quaintly Victorian (Kenner 289–90). In short, as Levi writes, Eliot's later plays are overly confined by their "subject matter, which is determined by the class-bound conventions of drawing room comedy he chose to transform." As a result, they "exclude too much of life" (133–34).

Any assessment of Eliot's theatrical undertaking, however, must also take into account that Eliot did not *expect* to succeed—not, at least, according to the usual aesthetic definitions of success. His public comments on his own drama repeatedly characterize his project as one of early trailblazing rather than perfection; he imagined himself as rather a Kyd than a Shakespeare. He spoke often of, and to, a succeeding generation of poetic dramatists who, "having the benefit of our experience," would solve the problems that Eliot had helped to define and with which he had made palpable but limited headway ("Poetry and Drama" 82). "I think that the work of still another generation will be needed," he wrote, "before poetry can hope to be established on our popular stage as it was three hundred and more years ago" ("Aims" 10). For Eliot's purposes, then, his success was to be measured not merely by the virtues of his own plays, but by the lessons they held for future verse dramatists, and by their contribution to the slow process of attracting and preparing a public. To Helen Gardner, Eliot seemed to discuss his work "with the simplicity and seriousness of someone who cares more for the things which he has tried to do than for his own success" ("Aged" 8). If this impression appears to betray an excessive reverence for the graciously humble master, it is at least characteristic of Eliot to take the long view.[30] And it is remarkable that Eliot should have been so willing to sacrifice his track record in impeccable artistry, painstakingly acquired through his small oeuvre of highly polished poems, in order to break rough ground for a new art form.

For a brief hour, the venture appeared to have paid off. One could say confidently, in the wake of *The Cocktail Party*, and with the temporarily overrated *Confidential Clerk* on the horizon, that "it cannot be denied that Eliot's plays have spread his name and influence far beyond the audience that his poetry reached" (Lehmann 5). But few who know Eliot's name a half-century later know it because of his playwriting. The thorough discounting of Eliot the dramatist, in part an overreaction to the plays' overgenerous reception, may also be an effect of their failure to bear progeny—to alter the course of English drama in the long run. The "kitchen sink drama" of the late 1950s famously swept all before it, leaving Eliot and his fellow verse dramatists stranded in its wake, remnants of British theater's bad old days. This changing of the guard provides the context for Kermode's conclusion in 1959 that Eliot had sabotaged his poetic drama through his consideration of the middle-class audience: the same charge was then being leveled against prose-dramatist Terence Rattigan for his concern with the typical middlebrow playgoer he whimsically called "Aunt Edna." In any case, the revival in poetic drama was an almost total loss.

To Eliot, it appeared that the movement had been wrecked from within. Ronald Duncan tells of Eliot's embarrassment at being "bracketed with Christopher Fry," whose advent, he felt, did far more harm than good:

> Eliot and I had tried to make verse in the theatre a pliable vehicle of our contemporary feeling. We had both turned our backs on *Murder in the Cathedral* and *This Way to the Tomb* and set ourselves the task of writing modern plays in which the verse was not decoration upon the theme but

simple, unrhetorical and lucid. In *The Cocktail Party* and *Stratton* we felt we were moving towards language which had the discipline of prose but could carry the charge of a hand grenade when required. But the success of Fry's *The Lady's Not for Burning* [1949] put the clock back. We deprecated these verbal fireworks, this concern with imagery for the sake of coining it. My own aversion to this was tempered by my knowing Fry personally and liking him considerably. But Eliot had no inhibition here.

"He'll get over this style," I said.

"But the damage will be done."

He was quite correct. The damage was done. Fry's brief success associated poetry on the stage with rhetoric and verbal puff again. Within five years both Eliot and I found it difficult to get a production—Fry himself found it impossible.[31] (385)

The notion that the collapse of public interest in verse drama could be attributed to Fry's technical failings and the bad associations they generated is obviously too convenient. But it must have been easier for Eliot and Duncan to believe that the public had rejected Fry than that the entire revival of verse drama, which they had both felt was making progress, had been nothing more than a passing fad, a curiosity without a future. In 1952 Eliot had written, on another subject, "it is, after all, worth while exploring a blind alley, if only to discover that it is blind" ("Introduction to *Leisure*" 12). But these words, with which Eliot predicts the "exhaustion" of logical positivism, he would never pronounce on behalf of contemporary poetic drama. At no point was he prepared to concede the blindness of that particular alley.

What Eliot never found, perhaps because he never sought it, was a way to combine the jazzy dynamism of *Sweeney Agonistes* with the public reach of *The Cocktail Party*. And what his critics have seldom done, because they have seldom tried, is to grasp the implications of Eliot's "disastrous" course. The plays were written off too quickly because, as we will see in the next chapter, the Eliot who attempted to make a popular form of his art was not the Eliot his intellectual contemporaries wanted to see: the champion of high culture, the bulwark against the booboisie, the symbol of no compromise with kitsch. Eliot's career, when the plays are not arbitrarily excluded, reaches across the cultural divide and urges an attitude toward popular culture far more open and unpatronizing than his mid-twentieth-century readers, so often operating under a siege mentality, could permit themselves to acknowledge.

THE T. S. ELIOT IDENTITY CRISIS

He became his admirers.

—W. H. Auden, "In Memory of W. B. Yeats" (1939)

MEN WITH INITIALS

One day in 1952, after a church service in New York, Eliot's host brought him to meet the rector's wife, who "proceeded to introduce each of her three children in turn to 'Mr. C. S. Lewis,' adding that it was a day they would all remember!" Eliot received the misplaced compliment and allowed the mistake to pass uncorrected (Levy and Scherle 28). Joining the rector's wife in her pleasant confusion of two double-initialed English writers, critics of modernism have regularly introduced readers to a T. S. Eliot who is really, I would suggest, Mr. F. R. Leavis. Although the reasons for this confusion are understandable, it remains a blunder. And true to form, Eliot himself did little to rectify the error.

Leavis's literary criticism and his editorial leadership of *Scrutiny* were extraordinarily effective in advancing the claims of modernism in England, and in establishing the canonicity of Eliot, Lawrence, and other contemporary writers. And it is Leavis, not Eliot, whose major works of the 1930s— especially *For Continuity* and *Culture and Environment*—established the dominant critical approach to popular culture for the succeeding three decades.[1] These influential works codify the pervasive "standardization and levelling-down" of culture in the age of technology (*Culture* 2–3); the narcotic effect of popular culture, which for the majority becomes a form of "substitute-living," a compensation for the actual poverty of modern existence (*Culture*

99–100); and the requisite vigilance of the besieged minority who sustain the vitality of high culture against the tide of general decline ("Mass Civilisation" 38–39). The martial imagery so often associated with Eliot—that of a self-appointed epic hero "fortifying" cultural "boundaries," "policing" the "borders," and attempting a "rescue" or "defense" of institutional art— is rooted in these Leavisite metaphors rather than in the substance of Eliot's own work. Modern culture, in the Leavisite worldview, is a Waste Land, and indeed, Eliot's poem, whatever it may have meant to the poet, supplies a ubiquitous metaphor for the state of culture as seen through the eyes of mid-twentieth-century intellectuals. The Waste Land, as Kenneth Koch was later to observe ironically, "gave the time's most accurate data" (2).[2] Leavis himself draws liberally on Eliot's cultural criticism, behind which he clearly perceives a near forebear and a powerful ally.[3]

There is thus a tradition, beginning with Leavis himself, of reading Eliot as a proto-Leavis, and in this way of crediting Eliot with—or blaming him for—an intellectual movement to which his actual contribution was both modest and ambiguous. It is Eliot who now appears as the iconic figure for a militant advocacy of high culture against low in the accounts of both neo-conservatives and neo-Marxists. A typical remark on the Left, for instance, applauds the "aesthetic populism" of 1980s cultural studies for rejecting "the blanket dismissal of popular culture by elitists in the Eliot tradition, a dismissal which effectively stigmatized all current forms of popular art" (Fowler 166). How Eliot can have set the example for a comprehensive rejection of popular culture is not altogether easy to explain, and I will spend much of this chapter trying to account for this common allegation.

It must first be reemphasized how ill this account sits with the realities of Eliot's life and career. Eliot, as I have been arguing, was always ambivalent toward popular culture rather than mindlessly oppositional, and every phase of his career found him productively engaged as an artist with one or more of the modern popular genres. We have already considered Eliot's formative dialect with emergent jazz; his warmth toward music hall, vaudeville, and other species of popular stage entertainment; his broad negotiations with the popular in essays like "Wilkie Collins and Dickens," "Marianne Moore," and "Marie Lloyd"; and his ambition to write "popular plays" at whatever cost to his literary reputation. This list by no means exhausts the "current forms of popular art" that Eliot failed to "stigmatize."

Another long-term interest, for example, was comic strips, which the Eliotic persona of "Portrait of a Lady" could be found reading "any morning in the park." The younger Eliot was in fact captivated by Krazy Kat, Mutt and Jeff, and other early classics of the genre (Aiken, Ushant 133). By the early thirties he was devoted to the work of James Thurber, to whom he sent fan mail, and whom he later extolled in *Time* magazine ("Priceless").[4] Privately, he also applauded Walt Kelly, the creator of Pogo (no relation) Possum, as having skills in wordplay comparable to James Joyce's, and he traced the humorist's lineage through the work of Rube Goldberg and George Herriman (Levy and Scherle 46–47).[5] Another newspaper feature to which he was almost ostentatiously addicted was the crossword puzzle.[6]

Evidence of Eliot's devotion to detective fiction abounds, ranging from the anecdotes of friends who apparently considered Eliot's attachment to the genre an amusing peccadillo, to Eliot's own estimates of particular authors and his claims to an encyclopedic mental store of Sherlockiana.[7] His taste ran from the classic (Poe, Collins, Conan Doyle) to the contemporary (Simenon, Christie, Sayers, Cheyney, and Chandler).[8] Detective fiction, it must be granted, had a strong run as a midcentury intellectual vogue, and Leslie Fiedler could fairly complain in 1970 that "the detective story . . . has by our time become hopelessly compromised by middlebrow condescension: an affectation of college professors and presidents" (469). But Eliot, while not without his own cache of affectations, was too far ahead of the curve in this instance to have been merely posing; if anything, he may be said to have helped *create* the intellectual vogue for detective fiction.[9] He publicly declared his enthusiasm for the genre as early as 1927, close to the beginning of what is now considered its "Golden Age." Eliot sensed this incipience (which he dated to "the last year or two") and was even willing to forgo his customary pessimism to assert that the detective novel was improving rather than declining ("Homage" 140). In the *Criterion*, he attempted to codify some "general rules of detective technique" that characterize the best of the genre (141–42). And though many efforts along those lines were published in the next few decades, Eliot's attempt quite possibly qualifies as the first—and as almost the only one not contributed by a professional novelist (Tepper 10–11).[10]

Many other modernist critics would soon write on detective fiction, most using it to exemplify the vices of contemporary mass culture. Leavis and Denys Thompson suggest that to read a "thriller" is worse "than not to read at all" (*Culture* 143); Dwight Macdonald finds the genre, as practiced by Hammett, Spillane, and others, "rank, noxious [and] 'sensational,'" a product of massification and a "general degradation in ethics" ("Theory" 67–68); George Orwell, too, complains of a decline at the moral level (203). In a well-known 1950 essay called "Who Cares Who Killed Roger Ackroyd?" Edmund Wilson—who elsewhere refers to the "cult of Sherlock Holmes" as "infantile" (*Classics* 290)—compares the lure of detective novels with the effects of alcohol and opium (263–64).[11] And he concludes by linking arms defensively with enlightened readers:

> Friends, we represent a minority, but Literature is on our side. With so
> many fine books to be read, so much to be studied and known, there is
> no need to bore ourselves with this rubbish. (264–65)

Wilson less colorfully disputes a point he finds recently made by three writers—Somerset Maugham, Joseph Wood Krutch, and Bernard De Voto—who are sympathetic to detective fiction: "that the [serious] novel has become so philosophical, so psychological and so symbolic that the public have had to take to the detective story as the only department of fiction where pure story-telling survives" (261). Eliot, as we have seen, had made just the same argument in "Wilkie Collins and Dickens," nearly a quarter century earlier. And his subsequent references to the detective novel uniformly treat the genre earnestly and thoughtfully. Reading them, I think, one is the more inclined to regret that Eliot never applied himself to the analysis of popular culture with the regularity of a Seldes.[12]

Even when the term "mass culture" is introduced as tertium quid alongside the high-culture/popular-culture binary, Eliot's point of view remains complex, irreducible. True, Eliot attacked the mass media in terms that are consonant with the "mass-culture critique" with which he is so often associated—the line of thought that runs from Adorno and Leavis to Macdonald and Clement Greenberg. In one typical passage of this sort, Eliot charged:

> Mechanisation comes to kill local life: with the universal picture palace,
> you may travel the world over and be unable to avoid Shirley Temple;
> television may have a still more deadly effect on local life; and just as food
> comes to be something you have got out of a tin, and not something you
> have grown for yourself, so drama may mean for millions of people
> something out of a box or thrown onto a screen. ("Religious Drama" 17)

His chosen exemplars here (film, canned foods, and television) rank among Eliot's perpetual bugbears, and they are all, certainly, common enough targets among the mass-culture doomsters of his century. Nevertheless, Eliot was a strong supporter of radio from as early as February 1929, when he offered his unsolicited services to the BBC as a lecturer. As Michael Coyle has documented, Eliot made at least eighty-three broadcasts between that year and 1963, in what must be counted "one of the most sustained and principled engagements in modern literary history" between a major writer and a mass medium (" 'This rather elusory' " 32–33). Coyle details the trouble Eliot took with his broadcasts (for which, incidentally, he received little remuneration); his attempts to fathom the unique qualities of radio as a medium, recognizing that "despite its reliance on technology, there is something potentially intimate in the way a radio talk brings the speaker into people's homes" (35); and his remarkable success with radio audiences (39–40).[13] Recent scholarship by Patrick Collier suggests that Eliot's attitude even toward journalism was more complicated than is often supposed (188). Tempted as he was, then, by the siren song of the mass-culture critique, Eliot was willing to engage critically with the mass media—attempting, even if not always successfully, to be selective and not extravagant in his condemnations. He sought, in other words, to *discriminate* among cultural forms based on social and aesthetic criteria, accepting radio while rejecting television, music hall while rejecting film, crime novels while rejecting other varieties of popular fiction, and so on. Though in retrospect they do not always seem consistent or even rational, his choices bespeak a desire to respond reflectively, rather than reflexively, to the popular arts. Eliot's critical orientation is thus comparable in significant ways with the early works of cultural studies (e.g., with Hoggart's *Uses of Literacy* or Hall and Whannel's *Popular Arts*), which also struggle toward an equitable negotiation with the popular from a position of traditional critical discrimination.

Eliot's ambivalence makes even his late cultural criticism rather more nuanced than certain ubiquitously cited passages would lead one to believe. Yet it should be said at once that the Leavisite Eliot is not hard to find if one goes looking for him. His frequently quoted diatribes against film, for example, occur early and late in his oeuvre. Cinema, for Eliot, is "mere distractive amusement," pure escapism; unlike live entertainment, it is absorbed passively; it has a narcotic or hypnotic effect on the minds of its audiences; and so on.[14] Such criticisms were already commonplace by the time Eliot took them up, and they remained so until the 1950s, when they attached themselves to television.

Like many modernists across the political spectrum, Eliot shares a brand of cultural pessimism summed up in parts of his *Notes towards the Definition of Culture* (1948):

> We can assert with some confidence that our own period is one of decline; that the standards of culture are lower than they were fifty years ago; and that the evidences of this decline are visible in every department of human activity. I see no reason why the decay of culture should not proceed much further, and why we may not even anticipate a period, of some duration, of which it is possible to say that it will have no culture. (CC 91)

Here and elsewhere, Eliot remarks gloomily on the modern "tendency to mass production and lowering of standards" ("T. S. Eliot, 70 Today"), eventuating in the destruction of "our ancient edifices to make ready the ground upon which the barbarian nomads of the future will encamp in their mechanised caravans" (CC 185). He tends to sound this note loudest when evaluating modern culture in the abstract, a project that leads naturally to heavy-handed generalizations invoking the critical shibboleths of the day. A 1958 interview, for instance, finds him recalling Ortega y Gasset's "remarkable book" The Revolt of the Masses (1929), inveighing against the appeal of the profit-driven media "to the lowest common denominator," and bemoaning "a deterioration . . . in the quality of amusement as it becomes more mass entertainment" (qtd. in Paul 14). In such statements, Eliot added his imprimatur—which carried, to say the least, considerable authority—to a view of contemporary culture that had become the centerpiece of an extraordinary critical consensus. Nonetheless, the Eliot of the mass-culture critique cannot be taken to represent the whole or the essential Eliot without ignoring a good deal else in his poetry and criticism. While Eliot must be held partly responsible for the mythology surrounding his cultural outlook, we will have to look to outside forces as well if we are to understand fully how that mythology took hold.

GENESIS OF A MYTH

The evidence suggests that the familiar representation of Eliot as the unalloyed champion of elite culture was already fixed in the minds of both supporters and adversaries before 1930, and for a number of reasons. First, there was the obscurity and the obvious erudition of his poetry, often perceived as a deliberate attempt to exclude the "ordinary reader" out of snobbery.[15] Second, there was his expatriatism, which, particularly for U.S. readers, aligned him with European high culture—with, in Harriet Monroe's words, "old things, the old ways, in literature, art and life" (212)—against "America" and the cultural developments associated with it. Third, there was the disgust for material existence and ordinary experience detectable throughout his poetry, which associated Eliot with the mind over and against the senses, and reinforced accusations of excessive "intellectualism." Fourth, and closely related, was Eliot's general kulturpessimismus, a worldview generally associated in his time with a dislike and resentment of popular culture. And finally, there was Eliot's early prose, which, even when not defiantly aestheticist, delved with its steadfastly "literary" focus, its emphasis on "tradition," and its impeccable detachment into matters redolent of the ivory tower.

Each of these causes for blame was just as often, with a slight shift of terms, singled out for praise, without any real challenge to the underlying characterization of Eliot or his work. Even those early advocates who disputed the charge of willful obscurity, for example, rarely suggested that a work like The Waste Land might someday speak to anything beyond a coterie audience.[16] On the contrary, as G. W. Stonier noted in 1933, such phrases as

"Eliot is an exacting writer" and "he makes no concessions to the reader" were among the favorite commendations of Eliot's adherents (141). The tendency of enthusiasts to embrace Eliot's elitism while ignoring the many factors that complicated or mitigated it only helped to stiffen his reputation.

Once the image of Eliot as a cultural purist had formed, it proved quite durable. As clearly as Eliot announced his own dissatisfaction with strictly "literary" criticism in the late twenties, for example, his critics were remarkably slow to recognize the evolution of his concerns. Even Edmund Wilson, one of Eliot's most perceptive readers, was protesting in 1931 that Eliot's criticism sought "to impose upon us a conception of poetry as some sort of pure and rare aesthetic essence with no relation to any of the practical human uses for which, for some reason never explained, only the technique of prose is appropriate" (*Axel's Castle* 118–19). Despite its once "salutary effect," Eliot's "anti-Romantic reaction" was now "leading finally into pedantry and into a futile aestheticism" (122). This was three years after Eliot's 1928 preface to *The Sacred Wood* spoke of his current project as "the relation of poetry to the spiritual and social life of its time and of other times" (viii), and a full nine years after the appearance of Eliot's "London Letters" in the *Dial*.

Such persistence of vision appears less surprising when one considers how rapidly Eliot had been if not canonized then at least anointed as leader of a movement. As early as 1920, Louis Untermeyer could say that Eliot "threatened at the age of thirty-one to take on the proportions of a myth" ("Irony" 126). And the gist of that "myth" is well summed up by the reference in a 1927 article to "the whole intellectualist movement which Mr. Eliot represents both for England and for America" ("Literature and Tradition"). Conceptions of such a figure do not change easily. The name "T. S. Eliot" had come rapidly to stand for high intellect and high taste, and nothing that the mortal Eliot did or said was likely to alter that.

Even Eliot's friends and associates misconstrued him. In 1942, for instance, when Martin Browne and Ronald Duncan discussed the idea of producing a revue to be written by Duncan, Eliot, and Christopher Fry with music by Benjamin Britten, Duncan told Browne: "You can count on me, but I can't imagine Possum unbending that much, though *Sweeney* [*Agonistes*] proves he could write it." When the proposal was brought to Eliot, he responded enthusiastically, to the surprise of the other collaborators—even Browne, who, as producer of *The Rock*, ought to have known better (Duncan 171).[17] Gilbert Seldes, likewise, never noticed the strain of agreement between his own outlook and Eliot's. In his correspondence with Eliot, Seldes was defensive not only about his own contributions to the mass media (via the Hearst syndicate) but even about what he called his "vulgarization of Lysistrata," a modern adaptation of the Greek play (Kammen 165).[18]

Would the author of an "Aristophanic Melodrama" object to Aristophanes on Broadway? Apparently Seldes thought so. In his unpublished memoirs, dictated circa 1965, he cited Eliot as exemplifying one type of critic hostile to the popular arts. Seldes's Eliot sounds more like Clive Bell than like himself: he fears "the destruction of all that is noble and beautiful in mortal life presumably because these things are so fragile, they cannot even bear being admired by the multitude" (qtd. in Kammen 389–90). By this point Seldes was accustomed to reacting against a fetishized Eliot and was no longer even conscientious about it. In *The Great Audience* (1951) he had written of Dwight Macdonald's "Theory of Popular Culture," "T. S. Eliot has said that it is the only position opposed to his own for which he has much respect" (261). If it were so, it was a grievous fault; but Eliot's actual words, from the preface to *Notes towards the Definition of Culture*, were merely, "Mr. Macdonald's theory strikes me as the best *alternative* to my own that I have seen" (CC 83; Eliot's emphasis).

Eliot was lionized by young academics in the 1920s in part because, as Gail McDonald has argued, his critical prose "was telling them what they needed to hear" (180). In *The Sacred Wood*, Eliot set out to establish a new literary criticism "more serious" than the prevailing "impressionistic and 'appreciative'" styles; he made clear by precept and example that literary studies was a "serious business" that had "important consequences for civilization" (McDonald 57–59). Eliot campaigned repeatedly in his early essays for professionalism in both the creation and the study of literature, returning often to the point that "we must learn to take literature seriously" ("Professional"). This goal was to be realized on a scale of which he probably never dreamed. By midcentury, Eliot was revered for having restored to literature a cultural authority that had long been in decline, its prestige usurped by the sciences. Without his direct participation or even his whole-hearted support, Eliot now found himself conscripted as titular leader in the establishment of literary criticism as an academic discipline of which "seriousness" was the mantra.[19]

There were further reasons, in the 1930s and early 1940s, for maintaining the highest possible standards of "seriousness" in literary criticism. During their rise to power, as Gerald Graff points out, the New Critics were still under pressure "to measure up to the institutional criteria" set by the philological "scholars" who remained, at this point, their superiors in the academy, and who frowned on "criticism" as the province of amateurs (145). As the champions of literary modernism, still for the most part an object of academic suspicion and hostility, the New Critics needed all the more earnestly to demonstrate the sobriety of their enterprise.

Beyond these institutional forces, there were other promptings to "seriousness" of even graver consequence. There was, especially, the ideological construction of poetry as a response to social conditions; for The Waste Land, as McDonald has shown, "was appropriated as an artistic triumph over the ruinous vulgarities of modern life":

> The equipoise of irony, ambiguity, paradox—the essential vocabulary of New Criticism—became a synecdoche for artistic transcendence of worldly chaos. The poem, more powerful than the numerous quotidian forces it transcends, became the home of the sacred, the missing scripture of the New Humanist clergy. (193)

Art, so viewed, was a momentous and urgent matter, and criticism a serious business indeed. No wonder, then, that the Eliot who seemed significant to his midcentury admirers was the solid traditionalist who addressed himself with great intensity and near-scientific precision to the study of text and culture, rather than the indeterminate, culturally ambiguous character whose shifting outlines we have been tracing in this book. Popular culture of course formed a part of the "ruinous vulgarities" that the well-wrought artwork was supposed to transcend. What could a professional critic, addressed to the "artistic transcendence of worldly chaos," have to do with the "Shakespearian Rag" but to ironize it? And so, then, must Eliot, who, if he was to be the tutelary god of the new regime, had to be assimilated to its values.

And thus Eliot, as both critic and poet, was domesticated by the academic critical machine he himself had done so much to prime—a process noted by at least a few observers at the time. G. W. Stonier remarked that where Eliot's poetry had once been "acclaimed as revolutionary, surprising, odd," by 1933 it was "the classicism, the detachment and formality of Eliot's thought and expression, that [was] emphasized":

> He appears now as the *poet of tradition*, each word is answerable for in some earlier context, the stones of The Waste Land are comfortably cemented on to the edifice of the world's literature. (144–45)

And John Berryman wrote perspicaciously in 1948 of "a certain desire in the universities to disinfect Mr. Eliot by ignoring his disorderly and animating associations" (826). Though much of the ossifying of Eliot's reputation may be attributed to the needs and goals of his critics, a further observation of Berryman's reminds us again how Eliot collaborated in his own taming. In the "pious exegetical studies" of his contemporaries, Berryman noted, "Eliot is found 'unified' and 'impersonal' everywhere, unutterably 'traditional,' and so on, all his favorite commendations" (828).

From a post–New Critical point of view, the poetic "disinfection" that Berryman and Stonier observed is seen nowhere more clearly than in the reception history of The Waste Land. As Ruth Nevo argues in "The Waste Land: Ur-

Text of Deconstruction," a 1982 essay, the poem is easily read as a work of avant-garde experimentation that in many ways anticipates poststructuralist themes and strategies:

> It is totally, radically nonintegrative and antidiscursive, its parts connected by neither causes, effects, parallelism, nor antithesis. It is a cinematographic mélange or montage of glimpses, gestures, images, echoes, voices, phrases, memories, fragments of speech, song, quotation, appearances, and disappearances. (98)

Nevo sees the poem's "disunification, or desedimentation, or dissemination" as its raison d'être (97). Along similar lines, Helen Vendler has more recently found in The Waste Land "the successful prototype of the homeless postmodernist assemblage" (161). And Harriet Davidson has shown that the poem thematizes in its almost every detail a conflict between psychocultural impulses that she labels the "proper" and the "improper": on the one hand, "its respect for tradition, and its recoil from the chaos of life"; on the other hand, its "fascination with mutation, degradation, and fragmentation" (122). The poem's strength, for Davidson as for Nevo, derives from its refusal to resolve the resulting tensions. Both critics find it unfortunate that criticism of the poem, over the years, has tended to efface its more disruptive and eclectic elements. The Waste Land, as Nevo writes, "exploded upon the world with an effect of total incomprehension"; yet "[i]n the heyday of New Criticism it was customary to attempt to unify" the poem (96–97). Without denying the achievement of the important readings of Cleanth Brooks and others, which made sense of The Waste Land for countless readers and ensured the poem's position as one of the key texts of its century, she regrets the multiplication of "recuperative strategies" that have undermined the fundamental radical indeterminacy of the poem (100). Davidson similarly explains:

> Early New Critical readings of the poem canonized the poem as the exemplar (even origin) of a kind of high modernism that powerfully depicts and rejects modern life, valorizing myth over history, spatial form over time, an orderly past over a chaotic present, and the transcendence of art over the pain of life—what I would call the proper over the improper. (123)

Later critics from Terry Eagleton to Sandra Gilbert, she adds, have tended to accept this influential reading, dismissing The Waste Land, as a result, as a "monolithic representative of the long dominant New Critical values" (123).[20]

Although Davidson does not specifically mention popular culture, its inclusion alongside the more traditional, scholarly, and esoteric elements of

The Waste Land clearly violates conventional boundaries and constitutes in it-self a powerful "impropriety" in Davidson's sense. Only recently, though, have critics been able to perceive again what made *The Waste Land* shocking for its first readers, who confronted the poem without the critical apparatus that later made the confrontation safe. As Alex Zwerdling observes:

> A poet of Eliot's generation should have subordinated "foreign" works to the native tradition, recent writing to the canon, popular to high culture. But he denies primacy to any of these dispensations. The vitality of the poem owes much to his refusal to honor the expected hierarchy. Cross-cutting increases the instability, for example in the leap from Shake-speare's *Tempest* to a popular song. . . . Or the jump in the opposite direction, from the drunken farewells of the characters in the pub scene, to Ophelia's last words. (296–97)

There was indeed a good deal more of this particular shock in the uncut drafts of *The Waste Land*, and Eliot, who made or acceded to the revisions that in effect "tame[d] some of the unruliness of the poem"—including the publication of the Notes—is as responsible as anyone for setting the course of its reception (Davidson 124). Yet the "vitality" that Zwerdling recognizes survives in the finished poem, if only we do not try to make it disappear.

> O the moon shone bright on Mrs. Porter
> And on her daughter
> They wash their feet in soda water
> Et O ces voix d'enfants, chantant dans la coupole!
>
> (CPP 43)

The effect of such a "leap" across cultures and levels of culture, as Vendler comments, is "thrilling," with a peculiar frisson that is "not available in English poetry before Eliot" (150).

Where Eliot seemed least explicable to the apostles of seriousness was, naturally, in his persistence with the theater, and particularly in his perverse determination to write a popular comedy. There was no alternative for crit-icism but to write off the plays as a group, and to neglect them individually in proportion to their apparent lack of seriousness. *Murder in the Cathedral* could be readily accepted as the token drama in the Eliot canon; *The Family Reunion* was a pardonable excrescence of *Four Quartets*; the later plays were trifles, *The Rock* and *Sweeney Agonistes* practically unmentionable. Excepting Hugh Kenner's *Invisible Poet*, midcentury criticism stubbornly upheld Eliot's "seriousness" in the teeth of his plays, the central creative project of his last twenty-five years. To William Barrett, the reception of *The Cocktail Party* seemed nothing less than a paradox: "on the one hand, the play seems to have been carried to a critical and commercial success by the author's name, but on the other hand seems to be finally approved of by the standards of Broadway, which are hardly those of Eliot" (354). Never, it seems, the twain shall meet. D. G. Bridson made even shorter work of *Sweeney*, suggesting that as "a man of high seriousness," Eliot was simply out of his element. Joyce, in *Ulysses*, might have his Aristophanic moods; but "an Aristophanic melodrama by Mr. Eliot . . . ! [*sic*] Sooner a parody of the Sermon on the Mount by St. Thomas Aquinas!"

There were other ways, too, in which Eliot made his own adoption as an exalted institution difficult. He repeatedly voiced skepticism about the "use" of poetry in the modern age, and his commitment to poetry (except as a medium for drama) appeared increasingly qualified. He continually held at arm's length the university communities that so fervently honored him, retaining his employment as publisher and editor when he could have accepted any number of academic sinecures, and taking occasional potshots at academic criticism, and formalist approaches specifically, in his late essays.[21] Inconveniently, he even disapproved of modern poetry, including his own, as a classroom subject.[22] Despite his influential call for more "professional standards" in criticism, the absorption of the literary world into the academic was not, as Frank Lentricchia has remarked, what Eliot had in mind: "As the keeper of what are called canonical texts, the university has become what Eliot would never have approved of for his idea of a healthy society: the cordoned-off preserver of literary culture, the institution that unavoidably puts at the margin what it preserves" (268). But the living Eliot with his messy views was no match for his crystalline legend: it was the Eliot selectively reconstructed by his followers who counted.

For a time, the Eliot legend served virtually everyone's purposes. The solidifying intellectual consensus on cultural hierarchy made Eliot its honorific captain, a human embodiment of legitimate culture standing fast against the onrushing tide of totalitarian mass culture. Even midcentury leftists, who had no use for Eliot's politics, found him indispensable as an emblem of high art at the pinnacle of its purity.[23] For Clement Greenberg, kitsch has triumphed in a culture where "Eddie Guest and the Indian Love Lyrics are more poetic than T. S. Eliot and Shakespeare" (106). Greenberg opens his seminal 1946 essay "Avant-Garde and Kitsch" with the seeming paradox that "One and the same civilization produces simultaneously two such different things as a poem by T. S. Eliot and a Tin Pan Alley song." "[W]hat perspective of culture," he wonders, "is large enough to enable us to situate them in an enlightening relation to each other?" (98). At almost the same moment and at the other end of the political spectrum, Cleanth Brooks was asking in *The Well-Wrought Urn* (1947): "For what is the sensibility of our age? . . . Do we respond to T. S. Eliot, [or] Dashiell Hammett?" (232). The irony of the examples chosen by Greenberg and Brooks for contrast with Eliot is entirely unconscious: neither man could see that the distinctive excellence of Eliot's work owed a great deal to the popular song and detective fiction to which it was supposed to furnish the ultimate contrast.

The interviews Eliot gave after the Second World War show vividly how the mantle of *defensor fidei* was pressed upon him, and how, conflicted as ever, he managed both to accept and to chafe at it. In 1959, for instance, Donald Hall cited two passages from Eliot's essays before asking whether the standardization of English speech by the mass media made "the problem of the poet and his relationship to common speech more difficult." Eliot's half-hearted acquiescence—"You've raised a very good point there"—was insufficient to satisfy his interviewer, who replied, "I wanted *you* to make the point." "Yes," Eliot observed, "but you wanted the point to be made." Having caught the interviewer at his game, Eliot then amiably agreed to "take the responsibility of making it" by restating Hall's point (108).[24]

Nothing, however, documents the determination of the midcentury cultural consensus to bend Eliot to its own purposes quite like Eliot's 1961 interview with Tom Greenwell of the *Yorkshire Post* ("Talking Freely").[25] The core of the interview focused on one of Eliot's long-time favorite topics, which Greenwell raised by asking, "What do you feel to be the function of poetry?" This did not, by itself, appear to be a leading question, and Eliot answered it as he had many times before: "The function of poetry is to give pleasure." He added that such pleasure was not mere gratification, but "an enhancement of life [and] an enlargement of our sensibility."

Greenwell, who had apparently been expecting a quite different answer, was not mollified by this explanation. "But in your own works," he replied, "you don't strictly aim at being read for pleasure?"

"Don't I?" Eliot shot back, before conceding, "Certainly not 'strictly'!"

"I am sure you don't think primarily in terms of entertainment," Greenwell insisted.

"Well," Eliot agreed, "in my non-dramatic poetry I think primarily in terms of something I want to say. . . . But, of course, poetry must entertain or it won't be read."

The association of poetry with entertainment was evidently not something that Greenwell could let stand, and the interviewer now began to quarrel with his subject. "The fact that it entertains may be quite incidental."

"It is necessary, surely?"

"But this is not the object?"

"A piece of music that nobody wanted to hear," Eliot countered, "would rather fail of its purpose, wouldn't it?"

"But the idea of entertaining the public is not the thing that stimulates you to write?"

Eliot now made another attempt to conciliate his interviewer. "No, it's not organised like a Music Hall turn, certainly. I think that what stimulates me to write a poem is that I have something inside me that I want to get rid of. It is almost a kind of defecation, if you like." He then tried to deflect the conversation slightly by remarking that in poetry one seldom "knows exactly what one wants to say, until one has said it."

Surprisingly, Greenwell refused to accept Eliot's olive branch, overlooking both the uncontroversial point about authorial intention and the unappetizing analogy between writing and excretion to return to the earlier issue, which, clearly, continued to rankle. "But that thing inside you is not the need nor the desire to entertain?"

Eliot held his ground and continued to feint. "No, no, it isn't. But, at the same time, unless a poet feels that what he gets out is going to convey something, or mean something to others, then he hasn't really got it out. It's got to be in such a form that other people can take it."

Sensing that he now had Eliot nearly at the point of saying something that might finally lay to rest the notion of poetry as entertainment, Greenwell persisted, "But you yourself don't make many concessions to the people who want to be entertained." And in case this flattery, elevating Eliot over those people (evidently a contemptible sort) were insufficient, he added gratuitously, "Rather like Donne, perhaps."[26]

If not prepared to withdraw his previous assertions, Eliot was at least ready to grant that a writer was no panderer: "I don't believe any good poet makes concessions in that way. Certainly not in non-dramatic poetry, because I think that is introducing another element into it which would be irrelevant."[27] That said, the interview was finally permitted to pass on to another subject.

One senses in this passage that Greenwell's expectations of Eliot were based very little on an acquaintance with Eliot's criticism—which, as we have seen, repeatedly stresses a connection between poetry and "entertainment" or "amusement"—and much more on a broad conception of who Eliot was and what he represented.[28] Whatever Greenwell himself considered to be the function of poetry, his creed obviously held poetry at a very safe remove from anything smacking of "entertainment." Clearly he believed that Eliot shared his commonplace notion of art as keeping its austere distance from such lowbrow appetites; and like Hall and many others, he looked to Eliot for some memorable statement of his own view.[29] When Eliot not only failed to produce such an endorsement but came out fully on the "wrong" side of the argument, Greenwell may well have suspected that Old Possum was having a pull at his leg.[30] Everyone knew, after all, that T. S. Eliot was the great champion of Art in its last stand against popular culture. Unhappily for Greenwell, his efforts to badger Eliot into playing this role backfired. The editor of the *Yorkshire Post*, who pulled out Eliot's phrase "Poetry Must Entertain" and splashed it in bold type across the middle of the interview, stretching nearly all the way across the page, saw all too clearly where the story lay.

CLASS, CULTURE, KIPLING

It was Eliot's extended social criticism in *The Idea of a Christian Society* (1940) and *Notes towards the Definition of Culture* (1948) that confirmed his supposed cultural antipopulism once and for all. Yet his views on popular culture even in these frankly conservative texts does not embarrass the portrait I have been sketching of a reflectively ambivalent and usable Eliot. I will focus here on *Notes towards the Definition of Culture*, which bears most directly on the issues we have been considering. The crucial tenet for our purposes is Eliot's starting point in the book: his rejection of the notion that culture is "the property of a small section of society." From here Eliot struggles mightily, though with uneven success, to leave behind the narrow, Arnoldian equation of culture with the fine arts and to embrace the broader, modern, sociological definition of culture as "all the characteristic activities and interests of a people" (104).[31] The consequences of this new conception are less democratic, for Eliot, than one might suppose. From the premise that "[t]he primary channel of transmission of culture is the family," Eliot goes on to argue that a culturally "vigorous" society of any complexity demands the maintenance of a class structure (115–17); a culture, if it is to survive, requires "groups of families persisting, from generation to generation, each in the same way of life" (121–22).

Though defined in the first place by their political (i.e., power) relations, the social classes are distinguished also by their degree of "consciousness," with citizens at the lower levels following out the cultural patterns of their class unselfconsciously, and those at the higher levels more critically aware of their relation to their culture, society, and history (110–11). In a "healthy" society, the high culture (i.e., the "more conscious" level) develops out of the popular culture organically, and, in turn, "enriches" the "lower levels"; "thus the movement of culture would proceed in a kind of cycle, each class nourishing the others" (110). It follows that a culture, as a whole, is the product and property of the entire population, but also that the direct participation of each stratum will be confined, for the most part, to its own cultural level (111).

Clearly, much of this argument exists in utero even in Eliot's essays of the twenties. The statement in "Marianne Moore" that "fine art is the refinement, not the antithesis, of popular art," for instance, is preceded by a political analogy: a "real aristocracy," Eliot asserts, "is of the same blood as the people over whom it rules: a real aristocracy is not a Baltenland aristocracy of foreign race" (395). The dependent relationship between fine art and popular culture posited here, in 1923, reappears, similarly politicized, in Notes:

> Error creeps in again and again through our tendency to think of culture as group culture exclusively, the culture of the "cultured" classes and élites. We then proceed to think of the humbler part of society as having culture only in so far as it participates in this superior and more conscious culture. To treat the "uneducated" mass of the popular as we might treat some innocent tribe of savages to whom we are impelled to deliver the true faith, is to encourage them to neglect or despise that culture which they should possess and from which the more conscious part of culture draws vitality. (CC 183–84)

As such passages attest, Eliot continues to recognize that popular culture has independent value, and that sophistication, whether labeled "refinement" or "consciousness," is not a self-evident marker of superiority.[32] The notion that the "more conscious part of culture" takes its "vitality" from the popular culture echoes "Marianne Moore" at a quarter century's remove. But the incidental politics of the "Moore" essay—its casual approbation of "real" aristocracy rooted in the same stock as its peons—has calcified, in the later work, into an argument that class distinction must be preserved because Eliot cannot imagine that culture at any level can exist without it.

Although Eliot speaks in Notes of a reciprocal relation—a symbiotic "cycle" of mutual nourishment—among the different levels of culture, his characterization of the social classes seems to work against such an understanding. Since the lower cultural levels are by definition unconscious, it seems inevitable that any development of the national or common culture will trickle down from the top, where self-criticism, innovation, and influence from outside the nation, which Eliot always prizes, are possible. The lower class that Eliot conceptualizes seems quiescent in its response to life and passive in the acceptance of its culture, and in both these respects, Eliot's vision appears to be rooted in and limited by the Cockney myth of the music-hall stage.

The class structure that Eliot advocates is both stable and permeable: "each class should have constant additions and defections; the classes, while remaining distinct, should be able to mix freely; and they should all have a community of culture with each other which will give them something in common, more fundamental than the community which each class has with its counterpart in another society" (123–24). His insistence on class distinction, in other words, is paired with an insistence on the continuity of culture across class boundaries: "it is only by an overlapping and sharing of interests, by participation and mutual appreciation, that the cohesion necessary for culture can obtain" (CC 96). Interestingly, although he considers the ideal of a classless society a liberal folly, Eliot reserves the term "cultural disintegration" not for situations where class boundaries have broken down but for those in which they have become impassable. In *The Use of Poetry and the Use of Criticism*, he had argued that a popular dramatic poetry "could cut across all the present stratifications of public taste—stratifications which are perhaps a sign of social disintegration" (146). And *Notes* defines "cultural disintegration"—"the most radical disintegration that a society can suffer," the disintegration that is "the most serious and the most difficult to repair"—as arising "when two or more strata so separate that these become in effect distinct cultures" (98). Eliot's ideal society is stratified, but the parts are never quite separate as the fingers.[33] There is an obvious analogy in this argument to Eliot's previous writing on the cultural divide, which, as we have seen, had recognized the historical artificiality of the received high-low binary without quite liberating itself from its grasp. In this respect Eliot's earlier thinking can be said to conform to one view repeatedly expressed in the "advanced" periodicals of the 1920s: that an ideal culture is "universal throughout the society but divided into levels of quality that are . . . openly differentiated from each other" (Denney 168). Over time, as Eliot worked to systematize his ideas in a sociopolitical program, his notion of cultural strata grew more emphatic and inflexible, so that when his critical oeuvre as a whole is interpreted (as it often is) in light of the more sustained later works, he appears more predictably conservative than he actually was.

This hardening of position becomes particularly noticeable when Eliot discusses the subject of education. Since members of the subordinate classes do not need to be fully "conscious"—since making them so would, in fact, undermine their class's relatively "unconscious" culture—Eliot inveighs against "the dogma of equal opportunity" in education (CC 180). For Eliot, the left-liberal argument that "in the society of the future the culture which has been in the possession of the few must be put at the disposal of everybody" is a fallacy dependent on the older notion of culture, which excludes the popular and denies it intrinsic value (105). It is not only the popular culture, however, that is threatened by the universalizing of education; Eliot adds that "to aim to make everyone share in the appreciation of the fruits of the more conscious part of culture is to adulterate and cheapen what you give" (184)—an assertion that seems to thrust the higher or "more conscious" level of culture right back onto its pedestal.

Eliot's system of cultural "levels" that correspond closely to social classes impels such conclusions in *Notes towards the Definition of Culture*. And indeed, Eliot had long voiced a dour skepticism toward the expansion of higher education, which imperiled the traditional classical education he himself had received and which he always valued. Yet Eliot had once, and not long before, espoused a much more fluid relation between culture and audience. He had remarked in 1940, for example, on the impossibility of classifying readers into "those who read for mere pastime and those who read for information and those who read in order to enjoy literary art"; every reader reads for different purposes at different times (qtd. in Hawkins, "Writer" 773). And in 1941 he had argued, similarly, that "[t]he audience for the more highly developed, even for the more esoteric kinds of poetry is recruited from every level," and that "the composition of this audience has . . . no relation to any social and economic stratification of society" ("Rudyard Kipling" 232). The audience for popular forms like music hall, detective fiction, or ballads, meanwhile, quite obviously cut across any social classification one could suggest. This is all consonant with Eliot's earlier conception of the "large and miscellaneous" audience he desired in *The Use of Poetry and the Use of Criticism*. In *Notes*, Eliot tries to make space for a "miscellaneous" public for high culture by positing the need for an independent intellectual elite to supplement the social classes. He is finally content, however, to observe that such an elite will, in all likelihood, draw its membership almost entirely from the dominant class (114–15).

In short, the later Eliot of *Notes* "does not," as Terry Eagleton puts it, "believe that more than a small minority can ever be . . . capable of subtle and complex response" ("Eliot" 281). And the composition of that "small minority" appears far less various in *Notes* than it had in the Eliot of ten or twenty years before. In *Notes*, a society's high culture is, fairly unproblematically, the culture of its dominant economic class. Eliot's conception of cultural levels corresponding to social classes is fundamentally too simple a metaphor to describe any actual society of the present or future.[34] It also fails to tally with Eliot's own experiences, either of his university extension students early on, or of his audiences for *The Rock* and *Murder in the Cathedral* much later.

Although Eliot's cultural solution in *Notes*—essentially to shore up the fragments of a class structure that was already, as he understood, failing—is uncompelling, his position seems to me less duplicitous than it does to certain recent critics who believe that Eliot pleads a concern for "culture" as an excuse for political reaction. One might rather suggest, I think, with still better reason, that it is his concern for culture, however well or ill placed, that explains much of Eliot's politics. In any case, distress over the loss of subcultural difference in the face of economic and social convergence is hardly a right-wing monopoly.[35]

In registering a stepped-up alarm over "mass culture" in his late works; in reacting impulsively against new developments such as television; and in nurturing a confidently pessimistic view of the future of *all* culture in a mass society, Eliot had plenty of company at midcentury, when, in the face of totalitarianism, a phobic response to popular culture was intellectual gospel in both Britain and the United States. The degree to which the "serious and grim picture of culture under capitalism" was held in common by thinkers on both the Left and the Right is implicit in T. J. Clark's concise oxymoron, "Eliotic Trotskyism" ("More" 178).[36] This context remembered, Eliot actually seems less doctrinaire on cultural matters than most of his contemporaries, including his own critics on the Left. Harold Laski, for example, critiques Eliot's argument against universal education as follows:

> To train a man to be a "skilled agricultural labourer" does not mean that we waste our energies and our substance if we teach him also to appreciate the beauties of Shakespeare or Dickens, to recognise why Goya was a greater artist than W. P. Frith, to realise that the music of Bach and Beethoven can bring things into his life more precious than he will find in the music of Sousa or George Gershwin, to explain to him at least in large outline, what science is, and how it has developed, and to give him some sense of the movement of world-history, not least of the place of his own country in that movement. (129)

No irony is intended here in the choice of Shakespeare and Dickens to represent the cultural summits that popular literature will never attain. Laski manages only to replace Eliot's social elitism with a cultural elitism of which Eliot himself, even in his late work, usually manages to steer clear.

As a case in point, we may take Eliot's introduction to his anthology *A Choice of Kipling's Verse* (1941), an essay that represents probably his most extended treatment, late or early, of a specific high/low problematic. Writing five years after Kipling's death, Eliot is compelled to defend the older poet, whose reputation had sunk a long way since his 1907 Nobel Prize, and who was now widely dismissed as a crude and fusty versifier. Eliot confronts this indictment by arguing, in the first place, that a writer of verse may still be an artist; it is not only "poetry," narrowly conceived, that has cultural value and consequence. This is a point that Eliot stressed more than once; in a 1940 interview, for example, he suggested that "the writer as artist" appeared not only as poet and novelist but as "the historian, . . . the philosopher, the scientist; even the judge rendering a decision, the chairman writing a company report, the explorer recording his daily observations, or the naval officer recounting an action" (qtd. in Hawkins, "Writer" 774). By limning Kipling as a first-rate "ballad-maker," Eliot is able to contest his classification as an inferior poet, condemned "by reference to poetic criteria which do not apply" to his work ("Rudyard Kipling" 228). He goes on to uphold the ballad itself in terms quite similar to his praise of melodrama fourteen years earlier in "Wilkie Collins and Dickens": the ballad is not merely a primitive form that a developing culture eventually surpasses; it represents, rather, "a permanent level of enjoyment of literature" (231).[37]

Eliot is at pains here to insist that there is no clear boundary between the refined and the unrefined genre: "with Kipling you cannot draw a line beyond which some of the verse becomes 'poetry'" (234). The mutual penetration of the fine art and the popular genre, he suggests, is healthy for both (251). Here—again as in "Wilkie Collins and Dickens"—Eliot wishes to maintain distinctions without the rigid dichotomies that lead an art into decadence.[38] And he declares self-consciously that there is no hierarchy to his categories:

> It should be clear that when I contrast "verse" with "poetry" I am not, in this context, implying a value judgement. I do not mean, here, by verse, the work of a man who would write poetry if he could: I mean by it something which does what "poetry" could not do. The difference which would turn Kipling's verse into poetry, does not represent a failure or deficiency: he knew perfectly well what he was doing; and from his point of view more "poetry" would interfere with his purpose. (251; emphasis Eliot's)

If this is not *entirely* convincing (one wonders, especially, about that italicized "in this context"), its general purport is plainly to affirm the independent value of the popular art. "We sometimes speak," Eliot notes, "as if the writer who is most consciously and painstakingly the 'craftsman' were the most remote from the interests of the ordinary reader, and as if the popular writer were the artless writer. But no writer has ever cared more for the craft of words than Kipling" (234)—a point supported by a careful analysis of "Danny Deever." One groans when such broad-mindedness is spoiled by, for instance, the assertion that "[w]hat is unusual about Kipling's ballads is his singleness of intention in attempting to convey no more to the simple minded than can be taken in on one reading or hearing" (232).

The thrust of Eliot's essay was not lost on his contemporaries, who evidently had some difficulty piecing this Eliot together with the Eliot they thought they knew.[39] For the *New York Times*, Eliot's "enthusiastic introduction to a selection of Kipling's verse" seemed remarkably abberant for a man so often labeled a "high-priest of the most esoteric art for art's sake" (Lehmann 5). Louise Bogan, writing for the *New Yorker*, was candidly perplexed:

> "A Choice of Kipling's Verse Made by T. S. Eliot" is a startling title, both to those who admire Kipling and those who admire Eliot. The juxtaposition of the two writers' names is one which the wildest flight of the imagi-

nation could not have conjured up some years ago.[40] Eliot's remarks, in the long introductory essay to the collection, about the talents of the man he calls "a great verse writer," are, though expressed in the quiet tone of ordered logic, often surprising; they will someday stir up controversy. (76)

The controversy Bogan foresaw never materialized, as his "Kipling," like everything else that is not easily assimilated to Eliot's elitist reputation, soon evaporated into obscurity. Bogan herself clearly had no idea what to make of this text, concluding only that it was "strange" to find Eliot "bending the subtle resources of his intelligence" in such a "hopeless cause" (78). And no wonder, for as the prevailing judgment had it, Kipling represented a stage in the degeneration of high culture. Leavis, for one, expressed the view that by adulterating poetry with popular elements, Kipling had facilitated the decline of Art into advertising ("Mass Civilisation" 23). That T. S. Eliot of all people would defend such a miscreant must have seemed unfathomable. The reality of Eliot's resistance to the near-universal intellectual condemnation of the "lowbrow" was unavailable to Bogan and her contemporaries.

The later Eliot nevertheless ranges himself more than ever as an opponent of aestheticism, seeking to dispel the myth that art arises from a writer's conscious effort to produce an aesthetic object for a limited readership in search of aesthetic experience. A writer, Eliot told Desmond Hawkins,

> always has some other purpose in writing than merely to create "art." . . . And above all I don't want you to think of the literary artist as a man who writes for a select few, either deliberately or because he can't help himself. ("Writer" 773)

Eliot's religious conviction only reinforces his stand against aestheticism. Once an artistic obstacle, the "religion of art" now becomes a secular heresy, and l'art pour l'art an evasion of moral obligation.

At the same time, Eliot tries to carve out a space between purely aesthetic and purely propagandistic conceptions of art, repeating continually during the last thirty years of his life that the writer's "direct duty is to his language, first to preserve, and second to extend and improve" ("Social Function" 20).[41] Poets, especially, contribute a vocabulary of feeling to the common speech, renewing the ability of their language to express the reality of their particular time and place:

> For our language goes on changing; our way of life changes, under the pressure of material changes in our environment in all sorts of ways; and unless we have those few men who combine an exceptional sensibility

with an exceptional power over words, our own ability, not merely to express, but even to feel any but the crudest emotions, will degenerate.[42] ("Social Function" 21)

This position is arguably an updated romanticism, but it never collapses into aestheticism because Eliot consistently presents it in terms of the artist's public responsibility. The development of language, he emphasizes, is a process in which an entire society participates. Though writers of all kinds play the leading role "in preserving, refreshing, and developing the language," they work in a "continuous collaboration" with "everybody who speaks it—a collaboration none the less genuine for most people being unaware of what is going on" (qtd. in Hawkins, "Writer" 774).[43] Thus the "social usefulness" of the writer "goes far beyond the number of readers who consciously appreciate his artistry, which goes beyond the circle of those who read his work at all, which extends even, in time, to those people for whom he becomes merely a name on a public monument" (774).[44] Poetry, in particular, "makes a difference to the speech, to the sensibility, to the lives of all the members of a society, to all the members of the community, to the whole people, whether they read and enjoy poetry or not" ("Social Function" 22).

Lyndall Gordon identifies this "concern for language" as the most admired theme of Eliot's late criticism (Imperfect 490–91). Naturally so, for it offered a vision of writing, and of the writing of poetry most of all, as a noble and consequential public service at a moment of transition, when poets and critics alike felt the need for such justification (McDonald 192). Never mind that Eliot meanwhile continued to maintain that the one really consequential venue for contemporary poetry was the theater: his vision of poetry as a mission was what resonated. It was soon found that Eliot himself provided the best illustration of poetry's cultural significance:

> [Eliot's] influence is not confined to intellectual circles; it has touched the lives and thoughts of many who have only half-understood the poetry and many who have not even read it. . . . [T]he influence of Mr. Eliot has reached an enormous public, filtering down through the work of hundreds of poets, novelists, dramatists, radio-script-writers, journalists and even advertising agents. I have spotted it also in films, dance lyrics, sermons and blurbs. (Nicholson 232)

To whatever extent this may have been true, it is certain that the midcentury writers and critics who appreciated Eliot's perceived support for their own life's work did yeoman's service in propagating Eliot's reputation among the multitude (through a similar trickle-down process) as the granite god of high culture that Cynthia Ozick would later recall. Indeed, one of the many paradoxes of Eliot's career is that it was the austere and aloof elitist, and not the low-comedy or Raymond Chandler enthusiast, that became the public face of his own celebrity. It was, in other words, Eliot at his furthest remove from popular culture who became a popular figure.

MR. ELIOT AND THE CHEESE

In a 1958 essay, Edmund Wilson suggested that there were two persons contained in the mind and body of T. S. Eliot. One was "the author of *The Sacred Wood, The Waste Land, The Cocktail Party,* and other excellent things." The other, whom Wilson dubbed "Mr. Eliot," was

> the public figure, the pillar of British culture, and the remote inscrutable deity who presides over the American academic guild of what its members like to call criticism. The point is that Eliot is a genuine person, whose work is of exceptional interest, but that the public "Mr. Eliot" is a fictional character, a creation of T. S. Eliot's. (Bit 375–6)

As an artist, Wilson argued, Eliot was "essentially a dramatist," and he had become, over time, "an actor in his own person," developing his "public self as a theatrical character, or characters" (382–83). Wilson had in fact noticed the qualities of the "actor" and "self-invented character" in Eliot as early as 1933 (*Letters* 203). And by 1958 "Mr. Eliot" had developed a sizable repertoire of roles: the "Anglican clergyman"; the "formidable professor"; "Dr. Johnson," the canonizer and arbiter of taste; the "genteel Bostonian"; "Old Possum," the Eliot who "plays dead but . . . indulges his private ribaldry"; "the Christian," an "apologetic humble person"; and finally the "oracle," who pronounces on contemporary social problems, aware that "every tiny poem, every slender pamphlet of an essay that he drops into the literary world, will be received with profound respect and read with devoted attention" (Bit 383–84).[45]

Wilson's supposition of a singular authentic Eliot behind the mask, or masks, now appears oversimple; one might rather suggest that all of these personas, including what Wilson calls the "genuine person," were elements in the complex subject that was T. S. Eliot and played their part in authoring Eliot's works.[46] The *Four Quartets,* for example, would be inaudible without the contributory voices of the "Anglican clergyman," the "formidable professor," and "the Christian," at the very least. Eliot was a compulsive self-fashioner and a deft one, but the selves that he fashioned were not merely facades concealing some shrouded essential self.

Some Eliotic selves more than others, however, were meant for public consumption. And so, for an ever-expanding, less and less exclusive public, it was a particular "Mr. Eliot" who became the familiar, the instantly recognizable figure. Solemn, cerebral, recondite, emphatically decorous and punctilious in all things, Eliot in this aspect was the quintessential high-brow, to such an extent that the imaginary highbrow intellectual began to wear Eliot's face. Eliot certainly overplayed this character; crucially, though, he overplayed it with tongue in cheek. "Mr. Eliot" knew, and let you know he knew, that he carried his seriousness to the point of absurdity. It was in this way that Eliot turned himself, as the human incarnation of high culture, into a species of popular culture. He was almost, one might say, a caricature from the music-hall stage.

A series of short columns in the New Yorker suggests that even in 1932–33, during his temporary return to the United States, Eliot's reputation for extreme decorum and abstruseness could make him an object of bemused affection and thus a sort of cultural treasure, both estimable and amusing. Reporting on Eliot's embarrassed, apologetic encounters with Harvard students ("Tea") and the bewilderment he inspired in children ("Error") and working folk ("Poet and Janitor"), the New Yorker pieces are able to treat Eliot as fun precisely because he is, both as a person and as a cultural figure, so terribly and self-consciously serious. The reporter was taking his cue from Eliot himself. It was in January 1933, the same month that the New Yorker began to report on his misadventures in Cambridge, that he published his Five-Finger Exercises, containing his self-portrait in the manner of Edward Lear, the "Lines for Cuscuscaraway and Mirza Murad Ali Beg," beginning:

> How unpleasant to meet Mr. Eliot!
> With his features of clerical cut,
> And his brow so grim
> And his mouth so prim
> And his conversation, so nicely
> Restricted to What Precisely
> And If and Perhaps and But.

(CPP 93)

This persona, Eliot's face of celebrity, would serve him well for the remaining thirty-two years of his life: it offered him a kind of privacy screen behind which his growing public, enjoying the spectacle before them, would not wish to pry. A choice subject of entertaining squibs in the middlebrow press, Eliot was presented, and presented himself, as quirky and comically inscrutable, with a touch of somewhat affected, or at least exaggerated, melancholy.[47] His authority and importance were taken for granted; and since his thoughts were assumed to be too deep for mere mortals to fathom, it was the seriocomic exterior that reporters latched on to. Eliot's very obscurity, which had put off so many of his early readers, thus became, in time, a part of his lovable legend. It helped immeasurably that Eliot so clearly enjoyed being "Mr. Eliot"—that Time could report:

He gave reticent teas, at which young Harvard intellectuals silently watched the silent poet eat cake. Eliot seemed to enjoy flaunting his English ways: "I tend," said he, "to fall asleep in club armchairs, but I believe my brain works as well as ever, whatever that is, after I have had my tea." ("Tom to T.S.")

The element of self-mockery in the "Mr. Eliot" persona undercut even as it preserved his authority, and welcomed outsiders who would otherwise have found Eliot incomprehensible or intimidating to look on him with a knowing smile. Without this element, it is inconceivable that this recondite figure, whatever the extent of his critical esteem, should have developed into an international superstar.

"Mr. Eliot" could become a popular figure in part because he was based on a number of conventional character types: the enigmatic artist, the old fogy, the bookish scholar, the eccentric English gentleman. This last type was as important to Eliot's celebrity as the first. Its specific nature is nowhere more visible than in his 1935 disquisition on cheese. Here, in a letter to the London Times, Eliot offered his support for Sir John Squire's "manly and spirited defence of Stilton cheese" while expressing apprehension toward Squire's proposal for a public monument:

> I do not suggest for a moment that the inventor of Stilton cheese is not worthy of a statue. I only criticize the proposal on the ground of the transitory character of the result. Certainly all the business of public subscriptions, speeches, broadcasts, the wrangling over designs, the eventual unveiling with a military band, and the excellent photography in The Times—this is all exciting indeed. But once a statue is erected, who in this country ever looks at it?

Clearly a "Stiltonian monument" will not do; what is needed, "if cheese is to be brought back to its own in England," is "the formation of a Society for the Preservation of Ancient Cheeses."

> There is a great deal of work which such a society, and its members individually, could do. For instance, one of its first efforts should be to come to terms, by every possible persuasion, with the potteries which supply those dishes with three compartments, one for little biscuits, one for pats of butter, and one for little cubes of gorgonzola, so called. The production of these dishes could be stopped by a powerful organization of cheese-eaters. Also troops of members should visit all the hotels and inns in Gloucestershire, demanding Double Gloster [sic]. (On two occasions I have had to add the explanation: "it is a kind of cheese.")

Having gone on to assert briefly the inferiority of "even the finest Stilton" to "the noble Old Cheshire when in prime condition," the letter ends by acknowledging that "this is no time for disputes between the eaters of English cheese," for "the situation is too precarious." In this concentrated performance, Eliot caricatures a venerable tradition of English cultural protection movements (we saw in chapter 3 his skepticism toward Cecil Sharp's folk revivalism) as well as his own investment in such echt-British traditions as music hall, Sherlock Holmes, gentlemen's clubs, and the rolled umbrella.[48] Eliot's knowingly overwrought oddness was a quintessentially English parody of Englishness.

Numerous anecdotes involving cheese are recounted in the memoirs of Eliot's friends and acquaintances. Like Hugh Kenner's narrative describing the poet's interrogation of an unidentifiable "anonymous cheese" at the Garrick Club, all of these evoke Eliot's tone of ostentatious gravity—his deadpan, paradoxically, the one unmistakable sign of his facetiousness. "What was peculiar to TSE in this sort," wrote I. A. Richards, "was the delicately perceptible trace, the ghostly flavor of irony which hung about his manner as though he were preparing a parody"—as when Eliot declined Richards's invitation to visit with him in Peking in 1929 on the grounds that he did "not care to visit any country which has no native cheese" (6).[49] Eliot had himself once suggested that "whenever any one is aware of himself as acting, something like a sense of humour is present" ("'Rhetoric'" 29). This sense of humor, or something like one, joined with Eliot's prominence as poet and critic to make possible T. S. Eliot, the phenomenon.

The influence of Eliot's character on his reputation, naturally, has diminished steadily since his death. Readers of Eliot today do not stand in the shadow of a master's unassailable eminence and, to an extent unimaginable a half-century ago, are not cognizant of the once-conspicuous personality. It would be naive, however, to conclude that "Mr. Eliot," even if he has relinquished direct control over Eliot's reception, has no lingering effect on "our" Eliot. The very qualities of high seriousness, formality, and measured control that once made Eliot the "perfect icon of high culture" for the New Critics and their generation later helped to make him, as McDonald has shown, "a large and inviting target for assaults on the axiology of high culture" (203). Eliot's exceedingly "proper" public persona called forth and lent credence to readings of his poems that foregrounded their traditionalism, structural unity, classicism, and erudition, downplaying their formal instability, psychological disruption, linguistic experimentation, sexual transgressiveness, and interrogation of cultural hierarchies. In Davidson's terms, "Mr. Eliot" authorized a construction of Eliot's work that emphasized its "propriety" and left its "impropriety" buried for decades (124–25).

One specific casualty of "Mr. Eliot's" combination of sobriety and irony, so far as critical perception is concerned, is Eliot's productive engagement with popular culture. For once it is perceived as a facet of the "Mr. Eliot" persona, Eliot's attachment to various popular forms is easily reduced to whimsy—a requisite peculiarity of the part he is playing. Detective fiction, vaudeville, popular song, music-hall comedy, even playwriting, need be taken no more seriously than Stilton cheese; such caprices are never to be understood as genuine commitments. Eliot's "delighted and highly critical immersion" in, for instance, a popular vaudeville act, the "Two Black Crows," struck Richards as merely another instance of his self-parodic "pose," comparable with his pretense on one occasion to be gravely preoccupied "with the exactly right temperature at which hot cross buns should be served" (6). Eliot, after all, was the "literary conscience of an era," a cultural stalwart regularly praised for maintaining "critical standards" in a vulgar age.[50] His oft-proclaimed love for detective fiction was therefore, to his contemporaries, a peccadillo, at best charming, at worst an irritating flaw in an otherwise sterling character. No one seems to have considered the possibility that Eliot's attitude toward the cultural divide might really be more flexible than the intellectual consensus of the time considered acceptable.

For the same reason, Eliot's lighter poems inspired only indifference or impatience in most of his critics, as when Rolphe Humphries singled out the two Edward Lear variations in *Five-Finger Exercises* as "ghastly incongruous" and "unworthy of one who may aspire to saintliness" (357).[51] (It was perhaps fortunate that Humphries knew nothing of Eliot's cruder verses, such as the lyric, contemporaneous with the *Five-Finger Exercises*, about a fart that shattered some stained-glass windows.[52]) *Old Possum's Book of Practical Cats* met with similar embarrassment. John Holmes, for one, thought it "strange" that "the desperately profound poet of despair" should have produced such work; he expressed doubt that Eliot had "the right to publish a playful book about cats, or a book playful about anything"; and he wished that its issuance had been "prevented" (15). Such work was an unseemly departure from the standard of seriousness and high purpose that Eliot was presumed to have set for himself, and a critic could render Eliot friendliest service by minimizing it, or by overlooking it altogether. Even today, and despite the Lloyd Webber musical, references to the *Cats* poems are exceedingly rare in the criticism.[53] Gordon's seven-hundred-page biography contains no reference to the *Five-Finger Exercises* (or to Edward Lear) and mentions the *Cats* poems only glancingly, to illustrate Eliot's relationship with their original young recipients.

CITIZENSHIP AND CELEBRITY: *FOUR QUARTETS*

Left to his own devices in 1939, after *The Family Reunion* ended its short, unhappy run, Eliot would have immediately begun work on a new play. Ironi-

cally, the Second World War, by banishing any plans he may have been forming for the stage, forced Eliot to channel his energies into poetry instead and
thus to produce what both he and many of his critics have considered his
greatest work, the Four Quartets (Paul 19; Ackroyd 254). Because, as we know,
Eliot had decided long before that he was unwilling to rest on the "highbrow" side of the cultural divide between poetry and the popular genres,
his crowning achievement lay, generically speaking, far to the side of the career path on which he had consciously embarked. A further irony, therefore,
lies in the fact that the Quartets then proved (arguably) a more popular work
than most of Eliot's plays. To clarify the place of Four Quartets in Eliot's oeuvre,
to account for their remarkable effect on Eliot's reputation, and to define the
limited senses in which the Quartets should be recognized as "popular" poetry are the important tasks that will bring this study of Eliot and popular
culture nearly to its conclusion.

The "popularity" of Four Quartets is intimately connected with the new
attitude the poems implicitly adopt toward the "lived culture" of Eliot's
neighbors. If Eliot's interest in the popular arts was of long standing, his
reconciliation with popular cultural practices was much slower in coming.
In his 1930 essay on Cyril Tourneur, Eliot speaks of the playwright's
"loathing and disgust of humanity" as a "consummately expressed" yet
"immature" response to life. Tourneur's characters are "spectres projected
from the poet's inner world of nightmare, some horror beyond words."
The keynote of The Revenger's Tragedy is "the loathing and horror of life itself,"
which Eliot calls an "important phase—even, if you like, a mystical experience—in life itself" (166). That such recoil from life and from humanity
can be called a "phase" gestures toward the possibility of redemption, or at
least of maturation. As so often in his essays, Eliot's account of Tourneur offers insight into his own life and career.

The Quartets, as Lyndall Gordon has noted, were "the final stage of a
moral cure," the decisive effort of a naturally aloof, even haughty spirit "to
enter into a sense of community" (Imperfect 436). This personal transformation was matched by a parallel change in Eliot's work—a trajectory especially obvious in his drama, as reviewers of The Rock had first begun to notice.
The same metamorphosis inevitably affected Eliot's remaining poetry,
which became increasingly tied up with his writing of plays. "Burnt Norton," the earliest of the Quartets, had its genesis in lines discarded from Murder in the Cathedral, while "East Coker" shares themes and even phrases with
The Family Reunion. The diction of Eliot's poetry thus gradually converges with
that of his drama, so that by the time Eliot composes the Quartets, any distinction between the language and materials of the two genres has nearly
evaporated (Malamud, Words 90):

Home is where one starts from. As we grow older
The world becomes stranger, the pattern more complicated
Of dead and living.

. . . .

There is a time for the evening under starlight,
A time for the evening under lamplight
(The evening with the photograph album).

(CPP 129)

The Quartets thus challenge the private/public dichotomy that had characterized poetry's difference from drama for Eliot since 1920: they may not be
"applied poetry," yet they do address themselves to an ample readership.
Critic Morton Zabel could observe in 1936, with only "Burnt Norton" to
hand, that Eliot had become "a more patient and explicit—that is, a more
popular—poet," abandoning "cryptic historical reference and erudition"
for a style of "dialectic lucidity." Eliot was "compelled, as churchman and
citizen," Zabel speculated, "toward popularizing and clarifying his language,
even though he has not descended to simplifying his metaphysical vision"
(170). And Eliot himself was conscious of the difference. When Donald Hall
asked him whether he thought that his work, including his poems, had
widened its appeal "from a narrower to a larger audience," Eliot agreed that
it had. His writing for the stage, Eliot thought, had "made a difference to the
writing of the Four Quartets," leading "to a greater simplification of language,"
relative to The Waste Land or Ash-Wednesday, and to a more open, equal, and conversational relationship with his readers (D. Hall 104–05).[54]

Eliot's struggle to purge his ingrained elitism, which had begun even before his conversion, would reach its ethical culmination, if not its aesthetic
high point, in such very late works as The Elder Statesman and "The Cultivation of
Christmas Trees," which are marked by a generous acceptance of common
life and ordinary—including middle-class—experience.[55] The Quartets, however, represent the best and fullest expression of his striving, often in passages
that juxtapose, without condescension, common and mystical experience:

You cannot face it steadily, but this thing is sure,
That time is no healer: the patient is no longer here.
When the train starts, and the passengers are settled
To fruit, periodicals and business letters
(And those who saw them off have left the platform)
Their faces relax from grief into relief,
To the sleepy rhythm of a hundred hours.
Fare forward, travelers! not escaping from the past
Into different lives, or into any future;

> You are not the same people who left that station
> Or who will arrive at any terminus,
> While the narrowing rails slide together behind you.
>
> (CPP 134)

Importantly, Eliot's persona now takes the "tube," eats dinner, prays, ages, fears, and suffers alongside his fellow citizens, and while these experiences do not satisfy his spiritual longings, they are not, like Tiresias's dreadful wanderings in the "Unreal City" of *The Waste Land,* a cause of horror. If the Eliot of *Four Quartets* is not quite Wordsworth's "man speaking to men," he is at least a citizen. His citizenship is even foregrounded, most of all in the moving air raid scenes of "Little Gidding." Gordon documents Eliot's "feeling his way" into the communal mood of a Britain under assault, and into communities of "ordinary people," as he composed this last of his major poems (*Imperfect* 382–84).

The results of Eliot's effort showed in the poems' reception. Like *Murder in the Cathedral,* *Four Quartets* had a peculiar success that, if it was not exactly "popularity," was something more than a succès d'estime. In Britain, the *Quartets* were read, at the time of their publication, as inspirational works that offered strength and solace at the most disheartening moments of the Second World War.[56] The effect of "East Coker," the first of the wartime *Quartets,* was especially notable. The poem sold 12,000 copies and went through five printings in less than a year, and if such numbers seem underwhelming by the standards of popular fiction, perhaps the poem's oft-noted impact can be attributed to the sort of indirect tone-setting, vision-disseminating power that Eliot considered the social function of the poet.[57] "The Dry Salvages," with its stoic call to perseverance in the face of failure and obliteration—its "Fare forward, travelers!"—and "Little Gidding," with its calm yet emotionally charged reflections on England and history, and its ultimate transcendence of time and place, offered further comfort that was badly needed and gratefully received:

> Thus, love of a country
> Begins as attachment to our own field of action
> And comes to find that action of little importance
> Though never indifferent. History may be servitude,
> History may be freedom. See, now they vanish,
> The faces and places, with the self which, as it could, loved them,
> To become renewed, transfigured, in another pattern.
>
> (CPP 142)

The medium of radio, which Eliot had embraced since its early days, now repaid his friendship, as broadcast readings of the wartime *Quartets* over the BBC network—to be supplemented, eventually, by commercial recordings—brought the poems to a measurably larger and more miscellaneous audience and drastically altered Eliot's "public image" (Durrell 61; Speaight, "Interpreting" 77). The sense that Eliot's work was highbrow fare that spoke to an intellectual elite never dissipated, but thanks to Four Quartets, the public that could envision itself as belonging to that elite was significantly enlarged.

It was not, then, The Cocktail Party but "East Coker" and the remaining Quartets that gave the final impetus to Eliot's rise to celebrity (Gordon, Imperfect 384–85). Though not a "popular" work in the usual sense, the Quartets prepared the ground so that his seemingly preordained Nobel Prize in 1948 only confirmed Eliot in the extraordinary renown that he carried ever after. One tangible measure of his celebrity is the success of the four plays Eliot permitted to be broadcast on BBC television.[58] A first broadcast of The Cocktail Party, for example, drew 3.5 million viewers in 1952, while a second, in 1957— when the play was no longer even new—reached eight million, almost a quarter of the adult population of the United Kingdom (M. Barry 85–86).[59]

Another sign of Eliot's celebrity was his consistent popularity—dating, again, from the enthusiastic reception of "East Coker" in 1940—as an invited speaker in academic, civic, and other public venues (Gordon, Imperfect 436). The lucrative possibilities open to public intellectuals on today's lecture circuit owe much to Eliot, who received a $2,000 fee (a sum till then unheard of) for the lecture he gave at the University of Minnesota in 1956. The sponsors got their money's worth, for an audience of nearly 14,000— a record that perhaps still stands for a literary-critical event—came to hear the Great Man deliver "The Frontiers of Criticism." To house the anticipated crowd, the lecture had to be given in the basketball arena, an accommodation repeated at the University of Texas in 1958, when over 7,000 turned up to hear Eliot speak in the stadium (Matthews 166). Eliot's allure clearly went beyond anything he might have said, however brilliant, about literature; it was Eliot himself, and what he was taken to represent, that was the attraction. One acquaintance who attended an Eliot reading at the YMHA in New York overheard a teenager in the audience remark to her friend, "It's not that I care about his poetry, I just want to get a look at him before he dies" (Straus 151).[60] And no wonder, for it is a rare individual, and a still rarer poet, whose birthday is reported on the front page of the New York Times (headline: "T. S. Eliot, 70 Today, Concedes He Looks on Life More Genially").

Occasional charges of highbrow elitism and "contempt for the common man" continued to dog Eliot; he even felt compelled to defend himself in a 1942 letter to the Partisan Review, which responds to Van Wyck Brooks's lecture "Primary Literature and Coterie Literature" and a London Times leading article called "The Eclipse of the Highbrow." Eliot's defense is not especially satisfying; he is left sputtering by the "puzzling" "warmth of feeling" in these two antimodernist diatribes, and can only retort that the grounds for their condemnation are not clearly defined. More cogently, he suggests that instead of "merely denouncing modern art," it would be more valuable to enquire "why it is what it is" ("Letter" 116)—the very project he had set himself in his "London Letters" of the early twenties and followed out ever since.[61] Eliot was already sensitive to such charges of elitism, which had been leveled earlier by Louis Untermeyer and others. "We expect a poet to be reproached," he had written only the year before, in "Rudyard Kipling," "for lack of respect for the intelligence of the common man, or even for de- liberately flouting the intelligence of the common man" (229). "The Eclipse of the Highbrow" found in modern art only "esoteric parlour games" for an intellectual elite and drew what Eliot called "the now famil- iar comparison of modern poetry to the crossword puzzle" ("Letter" 115).[62] Eliot's protestations that he could not imagine a poet deliberately "restrict[ing] his public by his choice of style of writing or of subject- matter" (UPUC 22) or that he had "never heard of a writer of genius who preferred to have only a small number of readers" (qtd. in Hawkins, "Writer" 773) must be read in the context of such criticism.

In the midcentury years, these charges did nothing at all to diminish Eliot's celebrity, precisely, I would suggest, because his celebrity was *based on* a perception that he was above the rabble who watched television and read bad novels. He was the anointed protector of the heavenly sphere of Art, a position for which contempt for the "common man" and the "common culture" does not count as a character flaw. The central importance of popular culture to Eliot's work and thought was thus lost entirely. Eliot's public—those thousands who flocked to his lectures, those millions who tuned in to *The Cocktail Party* on television, and the many more millions worldwide who knew him by his name and reputation—came to him be- cause (to recur to Cynthia Ozick's formulation) he *was* "high art" at a mo- ment when high art carried a "power and prestige" magnified many times by its being menaced from below. No wonder people came "to get a look at him before he died": his moment was, by definition, always passing, and his like would never be seen again. That he was the last of his kind was a condition of his fame.

THE UNEXPECTED GUEST

"Mr. Eliot," as Edmund Wilson recognized, got his start in Eliot's "original transformation of the American into a Britisher" (Bit 383–84). Certainly he loved to play the superior Briton. One report, which described Eliot as "never popular" in his interests, recounted his "winc[ing] at Americanisms" with an infuriating superciliousness during his 1932–33 stint in the United States ("Tom to T.S."). But Eliot was having his critics on; his letters to Pound and Woolf showed him refreshed and rejuvenated by America, amused by such foolery as a restaurant shaped like a bowler hat, and "keen to pick up the latest popular songs" (Gordon, *Eliot's New Life* 20). Some, indeed, have credited Eliot's protean identity to his very Americanness.[63] Along these lines, Alfred Kazin's description of Eliot is, I think, one of the most perceptive:

> He was an institution capable of great suffering. He was also a Yankee humorist, skilled in playing many parts between America and Europe. How mischievously he fitted into his English décor—he was a subtler international type than those chaste Jamesian heroes Eliot had been among the first to recognize as comic masks. Looking at Eliot, in his lounge suit, carefully constructing a personality for the public gaze, it seemed to me that James had imagined the role, Eliot now lived it. How far the Yankee imagination ranged in time as well as space—how easily an American took up any role on the English stage. Benjamin Franklin playing a rustic sage had nothing on this poker player from Missouri. America was right in that room and would never leave it. (139)

Eliot was himself aware of his "indestructible American strain," as he cheerfully acknowledged to those English friends who chose to call him on it ("Out of the Air"; Chiari 8). And he felt that his creativity, "in its sources, in its emotional springs," was rooted in America (qtd. in D. Hall 109–10).

Though one might have expected the opposite from an artist who had so conspicuously fled the premises, it was probably his American roots that allowed Eliot to view the "Americanization" of England with something like equanimity. Then as now, the term "Americanization" represented postindustrial modernizing and massifying tendencies, and particularly the growing power of popular culture, as a specifically American phenomenon (Ross 7). British critics anxious about the corruption either of traditional high culture or of working-class culture by the "homogenizing influence" of modern popular culture have long had recourse to this term, with its suggestion of foreign infestation. Popular culture, according to this understanding, is American mass culture (Storey 11). Eliot saw no reason to contest these definitions, as his 1928 preface to Edgar Ansell Mowrer's *This American World* shows.[64] Eliot, who has, at age forty, only just finalized his earlier choice by declaring British citizenship, does not question Mowrer's characterization of "Americanism" as a "malady" or an "ailment" (xi, xiv); yet he counsels a measured response and warns against overreaction: "The majority of foreigners think either of Americanization as something to be welcomed and exploited, or as a plague to be quarantined; and either point of view is apt to be superficial" (x). Eliot here anticipates the realization among more recent cultural critics that neither indiscriminate celebration nor unremitting opposition is a salutary response to the modern popular— that what is called for is rather a critical close reading guided by a considered ethics. And thus Eliot concludes his preface: "if one looks far enough ahead, none of these things that are happening seem either good or bad: they are merely change. Our task is simply to see what we are, and to know what we want in the immediate future, and to work towards that" (xv). The struggle to come to terms with a mass society is palpable in these lines, but Eliot manages, if just barely, to win the struggle. Even later in life, as we saw in chapter 1, he maintains an ability to wonder what will issue from the intermarriage of the American revolution in culture with the European tradition—what songs the offspring of the American robin and the English thrush will sing. Unlike many of his contemporaries, Eliot could countenance the possibility that the arrival of *turdus migratorius* did not mark the end of all song.

For Eliot to have resisted the mass-cultural pessimism of the postwar consensus as far as he did—a consensus that had made Eliot himself its hero—bespeaks a laudable independence; yet how qualified an achievement! With his critical intelligence and personal enthusiasms, Eliot might have broken through the mass-culture commonplaces of his time to a new and subtler mode of analysis, and yet he never quite rose to the occasion. His faith, in this respect, was weak—a point expressed cogently by Anthony Burgess:

> [T]here was always a "double-standard" in Eliot's approach to popular art which forbade a serious synthesis of the high and the low. He was something of a rogue, said Edmund Wilson,[65] but not perhaps enough of one. He flirted with the entertainments of the common people but then grew scared and ran away. . . .
>
> He was always promising to attempt a serious critical evaluation of the detective story, but he probably failed, as he did in his essay on Kipling, to find the right tools for dissecting what, being merely good, was the enemy of the best. He admired Conan Doyle's Sherlock Holmes stories but did not see how they could be literature. . . . He wrote a touching essay on the art of Marie Lloyd and in it lamented the death of the music hall, but he knew that a music-hall song could never be literature in the manner of a Shakespeare sonnet. From popular art he did not expect too much. Enjoying it, he temporarily doused his critical faculties. . . . It was a timid flirtation. (103–04)

Not all of this, I think, is on the mark. Burgess's explanation of Eliot's reticence, in particular, seems feebly conjectural; the notion that "merely good" (popular) culture is the "enemy of the best" (high art) is not to be discovered in any of Eliot's essays, nor did he ever exhibit the attributed reservations about the aesthetic value of music hall or detective fiction. But Burgess's conclusion points up an important deficiency in Eliot. He could see, but he feared to be seen, across the cultural divide. In his reams of prose, Eliot never sustains an analysis of popular culture for more than four or five pages, and his qualms about the elitist commonplaces of his time are obliquely and diffidently expressed. Eliot's openness to popular genres was voiced mostly in private fora (in letters, at parties, among friends), or in interviews and other occasional pieces, rather than in published essays or lectures, where it might have had an appreciable impact. The popular influence, as I have argued, is audible in, even crucial to, his poetry; but only in some of the *March Hare* poems, which he did not publish, and in *Sweeney Agonistes*, which he could not finish, does he dare bring it into the foreground. Even in his late comedies, where Eliot probably came closest to "crossing the border and closing the gap" (to adapt Leslie Fiedler's phrase), he could work only through drawing-room comedy, with its already antiquated resonances.

Emblematic, to my mind, of Eliot's flirtation and flight is his habit of working from extravagant popular allusions that he then expunged. The works that began their lives as "He Do the Police in Different Voices," "Wanna Go Home Baby?" and "All Aboard for Natchez, Cairo, and St. Louis" reached print as *The Waste Land*, *Sweeney Agonistes*, and *Ash-Wednesday*. That the languorous cadences of part I of *Ash-Wednesday* cunningly reproduce the celebrated deadpan of vaudeville comedian Charles E. Mack will be obvious to anyone who is familiar with the poem's working title and its source in the recordings of the "Two Black Crows"—and utterly imperceptible, given the poem's visible range of reference, to anyone who is not.[66] A bowdlerized "Mrs. Porter" survives in *The Waste Land*, but the epigraph "Casey Jones was a fireman's name; / In the red light district he won his fame" (with the facetious attribution "OLD BALLAD") never made it out of the draft synopsis of *Sweeney Agonistes*, where it once stood shoulder-to-shoulder with Aeschylus and St. John of the Cross (Crawford 169). The epigraph "I want someone to treat me rough. / Give me a cabman" (ascribed to a "popular song") vanished with Eliot's 1926 Clark lectures, which did not reach print until 1993. Had the lectures been published during Eliot's lifetime, one does not doubt that only his other epigraph, from the *Vita Nuova*, would have seen the light of day. Eliot made incidental use of another bawdy song, "The One-Eyed Riley," in his most popular play, but scrapped it for his title in favor of *The Cocktail Party*. Eliot's inspiration was tied to the popular forms that provided these various references, but he took them down, like scaffolding, or buried them out of sight. Intentionally or not, he thus spared his critics an uncomfortable confrontation with a segment of culture that they would not have joined him in embracing. For Eliot remained, in Burgess's slightly hyperbolic words, "the one poet and critic of the age who was qualified to recognize that certain reaches of popular art protected traditions of craftsmanship, intelligence, wit and taste that artists acclaimed by the intelligentsia had abandoned" (104). Although he never succeeded in bringing it fully into the open, Eliot's productive interchange with popular culture animates all of his major creative works.

Fittingly, the anomaly of Eliot's position came through even in the "Homage to T. S. Eliot" staged in the Globe Theatre by the London Library—one of Eliot's favorite causes—on June 13, 1965, five months after the poet's death. The program began with two pieces by Stravinsky, one written for the occasion, the other his choral setting of "The dove descending breaks the air," from "Little Gidding." Next came a selection of Eliot poems chosen by W. H. Auden and read by Paul Scofield, Laurence Olivier, and Peter O'Toole. The program ended with a performance of *Sweeney Agonistes*, with musical accompaniment by Johnny Dankworth's jazz band. Already, then, the attempt to pay appropriate homage to Eliot had introduced a few popular notes to queer the highbrow pitch. By common consent, however, the high point of the affair was a speech given by Groucho Marx.

When Eliot had first become addicted to the Marx Brothers is unclear; we know only from certain comments and incidents late in his life that he attended their movies at every opportunity. He had a special affinity for Groucho, whom he considered "a master of nonsense" and "a comic genius, a very rare thing" (Levy and Scherle 140).[67] It should be said that Eliot took nonsense seriously, numbering Edward Lear with Mallarmé and Herbert among the "very few" poets he always found himself returning to; writing a poetic tribute to Walter de la Mare, whose nonsense verse he particularly admired; and critiquing anthologies of nonsense in a *Criterion* review.[68] In the last five years of Eliot's life, his admiration for Groucho culminated in a fan letter, which led to an exchange of portraits, a series of warm and humorous letters, and, at last, a memorable dinner at the Eliots' home in London, at which Groucho tried and failed to get Eliot to discuss literature, Eliot tried and failed to get Groucho to reprise scenes from his movies, and the two men discovered common ground in their fondness for cats, cigars, and puns.[69]

Groucho, the "master of nonsense," was a scion of the vaudeville and variety forms to which Eliot had always been devoted; and like Eliot, he was an artist in language. At the London Library "Homage," his narrative of Eliot's shy courtship, capped off with a reading of "Gus: The Theatre Cat"—Old Possum's tale of a nostalgic survivor of the melodramatic stage Eliot had mourned in "Wilkie Collins and Dickens"—was a fitting eulogy for one important side of the deceased. And yet Groucho, as a *New Yorker* correspondent observed, came as a "staggering surprise to the audience." No doubt he was an unexpected guest at T. S. Eliot's memorial; and, too, his unextraordinary appearance came as something of a shock. "[G]arbed as conservatively as a bank president and speaking in the mild, cultured tones of a university professor" (Panter-Downes 86), Mr. Marx demonstrated forcibly that a Groucho could lie beneath a perfectly Eliotic exterior. A closer look at Eliot himself would have imparted the same revelation.

It was Eliot's lot, however, to be seen with partial vision, in both senses of *partial*. In 1932, Eliot's friend Paul Elmer More reported asking "a young student of very advanced ideas about art and life how he, as an admirer of Mr. Eliot, reconciled *The Waste Land* with [Eliot's] program of classicism and royalism . . . and Anglo-Catholicism." The student unhesitatingly replied, "I don't reconcile them; I take the one and leave the other" (27).[70] And thus, with respect to matters of culture, did most of Eliot's readers in his lifetime: they "took" the portentous, the elitist, the mandarin Eliot, leaving all others by the wayside. They needed this Eliot and so produced him; we who have inherited this Eliot do not need him and so reject him. The Eliot who tested and not infrequently transgressed the cultural divide has never been given his critical due, mostly because he has never been the Eliot that mattered. This Eliot is needed today, however, if Eliot is to matter at all.

ABBREVIATIONS USED FOR ELIOT'S WORKS

CC   *Christianity and Culture*
CPP   *The Complete Poems and Plays, 1909–1950*
LL   London Letters
SE   *Selected Essays*
UPUC   The Use of Poetry and the Use of Criticism
WLF   *The Waste Land: A Facsimile and Transcript*

NOTES

INTRODUCTION

1. In fairness to Foster, I should note his awareness that his time is one of "literary housecleaning and renovating." He observes, for example, that the stars of Eliot and Joyce are being eclipsed by those of Whitman and Lawrence (282). He does not believe, then, that nothing can change, but rather that the type and direction of change is controlled by the intelligence of a coherent literary culture for which the New Critics are primarily responsible. The "Beat phenomenon," for example—which Foster discusses in the past tense—was "so beautifully handled by all" that it had no chance to trash the "house" and is now safely and properly consigned to occasional appearances in college anthologies (274–75). Any change that Foster can envision is thus already well contained by the dominant critical and institutional structures. He is not fatuous; he is only unfortunate to be ideologically blinkered in a way that would soon become altogether obvious.

2. One wonders whether Karl Shapiro's acerbic rebuttal, titled "The Three Hockey Games of T. S. Eliot," induced any doubt in Foster's mind. "Eliot's triumph in the gymnasium proves nothing to me," Shapiro proclaimed, before going on to denounce Eliot—as indeed he often did—for elitist and antidemocratic tendencies, not so much in politics as in art (284). With the free-verse revolution of 1912, poetry "had successfully escaped the Academy"; Eliot, with Pound, had helped put it back, and "[t]he great audience was sent packing." As for Foster's ancillary heroes, Shapiro considered them Eliot's lackeys and dismissed them with the Orwellian ep-

ithet "Newcrit." Meanwhile "only one American poet succeeded in making his voice heard in protest—William Carlos Williams" (285). If this picture looks familiar, it's because the views sketched here by Shapiro soon routed the New Critical worldview to become postmodernist doctrine. Note, however, that as sharply as they differ in their valuations, Foster and Shapiro both characterize Eliot in the same way: as a champion of high-cultural exclusivity, coterie poetry, and an updated aestheticism. In a moment we will find the identical sameness-in-difference played out in another debate a generation later.

3. This is of course a debatable point, and one of the shrewdest replies to Ozick, that of Sebastian Knowles, has contested her thesis on just these grounds. "Reports of Eliot's death," Knowles avers, "are plain lies" (395). For Knowles, an exaggerated conception of Eliot's present irrelevance is nothing more than a convenient fiction his detractors are happy to rehearse.

As someone who has quite recently offered "a vestigial graduate seminar given over to the study of Eliot"—something that Ozick claims has been impossible to find since the early seventies—and who still finds enough of interest in Eliot to write about him, I sympathize with Knowles's position. Still, if Eliot today is not quite as dead, or as invisible, as Ozick (or Kramer) represents him to be, he certainly has come a long way down from the singularly venerated position he held a half century ago. Changing fashion and generational rebellion factor into, but do not entirely account for, the extent of this revaluation. As Ozick correctly perceives, Eliot has fallen so hard for the same reason he once rose so high: because of what he *represents*.

For a milder version of Knowles's point, see Parini, who also argues that Eliot "has hardly vanished," while suggesting that he has rather "fallen back into his rightful place in the pantheon of modern poets, a worthy voice beside Frost, Stevens, Moore, Williams, Pound, Yeats, and others" (3).

4. The identification is extended to encompass modernism as well. The defense of high culture is, for Kramer, tantamount to the defense of modernism (7), just as, for Ozick, the death of modernism is equivalent to the death of high culture. Kramer describes modernism and high art as "still very much alive, [though] nonetheless imperiled and under sustained attack" (6). Here, as elsewhere, he invokes the familiar Leavisite metaphors of siege and guardianship ("the defense of high art is a beleaguered minority position on the cultural scene and the enemies of modernism command enormous patronage and influence" [7]), metaphors that, as I argue in chapter 6, have long been misattributed to Eliot.

5. A revised version of Gendron's article now appears as chapter 4 in his *Between Montmartre and the Mudd Club* (83–101).

6. Michael Murphy, for example, writes: "[T]his consensus understanding of modernism . . . has come to seem too neat a narrative, too general and unqualified a diagnosis of the astonishingly multiple, dynamic, and complicated phenomenon that we agreed a long time ago it was something of a reduction to generalize as

'modernism.' It is a simple misrepresentation of the multiplicity of early-twentieth-century culture, and it demands qualification" (66).

7. Eliot is now so routinely paired in this context with the incomparably more fervid Ortega that only a rash of scholarly cribbing can account for it. One typical passage, echoing Huyssen, claims that Ortega and Eliot "epitomized" the "disdain for the popular" characteristic of mass-society critics (Marshall 37). But even Huyssen did not originate this pairing: it appears as far back as Alan Swingewood's 1977 diatribe, *The Myth of Mass Culture* (5–10). Thanks to its appearances in such trend-setting works of the late eighties as *After the Great Divide* and Andrew Ross's *No Respect* (50–52), the twinning of Eliot and Ortega seems likely to remain with us for some time.

8. Eliot is here linked with three younger "modernist critics" (I. A. Richards, F. R. Leavis, and Edmund Wilson) who are all, not coincidentally, associated with Eliot as early champions of his work.

9. As his recent publications indicate, Coyle has significantly revised his view of Eliot since the appearance in 1995 of his book on Pound.

10. Portents of the Eliot I am urging also appear in the work of the few critics, from Carol H. Smith to W. B. Worthen, whose main concern has been Eliot's theater. Eliot's drama—apart from *Murder in the Cathedral*, his most "poetic" play—has been neglected in literary criticism. But the drama critics have no wish to evade the fact that Eliot dedicated half his career to an attempt to create a "popular" art of his own. They tend to be more than usually aware not only of popular genres as elements of Eliot's plays but of the ambiguous cultural status of the plays themselves, and of the transformations in Eliot's thinking about art and society that underlay his extensive foray into the theater. Randy Malamud's *Where the Words Are Valid* is particularly instructive on this last subject.

11. This, I must emphasize, is *not* to suggest that we read inductively from Eliot to modernism. As Michael North has recently admonished, our questions about modernism and popular culture cannot be "settled by reference to the intentions of its most visible perpetrators," but must consider "institutions, modes of dissemination and production, such as publishers, galleries, and magazines" (*Reading* 207). Yet when Laura Cowan writes that "A revaluation of Eliot is in essence a revaluation of modernism" (140), she is only overstating a reality, because in the politics of literary criticism, Eliot still functions as modernism's lightning rod. For now, any thorough rereading of modernism is likely to involve, and to require, a rereading of Eliot. Even North's admonition, after all, comes near the end of a book whose subject, the year 1922, was driven in large measure by Eliotic considerations, and in whose pages Eliot continues to share pride of place with a select group of historical figures—even if these are not, in many cases, the usual suspects.

12. "The coexistence in one person," according to the *Oxford English Dictionary*, "of contradictory emotions or attitudes (as love and hatred) towards a person or thing."

13. In his important critical biography *Matthew Arnold*, Lionel Trilling notes that

"Rousseau's *Confessions* had laid the ground for the understanding of emotional ambivalence" for the nineteenth century (123).

14. *Webster's* gives the year as 1918.

15. These moods sometimes cohabit in the same work. Eliot's editorial "Commentary" in the June 1927 *Criterion*, for example, begins with an inspiring paean to social responsibility and ends with a pointless denunciation of "community singing" at soccer matches, in which practice Eliot somehow detects the footsteps of approaching doom.

16. As Anthony Lane writes in a review of Eliot's *Inventions of the March Hare*:

Is it too much to ask that we should entertain mixed feelings about a writer? I suspect that no other feelings are worth having; that a writer who arouses clean, uncomplicated feelings will, in the final reckoning, turn out to be unworthy of serious attention; and that Eliot offers us a strong opportunity to revive the ancient art of being of two minds. (91)

17. Francis Mulhern groups Eliot for similar reasons with Hoggart; these thinkers, though in obvious ways politically antithetical, together "define[d] the new terms of cultural reflection in post-war Britain" (xx).

18. The need for such a resituating of Eliot has been suggested before, notably by DuPlessis, for whom Eliot must be "further contextualized within racialized, gender-laden, popular, and American discourses" (82).

19. Throughout this book I will be using the term "popular culture" primarily in the sense of "popular arts" and less often in the broader sense that includes such objects of everyday experience as subway trains, costume jewelry, and seaside holidays. I will, in other words, be concerned mostly with "cultural texts" rather than "cultural practices." To deal justly with "lived" culture in Eliot—from the voyeuristic *flânerie* of the early poems to the horrified immersion of *The Waste Land*, and thence to the slow-growing reconciliation from *Murder in the Cathedral* and *The Rock* to the *Quartets* and the later plays, with suitable reference to the dozens of Eliot essays that touch on the subject—would require, and will have to await, another full-length study.

As a rule, I favor the term "popular culture" over "mass culture," a term I employ only as historical context dictates. I do this not only because I think it generally a good thing to avoid the supercilious overtones and dystopian connotations invoked by "mass culture" but also because I do not want those associations to set the tone for this particular discussion of Eliot. It is part of my argument that Eliot has been bracketed too readily with the mid-twentieth-century mass-culture critique. If the term "popular culture," on the other hand, runs the risk of invoking a naively celebratory critical discourse—and I hope we are past the point where this is inevitable—I still believe that the insertion of T. S. Eliot into such a discourse would be more salutary than otherwise.

On the terminological question see, e.g., Ross 233–34 (n. 4), and Naremore and Brantlinger 1–12.

20. In one of the earlier critical works to give some attention to this subject, John D. Margolis feels similarly compelled to write, "Unlikely as it may have seemed, Eliot's appeal to the music-hall was in earnest" (181).

21. The exception in all this is always *Murder in the Cathedral*, the one play whose "literary" qualities are sufficiently obvious that it can be read as a poem.

22. On bawdy verse, see Gill on Eliot's "King Bolo" stanzas; and Chinitz, "T. S. Eliot's 'Blue' Verses."

23. See Coyle, "T. S. Eliot on the Air" and "'This rather elusory,'" as well as his "T. S. Eliot's Radio Broadcasts, 1929–63: A Chronological Checklist," in Brooker, *T. S. Eliot* (205–13).

24. In addition to Coyle's work on Eliot and radio, see, for example, Schuchard's chapter "In the Music Halls" in *Eliot's Dark Angel* (102–18); Knowles in *ANQ*; Faulk in *Modernism/Modernity*; Collier; the articles by McNeilly, Mackin, and Gill in Cooper's *T. S. Eliot's Orchestra*; and Jaidka's *T. S. Eliot's Use of Popular Sources*.

25. On the evolution of the highbrow/lowbrow dichotomy, see Levine, who writes, "Although the stated intention of the arbiters of culture [in the mid–nineteenth century] was to proselytize and convert, to lift the masses up to their level, in fact their attitudes often had the opposite effect. The negative stereotypes of terms like 'culture' and 'cultivated' took hold early; the term 'highbrow' was still young when it became a term of popular derision" (235).

26. I am not suggesting that *Cats* was all bad. The long Gus/Growltiger sequence in act 2 was particularly affecting and musically interesting; the staging and costumes were remarkably creative; many of the songs were attractive (including, of course, "Memory," despite its reduction of "Rhapsody on a Windy Night" to cliché); and the pastiche of musical styles throughout was clever and lively. On the other hand, several of the settings (e.g., "The Old Gumbie Cat," "Mungojerrie and Rumpleteazer," "Old Deuteronomy") were quite pedestrian; the long dance sequence representing the "Jellicle Ball" in act 1 was tedious; and the setting of the "moments of happiness" passage from "The Dry Salvages" was thoroughly pretentious. Neither the composer nor the director had any idea of what to do with "The Naming of Cats," which the feline cast muttered while slithering around the theater, apparently in the hope that no one in the audience would catch the words and wonder what bearing they had on the question, "What's a Jellicle Cat?" In many instances, too, the show clearly missed the point of Old Possum's lightly ironic humor. It was, on the whole, a partial success.

CHAPTER 1

1. A few examples spanning seven decades: Clive Bell (1921) places Eliot within a larger "jazz movement" in the arts (94). Stephen Spender (1935) finds Eliot "experimenting with jazz" in *Sweeney Agonistes* but does not elaborate (*Destructive* 187). Morris Freedman (1952) fails to distinguish jazz from operetta or even from

nursery rhymes; thus any sharp rhythms in Eliot's poetry are immediately declared to be "jazz." Carol H. Smith (1963) discusses Eliot's "jazz rhythms" cogently, though with reference only to *Sweeney Agonistes* (*T. S. Eliot's* 51–61). Marshall McLuhan (1974) comments perceptively on the relation of Eliot's art to his American background; however, his assertion that Eliot "said a great deal about jazz and blues, both in his prose and in his poetry" seems hyperbolic, and the connection he makes between Eliot and jazz remains an inspired hunch (122). Robert Fleissner (1990) alludes indefinitely to "some jazz or music-hall-revue syncopation in Eliot's early poetry" that "most readers can detect" (1).

2. Eliot's attitude may be gauged from his June 1919 comment to Ottoline Morrell: "I feel . . . especially depressed by my awareness of having lost contact with Americans and their ways, and by the hopelessness of ever making them understand so many things" (*Letters* 307).

3. Unfortunately, however, English civilization was in abeyance. As Eliot wrote in 1915, "I do not think that I should ever come to like England—a people which is satisfied with such disgusting food is not civilised" (*Letters* 88).

4. Apparently Eliot's acquaintances in England remained always conscious of his Americanness. In 1918, during a period of British curiosity about baseball, Eliot found himself "constantly called upon to explain terms" (*Letters* 237). Thirty years later, Desmond Hawkins noted that Eliot's "slightly too gentlemanly air reveals that his England has a tincture still of New England" ("Pope" 46).

5. In his memoir, Joseph Chiari records the feeling he and Eliot, even in his later years, shared: that "seen within the context of the highly evolved and complex English society to which we were both deeply attached, we nevertheless were two kinds of primitives, he from Missouri and I from Corsica" (12).

6. In the paragraph that follows, Eliot twice expresses regret at having to turn down an invitation for the following Sunday.

7. See Winans and Kaufman 14–15; and Linn 83–84.

8. Here, for example, is Eliot in 1934, aping Pound aping Uncle Remus: "Now, Mr. Orage, Sir, I am going to set round the chimbly and have a chaw terbacker with Miss Meadows and the gals; and then I am going away for a 4tnight where that old Rabbit can't reach me with his letters nor even with his post cards." The letter to the *New English Weekly* that this passage concludes is signed, "I am, dear Sir, Your outraged Possum" ("Use").

9. See Christopher Ricks's valuable "Chronology of T. S. Eliot's Poems 1905–1920" (Eliot, *Inventions* xxxix).

10. Though I do not take up here the gender issues raised by "Cousin Nancy," I have treated them elsewhere ("Dance" 323–24).

11. Five years later, Eliot is still complaining that his dancing skills have gotten "rather out of date"; he invites Mary Hutchinson to join him "at a place near Baker Street" where "[t]hey teach the new dances and steps, which I don't know and want to learn" (*Letters* 275).

12. Clearly Eliot is working out the argument of "Tradition and the Individual Talent" in both the letter to John Quinn just quoted and the letter to Eleanor Hinkley quoted earlier. The letters were written only two days apart (July 9 and 11, 1919) and the essay was published a few months later in the *Egoist*.

13. Dance was apparently an ongoing part of Eliot's life at least in the earlier days of his first marriage, and before the business of editing the *Criterion* caught up with him. According to the recollections of his friends, he and Vivien often passed a Sunday afternoon dancing to the gramophone in their apartment or at a Queensway dance hall (Spender, "Remembering" 58; Patmore 85–86). Many years later, after his second marriage, Eliot told the *Daily Express*, "I am thinking of taking up dancing lessons again, as I have not danced at all for some years" (Ackroyd 321).

For the earliest image of a dancing Eliot, see the narrative of Margaret Shapleigh quoted in Soldo (27). Soldo also notes Eliot's participation in the Brattle and Buckingham Hall social dances at Harvard (57).

14. In 1920s discourse the tom-tom, like the saxophone, often stands synecdochically for jazz. It appears that this association was valid a decade earlier for the Eliot of "Portrait."

15. In "Dramatis Personae" (1923), Eliot approvingly quotes a similar passage in which Cocteau argues that the vitality of the theater has passed into "Le cirque, le music-hall, [et] le cinématographe" (303).

16. Eliot himself considered Bell an intellectual lightweight: "Bell is a most agreeable person, if you don't take him seriously, but a great waster of time if you do, or if you expect to get any profound knowledge or original thought out of him" (*Letters* 450).

17. This seems to have occurred with some regularity; see, for instance, Richards 6, Read 15, and Duncan 278. At a party celebrating his receipt of the Nobel Prize in 1948, Eliot treated the assembled well-wishers to a rendition of "Under the Bamboo Tree" (Ackroyd 290), a tune he had learned more than forty years earlier and had meanwhile parodied in *Sweeney Agonistes*.

18. Of these phrases, the first three are specifically identified by the OED as originating in the United States. Eliot's usage of "get away with it" predates by two years the first citation in the OED (under "get," 61c); "I guess," meaning "I am fairly certain," is rooted in the New England habit of understatement (see "guess," 6). "Likely," in the sense of "probably, in all probability," has largely been replaced by "most likely" and Eliot's "very likely," which dates from the late 1800s (B. *adv.*, 2).

19. The connection Eliot makes between Donne and Laforgue in "The Metaphysical Poets" is based on both poets' ability to integrate thought and complexity of feeling in their verse (248–49). In a 1931 essay called "Donne in Our Time," Eliot extends this point about Donne in a way that suggests the technical resemblance to Laforgue to which I have alluded here: "Donne . . . first made it possible to think in lyric verse, and in a variety of rhythms and stanza schemes

which forms an inexhaustible subject of study; and at the same time retained a quality of song and the suggestion of the instrumental accompaniment of the earlier lyric" (16–17).

20. Several critics have remarked on the disparity between English and French verse, and Annie Finch, following the lead of C. K. Stead, has even argued that Eliot's negotiation of this difference produces his unique prosody (87). I suggest that Eliot's adoption of American jazz to fill the role that the music of the café-concert had played for Laforgue is what made this difficult feat practicable.

21. Even "worthwhile" was then a new and rather trendy expression.

22. Sigg's formulation, "It is not impossible that the strains of a rag could have floated on a breeze to Locust Street where they might drift through upstairs windows open on some 'soft October night' " ("Eliot" 21), seems to me unnecessarily fanciful. Nothing so picturesque need have taken place. Likewise overly tentative is his suggestion that "Somehow, somewhere, Eliot got rhythm" (22). It is impossible that Eliot should have remained entirely innocent of ragtime while growing up in St. Louis.

23. Eliot mentions Faust's in an April 1917 letter to his father (*Letters* 174).

24. Another of these tunes, the "Bully Song," helped launch May Irwin to national prominence in 1895 as "the stage mother of ragtime" (Ewen 84). Mama Lou never received credit, much less royalties, for these hits, to which she may well have contributed music and lyrics.

25. Credit for the song was hotly contested, leading to lawsuits on both sides of the Atlantic and, eventually, the legal judgment that the music and chorus belonged to the public domain. Of the many stories purporting to explain the birth of "Ta-ra-ra-boom-de-ay," several ultimately trace the song to, or at least through, Mama Lou's performance of it in St. Louis (see Goldberg 114–17; Spaeth, *History* 258–59).

26. Of W. C. Handy's "St. Louis Blues," Langston Hughes wrote in 1964:

> I have heard the "St. Louis Blues" on Japanese jukeboxes sung in Japanese, in Russia sung in Russian, and in the various languages of Europe. In French provincial cafes with their little orchestras, almost every time a party of American tourists walks in, they play the "St. Louis Blues" evidently under the impression that it is the American National Anthem. ("I Remember" 154)

27. So Aldous Huxley, who knew the Eliots from about 1916, informed Stephen Spender ("Remembering" 58).

28. On Pound and the cultural divide, see Coyle, *Ezra Pound* (passim, but esp. 29–40).

29. Yet Grover Smith, certainly a careful scholar, similarly wonders if *The Waste Land* "might have made something of the materials Pound thought should go" (*Waste* 82).

30. In the typescript Eliot has slightly altered these lines: "I'm proud of all the Irish blood that's in me, / There's not a man can say a word agin me" (*WLF* 5).

31. For example, in his August 1922 "London Letter," Eliot praises Joyce on grounds that are entirely different from those he chooses in "*Ulysses*, Order, and Myth." Essentially, he sees *Ulysses* as a pastiche whose main use to "the intelligent literary aspirant" is to provide a compendium of negative examples (329). His recommendation of the book the next year as providing a positive model for contemporary art is not even hinted at here. Months after completing *The Waste Land*, then, Eliot still had not lit on the mythical method and its vital importance to contemporary art.

Of "*Ulysses*, Order, and Myth," Astradur Eysteinsson notes: "Critics are untiring in replaying [Eliot's] argument and using the essay as a kind of model or program for the modernist work. And as such the essay becomes a particularly convenient text to draw on for those arguing for a militant reaction against modernism" (124). But while Eliot's "*Ulysses*" has had an "astounding" impact on the "criticism and reception of modernist works," it is not at all clear that the essay succeeds in identifying or explaining the modernism of *Ulysses, The Waste Land,* or any other text.

32. Because the opening page of the manuscript is canceled, apparently in Eliot's hand, and because we do not have Pound's comments on it, critics have usually assumed that Eliot decided to drop the passage on his own. I am inclined to agree, however, with Barry, who strenuously urges the contrary (244–46). Considering the pattern of the poets' collaboration, it seems fair to say that for Eliot to have dropped an entire scene unilaterally would have been most uncharacteristic. And while it is true that the pencil streaks that dispose of the first page are Eliot's, this does not rule out the possibility that Pound, having gone over a carbon copy (as he did in other instances), had first discussed the passage with Eliot in Paris.

33. Eliot's depiction of Fresca on the toilet in the rejected opening of "The Fire Sermon" may be another attempt to borrow a page—a much earlier page—from *Ulysses*. Again, however, Eliot cannot muster the equanimity with which Joyce treats Bloom's defecation. For Eliot, the fact that Fresca, Fresca, Fresca shits provides only an occasion for misogynistic satire.

34. Charles Sanders attempts to prove that the unedited *Waste Land* imitates the format of the minstrel show in detail. North's less literal claim strikes me as far more convincing.

35. As Sebastian Knowles has argued, Eliot's note to the "Mrs. Porter" song, gesturing at a source in Australia, is a comic misdirection ("Then You Wink" 24–25).

36. The exception on the deleted page is "The Maid of the Mill," which belongs to a Victorian sentimental tradition quite distinct from the modernity evoked by the other song quotations. This reference is clearly meant to seem a bit old-fashioned or even nostalgic.

37. This is the gist of, for instance, Sigmund Spaeth's argument in "Jazz Is Not Music" (268–69).

38. By suggesting that the poem consists entirely of ventriloquism rather than original utterance, Eliot's working title, "He Do the Police in Different Voices,"

seems to anticipate such accusations and to deflect them with irony—exactly as Eliot later said he had intended to do with his Notes ("Frontiers" 109).

39. Or as Leslie Fiedler wrote in 1970: "As early as T. S. Eliot, to be sure, jazz rhythms had been evoked [in poetry], as in 'O O O O that Shakespeherian Rag—It's so elegant, So intelligent . . . ,' but Eliot is mocking a world he resents" (482).

40. Unless, that is, Othello's line "Bring the rag right away" is meant to parody his demands for the missing handkerchief in act 3, scene 4. But that level of subtlety would be so alien to the rest of the song that I am inclined to write off this parallel as a lucky accident.

41. Sigg, too, argues that Eliot's "ragtime fragment" is not merely an object of ridicule:

"O O O O" the line begins, the wind moaning under the door but also bringing a song of convivial life to penetrate the bleak marital flat. The introductory "But" contrasts ragtime's lively, frisky charm to the strained, baleful couple, starved for a bit of fun. . . . Beware of false reverence about art, the lines also seem to say, rebuking genteel misapprehension by joining two remote art forms, ragtime and Shakespeare. (21)

42. Eliot was baptized on June 29 and confirmed the next day by the bishop of Oxford (Ackroyd 162). He declared British citizenship in November (165; Gordon, *Imperfect* 223).

43. So, at any rate, explained Constant Lambert, whose jazzy *Rio Grande* (with text by Edith Sitwell's brother Sacheverell) remains to this day *his* best-known composition.

44. For more on the sexual politics of Eliot's rejection of jazz, see Chinitz, "Dance" 322–26.

45. Note, for example, that he did not *go* to school in New England: he "was sent" there.

CHAPTER 2

1. The analogy to camouflage is Pound's as well; he wrote in a 1923 letter, "*The Criterion* has to be so heavily camouflaged as Westminster Abbey, that the living visitor is not very visible" (*Selected Letters* 187).

2. Eliot's reading of cultural history is corroborated by recent scholarship. Lawrence Levine has shown that the divisions between levels of culture in America were indeed "much more fluid, much less rigidly hierarchical" until late in the nineteenth century (Levine 107). A similar fluidity obtained in certain areas of nineteenth-century English culture. As Ronald Pearsall explains, "There was no demarcation in Victorian England between popular and serious music, and the listener who wiped away a tear after a stirring performance of a drawing-room ballad was

quite willing to stir himself for a Beethoven symphony" (123). Again, though, the cultural hierarchies had solidified by the end of the century (135).

3. See "Homage to Wilkie Collins" and "Recent Detective Fiction" in the January and June issues of Criterion 5. Later publications that continue this project include a review of The Canary Murder Case in Criterion 6; and a review of three novels and a short story collection, the review essay "Sherlock Holmes and His Times," and reviews of The Greene Murder Case and The Beast With Five Fingers in Criterion 8. Although many of the reviews are unsigned, they are clearly Eliot's work; they sometimes even refer back to the signed pieces using such phrases as "as we have already observed."

4. Similarly, Eliot told the New York Times in 1958 that he was reading "[s]ome poetry, but little fiction—you would be surprised how much I haven't read" ("T. S. Eliot, 70 Today").

5. Given Eliot's professional duties at Faber and Faber, this claim cannot have been strictly true; to cite only one counterexample, Eliot had edited, and therefore read, the "serious prose fiction" of Djuna Barnes. Doubtless he meant that he read no "serious" fiction outside the office. But since he kept up after 1927 with, for instance, the work of Joyce and Wyndham Lewis (whom Faber did not publish), even so limited a restatement could not be taken quite literally. For Joyce, see, e.g., "Milton I" 142–5; for Lewis see "Books."

6. See Ackroyd 279; Gordon, Imperfect 110; Levy and Scherle 66.

7. He anticipates this subject as early as October 1920, when he writes to Scofield Thayer agreeing to undertake the task of writing a regular "London Letter" (Letters 413–14).

8. We will return in the next chapter, and again in chapter 6, to the politics of Eliot's argument.

9. Eliot routinely undermines the linguistic constructs that separate literary genres from subliterary ones: "the frontier of drama and melodrama is vague" ("Wilkie Collins" 415); "[t]he distinction between 'journalism' and 'literature' is quite futile" ("Charles Whibley" 439); "I don't think that you can divide writers sharply into two kinds, those who are artists and those who are not" (Hawkins, "Writer" 773); to mark the boundary between "poetry" and "verse," "we should be dealing with matters as imprecise as the shape and size of a cloud or the beginning and end of a wave" ("Rudyard Kipling" 251); and so forth.

10. Ironically, although Thompson goes on to argue that "Contempt for popular culture is certainly not a universally shared aspect of modernism," he overtly excludes Eliot from the company of dissenters (35).

11. Seldes argues that Joyce develops the lead of Flaubert and James in bringing the novel to its "culmination," after which the genre will "take . . . a new form" (211); he finds the whole work expressive of "tragic gaiety" (212); and he predicts that "the innovations in method and the developments in structure which [Joyce] has used with a skill approaching perfection are going to have an incalculable effect

upon the writers of the future" (212). These phrases all find echoes in Eliot's "*Ulysses*, Order, and Myth," published a year later.

12. He believes, for example, that in every age the "great" arts can be distinguished by their Arnoldian high seriousness from the "lively" (Kammen 93). He claims, too, that "except in a period when the major arts flourish with exceptional vigour, the lively arts are likely to be the most intelligent phenomena of their day" (*Seven* 294).

13. Seldes's nominees for "bogus arts" bear out the charge of arbitrariness; they include "vocal concerts, pseudo-classic dancing, the serious intellectual drama, the civic masque, the high-toned moving picture, and grand opera" (*Seven* 265). It is impossible to escape the sense that this list originates in personal proclivities and not in any intrinsic qualities of the arts in question. Such phrases as "pseudo-classic" and "serious intellectual," moreover, smack of circular reasoning.

14. This was not, incidentally, the only occasion on which an Aiken review in the *Criterion* diverged from Eliot's own valuation of the book under consideration. *The Great Gatsby*—a "serious" novel about which Eliot was uncharacteristically enthusiastic—elicited a lukewarm response from Aiken in October 1926.

15. Seldes's first column, in the January 1925 *Criterion*, refers to Eliot's invitation (284). He wrote two subsequent "New York Chronicles," published in January and October 1926, and an "American Chronicle" in February 1928.

16. This remains true despite anything one might say about the interpenetration—amply demonstrated in the past decade of modernist studies—of modernism and popular culture.

17. The cases of Conrad, Joyce, and Lawrence are discussed by Wexler; for Joyce, Woolf, and Yeats (as well as Eliot), see Tratner; for Pound, see Coyle. All three of these critics, taking quite disparate approaches, draw broad conclusions about modernism that support the claims I am making here.

18. He circumspectly avoids mentioning either writer by name. But noting the sensational success of *East Lynne* and its translation "'into every known language,'" he remarks, "We believe that several contemporary novels have been 'translated into every known language'; but we are sure that they have less in common with *The Golden Bowl*, or *Ulysses*, or even with [George Meredith's] *Beauchamp's Career*, than *East Lynne* has in common with *Bleak House*" ("Wilkie Collins" 410).

19. In a 1919 letter to John Rodker, for example, he explains his decision to call his new book *Ara Vus Prec* by pointing out that it is "non-committal about the newness of the contents, and unintelligible to most people" (*Letters* 338).

20. Eliot seems first to have conceived of something like the "London Letters" in 1918, when he wrote to Scofield Thayer, "I think that if I composed something in the hope of your printing it I ought to exploit my geographical position rather than send you my projected series on the Jacobean Dramatists," although his idea of its content at this point was more strictly literary (*Letters* 236). By 1920, Eliot was hop-

ing to "write occasional London letters" for "some American paper" (397), and when Thayer offered him the chance later that year he was "glad" to accept (413).

21. John D. Margolis's gloss on this remark, "Eliot's goal was no less than that of re-educating his society" (21), seems to me rather generous. Eliot's bluster, so alien to his later, cautious persona, resembles rather the Pound of the same period, who writes, for example, "Modern civilisation has bred a race with brains like those of rabbits and . . . we artists who have been so long despised are about to take over control" ("New Sculpture" 68). As Leonard Diepeveen has argued, the Eliot of the teens targets a small, well-schooled literary audience, addresses its interests, and subtly trains it to receive the modernist projects of himself and his allies. He does this by encouraging his readers "to imagine themselves as part of a professional elite" that transcends an unthinking general readership (47–52). His success with this rhetorical strategy is unparalleled—although, as Diepeveen points out, it also left behind a string of unattractive remarks and a haughty tone that has alienated later readers (38–39).

22. See, for example, "Milton II," where Eliot tackles his original formulation of the "dissociation of sensibility" (152–53). Clear examples of the aestheticizing of history appear in Eliot's 1918 "Note on Ezra Pound" (4), as well as in "Tradition and the Individual Talent" ("Precisely, and they [the dead writers] are that which we know") (6). In a late essay, F. R. Leavis commented harshly on the latter passage: "We are forced to put the obvious and damning interpretation on this by the context and the essential aim (a matter for diagnosis) of the whole essay, which, under cover of a stern doctrine of disciplinary rigour and an ascetic posture (it is not a conception) of 'impersonality,' is to absolve the artist from responsibility towards life" (*Valuation* 121–22). I think there is some justice to this comment so far as "Tradition and the Individual Talent" is concerned. But Leavis, overlooking several major shifts in Eliot's critical thinking, takes this passage as paradigmatic of Eliot's general weakness as a theoretician.

23. Interestingly, McAlmon depicts Eliot as a "victim" of the cultural divide. Art, he argues, has "developed professionally two ways": the way of "popular appeal" and the way of "erudition" (9). Eliot is "slowly committing a literary suicide smothering fine sensitivities by being a professional litterateur" (10). Eliot discussed this diagnosis with McAlmon—whom he found to be "of promising general intelligence and very amiable personality"—and invited him to dinner (*Letters* 453–54).

McAlmon, for his part, found Eliot surprisingly likeable and expressed regrets for his published comments (McAlmon and Boyle 7–8). Yet he was never reconciled to what he regarded as the "cerebral tearfulness" of Eliot's poetry, its "liverish and stomach-achey wail," or to his political and religious conservatism (10).

24. Many passages could be cited, but one of the clearest appears in Eliot's November 1927 "Commentary" in the *Criterion*: "The man of letters to-day is interested

in a great many subjects—not because he has many interests, but because he finds that the study of his own subject leads him irresistibly to the study of the others; and he must study the others if only to disentangle his own, to find out what he is really doing himself" (386). Such study, though distracting, is ultimately necessary: "We can only hope that all this labour will make it possible for us to return more tranquilly to our own business, such as writing a poem, or painting a picture" (387).

25. Eliot excepts only "dramatic literature" from this proscription, for which see below and chapter 5.

26. In the *Dial* Eliot had disparaged Robert Frost, of all poets, on the grounds that he was insufficiently entertaining. "Mr. Frost seems the nearest equivalent to an English poet, specializing in New England torpor; his verse, it is regretfully said, is uninteresting, and what is uninteresting is unreadable, and what is unreadable is not read. There, that is done" ("LL [Apr. 1922]" 513). Surely this must rank among Eliot's least prescient judgments.

27. The residual effects of nineteenth-century conceptions of art, Eliot argues, block our enjoyment of Dryden.

28. In its definition of "mug's game" ("a thankless task; a useless, foolish, or unprofitable activity"), the *OED* cites Eliot's *Elder Statesman*, in which the character Gomez calls forgery a "mug's game" (*Elder* 32).

29. The accuracy of Leslie Fiedler's claim that "Poetry was, of course, never a popular art, in any meaning of that word" likewise turns on what one means by "poetry" (411). If ballads or blues are poetry—or, for that matter, if Shakespeare's plays, Homer's epics, or the psalms are poetry—then Fiedler's statement demands qualification.

30. It must be admitted, though, that Eliot's distrust of aestheticism is visible as early as "Portrait of a Lady," where the lady's cloistered notion of art is held up for ridicule in her first speech (CPP 8). Her suggestion that Chopin should be enjoyed only among a few discerning friends seems oddly reminiscent of Yeats's theater.

31. Eliot's numerous pieces on individual verse dramatists from Euripides to Middleton Murry can also be usefully regarded as case studies in "applied poetry," though some are more occupied with formal questions than others.

32. I am not here counting the *Cats* poems, which I do not mean thereby to devalue. Nor am I including the "Choruses from *The Rock*" since they were written as part of a play. The remaining poems range from *The Waste Land* to the brief "Lines to a Persian Cat." There is an obvious arbitrariness to my (or any) method of counting. Perhaps it will help to point out for comparison's sake that Yeats, whom Eliot survived by a quarter century, wrote nearly 200 poems after 1920; that Stevens, whom Eliot outlived by a decade, wrote over 300; and that Pound wrote over 100 of his *Cantos*. Even Marianne Moore, like Eliot not a prolific poet, managed about 120 poems between 1920 and 1965. I offer these totals only as a rough measure of poetic output.

33. This was in response to Bennett's bluntly informing Eliot that he "couldn't

see the point" of The Waste Land. "He said he didn't mind what I said as he had definitely given up that form of writing, and was now centred on dramatic writing"
(Journal 786).

34. "Burnt Norton" originated in material dropped from Murder in the Cathedral.
The remaining Quartets were composed during wartime, when Eliot foresaw no opportunity for the staging of a new play.

35. In 1933 Eliot reviewed A. E. Housman's Name and Nature of Poetry. On Housman's dry declaration, "I have seldom written poetry unless I was rather out of
health," Eliot commented, with equal understatement, "I believe that I understand
that sentence" (154).

36. On Eliot's early conviction that "Prufrock" would prove his "swan song,"
see Letters 58, 69, 141, 151; and D. Hall 98. For accounts of Eliot's "dry spells" in
1917, 1920, 1923 and 1924, see Ackroyd 77, 108, 135, 144. The fruitless periods
that preceded "Journey of the Magi," The Rock, and "Burnt Norton" are described by
Eliot in "The Three Voices of Poetry" (91) and in his conversation with John
Lehmann (5); see also Ackroyd 163, 225. Eliot spoke in general terms of his dry
spells to Helen Gardner as well (8).

37. Of the "Three Main Points" that "may never be forgotten in the criticism of
our Drama," J. A. Symonds, for example, gives pride of place to the idea that English
drama "grew up beneath the patronage of the whole nation; the public to which
these playwrights appealed was the English people, from Elizabeth upon the throne
down to the lowest ragamuffin of the streets." Without the "sympathy" of the
"whole people," in fact, drama "cannot flourish or become more than a merely literary product" (70).

38. As is typical with Eliot, the popular attribute of the literature competes for
attention with formal considerations and aesthetic valuation. At this stage, he seems
unable to take both angles at once. A comparison of Eliot's syllabi for his lectures on
Kyd and Marlowe demonstrates the shifting quality of his approach. Kyd, who is introduced as "The first important dramatist," is treated historically, with attention to
the "great popularity" of The Spanish Tragedy and the surprising (to Eliot) unpopularity
of the "realism" of Arden of Feversham, "a unique attempt at tragedy based on contemporary events" (qtd. in Schuchard 46). Marlowe, in contrast, is introduced as "The
greatest poet since Chaucer and the greatest dramatist before Shakespeare," and Eliot
consequently takes up such issues as "His originality"; "His verse in Tamburlaine"; and
"Monotony of Marlowe's dramatic verse compared with Shakespeare's at his best"
(46).

39. See also "Cyril Tourneur" (1930), where Eliot applauds two key scenes in
The Revenger's Tragedy as "remarkable feats of melodrama" (162).

40. A letter of the same year—in fact, the same remarkable letter to Mary
Hutchinson in which Eliot calls himself a "metic" and fears he may be a "savage"—
expresses the identical concern (Letters 317). The "crocodile isle" section of Sweeney
Agonistes, too, can be read as parodying the primitivist vogue.

41. Eliot was of course by no means the only artist or theoretician to make use of these principles; such ideas were, on the contrary, very much in the air, from Wagner's concept of the *Gesamtkunstwerk* to the admiration of both French and English symbolist poets for dance, which they took to represent "art in an undissociated and unspecialized form" (Kermode, "Poet" 1–7). Eliot's serious marshaling of anthropological thought against the cultural divide is nevertheless of unique interest, and it reaches some unanticipated conclusions.

42. See also Eliot's 1923 article "The Beating of a Drum" (12).

43. See Perl, chapters 3–4 (esp. 58–65 and 73–78). Just as he historicizes such shibboleths as *"L'art pour l'art,"* over time Eliot subjects even his own essays to the same treatment, qualifying them as products of their moment and pointing out the ways in which their validity is circumscribed by their immediate contexts (see, e.g., "To Criticize" 16; and "Milton II" 159–60). He attempts, though less convincingly, to do the same with his political views—for example, on class structure (Paul 16–17).

44. Marc Manganaro points out that in some ways Eliot's persistent attention to the "inherent difficulty of representing [the] 'other' " anticipates today's concern with the problem of ethnographic representation (418).

45. The *primitive* or *savage* is of course a nebulous category, under whose banner various cultures tend to blur in an undifferentiated mass. Eliot's anthropological studies did not deliver him from the usual conflations and easy generalizations; on the contrary, the anthropologists he was reading were themselves susceptible to such thinking. The uncomplicated equation of ancestral with present-day tribal cultures is one common simplification to which Eliot was prone. For the problematics of the term *primitive* and its kin, see Torgovnick 3–23 and 257 n. 45.

46. As Robert Crawford notes, Eliot, in addition to making this point himself, seems to have been "only too pleased" to publish concurring opinions in the *Criterion* (178). Crawford has catalogued numerous instances in Eliot's poems; but see also DuPlessis (98–105).

47. See "Rev. of *Group Theories*" 116. The review dates from 1916, but Eliot reiterates this critique a decade later ("Introduction to *Savonarola*" viii), and it may be traced back as far as 1913 and his Harvard seminar paper on the "Interpretation of Primitive Ritual" (Crawford 91–92).

48. Compounding the self-contradiction, "Tradition and the Individual Talent" and "War-Paint and Feathers" were composed and published almost simultaneously in 1919. See *Letters* 317–18, 351; Gallup 204–05.

49. The sentence from *The Idea of the Christian Society* reads in full: "And without sentimentalising the life of the savage, we might practise the humility to observe, in some of the societies upon which we look down as primitive or backward, the operation of a social-religious-artistic complex which we should emulate upon a higher plane" (CC 49). The same contradictory tendency we noted in texts thirty years older is visible here: "we" need to observe primitive societies without conde-

scending to them, to learn from them without falsifying them, and to emulate them in areas where they are superior; yet the emulation must be practiced upon a "higher plane." The inconsistency is now backed by religious authority, for Eliot has adopted Christianity as a point of view from which to establish hierarchy, and cultural relativism is in that sense no longer a real possibility for him.

50. Naremore and Brantlinger similarly associate modernism with the "art-for-art's-sake movements of the late nineteenth century" and suggest that modernism "always cultivates what Adorno (a modernist himself) described as an 'autonomous' social role" (9). Avant-garde art differs in that it "problematizes the authority of autonomous art" (10). The authors cite the work of Bürger and Huyssen (who himself cites Bürger) in making these claims; and it is fascinating to watch this argument replicating itself in the critical literature since the publication of *After the Great Divide* in 1986. Its insistence on an absolute distinction between modernism and the avant-garde (Huyssen's "never," Naremore and Brantlinger's "always") has been questioned by Eysteinsson, North (in *Reading* 1922), and others.

51. On the politics and aims of the Cocteau group, which have a number of points of overlap with Eliot and his circle, see Gendron, *Between* 94–99.

52. Huyssen's notion of a great divide between American and European modernism, however—including the suggestion that "the enthusiasm of the European avant-garde" for popular culture "somehow skipped over American modernism"—has been challenged by North (*Reading* 206–07).

CHAPTER 3

1. The contribution of folk plays to modern drama was commonly overstated. It is unclear whether Eliot was more aware of the romantic view, popularized by Jacob Grimm, that European village ceremonies contained "the first vague beginnings of the whole of modern drama," or of the rejoinder of later sociologists that Grimm's contention was "demonstrably wrong" (Chambers, *Medieval* 182).

2. As Sharp explains, "The earliest forms of folk-dance bear upon them unmistakable signs of a religious origin; indeed, some of them are still performed ritually, as pagan ceremonies of a quasi-religious or magic character, usually associated with the cultivation and fertility of the soil, and performed at particular seasons of the year" (4–5). See also Brody 3, and 96–98 on the sword dance in particular. Even some of the performance details are Eliotic: many versions, for example, include a Tiresian figure played by a cross-dressed man. In his study of these English ceremonial dramas, E. K. Chambers calls this figure "the Man-Woman, that unquiet spirit, for whom there is no obvious function, but for whom a place always has to be found" (*English* 153).

3. On the history and comic nature of the Doctor figure, see Brody 55–57. Eliot's conjectures on this subject appear to have merit.

4. Sharp's disdain for "the Jazz" has a similarly nationalistic edge. Eliot's phrase

"Chelsea-cum-Golders Green" implies that Sharp's artistic nonconformity is merely a matter of surface, like the ersatz bohemianism of a pretentious bourgeois.

5. Recall Eliot's similar objections to the commodification of "primitive" cultures in "War-Paint and Feathers," discussed in the previous chapter.

In the end, Eliot's skepticism toward the revival of folk dances appears to have been better warranted than Sharp's enthusiasm. Looking back on the movement with fifty years' perspective, Ronald Pearsall concludes that "The injection of new life into folk dancing by dedicated folklorists was disinterment rather than rejuvenation, and any claims that they were preventing old customs from dying out should be discounted" (218).

6. So seen, the poem mourns the irretrievability of live ritual in a modern culture in which all ritual is alien. I will develop such a reading at the end of chapter 4.

7. I say "even" because, with his aversion to cinema (discussed later in this chapter), Eliot acknowledged Chaplin's genius only reluctantly.

8. Similarly, "There is, 'waiting' for poetry on the stage, a quite sufficient number of persons to fill a playhouse; there are even a few willing to subsidize the performance of any play of the mildest promise" ("Poetic Drama" 635).

9. For Eliot's ginger criticism of Murry's *Cinnamon and Angelica*, see "The Poetic Drama." Eliot blames Murry's failure (without actually calling it a failure) on the near impossibility of writing a play outside a thriving dramatic tradition. It is because Murry knows that his actual audience will be only a few refined litterateurs— and because, as Eliot politely suggests, Murry self-consciously resists the encroachment of this improper audience—that he falters. Murry, to his detriment, is not checked by "the necessity of *entertaining* an audience cruder than himself" (635).

10. The difficulty with this particular sentence arises from its exclusion of the popular genre from the sphere of "art." Elsewhere—in "Marie Lloyd," for instance—Eliot does describe music-hall comedy as an art form.

11. All subsequent printings of "Marie Lloyd" have five further deletions from the *Dial* version. The first is a lengthy paragraph on Lloyd's funeral, evidently culled from a British newspaper ("London Letter [Nov. 1922]" 599). The second is the speculation on Lloyd's performances in the United States discussed below (600). The third is an interjected "thank God," which had approved the absence of any "cinema records" of Lloyd's act (601). The fourth is the observation that Lloyd was a native of London and got her start at age ten performing for a Hoxton audience similar to the working-class public that supported her to the end (601). The fifth is the adjective "amorphous," which had redundantly modified the noun "protoplasm" in describing the middle class (602).

The differences between the *Dial* and *Criterion* versions of "Marie Lloyd" have been discussed to somewhat different ends by Sebastian Knowles, who reads Eliot's self-abnegating final sentence as rather more calculating than I do ("'Then You Wink'" 28–30).

12. This may be; nevertheless, Lloyd's several tours of the United States were

quite successful in their own right, as was her tour of Australia (Farson 46, 81, 98). It is true, though, that she adapted her material to her foreign audiences, to make it less dependent on their familiarity with the Cockney type.

13. Recently several critics have disputed this point, and while there is no harm in correcting hyperbole, I fear that the trend is now to overcompensate. Eliot emotionally overstated the consistency of Lloyd's appreciation by working-class audiences, but the gist of his comments is accurate enough.

Dagmar Kift writes of Lloyd:

> Her career flourished primarily in the atmosphere of the West End variety theatres and, according to many anecdotes, she suffered quite badly from the shock of discovering that her style was not to the fancy of the working-class audiences in the East End. (170)

There are in fact some such anecdotes; they do not add up to a "many." The anecdotes that do exist date from early in Lloyd's career, well before Eliot's time (see, e.g., Macqueen-Pope 73–74). And though Sebastian Knowles and Jonna Mackin both cast doubt on Eliot's formulation by citing a famous incident in Sheffield when Lloyd was "given the bird," that reception was not generally representative: Lloyd was unquestionably, as Kift puts it, "the darling of the public all over the country" (170–71). Lloyd was herself an East-Ender, and whatever her reception on particular occasions, Eliot correctly understood her to be a revered figure for the London working class, who perceived her as one of their own who had never turned her back on them.

14. In another report, Eliot offered the criticism that his students, although "extremely intelligent," were also "somewhat passive" and "not prepared for study" (qtd. in Schuchard 31–32). Later reports, however, find him again "very well pleased with the work of the majority of the class" (37).

As Ronald Schuchard points out, Eliot's public remarks on his adult students are less affectionate than his private ones; in the *Egoist*, for example, Eliot "referred disparagingly to a passage on Tennyson in Alice Meynell's *Hearts of Controversy* as 'what a University Extension audience would like' " (50). Schuchard speculates that "Eliot's sense of his students' general lack of seriousness or commitment to literature [may have] clouded his remembrance of the 'immense pleasure' his lectures once gave him." However that may be, it seems likely Eliot was also assuming a superior pose, as he often did, for the *Egoist*'s avant-garde readership.

15. Over time Eliot found himself exhausted by the effort demanded by lecturing, and within a few months his exclamations over his pupils gave way to complaints about his workload. He found that his work at Lloyds Bank left him with more time and energy for his writing (*Letters* 193).

16. The effect lasted for at least three years: in 1919 he described his political views as "Liberal and strongly opposed to the Government in almost everything" (*Letters* 336). This statement is qualified, however, by Eliot's distaste for the current

railway strike; while accepting the legitimacy of the strikers' demands he apparently opposed their "summary methods"—a position that testifies little for the depth of his Labourite leanings.

17. On the character of Islington from the 1880s through the 1920s, see Cohen 117–24. Even in the late 1940s, F.O. Matthiesson could describe Islington as "one of the poorer boroughs of London" (80).

18. Eliot does not seem to have been aware, or did not care to recognize, that the boundary between the working class and the lower middle class, and between their cultures, was far from impermeable (Höher 85).

19. These arguments are not without troubles of their own. The main difficulty with Senelick's is his own claim to be able to adjudicate authenticity. Music-hall songs often reflect a conservative sensibility; therefore, he concludes, the working class cannot have produced (nor pleasurably consumed) music-hall songs. The only evidence offered here is Senelick's certainty that no class would adopt an ideology that, from his vantage point, thwarts its own interests.

The discourse of authenticity, in which intellectuals step in, or down, to determine which "popular" forms are genuinely popular and which represent the falsifications of the culture industry, is always problematic, however benevolent the intrusion. Even Clark, in his sophisticated and carefully historicized argument, is forced by his emphasis on forms of class control to mediate between *real* proletarian culture (the popular forms that the middle class eventually appropriates) and the synthetic popular mounted in the cafés.

20. Peter Bailey, too, criticizes the hard-line representation of music-hall songs as an "almost wholly artificial product with little or no demotic authenticity," noting its resemblance to the "mass culture critique which disallows that the production of culture is a dynamic process in which the consumer continues to play a constitutive role, and the 'authentic' is a property of ever imperfect and contested definition" (xv–xvi).

21. MacDermott's "We Don't Want to Fight" gave the word "jingo" to the English language. "We don't want to fight, / But by jingo if we do . . . " threatens the rousing chorus.

22. This is argued in "Marie Lloyd" as well as in "A Dialogue on Dramatic Poetry," where the character C insists that even music-hall bawdiness "is a tribute to, an acknowledgment of, conventional British morality" (37).

23. "Marie Lloyd," for example, predicts the death of civilization through its capitulation to mass culture, and the March 1921 "London Letter" associates the disintegration of class distinction with the "second Flood" (451).

24. In a 1936 radio address to sixth-form students, Eliot explains that "[t]he cinema gives an illusion not of the stage but of life itself. When we see a great music-hall comedian on the stage . . . we feel that he is conscious of his audience, that a great deal of the effect depends upon a sympathy set up between actor and au-

dience, and we like to feel that some of his gags are spontaneous and were not thought of the night before. But when we see Laurel and Hardy, it is not Laurel and Hardy acting for *us*, it is Laurel and Hardy in another mess" ("Need" 994).

25. In 1903, Beerbohm revisited the Metropolitan and found it one of the few sites where the old-style, pre-"Variety" programs still prevailed. He recorded this discovery in a column titled "The Older and Better Music Hall" (300).

26. I want to avoid any naive claim to the effect that Eliot simply merged into "the people" when he attended music-hall performances. It is not clear that any intellectual can cross over into the realm of the popular in complete innocence, without carrying something across—preconceptions, ideologies, axes to grind—and Eliot, for one, certainly achieved no such thing. To become a theorist of a popular form, or even an advocate, is already to assume an unconventional relation to it.

27. For more on the "music-hall lament," see Faulk, "Modernism" 607–14. This valuable study historicizes and contextualizes "Marie Lloyd" in order to argue that the essay marks a key moment of transition in the relations of intellectuals to popular culture (616–17).

28. According to Koritz's post-aesthetic reading, the real purpose of essays like "Marie Lloyd" is to stave off the middle class while forging a new intellectual elite; Eliot's alliance with the working class is purely strategic. These arguments are well, but not flawlessly, defended. Koritz claims, for example, that Eliot ranked Marie Lloyd below ballet dancer Léonide Massine because Massine's performance style was "impersonal" while Lloyd's depended on her personality (142). (This is of course a matter of gender as well.) But this particular hierarchy is imposed on Eliot's writings by Koritz's predisposition to find it there. Eliot's adulation of Lloyd is never, in fact, tempered by a preference for Massine; and Lloyd, as much as Massine, is the guiding spirit of Eliot's own "future stage."

There is, as we have seen, a discrepancy between, on the one hand, Eliot's praise of music hall for the strong bond it fosters between artist and audience, and on the other hand his preference for "impersonal" or aloof performance styles in other genres such as theater and ballet. Koritz's treatment of this conflict is valuable; yet although she first identifies such contradictions as "symptoms of ideological commitments that are not, and perhaps cannot be, reconciled with each other" (139), she *does* finally reconcile them along the expected Marxist lines: in the end, Eliot's commitment to his class (the "traditional intellectual") explains pretty much everything, and what had appeared to be ambivalence turns out to have been mere subterfuge, an attempt to conceal allegiances. Marie Lloyd and the music hall are only means to political ends: "What Eliot fears is the merging of the lower class with the middle class, and his attempts to appropriate music hall for high art can be read as a rearguard action against this cultural alliance" (151). Eliot professes admiration for Lloyd in *response* to his fear of middle-class hegemony, which is the "more important object" of his essay (142). Similarly, "It is . . . this fear of middle-class power that mo-

tivates him to object to a distinction between proletarian and aristocratic art in his review of Marianne Moore's poetry" (152, emphasis added). Koritz's argument, driven by political suspicion, thus arrives at what I call a partial truth.

CHAPTER 4

1. See, e.g., Winans and Kaufman 1.

2. My account of Sweeney's career is generally indebted to Linn, to Woodward, and to Winans and Kaufman.

3. Linn 2; Winans and Kaufman 24–25.

4. T. "Daddy" Rice had appeared in England as early as 1836. But the Virginia Minstrels, as Michael Pickering points out, transformed minstrelsy from a solo novelty act into "an autonomous institution with established conventions, a specific style of performance, and sufficient magnetism and repute soon to warrant the staging of an entire show in separate halls or theatres" (72–73).

5. On the development of Eliot's Sweeney character between 1917 and 1926, see C. Smith, "Sweeney" 92.

6. Eliot never explicitly identified his sources for Sweeney. He came closest in one quizzical reference to "a professional pugilist, mildly successful" (Coghill 86), a figure often identified—though never by Eliot—with Steve O'Donnell, Eliot's erstwhile boxing trainer. Grover Smith calls Eliot's comment "overgrave and perhaps rather sportive," and I agree that it should not be taken as definitive (*T. S. Eliot's* 114). Yet just as it is difficult to doubt the contribution of Sweeney Todd to Sweeney's ghoulish personality, the presence of Joel Walker Sweeney seems to me manifest in the text. That his banjo-toting younger brother was named Sampson Sweeney is a wonderful coincidence and must surely have seemed so to Eliot.

7. To this, Eliot adds, "And a stimulus to do my part to bring about the conditions which will make this work possible." Does Eliot mean by this only that he will try to improve the conditions of his own life? (It would be another two and a half years before he would leave Lloyds Bank.) Or does he mean that he will redouble his efforts to "mak[e] the modern world possible for art" ("*Ulysses*" 178)—to bring about the cultural transformation discussed in chapter 2? His move into drama, as I have been arguing, was motivated in part by the desire to transform the relation of society and art.

8. Ackroyd cites Eliot's letter of 28 April 1936 to Paul Elmer More (146).

9. One might also refer to musical comedy, then a recently devised compound of revue, burlesque, and minstrel show elements, to which it conjoined a light plot together with lyrics and dialogue in the American idiom (Ewen 117–18).

10. The comic operas of Gilbert and Sullivan are likewise rooted in burlesque. The concluding "nightmare" chorus of *Sweeney Agonistes* parodies their *Iolanthe*.

11. This is not to suggest that Eliot's technique is more sophisticated than Joyce's, but only that it extends the "method" that Eliot attributes to Joyce in "*Ulysses*,

Order, and Myth." Eliot's multidimensional technique in Sweeney Agonistes, actually, seems to me more truly Joycean than the "mythical method" as he defines it in his essay.

12. Bennett records Eliot's saying that some of the play's lines might be "accentuated by drum beats" (Journal 786). Eliot indicated later to director Hallie Flanagan that he had imagined the entire play "accompanied by light drum taps to accentuate the beats" (Flanagan 83).

13. See Malamud, T. S. Eliot's Drama 36–37.

14. "You said it," "gotta," and "gonna" all date from the teens and twenties; "all right," "swell," and "slick" originate in the mid- to late 1800s but take on renewed currency in the Jazz Age; "pinch" comes earlier (ca. 1850) but remains popular. "Do in" is British but still a fairly new term (the first instance cited in the OED is from 1905).

Everett argues that the play's style is essentially American, its strongest affinities being with the work of such writers as Ring Lardner and Anita Loos (254–59).

15. When the "Fragment of an Agon" appeared in the January 1927 Criterion, it was identified as being "From Wanna Go Home, Baby?" The "Fragment of a Prologue" had been published in the October 1926 issue without any additional information other than the tag, "To be continued." The change of title replicates the substitution of The Waste Land for He Do the Police in Different Voices: in both cases the suggestive and literary replaces the definite and colloquial. As Everett points out, "Baby" as an endearment is clearly an Americanism (246).

16. In the song "My Old Dad," "[a] man is drowned, his son breaks a pole in fishing for him, the man is revivified in some strange manner, encounters the Devil, and then is marked with vegetative and fish-like characteristics" (Lyon 155).

17. This term, along with the epithet "smoked Irishman" for the African American, "indicated the fundamental affinity in the popular mind between these groups" (Lott 95).

18. In his 1919 essays on Jonson (129) and Marlowe (105), Eliot had already complained of the inadequacy of such labels as "comedy," "tragedy," and "farce." For an extended discussion of Eliot's attempts to break down these "abstractions," see Schuchard 87–101.

19. Turn-of-the-century music-hall observers could even identify the moment when "the American cross-talk ousted the Irish" (Mair 127).

20. Despite his ties to New England, the Missouri-born Eliot accepted and even nurtured an image of himself as a Southerner. In his 1928 letter to Herbert Read (quoted in chapter 1), Eliot spoke of having been "born in the South" and of speaking like a "southern boy with a nigger drawl" (Read 15). And in his freshman year at Harvard, Eliot joined the Southern Club, whose "sole criterion of membership . . . was that one had Southern blood" (Soldo 58). One wonders whether Eliot may therefore have felt—perverse as this now seems—more than usually entitled, even for an American, to make use of "Negro" materials.

21. For Grover Smith, for instance, jazz in *Sweeney Agonistes*, as in *The Great Gatsby*, reveals the vapidity of the age (*T.S. Eliot's* 114). Carol Smith assimilates the play's jazz element to "machine-like rhythms" that provide "a telling commentary on [Eliot's] attitude toward modern life" ("Sweeney" 90).

22. Eliot made this remark during an interview for Dublin radio, January 1936.

23. Gates pays Eliot a powerful compliment in asking "where in dialect poetry, with the notable exception of Sterling Brown, a black poet used his medium as effectively as Eliot did in *Sweeney Agonistes*" (289).

24. For the symbolist roots of Eliot's argument, see Kermode, "Poet and Dancer," as well as Koritz, passim. It appears that Eliot's enthusiasm for the Nö drama, expressed in his 1917 essay, had not worn off by the time he wrote *Sweeney Agonistes.*

As Kermode has shown, the opposition of empathy to abstraction in art comes to Eliot in part from Wilhelm Worringer via T. E. Hulme (*Romantic* 121–23).

25. As "Marie Lloyd" shows, Eliot did recognize and even relish the naturalism of Lloyd's act:

> To appreciate, for instance, the last turn in which Marie Lloyd appeared, one ought to know what objects a middle-aged woman of the charwoman class would carry in her bag; exactly how she would go through her bag in search of something; and exactly the tone of voice in which she would enumerate the objects she found in it. This was only part of the acting in Marie Lloyd's last song, "One of the Ruins that Cromwell Knocked Abaht a Bit." (406)

26. Even the card reading in the opening scene, as Grover Smith points out, corresponded to the casting of lots for a sacrificial victim (*T. S. Eliot's* 115). See also C. Smith, "Sweeney" 95–96.

27. On the play's paradoxical positioning of the audience, see also Crawford 179–80; and Jaidka 107.

28. Paraphrasing Eliot's letter of Nov. 30, 1924, Ronald Bush explains that when Eliot "sent Ottoline Morrell the *Hollow Men* typescripts, he told her that his new sequence of poems was an avocation of his more revolutionary play, which he had been too weak to go on with" (97).

29. Bush, however, is "inclined to regret" the poem's turn away from an internal spiritual quest patterned after the *Vita Nuova*—a view I certainly do not share.

30. See his "Preface to the Edition of 1964" in *The Use of Poetry and the Use of Criticism.*

31. A claim based on observation in the absence of statistics. The opening line of *The Waste Land* seems to be a favorite with meteorologists, who miss its irony, while variants of "*Not with a bang but a whimper*" are ubiquitous in all areas of reporting, from sports to politics to finance.

32. The representational costumes worn by some mummers' troupes are a late "decadence" that alters the effect of the ceremony (Brody 22).

33. The "startling and mysterious" appearance of the Marshfield Paper Boys, for example, is "achieved with a mass of shredded paper (often newspaper) which begins at the top of the conical headdress and shoulders and falls all the way down the body until nothing can be distinguished beneath it but a pair of farm boots." The costume has been compared to "the dress of figures like the Bavarian Wild Man and the African medicine man" (Brody 23).

34. In "The Beating of a Drum" (1923) Eliot reviews W.O.E. Oesterley's *The Sacred Dance,* which includes accounts of religious dances around sacred trees and quotes a passage from *The Golden Bough* that remarks how "often with the decay of old faiths the serious rites and pageants of grown people have degenerated into the sports of children" (qtd. in Oesterley 71).

35. For a summary of the play's publication history, see Malamud, *T. S. Eliot's* 51. Note that as late as 1932, Eliot was still calling the second section "Fragment of an Agon (From *Wanna Go Home, Baby?*)"; see Gallup 163, entry Ba7.

36. In 1933 Eliot had given Flanagan only a twenty-five-line concluding scene in order to round off the play; that text is quoted in Flanagan (83–84) and in C. Smith (62–63). The Group Theatre's production of the following year ended with Sweeney's offstage murder of Doris—an action invented by director Rupert Doone and not authorized by Eliot.

For a detailed discussion of "The Superior Landlord," see Sidnell 100–02 and 263–65. Sidnell's argument that the scenario dates from 1934 and not earlier seems to me conclusive.

CHAPTER 5

1. Even Dahlberg's unconscious reduction of Eliot's plays to "volumes," as though print were their proper medium, is revealing.

2. For an extended discussion of the "art versus money" ideology, see Wexler's *Who Paid for Modernism?* to which I am generally indebted.

3. As Edmund Wilson wrote to Malcolm Cowley on January 5, 1951: "I yesterday had a letter from Allen announcing his conversion [to Roman Catholicism]. . . . He never could forgive any kind of success: when *The Cocktail Party* was a box-office smash, he even threw over Eliot—so I suppose that after that there was nothing for it but Christ" (*Letters* 496). In the end, however, Tate's separation from Eliot proved temporary.

4. As H. S. Davies, for example, later commented, Eliot could "hardly have been unconscious of the possible change, the possible choice—I never remembered him missing much subtler points than that" (362–63).

5. Ballet, it should be noted, was a common and not unpopular music-hall attraction.

6. "In Trinity Church," interestingly, had been a key song in establishing the Cockney type for the stage (Pearsall 59). For Eliot's particular satisfaction with his

version, see Browne, *Making* 12. The practice of refurbishing familiar tunes with up-dated lyrics was itself a music-hall tradition—one to which Eliot had had recourse already in *Sweeney Agonistes* and in the final nursery-rhyme chorus of *The Hollow Men*. Jones ascribes this practice to the impoverishment of early music-hall singers, who lacked the resources to hire composers (490). Pearsall traces it back to the much older genre of ballad opera and up through the nineteenth-century burlesque (64).

For more on music-hall elements in *The Rock* see also Malamud, *Words* 35.

7. Eliot's attempts to write in Cockney dialect were controversial from the be-ginning. Shortly before the show's opening, Rev. Vincent Howson, who played Bert, complained to director Browne that Eliot's dialogue was "not true cockney," and he insisted on altering many lines to suit his own ideas of "true cockney" (Browne, *Making* 14). In his prefatory note to the published version, Eliot got in a dig in return by suggesting that Howson had "so completely rewritten, amplified and con-densed"—he did not say "improved"—"the dialogue between himself ('Bert') and his mates, that he deserves the title of joint author" (5). Browne, for his part, felt that Eliot's original text sounded no less authentic than Howson's, but he saw no alter-native under the circumstances but to compromise with his leading man. Contem-porary reviewers generally considered the (rewritten) Cockney scenes the weakest in the play; whether the fault lay with Eliot's ear or with Howson's tinkering—or perhaps, in some cases, with the critics' own prejudices—is difficult to say.

8. Of course, Eliot's decision to include the choruses in his *Collected Poems* while allowing the full text to go out of print can only have encouraged this approach. But that decision may have been influenced in turn by the play's reviewers.

9. See also Malamud, *Where* 39–40.

10. See Browne, *Making* 54–56; Malamud, *Drama* 84.

11. The "jazz rhythms" of the Four Knights' "Come down Daniel" chant in act 2 have often been cited as further evidence of popular influences, but I would not make too much of them. Unlike the pervasive rhythms of *Sweeney Agonistes*, these are used to produce a merely local effect. They are, in addition, processed through Vachel Lindsay's "Daniel" (also called "Daniel Jazz") and thus at an obvious literary remove from any popular source.

12. John D. Margolis writes, "One may reasonably suspect that the speaker la-beled E utters Eliot's sentiments" (183). Although this assertion would support my point, I think it an error, no less than Kristian Smidt's equally confident claim that "the character who represents the author most closely" is B (66). The "Dialogue" expresses Eliot's debates with himself, and *each* interlocutor displays aspects of Eliot and voices positions he adopts or considers in various essays.

13. Eliot discusses the resemblances of diction and style between *Murder* and *Everyman* in "The Aims of Poetic Drama" (11).

14. For more detailed accounts of these productions, see Malamud, *Drama* 70–75; Browne, *Making* 63–67, and "T. S. Eliot" 124–30; Speaight, "With Becket" 186; and Gordon, *Imperfect* 277–81.

15. The Winter Garden Theatre on Broadway, where *Cats* played for seventeen years, accommodates over 1,550 patrons.

The 1936 staging of *Murder* by the Federal Theatre Project in New York, too, enjoyed a surprising but nevertheless limited success. A side-bar to Richard Watts' review in the *Herald Tribune* notes that the play "has confounded the Broadway prophets by becoming a full-fledged hit. There was standing room only on the second night of its engagement at the Manhattan Theater, and 2,500 people were turned away from the playhouse last Monday, when citizens on relief were admitted free of charge. Originally scheduled to close Tuesday, it will continue until April 11"—that is, for a run of roughly three weeks, hardly the duration of a "full-fledged hit."

16. In commending a 1953 revival of *Murder*, Brooks Atkinson directly takes on Eliot's concern with the entertainment value of his play. Countering the Eliot of "Poetry and Drama," Atkinson notes, "It is a matter of record that some people were not bored by the original production." But the new production, starring Robert Donat, was even better, proving "that any play of literary and spiritual distinction can be made to fit the theatre, if accomplished directors and actors take hold of it." The conclusion that his play could be "made to fit" the theater can only have been a small consolation to Eliot, like Atkinson's reassurance that "as a poet of intellectual eminence he is entitled to write in classical forms" ("Triumph"). Eliot, as we have seen, did not wish to be granted these sorts of dispensations.

17. Or again, "underneath the action, which should be perfectly intelligible, there should be a musical pattern which intensifies our excitement by reinforcing it with feeling from a deeper and less articulate level" ("Need" 994).

18. This point is reminiscent of the striking suggestion in *The Use of Poetry and the Use of Criticism* that the "meaning" of a poem may function chiefly "to satisfy one habit of the reader, to keep his mind diverted and quiet, while the poem does its work upon him: much as the imaginary burglar is always provided with a bit of nice meat for the house-dog" (144).

19. Eliot ultimately came to believe that the play's "deepest flaw" was a failure to bring the original myth fully into a modern reality. The intractable difficulty of representing the Furies in performance, he felt, exemplified the problem ("Poetry and Drama" 84). See also Malamud, *Words* 108; and Gordon, *Imperfect* 329–31.

20. This characterization of *The Cocktail Party* had indeed passed its first test a few months before, when the play debuted at the Edinburgh Festival. The reviewer for the *Scotsman* solicited the reaction of a local "housewife" who had attended the play—an avowed nonexpert who "doesn't get to the theatre very often" and who "gave us her comments over the clamour raised by a naughty child or two." He reported her verdict as follows:

> She said that she liked the play immensely. She didn't pretend to understand it all, but it had sent her away from the theatre with her mind in a furious state of activity and her heart aglow. It had been very hot and stuffy where she was sitting,

but all the time she was very conscious of seeing a theatre put to its real purpose which she doesn't always feel. (6)

21. *Newsweek*, similarly, complained that the play was "written down a bit to cater to the masses." Eliot's mistake was "to play showman at the expense of the detached genius who wrote 'Murder in the Cathedral' and 'Sweeney Agonistes' " ("First Nights").

22. In addition to his call in "Wilkie Collins and Dickens" for a narrowing of the gap between popular and "serious" fiction, Eliot had written, "You cannot define Drama and Melodrama so that they shall be reciprocally exclusive; great drama has something melodramatic in it, and the best melodrama partakes of the greatness of drama" (417–18).

Gordon, who points out the mystery element in the earlier plays, considers these merely "sops to an audience incapable of divining the true mystery which is the recess of consciousness" (*Imperfect* 481). Though some of his remarks have a supercilious tone ("If the audience gets its strip tease it will swallow the poetry"), Eliot rather enjoyed the "strip tease" element himself and was, I think, not insincere in trying "to keep in mind that in a play, from time to time, something should happen; that the audience should be kept in the constant expectation that something is going to happen; and that, when it does happen, it should be different, but not too different, from what the audience had been led to expect" ("Poetry and Drama" 85). In my view, his use of mystery conventions is part of an attempt—not always successful, but not necessarily condescending—to make his plays satisfying as drama.

23. To put the play's run in perspective, *Death of a Salesman*, which opened in 1949, ran for 742 performances; and *The Member of the Wedding*, which opened two weeks before *The Cocktail Party*, ran for 501 performances. Of course both these plays are in prose, but it was with prose drama that Eliot avowedly wished to compete. The comparison with a blockbuster musical is perhaps unfair, but *South Pacific*, another holdover from 1949, ran for 1,925 performances. Yet *The Cocktail Party* still qualifies as a hit play, and it fared better than many quite respectable contemporaries, including William Inge's *Come Back, Little Sheba* (191 performances) and Clifford Odets's *Country Girl* (235). Eugène Ionesco's anti-theatrical breakthrough, *La Cantatrice Chauve*, first performed in 1950 in Paris, was not, of course, a popular success.

24. When the printed edition of *The Confidential Clerk* appeared on the list in 1954, it was "the first play to do so since *The Cocktail Party*" (Malamud, *Drama* 151).

25. William Barrett had rendered a similar judgment on the original production of *The Cocktail Party*, where he found Eliot's "creative powers" to have reached "their lowest ebb" (359). With its "starkness of rhythm and syncopation," by contrast, *Sweeney Agonistes* represented Eliot's "greatest achievement as a dramatic poet" (355).

26. There are also the innovations of *Sweeney*'s diction to be regretted, as Ronald Hayman writes:

In all his plays except *Sweeney* Eliot opted for a literary language, making larger and progressively more disastrous compromises in his attempts at approximating to conversational English. He left it for Pinter and subsequent playwrights to explore the possibilities of uneducated speech. (2)

27. In a variation on this theme, Martin Browne's appraisal of Eliot's dramatic work culminates in the judgment that it had peaked with *The Family Reunion*; that that play's austere ritualism "surely indicates the direction in which Eliot might fruitfully have moved"; and that "the truth about Eliot's drama [is] that its permanent value lies in its poetry" (*Making* 343). This conclusion cannot have brought much satisfaction to Eliot's shade.

28. It seems typical of Eliot to have selected a form of entertainment that, like music hall in 1922, had run through a long tradition and was on the verge of being superseded.

29. I am not suggesting that Eliot should have attempted precisely the same stunt again; he himself rightly pointed out that this special effect could not be duplicated in another play ("Poetry and Drama" 81).

30. *The Idea of a Christian Society*, for example, begins with the sentence: "The fact that a problem will certainly take a long time to solve, and that it will demand the attention of many minds for several generations, is no justification for postponing the study" (CC 5).

31. Duncan is presumably referring to Henry Sherek's difficulty in securing a suitable London venue for *The Elder Statesman* (it eventually ran for two months at the Cambridge Theatre), and to his inability to mount a Broadway production of any kind (see Browne, *Making* 341–42).

CHAPTER 6

1. *Culture and Environment* was coauthored with Denys Thompson. Because of Q. D. Leavis's obvious association with her husband, her important *Fiction and the Reading Public* should perhaps be mentioned here as well, though her work is of course her own.

2. Newton Minow, FCC chair under President John F. Kennedy, famously denigrated television as a "vast wasteland" in 1961.

3. Leavis asks, for example:

Are we then to listen to Spengler's . . . admonition to cease bothering about the inevitable future? That is impossible. Ridiculous, priggish, and presumptuous as it may be, if we care at all about the issues we cannot help believing that, for the immediate future, at any rate, we have some responsibility. ("Mass Civilization" 46)

This passage recalls all too readily Eliot's stirring "Commentary" in the June 1927 *Criterion*, which follows the identical course from a rejection of the "Spenglerish" notion that "tout est foutu" (this is "a fatalism which is unacceptable") to the asser-tion "that man is responsible, morally responsible, for his present and his immedi-ate future" (283). But Leavis saw no reason to hide his debt to the man he upheld as the courageous leader of the cultured minority. The *Criterion*, for Leavis, is one of the few remaining outposts of living culture in England; it "carries on almost alone" ("Mass Civilization" 32).

4. Thurber, it appears, greatly appreciated Eliot's advocacy and considered Eliot's words in *Time* "the best estimate of his work ever" (Bernstein 361). See also Bernstein 219 and 442–43; and Thurber 184.

5. At the same time, interestingly, Eliot condemned the work of Walt Disney, in which he thought he detected "a streak of cruelty" (47).

6. For an account of the *Times* crossword as an element of Eliot's daily routine, see "Reflections" 22. His absorption in a Penguin puzzle book while recovering from an illness is documented in Ackroyd 331.

7. For examples of various kinds, see, e.g., Ackroyd 167, 279, 331; Gordon, *Im-perfect* 354; Jay, *T.S. Eliot* 138; Matthews 122; Levy and Scherle 66; Durrell 64; Eliot, "Books"; and "Reflections" 26.

8. According to his autobiographical note for his twenty-fifth Harvard class reunion, Eliot also particularly enjoyed the adventures of Arsène Lupin, the gentleman-burglar created by Maurice Leblanc (Matthews 122).

9. Indeed, his name was often invoked alongside those of Franklin Roosevelt, Woodrow Wilson (Fiedler's "presidents"), and André Gide by educated fans of de-tective fiction seeking to legitimize their own taste.

10. Eliot's rules include such principles as "The story must not rely upon elab-orate and incredible disguises," and "The detective should be highly intelligent but not superhuman[; w]e should be able to follow his inferences and almost, but not quite, make them with him" ("Homage" 141–42). Each of these requirements is elaborated or defended in a short paragraph.

11. Eliot specifically recommended Christie's *Murder of Roger Ackroyd* to a friend in 1955 (Levy and Scherle 66).

12. Eliot said little about other "generic" forms of fiction, though the occa-sional comment that has been preserved suggests that he did not reject out of hand science fiction either. Despite his lifelong, largely ideological antipathy to H. G. Wells, for instance, in 1961 he called *The Time Machine* "a great story" and "a fearful, though a wonderful, imaginative, piece" (Greenwell, "Writing" 7).

13. Leavis, by contrast, dismissed radio broadcasting as "mainly a means of pas-sive diversion" that, like film, tended "to make active recreation, especially active use of the mind, more difficult" ("Mass Civilisation" 21). E. E. Cummings, similarly, bore an intense animosity toward radio (see, e.g., his *Selected Letters* 174–75 and 194–96; my thanks to Michael Webster for pointing out these references).

14. Besides the closing paragraphs of "Marie Lloyd" (407–08), see, for ex-ample, Eliot's October 1927 "Commentary" in the *Criterion* (290), "The Need for

Poetic Drama" (994), "Religious Drama: Mediaeval and Modern" (12), and his preface to *The Film of Murder in the Cathedral.*

15. In one typical comment in a review of *The Waste Land,* Gorham B. Munson thought it "a reasonable conjecture to say that Mr. Eliot does not want to communicate his suffering to the general reader. To such he desires to be incomprehensible." Eliot's "suffering" was meant to be understood only by "a chosen coterie of his similars" (207). Harold Monro, narrating his (presumably fictive) conversation with a friend who "came to me with the discovery that he and I could not hope to understand Mr. Eliot's poems," had his friend exit with the remark, "But at my back I always hear / Mr. Eliot's intellectual sneer" (164–65).

16. See, for example, the excerpts in Grant from Elinor Wylie (1923), Clive Bell (1923), and Louise Morgan (1926). And it was only 1920 when Mark Van Doren was predicting: "Mr. Eliot will never be popular at this rate. But when will he not have readers?"

17. Unhappily, the collaboration disintegrated when Fry failed in his promise to outline the project and delegate tasks to the others.

18. This production, incidentally, ran for an impressive 252 performances on Broadway.

19. Richard Foster's "Frankly, I Like Criticism," for example, praises the New Critics repeatedly for being "serious about literature" (280), for being "intensely and seriously interested in literature" (283), for "making the study of literature more serious" (281), and so forth. Conservative advocates continue even today to eulogize the New Criticism as the "most supple, serious, and responsive" of twentieth-century critical schools (Kimball 19), and the *Oxford Companion to English Literature* still identifies as Leavis's "most vital contribution" his "introduction of a new seriousness into English studies" (Drabble 581). I. A. Richards's credit for bringing "a new intellectual seriousness" to criticism was finally dropped in the *Companion's* sixth edition (2000).

Opposition to all this "seriousness" existed from the beginning. As early as 1929, Edmund Wilson was protesting that the New Criticism (not yet so called) was a jejune business—an opinion he never relinquished—and that the "disciples" of Eliot, who had carried their master's practice "to extremes," were largely to blame (*Letters* 170).

20. Louis Menand makes a related point: that *The Waste Land* has come to be read in the context of a narrow culture "defined for us by teachers and scholars— Richards, Brooks, Cassirer, Wellek. One effect of the supremacy of [this] culture, and of the academicism that produced it, was to rewrite modernism in the name of an esthetic epistemology and a theory of literature's educative function that modernism, in its initial inspiration, was a reaction against—the epistemology of Immanuel Kant and the educational philosophy of Matthew Arnold" (99–100).

21. The most notable example along these lines is "The Frontiers of Criticism" (1956), which dubs New Critical methodology "the lemon-squeezer school of

criticism" and writes off the formalist analysis of poetry as "a very tiring way of passing the time" best employed as "an exercise for pupils" (113). See also Perl 29–31.

22. See, e.g., Levy and Scherle 113.

23. For a discussion of the logic that brought the American political Left to back "highbrow," experimental modernism see Ross (e.g., 217–19).

24. Eliot's terms: "I do think that where you have these modern means of communication and means of imposing the speech and idioms of a small number on the mass of people at large, it does complicate the problem very much." Hall, still not quite satisfied, then wondered out loud "if there's a possibility that what you mean by common speech will disappear." Having thus tapped into Eliot's constitutional weltschmerz, Hall finally earned the conclusion he desired. "That is a very gloomy prospect," Eliot responded. "But very likely indeed" (109).

25. Part of a series titled "Talking Freely," this dialogue is rocky almost from the start, with the opinionated Greenwell apparently bent on getting Eliot to fulminate against "poetry that contains whole prose passages" taken from sources such as newspapers. Eliot, who had himself imported a catalogue of armaments into "Triumphal March," would have none of this, and Greenwell's mistake of citing Marianne Moore as exemplifying the alleged problem did nothing to help his cause with Eliot, long one of Moore's staunchest supporters.

26. Why Donne should be singled out as a model for the artist consciously aloof from the rabble is unclear, unless because this example would presumably appeal to Eliot.

27. Neither Eliot nor Greenwell suggested that this aesthetic purity might help to explain why Eliot had written exactly three "non-dramatic poems" in the past eighteen years. "The Cultivation of Christmas Trees," published in 1954, took its place as the last of Eliot's sequence of "Ariel Poems." "To Walter de la Mare" was published in 1948, and "To My Wife" in 1958. These last two works were ultimately grouped at the end of Eliot's Collected Poems under the heading "Occasional Verses" with three poems dating from the Second World War: "Defense of the Islands" (which, a headnote apologizes, "cannot pretend to be verse"), "A Note on War Poetry," and "To the Indians Who Died in Africa." Aside from the six brief pieces mentioned here, Eliot published no other (nondramatic) poetry after Four Quartets.

28. There is another embarrassing moment late in the interview when Eliot rather coldly denies having expressed a view that Greenwell insistently attributes to him.

29. Among the other examples one might mention, there is the 1958 interview cited earlier in this chapter as containing some authentic Eliotic grumbling about "mass culture." Here, as in the interview with Hall, the interviewer had to lead Eliot more than halfway down the path before the sage would impart the coveted wisdom. In this case, Eliot's diatribe on the "absence of values" in the mass media of a

"purely materialistic civilization" was preceded by the following oration from Leslie Paul:

> Well, there's a question that's begun to perturb me very much. It is not so much this business of a new pagan culture but rather what I would like to call a "cultureless culture." . . . What I really mean by that, I suppose, is this mass entertainment culture which is absolutely, as far as I can see, without any values at all—and yet is getting hold of the world. I think that it seems to be part of a whole process of spiritual drying-up, as if man no longer possessed or even wanted to possess any kind of spiritual inwardness, as though the whole business of inwardness or spirituality just bored him stiff. . . . Well, you're the poet of The Waste Land and what you have to say on this ought to be important. (Paul 13)

I do not mean to imply that interviewers like Paul or Hall somehow forced Eliot to take a position he did not agree with; the interview with Greenwell shows, on the contrary, that Eliot was not so easily conscripted. Still, the framing of a question does tend to shape the response, and Eliot was relentlessly nudged toward some pet point of his interviewers' that they wished, like Hall, to see him make. Not infrequently, these points had to do with the imminent cultural decline attributable to some dismaying change in contemporary society. Four of the eight questions Donald Carroll put to Eliot in 1962 take on this cast. Eliot sometimes takes Carroll's bait—as when he immediately agrees that "the jettisoning of classical education in the United States [is] likely to have a sterilizing effect on American literature"—and sometimes he refuses it:

> "Do you believe, as some writers have suggested, that our young poets today are too talented—that is, sophisticated in technique yet self-conscious in vocabulary?"
>
> "I have no belief about young poets as a crowd." (32–33)

But take it or leave it, Eliot was given every opportunity here and elsewhere to play the Grand Old Man frowning magisterially on the culturally irredeemable present.

30. In his preamble to the interview, Greenwell describes Eliot as having "a glint in his eyes that makes you suspect that you are about to sit down on a strategically positioned drawing-pin." Apparently this was the only way he could understand Eliot's stubborn insistence on poetry's need to entertain.

31. For a discussion of Eliot's inconsistency and its implications, see Eagleton, "Eliot" 286–89.

32. Or again: "[I]t is important to remember that we should not consider the upper levels as possessing more culture than the lower, but as representing a more conscious culture and a greater specialisation of culture" (CC 121).

33. See also Leslie Paul's "Conversation," in which Eliot tells his interlocutor that the class society toward which he is "emotionally disposed" "will be flexible; it

will somewhat blur the outlines of its classes. A very rigid class distinction is petrification" (16).

34. An observation in fact made long ago by Raymond Williams, who noted: "One thinks indeed, at times, of Eliot as the contemporary of Burke, who was himself idealizing and simplifying his actual society" (236). Williams also acknowledges the insight contained in Eliot's ideas about the uneven "diffusion of culture," agreeing that "[i]n any form of society towards which we are likely to move, it now seems clear that there must be, not a simple equality (in the sense of identity) of culture; but rather a very complex system of specialized developments—the whole of which will form the whole culture, but which will not be available, or conscious, as a whole, to any individual or group living within it" (237–38). But he then adds parenthetically, "This complex system has, of course, no necessary relation to a system of social classes based on economic discrimination" (238).

35. The prospective whitening of black identity was a recurrent concern of Langston Hughes, for example, though he worked for political changes that would make assimilation feasible. Jewish-American leaders have long experienced similar forebodings.

36. For Clark, who himself tends to see in popular culture more cause for concern than for celebration, this represents "a perfectly right and proper pessimism or right and proper degree of extremism in the posing of the cultural question" (189).

37. Another echo of "Wilkie Collins and Dickens," with its insistence on the "thriller" element without which the novel becomes "dull": "We know that [Kipling] is not dull, because we have all, at one time or another, by one poem or another, been thrilled" (239).

38. As to how Eliot distinguishes "verse" from "poetry" at all, he explains, "What fundamentally differentiates his [Kipling's] 'verse' from 'poetry' is the subordination of musical interest." A successful ballad tells a story with intensity; poetry, by contrast, focuses less on the tale than on the way it is told. "[T]here is a harmonics of poetry," Eliot claims, "which is not merely beyond [the] range" of the ballad; it would actually "interfere with" the ballad's "intention" (251).

39. Only months earlier, an unfriendly critic in the *Saturday Review* had adduced Kipling as precisely the sort of "inferior" figure by whom, according to Eliot's admirers at least, Eliot would never stoop to be influenced (Jackson 14).

40. Bogan is either unaware of or has forgotten Eliot's essay of 1919, "Kipling Redidivus."

41. See also, for example, Eliot's third Turnbull lecture (1933) in *The Varieties of Metaphysical Poetry* (289–90); "The Man of Letters and the Future of Europe" (1945) (333–34); and the climax of his powerful memorial lecture on Yeats (1940) (262).

42. Or: "[I]n developing the language, enriching the meaning of words and showing how much words can do, he [the poet] is making possible a much greater range of emotion and perception for other men, because he gives them the speech in which more can be expressed" ("What Dante Means" 134).

43. This view of 1940 improves on Eliot's formulation of 1933, where the process is entirely top-down, and the poet remains a persecuted outsider: "the function of the poet at every moment is to make the inarticulate folk articulate; and as the inarticulate folk is almost always mumbling the speech, become jargon, of its ancestors or of its newspaper editors, the new language is never learnt without a certain resistance, even resentment" (*Varieties* 289–90).

44. Although this conception of the artist's collaboration with the social rank and file resembles Eliot's account of the circulation of culture between the aristocracy and the other classes in *Notes towards the Definition of Culture*, neither argument is logically dependent on the other.

45. Others besides Wilson have attempted to catalogue Eliot's personas. Hugh Kenner's list comprises "the Archdeacon, the Publisher, the Clubman, the Man of Letters in Europe, the Aged Eagle, the Wag, and the Public-Spirited Citizen" (x). Igor Stravinsky's more offhand version includes "Old Possum, Tiresias, the churchwarden, [and] Sweeney" (92).

46. Gordon, too, seems to me a little too ready to dismiss most of Eliot's selves as "masks" or "casings" that obscure the "hidden life" of the spiritual aspirant who was Eliot's true self (*Imperfect* 259–60, e.g.).

47. See, for example, the series of droll articles published a few years later in the *New York Times Book Review* (Breit, "Interview" and "In and Out of Books"; Dempsey, "Feuilleton"). Even Henry, Eliot's protective brother, joined the game in March 1933 with a mock-serious letter to the *New Yorker*, politely but firmly rejecting the reporter's claim that Eliot, while entertaining students, relieved his nervousness by cracking his knuckles ("Kin Defends Bard's Knuckles").

48. According to his friend Hope Mirrlees, it was Eliot's deliberate demonstrations of Englishness that gave away his imposture: "On the anniversary of the Battle of Bosworth Field, when Richard III was killed, he used to always wear a white rose in honour of Richard III, the last English king" ("Out of the Air"). And Herbert Read, who found Eliot's American origins easy to forget, thought that "if anything gave him away it was an Englishness that was a shade too correct to be natural" (15).

49. Eliot apparently enjoyed this line, upon which William Empson remembered his elaborating: " 'I find I can no longer travel except where there is a native cheese. I am therefore bounded, northwards by Yorkshire . . . ' and the rest of the points of the compass were all tidy (I think he had a fair run to the south) but I no longer know what they were" (37; ellipses in original). For other recollections of Eliot's devotion to cheese, see Betjeman ("Usher" 91) and Hawkins ("Pope" 45).

50. It was Princeton University that, in bestowing an honorary doctorate on Eliot in 1947, eulogized him with these resonant phrases (see "T. S. Eliot, 'the literary conscience,' " published in *Vogue*).

51. Morton D. Zabel's review of *Collected Poems, 1909–1935*, dwells on these poems only long enough to dismiss them parenthetically as "a number of nonsense pieces . . . which hardly impress as important" (169–70).

52. See Gordon, *Imperfect* 259.

53. As Stephen Medcalf has previously noted. "Yet *Cats*," he muses, "is the only one of his works in which Eliot succeeded in being a poet for the whole community" (12)—a thought worth pondering, so long as we define the "poet" narrowly enough to exclude the playwright.

54. Eliot nevertheless warily refused to endorse the dictum that the literature of the future must be accessible to "the new large audience," replying neutrally, when V. S. Pritchett put the question to him, merely that it was "inhibiting to speculate on the kind of audience you write for" (qtd. in Pritchett 72).

55. See Abbott on *The Elder Statesman* (111) and Maxwell on "The Cultivation of Christmas Trees" (191–92). For early, preconversion evidence of Eliot's long struggle for a humbler and more life-accepting perspective, see, for example, Virginia Woolf's diary entry of 29 April 1925, which records a "long gaslit emotional rather tremulous & excited visit" from Eliot. "He has seen his whole life afresh," Woolf writes, "seen his relations to the world, & to Vivien in particular, become humbler suppler more humane" (*Diary* 3: 14).

56. The American reviewer who commented in 1943 that Eliot's work "lacks commonness in the good sense of that word as well as the bad" seems to have missed this point; yet he, too, concluded that the *Quartets* were "capable of charming, and teaching, many thousands among the great general reading audience" ("At the Still Point" 96).

57. For more on this poem's influence—and its sales—see Gordon, *Imperfect* 353–54; Matthews 131; and Settle 10.

58. Permitted, or perhaps suffered, since Eliot expressed his dislike of television early and often (see, e.g., "The Television Habit" [1950], "Independent Television" [1958], and "Television Is Not Friendly Enough" [1958]). The first two items are letters to the *Times*; the third is a brief response to a question posed by the editors of the London *City Press*, in which Eliot's response appears alongside comedian Peter Sellers's under the headline, "Sellers (The Goon) Attacks TV—Eliot (The GOM) Supports Him." Sellers was then host of the "Goon Show" on British radio; Eliot, at 70, was the "Grand Old Man [GOM] of English Literature."

See also Lyons, to whom Eliot memorably described TV as "a medium of entertainment which permits millions of people to listen to the same joke at the same time, and yet remain lonesome." Eliot did confess, however, to watching broadcasts of boxing matches.

59. John Xiros Cooper's *T. S. Eliot and the Ideology of Four Quartets* contributes important refinements to the accounts of Eliot's wartime and postwar reception that I have been citing. Cooper argues that Eliot's poems spoke directly and consolingly to an international "mandarinate" anxious about the future of the existing social order following the shocks it had received in the 1930s and the early 1940s. The almost immediate canonizing of the *Quartets* was a measure of Eliot's success in reaching this group. Recognition of Eliot's achievement must have spread rapidly outward

from this group, however, given the impressive audiences that would soon tune in to radio and television broadcasts of his works.

60. To her credit, Dorothea Straus, who recorded this comment, recognized that her own interest in Eliot was scarcely superior to the teenager's: "I had not returned to Eliot since my college days but now that my husband [Roger W. Straus] had become his publisher I was eager to see the great man in the flesh" (151).

61. Dwight Macdonald, also responding to Brooks in the *Partisan Review*, makes a similar argument from a familiar midcentury Marxist standpoint that upholds the value of modernist writing as the most "truthful" representation of bourgeois society in its decay ("Kulturbolschewismus" 445–46). He also avers, as Eliot does not, that modernists have small audiences "because popular cultural values are debased" (445).

62. The crossword puzzle and modernism were, at least, close contemporaries: the first citation of "crossword" in the OED dates from 1914, and the form reached its first peak of popularity in the twenties (Medcalf 12).

63. See, e.g., Douglas 111–15 on Eliot, and also 448–49 on Gilbert Seldes's vision of American identity as "an almost infinitely multiple act of impersonation," in which light "the essence of the stable American identity was to have no stable identity at all." The notion, which Douglas finds implicit in Seldes, that the "'natural self' of the American" is a kind of actor in a variety show seems a particularly suggestive way to understand "Mr. Eliot."

64. In *Culture and Environment*, Leavis and Thompson call special attention to this book, in which they read a warning about "the drift of modern civilization"—a warning of such importance that the book "should be read by all candidates for University Scholarships or for examinations that include an Essay or a General Paper" (26).

65. Wilson's actual word was not "rogue" but "rascal": "The truth is that there is a rascal in Eliot. . . . It was the young rascal who wrote the disturbing poems, full of ironies and moral shocks; it is the old rascal who puts on the public show with which we are here concerned" (Bit 388). In the same spirit, he wrote to Van Wyck Brooks—on whom the observation was certainly wasted—that there was "a scoundrel and actor in Eliot" (*Letters* 548).

66. Listening to Moran and Mack, the "Two Black Crows," alongside Eliot's recording of his poem makes the relationship especially clear.

Many of Eliot's friends were treated to (or, in some cases, puzzled by) the poet's lengthy renditions of "Two Black Crows" routines, which Eliot—having mastered the timing and intonation of the comics through frequent practice—recited "in a well-rehearsed and professional manner" (Levy and Scherle 107; see also Richards 6). In the observation that the rhythms of *Ash-Wednesday* reflect Eliot's debt to Mack, I am preceded by Susan Clement (58).

67. Apparently Eliot "particularly relished" *A Night at the Opera* (1935) (Levy and Scherle 140). The purists who insist that the Marx Brothers' best pictures were the

five they made with Paramount (1929–33) tend to see *A Night at the Opera*, the first of the more polished MGM productions, as the beginning of the end. In the realm of film, Eliot was of course no purist.

68. For the remark about Lear, see Stravinsky 92. The poem to de la Mare is in *Collected Poems* 219–20. The review of the Everyman anthology, *A Book of Nonsense*, which compares this book unfavorably with Carolyn Wells's earlier *Nonsense Anthology*, while unsigned, is certainly by Eliot. Eliot also reviews de la Mare's *Stuff and Nonsense* favorably in the same article: de la Mare "has succeeded" in creating a form of nonsense "quite his own," and this achievement is an integral part of his "whole work" as a poet.

69. Many of the letters, together with Groucho's uproarious description of his "literary evening" with the Eliots, appear in *The Groucho Letters* (154–64).

70. Stephen Spender writes similarly that to his generation, Eliot was simply "the poet of poets," and that "all disagreements about [Eliot's] opinions seemed superficial and could be shrugged off" ("Remembering" 57).

WORKS CITED

A. M. Rev. of *The Rock*, by T. S. Eliot. *Blackfriars* 15 (1934): 642–43.

Abbott, Anthony S. *The Vital Lie: Reality and Illusion in Modern Drama*. Tuscaloosa: U of Alabama P, 1989.

Ackroyd, Peter. *T. S. Eliot: A Life*. New York: Simon, 1984.

Aiken, Conrad. "King Bolo and Others." March and Tambimuttu 20–23.

———. "After 'Ash-Wednesday.'" *Poetry* 45 (1934): 161–65.

———. Rev. of *The Great Gatsby*, by F. Scott Fitzgerald. *Criterion* 4 (1926): 773–76.

———. Rev. of *The Seven Lively Arts*, by Gilbert Seldes. *Criterion* 3 (1924–25): 148–50.

———. *Ushant: An Essay*. New York: Duell, 1952.

"At the Still Point." *Time* 7 June 1943: 96–101.

Atkinson, Brooks. "Comedy by T. S. Eliot with Ina Claire, Claude Rains and Joan Greenwood." *New York Times* 12 Feb. 1954: 22. Rpt. in *New York Theatre Critics' Reviews* 15 (1954): 372.

———. "Triumph at Old Vic." Rev. of *Murder in the Cathedral*, by T. S. Eliot. *New York Times* 26 Apr. 1953, sec. 2: 1.

Auden, W. H. *Selected Poems*. Ed. Edward Mendelson. New York: Vintage, 1979.

Ayers, Robert W. "*Murder in the Cathedral*: A 'Liturgy Less Divine.'" *Texas Studies in Literature and Language* 20 (1977–78): 579–98.

Bailey, Peter, ed. *Music Hall: The Business of Pleasure*. Philadelphia: Open UP, 1986.

Barnes, Clive. "Theater: The A.P.A.'s 'Cocktail Party.'" *New York Times* 8 Oct. 1968: 42.

Barrett, William. "Dry Land, Dry Martini." *Partisan Review* 17 (1950): 354–59.

Barry, Michael. "Televising *The Cocktail Party*." Braybrooke 85–88.

Barry, Peter. "The *Waste Land* Manuscript: Picking up the Pieces—in Order." *Forum for Modern Language Studies* 15 (1979): 237–47.

Beerbohm, Max. "In a Music-Hall." *More Theaters 1898–1903.* New York: Taplinger, 1969.

———. "The Older and Better Music Hall." *Around Theatres.* 1924. London: Hart-Davis, 1953. 298–301.

Bell, Clive. "Plus de Jazz." *New Republic* 21 Sept. 1921: 92–96.

Bennett, Arnold. *The Journal of Arnold Bennett.* New York: Literary Guild, 1933.

———. *Letters of Arnold Bennett III, 1916–1931.* Ed. James Hepburn. London: Oxford UP, 1970.

Bennett, Tony. "Popular Culture: History and Theory." *Popular Culture: Themes and Issues.* Block 1, unit 3. Milton Keynes: Open UP, 1981.

Berlin, Irving. "Alexander's Ragtime Band." New York: Snyder, 1911.

Bernstein, Burton. *Thurber: A Biography.* New York: Dodd, 1975.

Berry, Ellen E. "Modernism/Mass Culture/Postmodernism: The Case of Gertrude Stein." Dettmar 167–89.

Berryman, John. "A Peine Ma Piste." Rev. of *T. S. Eliot: A Selected Critique,* ed. Leonard Unger. *Partisan Review* 15 (1948): 826–28.

Bérubé, Michael. *Marginal Forces/Cultural Centers: Tolson, Pynchon, and the Politics of the Canon.* Ithaca: Cornell UP, 1992.

Bethell, Samuel L. *Shakespeare and the Popular Dramatic Tradition.* Durham, NC: Duke UP, 1944.

Betjeman, John. Foreword. *British Music Hall.* By Raymond Mander and Joe Mitchenson. London: Studio Vista, 1965. 6–8.

———. "The Usher of Highgate Junior School." March and Tambimuttu 89–92.

Blackmer, Corrine E. "Selling Taboo Subjects: The Literary Commerce of Gertrude Stein and Carl Van Vechten." Dettmar and Watt 221–52.

Bogan, Louise. Rev. of *A Choice of Kipling's Verse,* ed. T. S. Eliot. *New Yorker* 2 Oct. 1943: 76–78.

Bratton, J. S. "English Ethiopians: British Audiences and Black-Face Acts, 1835–1865." *Yearbook of English Studies* 11 (1981): 127–42.

Braybrooke, Neville, ed. *T. S. Eliot: A Symposium for His Seventieth Birthday.* 1958. Freeport, NY: Books for Libraries, 1968.

Breit, Harvey. "In and Out of Books." *New York Times Book Review* 26 June 1955: 8.

———. "An Interview with T. S. Eliot—and Excerpts from His Birthday Book." *New York Times Book Review* 21 Nov. 1948: 3.

Bridson, D. G. "Views and Reviews: *Sweeney Agonistes.*" *New English Weekly* 12 Jan. 1933: 304.

Brody, Alan. *The English Mummers and Their Plays.* Philadelphia: U of Pennsylvania P, 1970.

Brooker, Jewel Spears. *Mastery and Escape: T. S. Eliot and the Dialectic of Modernism.* Amherst: U of Massachusetts P, 1994.

———. *T. S. Eliot and Our Turning World*. Ed. Jewel Spears Brooker. London: Macmillan, 2001.

Brooks, Cleanth. *The Well Wrought Urn: Studies in the Structure of Poetry*. New York: Harcourt, 1947.

Browne, E. Martin. *The Making of T. S. Eliot's Plays*. Cambridge: Cambridge UP, 1969.

———. "T. S. Eliot in the Theatre: The Director's Memories." Tate 116–32.

Buck, Gene, Herman Ruby, and David Stamper. "That Shakespearian Rag." New York: Stern, 1912.

Bürger, Peter. *Theory of the Avant-Garde*. Trans. Michael Shaw. Minneapolis: U of Minnesota P, 1984.

Burgess, Anthony. *This Man and Music*. New York: McGraw, 1983.

Bush, Ronald. *T. S. Eliot: A Study in Character and Style*. New York: Oxford UP, 1983.

Carpenter, Humphrey. *A Serious Character: The Life of Ezra Pound*. London: Faber, 1988.

Carroll, Donald. "An Interview with T. S. Eliot." *Quagga* 2 (1962): 31–33.

C[arter], B[arbara] B[arclay] Rev. of *The Rock*, by T. S. Eliot. *Blackfriars* 15 (1934): 499–500.

Chambers, E. K. *The English Folk-Play*. London: Oxford UP, 1933.

———. *The Medieval Stage*. Vol. 1. N.p.: Oxford UP, 1903.

Chiari, Joseph. *T. S. Eliot: A Memoir*. London: Enitharmon, 1982.

Chilton, John. *Sidney Bechet: The Wizard of Jazz*. New York: Da Capo, 1996.

Chinitz, David. "'Dance, Little Lady': Poets, Flappers, and the Gendering of Jazz." *Modernism, Gender, and Culture: A Cultural Studies Approach*. Ed. Lisa Rado. New York: Garland, 1997.

———. "T. S. Eliot's 'Blue' Verses and Their Sources in the Folk Tradition." *Journal of Modern Literature* 23 (1999–2000): 329–33.

Clark, T. J. "More on the Differences between Comrade Greenberg and Ourselves." *Modernism and Modernity: The Vancouver Conference Papers*. Ed. Benjamin H. D. Buchloh, Serge Guilbaut, and David Solkin. Halifax: P of the Nova Scotia College of Art and Design, 1983. 169–87.

———. *The Painting of Modern Life: Paris in the Art of Manet and His Followers*. New York: Knopf, 1985.

Clement, Susan. "'All Aboard for Natchez, Cairo and St. Louis': The Source of a Draft Heading of T. S. Eliot's *Ash-Wednesday*." *Notes and Queries* 43 (1996): 57–59.

Cocteau, Jean. *A Call to Order*. Trans. Rollo H. Myers. New York: Haskell, 1974.

Coghill, Nevill. "Sweeney Agonistes." March and Tambimuttu 82–87.

Cohan, George M. "Harrigan." New York: Mills, 1907.

Cohen, Phil. "Policing the Working Class City." *Crime and Society: Readings in History and Theory*. Ed. Mike Fitzgerald, Gregor McLennan, and Jennie Pawson. London: Routledge, 1981.

Collie, Michael, and J. M. L'Heureux. Introduction. Laforgue, *Derniers* 3–16.

Collier, Patrick. "T. S. Eliot in the 'Journalistic Struggle.'" *Challenging Modernism: New*

Readings in Literature and Culture, 1914–45. Ed. Stella Deen. Aldershot and Burlington: Ashgate, 2002.

Cooper, John Xiros. *The Ideology of Four Quartets*. Cambridge: Cambridge UP, 1995.

———, ed. *T. S. Eliot's Orchestra: Critical Essays on Poetry and Music*. New York: Garland, 2000.

Cowan, Laura. "Eliot." *American Literary Scholarship 1994*. Ed. David J. Nordloh. Durham, NC: Duke UP, 1996. 139–47.

Coyle, Michael. *Ezra Pound, Popular Genres, and the Discourse of Culture*. University Park, PA: Pennsylvania State UP, 1995.

———. "'This rather elusory broadcast technique': T. S. Eliot and the Genre of the Radio Talk." *ANQ* 11 (1998): 32–42.

———. "T. S. Eliot on the Air: 'Culture' and the Challenges of Mass Communication." Brooker, *T. S. Eliot* 141–54.

Craggs, Stewart R. "Façade and the Music of Sir William Walton." *Library Chronicle of the University of Texas* 25–26 (1984): 101–17.

Craig, Edward Gordon. *The Theatre Advancing*. 1919. New York: Blom, 1947.

Crawford, Robert. *The Savage and the City in the Work of T. S. Eliot*. Oxford: Clarendon, 1987.

Culler, Jonathan D., ed. *Harvard Advocate Centennial Anthology*. Cambridge: Schenkman, 1966.

Cummings, E. E. *Selected Letters of E. E. Cummings*. Ed. F. W. Dupee and George Stade. New York: Harcourt, 1969.

Dahlberg, Edward. *Epitaphs of Our Times: The Letters of Edward Dahlberg*. New York: Braziller, 1967.

Davidson, Harriet. "Improper Desire: Reading *The Waste Land*." Moody, *Cambridge* 121–31.

Davies, H. S. "Mistah Kurtz: He Dead." Tate 355–63.

Dempsey, David. "Feuilleton." *New York Times Book Review* 4 Feb. 1951: 8.

Denney, Reuel. "The Discovery of the Popular Culture." *American Perspectives: The National Self-Image in the Twentieth Century*. Ed. Robert E. Spiller and Eric Larrabee. Cambridge: Harvard UP, 1961.

Dettmar, Kevin J. H., ed. *Rereading the New: A Backward Glance at Modernism*. Ann Arbor: U of Michigan P, 1992.

Dettmar, Kevin J. H., and Stephen Watt, eds. *Marketing Modernisms: Self-Promotion, Canonization, Rereading*. Ann Arbor: U of Michigan P, 1996.

Diepeveen, Leonard. "'I Can Have More Than Enough Power to Satisfy Me': T. S. Eliot's Construction of His Audience." Dettmar and Watt: 37–60.

Dobrée, Bonamy. "T. S. Eliot: A Personal Reminiscence." Tate 65–88.

Douglas, Ann. *Terrible Honesty: Mongrel Manhattan in the 1920s*. New York: Farrar, 1995.

Drabble, Margaret, ed. *The Oxford Companion to English Literature*. 6th ed. Oxford: Oxford UP, 2000.

Duncan, Ronald. *How to Make Enemies*. London: Hart-Davis, 1968.

DuPlessis, Rachel Blau. *Genders, Races, and Religious Cultures in Modern American Poetry, 1908–1934.* Cambridge: Cambridge UP, 2001.

Durrell, Lawrence. "T. S. Eliot." *Atlantic Monthly* May 1965: 61–64.

Eagleton, Terry. "Eliot and a Common Culture." *Eliot in Perspective: A Symposium.* Ed. Graham Martin. New York: Humanities, 1970. 279–95.

———. *Literary Theory: An Introduction.* Minneapolis: U of Minnesota P, 1983.

"The Effort to Take Jazz Seriously." *Literary Digest* Apr. 1924: 29–30.

Eliot, Henry Ware, Jr. "Kin Defends Bard's Knuckles." Letter. *New Yorker* 25 Mar. 1933: 51.

Eliot, T. S. "The Aims of Poetic Drama." *Adam: International Review* Nov. 1949: 10–16.

———. "American Literature and the American Language." *To Criticize the Critic* 43–60.

———. "Answers to the Three Questions." *Chapbook* July 1922: 8.

———. "Arnold and Pater." *Selected Essays* 382–93.

———. "Audiences, Producers, Plays, Poets." *New Verse* Dec. 1935: 3–4.

———. "The Ballet." *Criterion* 3 (1924–25): 441–43.

———. "The Beating of a Drum." *Nation and Athenæum* 6 Oct. 1923: 11–12.

———. "Ben Jonson." *Selected Essays* 127–39.

———. "Books of the Year Chosen by Eminent Contemporaries." *Sunday Times* [London] 24 Dec. 1950: 3.

———. "Charles Whibley." *Selected Essays* 439–51.

———. "Charleston, Hey! Hey!" *Nation and Athenæum* 29 Jan. 1927: 595.

———. "Christianity and Communism." *Listener* 16 Mar. 1932: 382–83.

———. *Christianity and Culture.* New York: Harcourt, 1968.

———. *Collected Poems, 1909–1962.* New York: Harcourt, 1970.

———. "A Commentary [Jan. 1925]." *Criterion* 3 (1924–25): 161–63.

———. "A Commentary [June 1927]." *Criterion* 5 (1927): 283–86.

———. "A Commentary [Oct. 1927]." *Criterion* 6 (1927): 289–91.

———. "A Commentary [Nov. 1927]." *Criterion* 6 (1927): 385–88.

———. *Complete Poems and Plays, 1909–1950.* New York: Harcourt, 1971.

———. *The Confidential Clerk.* San Diego: Harcourt, 1954.

———. "Cyril Tourneur." *Selected Essays* 159–69.

———. "Dante." 1920. *The Sacred Wood* 159–71.

———. "Dante." 1929. *Selected Essays* 199–237.

———. "A Dialogue on Dramatic Poetry." *Selected Essays* 31–45.

———. "Donne in Our Time." *A Garland for John Donne: 1631–1931.* Ed. Theodore Spencer. Cambridge: Harvard UP, 1931. 1–19.

———. "Dramatis Personæ." *Criterion* 1 (1922–23): 303–06.

———. "'The Duchess of Malfi' at the Lyric: and Poetic Drama." *Arts and Letters* 3 (1919–20): 36–39.

———. "Durkheim." *Saturday Westminster Gazette* 19 Aug. 1916: 14.

———. *The Elder Statesman.* New York: Farrar, 1959.

————. "Euripides and Professor Murray." *Selected Essays* 46–50.

————. "Experiment in Criticism." *Tradition and Experiment in Present-Day Literature.* 1929. Freeport, NY: Books for Libraries, 1968. 198–215.

————. "Ezra Pound." *Poetry* 68 (1946): 326–38.

————. "Five Points on Dramatic Writing." *Scythe* 1 (1938): 10.

————. "Four Elizabethan Dramatists." *Selected Essays* 91–99.

————. "The Frontiers of Criticism." *On Poetry and Poets.* 103–18.

————. "Homage to Wilkie Collins." *Criterion* 5 (1927): 139–43.

————. "Independent Television." Letter. *Times* [London] 11 Nov. 1958: 11.

————. "The Influence of Landscape Upon the Poet." *Dædalus, Journal of the American Academy of Arts and Sciences* 89 (1960): 420–22.

————. Introduction. *Leisure the Basis of Culture.* By Josef Pieper. Trans. Alexander Dru. New York: Pantheon, 1952. 11–17.

————. Introduction. *Savonarola: A Dramatic Poem.* By Charlotte Eliot. London: Cobden-Sanderson, [1926]. vii-xii.

————. *Inventions of the March Hare: Poems 1909–1917.* Ed. Christopher Ricks. New York: Harcourt, 1996.

————. "John Dryden." *Selected Essays* 264–74.

————. Letter. *Partisan Review* 9 (1942): 115–16.

————. *The Letters of T. S. Eliot, Vol. I: 1898–1922.* Ed. Valerie Eliot. San Diego: Harcourt, 1988.

————. "London Letter [Mar. 1921]." *Dial* Apr. 1921: 448–53.

————. "London Letter [May 1921]." *Dial* June 1921: 686–91.

————. "London Letter [July 1921]." *Dial* Aug. 1921: 213–17.

————. "London Letter [Sept. 1921]." *Dial* Oct. 1921: 452–55.

————. "London Letter [Apr. 1922]." *Dial* May 1922: 510–13.

————. "London Letter [Aug. 1922]." *Dial* Sept. 1922: 329–31.

————. "London Letter [Nov. 1922]." *Dial* Dec. 1922: 659–63.

————. "The Man of Letters and the Future of Europe." *Sewanee Review* 53 (1945): 333–42.

————. "Marianne Moore." *Dial* Dec. 1923: 594–97.

————. "Marie Lloyd." *Selected Essays* 405–08.

————. "Marlowe." *Selected Essays* 100–06.

————. "The Metaphysical Poets." *Selected Essays* 241–50.

————. "Milton I." *On Poetry and Poets* 138–45.

————. "Milton II." *On Poetry and Poets* 146–61.

————. "Modern Education and the Classics." *Selected Essays* 452–60.

————. "The Music of Poetry." *On Poetry and Poets* 26–38.

————. "The Need For Poetic Drama." *Listener* 25 Nov. 1936: 994–95.

————. "The Noh and the Image." *Egoist* 4 (1917): 102–03.

————. "A Note on Ezra Pound." *To-day* Sept. 1918: 3–9.

————. "Observations." *Egoist* 5 (1918): 69–70.

———. *Old Possum's Book of Practical Cats*. 1939. San Diego: Harcourt, 1982.

———. *On Poetry and Poets*. London and Boston: Faber, 1957.

———. "The Perfect Critic." *The Sacred Wood* 1–16.

———. "The Poetic Drama." *Athenæum* 14 May 1920: 635–36.

———. "Poetry and Drama." *On Poetry and Poets* 72–88.

———. "Poetry and Propaganda." *Bookman* 70 (1930): 595–602.

———. "The Possibility of a Poetic Drama." *The Sacred Wood* 60–70.

———. Preface. *The Film of Murder in the Cathedral*. By T. S. Eliot and George Hoellering. New York: Harcourt, 1952. 7–10.

———. Preface. *This American World*. By Edgar Ansell Mowrer. London: Faber, 1928. ix–xv.

———. "Preface to the 1928 Edition." *The Sacred Wood* vii–x.

———. "The Problem of Education." *Harvard Advocate* 121 (1934): 11–12. Rpt. in Culler 69–72.

———. "Professional, Or . . . " *Egoist* 5 (1918): 61.

———. "The Publishing of Poetry." *Bookseller* 6 Dec. 1952: 1568–70.

———. "Recent Detective Fiction." *Criterion* 5 (1927): 359–62.

———. "Reflections on Vers Libre." *To Criticize the Critic* 183–89.

———. "Religious Drama: Mediæval and Modern." *University of Edinburgh Journal* 9 (1937): 8–17.

———. Rev. of *The Beast with Five Fingers*, by W. F. Harvey. *Criterion* 8 (1928–29): 175.

———. Rev. of *The Best Detective Stories of the Year: 1928*, ed. Ronald Knox and H. Harrington; *The Mystery of Orcival*, by Emile Gaboriau; *The Death of Laurence Vining*, by Alan Thomas; and *Inspector Frost's Jigsaw*, by H. Maynard Smith. *Criterion* 8 (1928–29): 760–61.

———. Rev. of *A Book of Nonsense*, ed. Ernest Rhys; and *Stuff and Nonsense*, by Walter de la Mare. *Criterion* 6 (1927): 570.

———. Rev. of *The Canary Murder Case*, by S. S. Van Dine. *Criterion* 6 (1927–28): 377.

———. Rev. of *The Greene Murder Case*, by S. S. Van Dine. *Criterion* 8 (1928–29): 174.

———. Rev. of *Group Theories of Religion and the Religion of the Individual* by Clement C. J. Webb. *International Journal of Ethics* 27 (1916): 115–17.

———. Rev. of *The Growth of Civilization* and *The Origin of Magic and Religion*, by W. J. Perry. *Criterion* 2 (1924): 489–91.

———. Rev. of *The Name and Nature of Poetry*, by A. E. Housman. *Criterion* 13 (1933): 151–54.

———. "'Rhetoric' and Poetic Drama." *Selected Essays* 25–30.

———. *The Rock: A Pageant Play*. London: Faber, 1934.

———. "The Romantic Englishman, the Comic Spirit, and the Function of Criticism." *Tyro* 1 (1921): 4.

———. "Rudyard Kipling." *On Poetry and Poets* 228–51.

———. *The Sacred Wood*. 1920. London: Methuen, 1950.

———. *Selected Essays*. New ed. New York: Harcourt, 1960.

———. "Seneca in Elizabethan Translation." *Selected Essays* 51–88.

———. "Shakespeare and the Stoicism of Seneca." *Selected Essays* 107–20.

———. "Sherlock Holmes and His Times." Rev. of *The Complete Sherlock Holmes Short Stories*, by Sir Arthur Conan Doyle; and *The Leavenworth Case*, by Anna Katherine Green. *Criterion* 8 (1928–29): 552–56.

———. "The Social Function of Poetry." *On Poetry and Poets* 15–25.

———. "Stilton Cheese." Letter. *Times* [London] 29 Nov. 1935: 15.

———. "Tarr." *Egoist* 5 (1918): 105–06.

———. "The Television Habit." Letter. *Times* [London] 20 Dec. 1950: 7.

———. "Television Is Not Friendly Enough." *City Press* [London] 28 Nov. 1958: 12.

———. "The Three Voices of Poetry." *On Poetry and Poets* 89–102.

———. *To Criticize the Critic*. New York: Octagon, 1980.

———. "To Criticize the Critic." *To Criticize the Critic* 11–26.

———. "Tradition and the Individual Talent." *Selected Essays* 3–11.

———. "Ulysses, Order, and Myth." *Selected Prose of T. S. Eliot*. Ed. Frank Kermode. New York: Harcourt, 1975. 175–78.

———. "The Use of Poetry." Letter. *New English Weekly* 14 June 1934: 215.

———. *The Use of Poetry and the Use of Criticism*. Cambridge: Harvard UP, 1933.

———. "The Value and Use of Cathedrals in England Today." *Friends of Chichester Cathedral Annual Report* 1950–51: 17–27.

———. *The Varieties of Metaphysical Poetry*. Ed. Ronald Schuchard. New York: Harcourt, 1994.

———. "War-Paint and Feathers." *Athenæum* 17 Oct. 1919: 1036.

———. *The Waste Land: A Facsimile and Transcript of the Original Drafts Including the Annotations of Ezra Pound*. Ed. Valerie Eliot. New York: Harcourt, 1971.

———. "What Dante Means to Me." *To Criticize the Critic* 125–35.

———. "Wilkie Collins and Dickens." *Selected Essays* 409–18.

———. "William Blake." *Selected Essays* 275–80.

———. "Yeats." *On Poetry and Poets* 252–62.

Elliott, Bridget J. "Much Ado about Money: Reading British Music-Hall in the Nineties." *Literature and Money*. Ed. Anthony Purdy. Amsterdam: Rodopi, 1993: 45–77.

Ellison, Ralph. *Shadow and Act*. 1953. New York: Vintage, 1972.

Empson, William. "The Style of the Master." March and Tambimuttu 35–37.

"Entertainment and Reality." Rev. of *The Cocktail Party*, by T. S. Eliot. *Times Literary Supplement* 31 Mar. 1950: 198.

"Error." *New Yorker* 21 Jan. 1933: 12.

Everett, Barbara. "The New Style of *Sweeney Agonistes*." *English Satire and the Satiric Tradition*. Ed. Claude Rawson. New York: Blackwell, 1984.

Ewen, David. *The Life and Death of Tin Pan Alley*. New York: Funk, 1964.

Eysteinsson, Astradur. *The Concept of Modernism*. Ithaca: Cornell UP, 1990.

Farson, Daniel. *Marie Lloyd and Music Hall.* London: Stacey, 1972.

Faulk, Barry Jameson. "Aesthetics and Authority: Fin-de-Siècle Intellectuals and London Music Halls." Diss. U of Illinois at Urbana-Champaign, 1994.

———. Letter. *PMLA* 110 (1995): 1052.

———. "Modernism and the Popular: Eliot's Music Halls." *Modernism / Modernity* 8 (2001): 603–21.

Fiedler, Leslie. *The Collected Essays of Leslie Fiedler.* Vol. 2. New York: Stein, 1971.

Finch, Annie. *The Ghost of Meter: Culture and Prosody in American Free Verse.* Ann Arbor: U of Michigan P, 1993.

"First Nights: The Confidential Clerk." *Newsweek* 22 Feb. 1954: 94.

Flanagan, Hallie. *Dynamo.* New York: Duell, 1943.

Fleissner, R. F. "Eliot's Appropriation of Black Culture: A Dialogical Analysis." Sess. on T. S. Eliot and Ethnicity. MLA Convention. Chicago. 28 Dec. 1990.

Forster, E. M. "Mr. Eliot's Comedy." *Listener* 23 Mar. 1950: 533.

Foster, Richard. "Frankly, I Like Criticism." *Antioch Review* 22 (1962): 273–83.

Foster, Stephen. "Ring de Banjo." 1851. *A Treasury of Stephen Foster.* New York: Random, 1946. 75–77.

Fowler, Bridget. "The 'Canon' and Marxist Theories of Literature." *Cultural Studies* 1 (1987): 162–78.

Freedman, Morris. "Jazz Rhythms and T. S. Eliot." *South Atlantic Quarterly* 51 (1952): 419–35.

Furia, Philip. *The Poets of Tin Pan Alley: A History of America's Great Lyricists.* New York: Oxford UP, 1990.

Galef, David. "Fragments of a Journey: The Drama in T. S. Eliot's *Sweeney Agonistes*." *English Studies* 69 (1988): 497–508.

Gallup, Donald. *T. S. Eliot: A Bibliography.* London: Faber, 1969.

Gardner, Helen. "The 'Aged Eagle' Spreads His Wings." *Sunday Times* [London] 21 Sept. 1958: 8.

Gates, Henry Louis, Jr. *Figures in Black: Words, Signs, and the "Racial" Self.* New York: Oxford UP, 1987.

Gendron, Bernard. *Between Montmartre and the Mudd Club: Popular Music and the Avant-Garde.* Chicago: U of Chicago P, 2002.

———. "Jamming at Le Boeuf: Jazz and the Paris Avant-Garde." *Discourse* 12 (1989–90): 3–27.

Gill, Jonathan. "Protective Coloring: Modernism and Blackface Minstrelsy in the Bolo Poems." Cooper, *T. S. Eliot's Orchestra* 65–84.

Giroux, Robert. "A Personal Memoir." Tate 337–44.

Goldberg, Isaac. *Tin Pan Alley: A Chronicle of American Popular Music.* New York: Ungar, 1961.

Gordon, Lyndall. *Eliot's Early Years.* Oxford: Oxford UP, 1977.

———. *Eliot's New Life.* Oxford: Oxford UP, 1988.

———. *T. S. Eliot: An Imperfect Life.* New York: Norton, 1999.

Graff, Gerald. *Professing Literature: An Institutional History*. Chicago: U of Chicago P, 1987.

Grant, Michael, ed. *T. S. Eliot: The Critical Heritage*. Vol. 1. London: Routledge, 1982.

Gray, Piers. *T. S. Eliot's Intellectual and Poetic Development, 1909–1922*. Sussex: Harvester, 1982.

Greenberg, Clement. "Avant-Garde and Kitsch." *Partisan Review* 6 (1939): 34–39. Rpt. in Rosenberg and White 98–107.

Greenwell, Tom. "Talking Freely: T. S. Eliot." *Yorkshire Post* 29 Aug. 1961: 3.

———. "Writing for the Stage." *Yorkshire Post* 30 Aug. 1961: 7.

Gross, John. "Eliot: From Ritual to Realism." *Encounter* 24 Mar. 1965: 48–50.

Gubar, Susan. *Racechanges: White Skin, Black Face in American Culture*. New York: Oxford UP, 1997.

Hall, Donald. "T. S. Eliot." *Writers at Work: The Paris Review Interviews*. 2nd Series. New York: Viking, 1963. 89–110.

Hall, Stuart. "Notes on Deconstructing 'The Popular.'" *People's History and Socialist Theory*. Ed. Raphael Samuel. London: Routledge, 1981. 227–40.

Hall, Stuart, and Paddy Whannel. *The Popular Arts: A Critical Guide to the Mass Media*. Boston: Beacon, 1964.

Hawkes, Terence. *Meaning by Shakespeare*. London: Routledge, 1992.

Hawkins, Desmond. "The Pope of Russell Square." March and Tambimuttu 44–47.

———. "The Writer as Artist." *Listener* 28 Nov. 1940: 773–74.

Hayman, Ronald. *British Theatre since 1955: A Reassessment*. Oxford: Oxford UP, 1979.

Henighan, Tom. "Shamans, Tribes, and the Sorcerer's Apprentices: Notes on the Discovery of the Primitive in Modern Poetry." *Dalhousie Review* 59 (1979–80): 605–20.

Hoggart, Richard. "Schools of English and Contemporary Society." 1963. *Speaking to Each Other*. Vol. 2. London: Chatto, 1970. 246–59.

Höher, Dagmar. "The Composition of Music Hall Audiences 1850–1900." Bailey 73–92.

Holmes, Anne. *Jules Laforgue and Poetic Innovation*. Oxford: Clarendon, 1993.

Holmes, John. "Eliot on Roistering Cats." Rev. of *Old Possum's Book of Practical Cats*," by T. S. Eliot. *Boston Evening Transcript* 15 Nov. 1939: 15.

Howarth, Herbert. *Notes on Some Figures Behind T. S. Eliot*. Boston: Houghton, 1964.

Hughes, Langston. *The Collected Poems of Langston Hughes*. Ed. Arnold Rampersad and David Roessel. New York: Vintage, 1994.

———. "I Remember the Blues." *Missouri Reader*. Ed. F. L. Mott. Columbia: U of Missouri P, 1964. 152–55.

———. "Rejuvenation through Joy." *The Ways of White Folks*. 1934. New York: Vintage, 1971. 66–95.

———. "Songs Called the Blues." *The Langston Hughes Reader*. New York: Braziller, 1958. 159–61.

Humphries, Rolfe. "Eliot's Poetry." *New Masses* 18 Aug. 1936: 25–26. Rpt. in Grant 356–59.

Huyssen, Andreas. *After the Great Divide: Modernism, Mass Culture, Postmodernism.*
Bloomington: Indiana UP, 1986.

Isaacs, J. *An Assessment of Twentieth-Century Literature.* London: Secker, 1952.

Jackson, Elizabeth. "Poetry and Poppycock." *Saturday Review of Literature* 25 Jan. 1941:
13–14.

Jaidka, Manju. *T. S. Eliot's Use of Popular Sources.* Lewiston, NY: Mellen, 1997.

Jay, Gregory S. "Postmodernism in *The Waste Land*: Women, Mass Culture, and
Others." Dettmar 221–46.

———. *T. S. Eliot and the Poetics of Literary History.* Baton Rouge: Louisiana State UP,
1983.

Jennings, Humphrey. "Eliot and Auden and Shakespeare." *New Verse* Dec. 1935:
4–7.

Johnson, James Weldon, and J. Rosamond Johnson. "The Congo Love Song."
New York: Shapiro, 1903.

Johnson, James Weldon, Bob Cole, and J. Rosamond Johnson. "Under the
Bamboo Tree." New York: Stern, 1902.

Johnson, Robert Underwood. "The Glory of Words." *Academy Papers: Addresses on
Language Problems by Members of the American Academy of Arts and Letters.* New York:
Scribner's, 1925.

Jones, Gareth Stedman. "Working-Class Culture and Working-Class Politics in
London, 1870–1900." *Journal of Social History* 7 (1973–74): 460–508.

Kammen, Michael. *The Lively Arts: Gilbert Seldes and the Transformation of Cultural Criticism in
the United States.* New York: Oxford UP, 1996.

Kaufmann, Michael Edward. "T. S. Eliot's New Critical Footnotes to Modernism."
Dettmar 73–85.

Kazin, Alfred. *New York Jew.* Syracuse: Syracuse UP, 1978.

Kenner, Hugh. *The Invisible Poet: T. S. Eliot.* London: Allen, 1960.

Kermode, Frank. "Poet and Dancer before Diaghilev." *Puzzles and Epiphanies.* London:
Routledge, 1962. 1–28.

———. *Romantic Image.* London: Routledge, 1957.

———. "What Became of Sweeney?" Rev. of *The Elder Statesman* by T. S. Eliot.
Spectator 10 Apr. 1959: 513.

Kift, Dagmar. *The Victorian Music Hall: Culture, Class and Conflict.* Cambridge: Cambridge
UP, 1996.

Kimball, Roger. "A Craving for Reality: T. S. Eliot Today." *New Criterion* Oct. 1999:
18–26.

Kissel, Howard. "Cats." *Women's Wear Daily* 8 Oct. 1982. Rpt. in *New York Theatre
Critics' Reviews* 43 (1982): 195–96.

Knowles, Sebastian D. G. "'Then You Wink the Other Eye': T. S. Eliot and the Music
Hall." *ANQ* 11 (1998): 20–32.

———. Rev. of "T. S. Eliot at 101," by Cynthia Ozick. *T. S. Eliot: Man and Poet: An
Annotated Bibliography of a Decade of T. S. Eliot Criticism: 1977–1986.* Ed. Sebastian D. G.

Knowles and Scott A. Leonard. Orono, ME: National Poetry Foundation, 1992. 394–95.

Koch, Kenneth. *Seasons on Earth*. New York: Penguin, 1987.

Koestenbaum, Wayne. "*The Waste Land*: T. S. Eliot's and Ezra Pound's Collaboration on Hysteria." *Twentieth Century Literature* 34 (1988): 113–139.

Koritz, Amy. *Gendering Bodies / Peforming Art: Dance and Literature in Early Twentieth-Century British Culture*. Ann Arbor: U of Michigan P, 1995.

Kramer, Hilton. "Cynthia Ozick's Farewell to T. S. Eliot—and High Culture." *New Criterion* Feb. 1990: 5–9.

Kramer, Hilton, et al. "A Note on *The New Criterion*." *New Criterion* Sept. 1982: 1–5.

Laforgue, Jules. *Derniers Vers*. Ed. Michael Collie and J. M. L'Heureux. Toronto: U of Toronto P, 1965.

———. *Oeuvres Complètes*. Lausanne: Editions L'Age d'Homme, 1986.

Lamos, Colleen. *Deviant Modernism: Sexual and Textual Errancy in T. S. Eliot, James Joyce, and Marcel Proust*. Cambridge: Cambridge UP, 1998.

Lane, Anthony. "Writing Wrongs." Rev. of *Inventions of the March Hare*, by T. S. Eliot. *New Yorker* 10 Mar. 1977: 86–92.

Laski, Harold J. *The Dilemma of Our Times: An Historical Essay*. 1952. New York: Kelley, 1968.

Leavis, F. R. "Mass Civilisation and Minority Culture." 1930. *For Continuity*. Freeport, NY: Books for Libraries, 1933. 13–46.

———. *Valuation in Criticism*. Ed. G. Singh. Cambridge: Cambridge UP, 1986.

Leavis, F. R., and Denys Thompson. *Culture and Environment: The Training of Critical Awareness*. London: Chatto, 1937.

Lehmann, John. "T. S. Eliot Talks about Himself and the Drive to Create." *New York Times Book Review* 29 Nov. 1953: 5+.

Lentricchia, Frank. *Modernist Quartet*. Cambridge: Cambridge UP, 1994.

Leonard, Neil. *Jazz and the White Americans*. Chicago: U of Chicago P, 1962.

Levenson, Michael H. *A Genealogy of Modernism*. Cambridge: Cambridge UP, 1984.

Levi, Peter. "Eliot's Late Plays." *Agenda* 21 (1985): 131–36.

Levine, Lawrence W. *Highbrow / Lowbrow: The Emergence of Cultural Hierarchy in America*. Cambridge: Harvard UP, 1988.

Levy, Eugene. *James Weldon Johnson: Black Leader, Black Voice*. Chicago: U of Chicago P, 1973.

Levy, William Turner, and Victor Scherle. *Affectionately, T. S. Eliot: The Story of a Friendship, 1947–1965*. Philadelphia: Lippincott, 1968.

Lightfoot, Marjorie J. "Charting Eliot's Course in Drama." Roby 119–23.

Linn, Karen. *That Half-Barbaric Twang: The Banjo in American Popular Culture*. Urbana: U of Illinois P, 1991.

Lipsitz, George. *The Sidewalks of St. Louis*. Columbia: U of Missouri P, 1991.

"Literature and Tradition." *Nation* 12 Oct. 1927: 355.

Litz, A. Walton. Introduction. "Tradition and the Practice of Poetry." By T. S. Eliot.

T. S. Eliot: Essays from the Southern Review. Ed. James Olney. Oxford: Clarendon, 1988. 7–10.

Lott, Eric. *Love and Theft: Blackface Minstrelsy and the American Working Class.* New York: Oxford UP, 1993.

Lucas, John. "Appropriate Falsehoods: English Poets and American Jazz." *Yearbook of English Studies* 17 (1987): 46–61.

Lyon, David N. "The Minstrel Show as Ritual: Surrogate Black Culture." *Rituals and Ceremonies in Popular Culture.* Ed. Ray B. Browne. Bowling Green: Bowling Green UP, 1980.

Lyons, Leonard. "The Lyons Den." *New York Post Magazine* 22 Sept. 1963: 7.

Macdonald, Dwight. "Kulturbolschewismus Is Here." *Partisan Review* 8 (1941): 442–51.

———. "A Theory of Mass Culture." *Diogenes* 3 (1953): 1–17. Rpt. in Rosenberg and White 59–73.

Mackin, Jonna. "Raising Life to a Kind of Art: Eliot and Music Hall." Cooper, *T. S. Eliot's Orchestra* 49–64.

Macqueen-Pope, W[alter James]. *Queen of the Music Halls.* London: Oldborne, 1957.

Mair, G. H. "The Music Hall." *English Review* 9 (1911): 122–29.

Malamud, Randy. *T. S. Eliot's Drama: A Research and Production Sourcebook.* New York: Greenwood, 1992.

———. *Where the Words Are Valid: T. S. Eliot's Communities of Drama.* Westport, CT: Greenwood, 1994.

Manganaro, Marc. "'Beating a Drum in a Jungle': T. S. Eliot on the Artist as 'Primitive.'" *Modern Language Quarterly* 47 (1986): 393–421.

March, Richard, and Tambimuttu, eds. *T. S. Eliot: A Symposium.* Freeport, NY: Books for Libraries, 1949.

Margolis, John D. *T. S. Eliot's Intellectual Development, 1922–1939.* Chicago: U of Chicago P, 1972.

Marshall, P. David. *Celebrity and Power: Fame in Contemporary Culture.* Minneapolis: U of Minnesota P, 1997.

Marx, Groucho. *The Groucho Letters.* New York: Simon, 1967.

Materer, Timothy. "T. S. Eliot's Critical Program." Moody, *Cambridge* 48–59.

Matthews, T. S. *Great Tom: Notes towards the Definition of T. S. Eliot.* New York: Harper, 1974.

Matthiesson, F. O. *From the Heart of Europe.* New York: Oxford UP, 1948.

Maxwell, D. E. S. "The Cultivation of Christmas Trees." Braybrooke 190–92.

McAlmon, Robert. "Modern Antiques." *Contact* 2 (1921): 9–10.

McAlmon, Robert, and Kay Boyle. *Being Geniuses Together: 1920–1930.* Garden City, NY: Doubleday, 1968.

McClure, John. Rev. of *The Waste Land,* by T. S. Eliot. *Double Dealer* 5 (1923): 173–74. Rpt. in Grant 170–72.

McDonald, Gail. *Learning To Be Modern: Pound, Eliot, and the American University.* Oxford: Clarendon, 1993.

McElderry, B. R., Jr. "Eliot's 'Shakespeherian Rag.'" *American Quarterly* 9 (1957): 185–86.

McLuhan, Marshall. "Mr. Eliot and the St. Louis Blues." *Antigonish Review* 62–63 (1985): 121–24.

McNeilly, Kevin. "Culture, Race, Rhythm: *Sweeney Agonistes* and the Live Jazz Break." Cooper, *T. S. Eliot's Orchestra* 25–47.

Medcalf, Stephen. "The Shaman's Secret Heart." *Times Literary Supplement* 2 Oct. 1992: 10–12.

Menand, Louis. "T. S. Eliot After His Time." *Raritan* 8 (1988): 88–102.

Monro, Harold. "Notes for a Study of 'The Waste Land': An Imaginary Dialogue with T. S. Eliot." *Chapbook* Feb. 1923: 20–24. Rpt. in Grant 162–66.

Monroe, Harriet. "Mr. Jepson's Slam." *Poetry* 12 (1918): 208–12.

Moody, A. D[avid]. "T. S. Eliot: The American Strain." *The Placing of T. S. Eliot.* Ed. Jewel Spears Brooker. Columbia: U of Missouri P, 1991. 77–89.

———, ed. *The Cambridge Companion to T. S. Eliot.* Cambridge: Cambridge UP, 1994.

Moore, Marianne. Rev. of *Sweeney Agonistes*, by T. S. Eliot. *Poetry* 42 (1933): 106–09.

More, Paul Elmer. "Cleft Eliot." Rev. of *Selected Essays*, by T. S. Eliot. *Saturday Review of Literature* 12 Nov. 1932: 233+. Rpt. in *T. S. Eliot: A Selected Critique.* Ed. Leonard Unger. New York: Rinehart, 1948. 24–29.

Mulhern, Francis. *Culture / Metaculture.* London: Routledge, 2000.

Munson, Gorham B. "The Esotericism of T. S. Eliot." *1924* July 1924: 3–10. Rpt. in Grant 203–12.

Murphy, Michael. "'One Hundred Per Cent Bohemia': Pop Decadence and the Aestheticization of Commodity in the Rise of the Slicks." Dettmar and Watt 61–89.

Naremore, James. *More Than Night: Film Noir in Its Contexts.* Berkeley: U of California P, 1998.

Naremore, James, and Patrick Brantlinger, eds. *Modernity and Mass Culture.* Bloomington: Indiana UP, 1991.

Nevo, Ruth. "*The Waste Land*: Ur-Text of Deconstruction." *New Literary History* 13 (1981–82): 453–61. Rpt. in *Modern Critical Views: T. S. Eliot.* Ed. Harold Bloom. New York: Chelsea, 1985. 95–102.

Newman, Ernest. "Summing Up Music's Case Against Jazz." *New York Times Magazine* 6 Mar. 1927: 3+.

Nicholson, Norman. "Words and Imagery." March and Tambimuttu 231–34.

North, Michael. *The Dialect of Modernism: Race, Language, and Twentieth-Century Literature.* New York: Oxford UP, 1994.

———. *Reading 1922: A Return to the Scene of the Modern.* New York: Oxford UP, 1999.

Oesterley, W. O. E. *The Sacred Dance: A Study in Comparative Folklore.* Cambridge: Cambridge UP, 1923.

Orwell, George. *Dickens, Dali and Others.* New York: Harcourt, 1946.

"Out of the Air: Eliot's Life." *Listener* 14 Jan. 1971: 50.

The Oxford English Dictionary. 2nd ed. Oxford: Clarendon, 1987.

Ozick, Cynthia. "T. S. Eliot at 101: 'The Man Who Suffers and the Mind Which Creates.'" *New Yorker* 20 Nov. 1989: 119–54. Rpt. in *Fame and Folly*. New York: Knopf, 1996. 3–49.

Ozick, Cynthia, and Hilton Kramer. "Cynthia Ozick, T. S. Eliot, High Culture: An Exchange." *New Criterion* Apr. 1990: 5–10.

Panter-Downes, Mollie. "Letter from London." *New Yorker* 26 June 1965: 82–89.

Parini, Jay. "T. S. Eliot Was Right: Questions of Cultural Literacy and Questions of Politics Cannot Be Divorced." *Chronicle of Higher Education* 25 Apr. 1990: B1+.

Patmore, Brigit. *My Friends When Young: The Memoirs of Brigit Patmore*. Ed. Derek Patmore. London: Heinemann, 1968.

Paul, Leslie. "A Conversation with T. S. Eliot." *Kenyon Review* 27 (1965): 11–21.

Pearsall, Ronald. *Victorian Popular Music*. Detroit: Gale, 1973.

Perl, Jeffrey M. *Skepticism and Modern Enmity: Before and After Eliot*. Baltimore: Johns Hopkins UP, 1989.

Pickering, Michael. "White Skin, Black Masks: 'Nigger' Minstrelsy in Victorian England." *Music Hall: Performance and Style*. Ed. J. S. Bratton. Philadelphia: Open UP, 1986. 70–91.

"Poet and Janitor." *New Yorker* 11 Mar. 1933: 12.

Pound, Ezra. "Musicians; God Help 'Em." *Townsman* Oct. 1938: 8–9.

———. "The New Sculpture." *Egoist* 1 (1914): 67–68.

———. *Selected Letters of Ezra Pound, 1907–1941*. Ed. D. D. Paige. New York: New Directions, 1950.

———. *Selected Poems*. New York: New Directions, 1957.

"Priceless Gift of Laughter." *Time* 9 July 1951: 88–89.

Pritchett, V. S. "'Our Mr. Eliot' Grows Younger." *New York Times* 21 Sept. 1958, sec. 6: 15+.

Purcell, Victor. *The Sweeniad*. 1957. Rpt in *How Unpleasant to Meet Mr. Eliot: Victor Purcell's The Sweeniad*. Ed. Sheila Sullivan. London: Allen, 1985.

Rainey, Lawrence. *Institutions of Modernism: Literary Elites and Popular Culture*. New Haven: Yale UP, 1998.

Ramsey, Warren. *Jules Laforgue and the Ironic Inheritance*. New York: Oxford UP, 1953.

Read, Herbert. "T. S. E.—A Memoir." *Tate* 11–37.

"Reflections: Mr. Eliot." *Time* 6 Mar. 1950: 22–26.

Richards, I. A. "On TSE." *Tate* 1–10.

Roby, Kinley E., ed. *Critical Essays on T. S. Eliot: The Sweeney Motif*. Boston: Hall, 1985.

Rev. of *The Rock*, by T. S. Eliot. *Listener* 6 June 1934: 945.

Rosenberg, Bernard, and David Manning White, eds. *Mass Culture: The Popular Arts in America*. Glencoe, IL: Free, 1959.

Ross, Andrew. *No Respect: Intellectuals and Popular Culture*. New York: Routledge, 1989.

Russell, Dave. *Popular Music in England, 1840–1914*. Kingston: McGill-Queen's UP, 1987.

Rye, Howard. "Fearsome Means of Discord: Early Encounters with Black Jazz."
    Black Music in Britain. Ed. Paul Oliver. Philadelphia: Open UP, 1990. 45–57.

Sagittarius. "Nightingale among the Sweenies." *New Statesman and Nation* 29 July
    1950: 118.

Saintsbury, George. "Dullness." *Criterion* 1 (1922–23): 1–15.

Sanders, Charles. "*The Waste Land:* The Last Minstrel Show?" *Journal of Modern Literature*
    8 (1980): 23–38.

Sayers, Michael. "A Year in the Theatre." *Criterion* 15 (1936–37): 648–62.

Schuchard, Ronald. *Eliot's Dark Angel: Intersections of Life and Art.* New York: Oxford UP,
    1999.

Schwartz, Delmore. *Selected Essays of Delmore Schwartz.* Ed. Donald A. Dike and David H.
    Zucker. Chicago: U of Chicago P, 1970.

"A Scotsman's Log: First Night." *Scotsman* [Edinburgh] 24 Aug. 1949: 6.

Seldes, Gilbert. *The Great Audience.* New York: Viking, 1950.

———. "New York Chronicle." *Criterion* 3 (1924–25): 284–89.

———. Rev. of *Ulysses,* by James Joyce. *Nation* 30 Aug. 1922: 211–12.

———. *The Seven Lively Arts.* 1924. New York: Barnes, 1957.

Senelick, Laurence. "Politics as Entertainment: Victorian Music-Hall Songs."
    Victorian Studies 29 (1975): 149–80.

Settle, Mary Lee. "How Pleasant To Meet Mr. Eliot." *New York Times Book Review* 16
    Dec. 1984: 10–11.

Shapiro, Karl. "The Three Hockey Games of T. S. Eliot." *Antioch Review* 22 (1962):
    284–86.

Sharp, Cecil J., and A. P. Oppé. *The Dance: An Historical Survey of Dancing in Europe.* 1924.
    Totowa, NJ: Rowman, 1972.

Sidnell, Michael J. *Dances of Death: The Group Theatre of London in the Thirties.* London:
    Faber, 1984.

Sigg, Eric. "Eliot as a Product of America." Moody, *Cambridge* 14–30.

Skaff, William. *The Philosophy of T. S. Eliot.* Philadelphia: U of Pennsylvania P, 1986.

Smidt, Kristian. *The Importance of Recognition: Six Chapters on T. S. Eliot.* N.p.: Tromsø,
    1973.

Smith, Carol H. "Sweeney and the Jazz Age." Roby 87–99.

———. *T. S. Eliot's Dramatic Theory and Practice.* Princeton: Princeton UP, 1963.

Smith, Grover. *T. S. Eliot's Poetry and Plays: A Study in Sources and Meaning.* 2nd ed. Chicago:
    U of Chicago P, 1974.

———. *The Waste Land.* London: Allen, 1983.

Soldo, John J. *The Tempering of T. S. Eliot.* Ann Arbor: UMI Research, 1983.

Spaeth, Sigmund. *A History of Popular Music in America.* New York: Random, 1948.

———. "Jazz Is Not Music." *Forum* 80 (1928): 267–71.

Speaight, Robert. "Interpreting Becket and Other Parts." Braybrooke 70–78.

———. "With Becket in *Murder in the Cathedral.*" Tate 182–93.

Spender, Stephen. *The Destructive Element.* London: Cape, 1935.

———. "Remembering Eliot." Tate 38–64.

Spurr, David. "Myths of Anthropology: Eliot, Joyce, Levi-Bruhl." *PMLA* 109 (1994): 266–80.

Steegmuller, Francis. *Cocteau: A Biography.* Boston: Little, 1970.

Stevens, Wallace. *The Collected Poems of Wallace Stevens.* New York: Vintage, 1954.

———. *The Necessary Angel: Essays on Reality and the Imagination.* New York: Vintage, 1951.

Stokes, John. *In the Nineties.* Chicago: U of Chicago P, 1989.

Stonier, G. W. "Eliot and the Plain Reader." *Gog Magog.* 1933. Freeport, NY: Books for Libraries, 1966. 140–55.

Storey, John. *Cultural Theory and Popular Culture: An Introductory Guide.* Athens, GA: U of Georgia P, 1993.

Straus, Dorothea. *The Paper Trail: A Recollection of Writers.* Wakefield, RI: Moyer Bell, 1997.

Stravinsky, Igor. "Memories of T. S. Eliot." *Esquire* Aug. 1965: 92–93.

Swingewood, Alan. *The Myth of Mass Culture.* Atlantic Highlands, NJ: Humanities, 1977.

Symonds, John Addington. *Shakspere's Predecessors in the English Drama.* London: Smith, 1884.

Symons, Arthur. "The Case of the Empire." *Saturday Review of Politics, Literature, Science, and Art* 10 Nov. 1894: 501–02.

———. *Selected Writings.* Ed. R. V. Holdsworth. Cheadle: Carcanet, 1974.

Tate, Allen, ed. *T. S. Eliot: The Man and His Work.* New York: Dell, 1966.

"Tea." *New Yorker* 7 Jan. 1933: 11.

Tepper, Michele. "T. S. Eliot and the Modernism of Detective Fiction." Sess. on T. S. Eliot and Popular Culture. American Literature Association. Baltimore. 23 May 1997.

Thompson, Jon. *Fiction, Crime, and Empire.* Urbana: U of Illinois P, 1993.

Thurber, James. *Selected Letters of James Thurber.* Ed. Helen Thurber and Edward Weeks. Boston: Little, 1980.

"Tom to T. S." *Time* 2 Jan. 1939: 35.

"Topics of the Times: Before Long They Will Protest." *New York Times* 8 Oct. 1924: 18.

Torgovnick, Marianna. *Gone Primitive: Savage Intellects, Modern Lives.* Chicago: U of Chicago P, 1990.

Tratner, Michael. *Modernism and Mass Politics: Joyce, Woolf, Eliot, Yeats.* Stanford: Stanford UP, 1995.

Trilling, Lionel. *Matthew Arnold.* 1939. New York: Harcourt, 1977.

"T. S. Eliot, 70 Today, Concedes He Looks on Life More Genially." *New York Times* 26 Sept. 1958: 29.

"T. S. Eliot, 'the literary conscience of an era.'" *Vogue* 1 Aug. 1947: 101.

Untermeyer, Louis. "Disillusion vs. Dogma." *Freeman* 6 (1923): 453. Rpt. in Grant 151–53.

————. "Irony De Luxe." *Freeman* 1 (1920): 381–82. Rpt. in Grant 126–30.

Vendler, Helen. "*The Waste Land* Revisited." *Yale Review* 79 (1990): 147–61.

Von Tilzer, Harry, and Vincent Bryan. "The Cubanola Glide." New York: Von Tilzer, 1909.

Watts, Richard, Jr. "Bringing the Middle Ages to Broadway." *New York Herald Tribune* 29 Mar. 1936: sec. 5: 1+.

Webster's Ninth New Collegiate Dictionary. Springfield, MA: Merriam-Webster, 1983.

Wexler, Joyce Piell. *Who Paid for Modernism? Art, Money, and the Fiction of Conrad, Joyce, and Lawrence.* Fayetteville: U of Arkansas P, 1997.

Williams, Raymond. *Culture and Society 1780–1950.* 1958. New York: Columbia UP, 1983.

Williams, William Carlos. "It's About 'Your Life and Mine, Darling.'" Rev. of *The Cocktail Party,* by T. S. Eliot. *New York Post* 12 Mar. 1950: M18.

————. [Tribute to T. S. Eliot.] *Harvard Advocate* 121 (1934). Rpt. in Culler 73.

Wilson, Edmund. "The Aesthetic Upheaval in France: The Influence of Jazz in Paris and Americanization of French Literature and Art." *Vanity Fair* Feb. 1922: 49+.

————. *Axel's Castle: A Study in the Imaginative Literature of 1870–1930.* New York: Scribner's, 1931.

————. *The Bit between My Teeth: A Literary Chronicle of 1950–1965.* New York: Farrar, 1965.

————. *Classics and Commercials: A Literary Chronicle of the Forties.* New York: Farrar, 1950.

————. *Letters on Literature and Politics, 1912–1972.* Ed. Elena Wilson. New York: Farrar, 1977.

Wilson, Timothy. "Wife of the Father of *The Waste Land.*" *Esquire* May 1972: 44–46.

Winans, Robert B., and Elias J. Kaufman. "Minstrel and Classic Banjo: American and English Connections." *American Music* 12 (1994): 1–30.

Woodward, Arthur. "Joel Sweeney and the First Banjo." *Los Angeles County Museum Quarterly* 3 (1949): 7–11.

Woolf, Virginia. *The Diary of Virginia Woolf.* Ed. Anne Olivier Bell. 5 vols. New York: Harcourt, 1977–85.

————. *The Letters of Virginia Woolf.* Ed. Nigel Nicholson and Joanne Trautmann. 6 vols. New York: Harcourt, 1975–80.

Worthen, W. B. "*Murder in the Cathedral* and the Work of Acting." *T. S. Eliot: Man and Poet.* Vol. 1. Ed. Laura Cowan. Orono, ME: National Poetry Foundation, 1990. 253–73.

Yeats, W. B. *Explorations.* New York: Macmillan, 1962.

Zabel, Morton Dauwen. "Poets of Five Decades." *Southern Review* 2 (1936): 160–87.

Zanger, Jules. "The Minstrel Show as Theater of Misrule." *Quarterly Journal of Speech* 60 (1974): 33–38.

Zwerdling, Alex. *Improvised Europeans: American Literary Expatriates and the Siege of London.* New York: Basic, 1998.

INDEX

Sagittarius (satirist), 130
Sainte-Beuve, Charles Augustin, 64–65
Saintsbury, George, 54–55, 70
Sanders, Charles, 201n. 34
Satie, Erik, 31
Sayers, Dorothy, 155
Sayers, Michael, 138
Schuchard, Ronald, 211n. 14
Schwartz, Delmore, 19
Scofield, Paul, 188
Seldes, Gilbert, 30, 60–62, 77, 87, 204nn. 12–13, 15, 229n. 63; on Eliot, 6, 60, 159–60; on Joyce, 60, 203–04n. 11
Sellers, Peter, 228n. 58
Seneca, Lucius Annæus, 110, 113–14
Senelick, Laurence, 97, 212n. 19
Shakespeare, William, 12, 70, 78, 86, 130, 141, 150, 207n. 38; as high culture, 47–49, 164, 171, 186; as popular culture, 44, 71, 88, 89, 137; in The Waste Land, 32, 45, 48, 163, 202n. 41
"Shakespearian Rag." See under songs mentioned
Shapiro, Karl, 193–94n. 2
Sharp, Cecil, 85–86, 88–89, 121–22, 178, 209n. 2, 209–10n. 4, 210n. 5
Shaw, Bernard, 101
Shaw, Martin, 132
Shelley, Percy Bysshe, 66, 90; The Cenci, 88
Sherbrooke, Michael, 119
Sherek, Henry, 147, 221n. 31
Sidnell, Michael, 217n. 36
Sigg, Eric, 37, 39, 46, 200n. 22, 202n. 41
Simenon, Georges, 56, 155
Sitwell, Edith, 50

Sitwell, Sacheverell, 202n. 43
slang. See vernacular, American
Smidt, Kristian, 218n. 12
Smith, Carol H., 195n. 10, 197–98n. 1, 216n. 21
Smith, Grover, 134, 200n. 29, 214n. 6, 216nn. 21, 26
song, popular: influence on Eliot, 13, 32–33, 35, 37–38, 42, 185; in Laforgue, 34–35; in The Rock, 132, 217–18n. 6; in Sweeney Agonistes, 15, 112, 115–17; in The Waste Land, 41–49, 163. See also ballads; coon songs; jazz; ragtime
songs mentioned: "Alexander's Ragtime Band," 28, 37; "Bill Bailey Won't You Please Come Home?" 115; "A Bird in a Gilded Cage," 43; "Brush Up Your Shakespeare," 48; "The Bully Song," 200n. 24; "By the Light of the Silvery Moon," 33; "By the Watermelon Vine," 43, 45; "Casey Jones" (parody), 187; "The Congo Love Song," 116; "The Cubanola Glide," 37, 43, 46, 115; "Dixie," 105; "Don't Dilly Dally," 98; "Frankie and Johnny," 39; "Harrigan," 42, 43, 46, 200n. 30; "A Hot Time in the Old Town," 39; "In the Shadows," 33; "In Trinity Church I Met My Doom," 132, 217–18n. 6; "I Want a Girl Just Like the Girl That Married Dear Old Dad," 43; "The Maid of the Mill," 201n. 36; "Memory," 197n. 26; "Mrs. Porter" (parody of "Red Wing"), 45, 49, 187, 201n. 35; "My Evaline," 43, 45; "My Old Dad," 215n. 16; "The One-Eyed Riley," 187; "One of the Ruins that Cromwell Knocked Abaht a Bit," 216n. 25; "Red Wing," 45; "Ring

Tucker, Sophie, 43
"Two Black Crows" (comedy act),
    179, 187, 229n. 66

"Ulysses, Order, and Myth," 38, 72,
    82, 84, 201n. 31, 203–04n. 11,
    214n. 7; on the "mythical
    method," 34, 42, 80, 201n. 31,
    214–15n. 11 (see also under Joyce,
    James)
Uncle Remus, 23, 198n. 8
Untermeyer, Louis, 41, 159, 184
Use of Poetry and the Use of Criticism, The,
    38–39, 63, 65, 124–25, 132,
    146, 184, 216n. 30, 219n. 18;
    poet as "popular entertainer" in,
    67, 68, 79–80, 95, 104, 107, 127,
    131, 169, 170

Van Doren, Mark, 223n. 16
Van Vechten, Carl, 5
vaudeville, 28, 46, 114, 179, 188; in
    Sweeney Agonistes, 107, 108, 110,
    112, 113
Vendler, Helen, 162, 163
Verlaine, Paul, 45
vernacular, American, 13, 19, 33,
    36–37, 112, 118–19, 184–85,
    199n. 18, 200n. 21, 215n. 14;
    Eliot's accent, 22, 27, 51, 215n.
    20. See also "racial ventriloquism"
Virginia Minstrels, 106, 114, 214n. 4
Volpone (Jonson), 70
Von Tilzer, Harry, 37, 43

Wagner, Richard, 45, 208n. 41
Wallace, Nellie, 89, 94, 95, 100
Walton, William, 50
Waste Land, The, 13, 29, 58, 84, 91,
    118, 119, 121, 127, 149, 175,
    181, 187, 189, 200n. 29, 201n.
    34, 215n. 15, 216n. 31; critical re-

sponses, 46, 60, 148, 158, 161–
    63, 201–02n. 38, 223nn. 15, 20;
    and cultural exile, 73, 104; and
    Eliot's development, 69, 95, 107,
    206–07n. 33; and "lived culture,"
    43–44, 182, 196n. 19; as mass-
    culture metaphor, 154, 221n. 2,
    224–25n. 29; and popular music,
    6, 32, 38, 41–49, 200n. 30, 201n.
    35–36, 202nn. 39, 41; "primi-
    tivism" of, 77–78; "That Shake-
    speherian Rag" (see under songs
    mentioned); social class in, 7, 43–
    44, 98–99, 134; and Ulysses, 42,
    201nn. 31–33
Watts, Richard, 138
Wells, H. G., 222n. 12
Wescott, Glenway, 58–59, 100
Wexler, Joyce, 217n. 2
Whannel, Paddy, 11, 157
Whiteman, Paul, 28
Whitlock, Billy, 106
Whitman, Walt, 35, 193n. 1
"Wilkie Collins and Dickens," 71,
    75, 108, 154, 171–72, 188, 203n.
    9; on the novel, 55–56, 61, 63,
    156, 204n. 18, 220n. 22, 226n. 37
Williams, Raymond, 10–11, 226n.
    34
Williams, William Carlos, 6, 144,
    193–94n. 2
Wilson, Edmund, 60, 159, 195n. 8,
    217n. 3, 223n. 19; on Eliot's per-
    sonas, 175, 184, 186, 229n. 65;
    on popular culture, 29, 30, 155–
    56
Wilson, Woodrow, 222n. 9
Wodehouse, P. G., 12, 56
Woods, J. H., 93
Woolf, Leonard, 130
Woolf, Virginia, 62, 43, 52, 69, 107,
    130, 185, 228n. 55